For Jessica, my one and only.

A lifetime supply of thanks to:

The wonderful people at Peachpit Press. My sincerest thanks to everyone there (and at Pearson) for their dedication to putting out quality books, for giving me these opportunities to publish, and for everything else they do. Specifically, I would like to thank Nancy Aldrich-Ruenzel, Marjorie Baer, Kim Lombardi, Gary-Paul Prince, and the other two dozen people whose names and jobs I may not know but should.

This book's editor, Rebecca Gulick. My job is easier and the book is better when I have the pleasure of working with you. I am very fortunate to have had that opportunity once again.

Bob Campbell, for his spot-on copy editing and attention to detail.

Pat Christenson, Production Coordinator Extraordinaire, for turning a disparate collection of text files and images into a usable, physical book.

Owen Wolfson, Compositor, and Karin Arrigoni, Indexer, for the work they do, which I almost understand (but not quite).

The readers of my other books who took the time to let me know how much they appreciated them (even if they followed that up with a support question) and for requesting that I write a MySQL book. I hope it's everything you were looking for.

Finally (whew!), thanks to everyone in the MySQL community—from those at MySQL AB to the participants of the various mailing lists. MySQL is yet another example of how great open source technology can be! Special thanks goes to Alexander Keremidarski, for his time and excellent technical review. I feel so much better having a person of your knowledge review everything!

VISUAL QUICKSTART GUIDE

MySQL

Second Edition

Larry Ullman

Peachpit Press

Visual QuickStart Guide
MySQL, Second Edition
Larry Ullman

Peachpit Press
1249 Eighth Street
Berkeley, CA 94710
510/524-2178
510/524-2221 (fax)

Find us on the Web at: www.peachpit.com
To report errors, please send a note to: errata@peachpit.com
Peachpit Press is a division of Pearson Education.
Copyright © 2006 by Larry Ullman

Editor: Rebecca Gulick
Copy Editor: Robert Campbell
Technical Reviewer: Alexander Keremidarski
Proofreaders: Liz Welch and Alison Kelley
Production Coordinators: Pat Christenson and Becky Winter
Compositor: Owen Wolfson
Indexer: Karin Arrigoni
Cover Production: George Mattingly/GMD Design

ISBN 0-321-37573-4

9 8 7 6 5 4 3 2 1

Printed and bound in the United States of America

TABLE OF CONTENTS

TABLE OF CONTENTS

INTRODUCTION

In the midst of the Information Age, where more and more data is being stored on computers, the need for high-speed, reliable databases has increased dramatically. For years, large companies, such as Oracle, Microsoft, and IBM, have been providing high-end data warehousing applications for mission-critical work. These programs were used primarily by Fortune 500 companies, which can afford their extreme cost and personnel demands. Meanwhile, within the open-source community, a new wave of small, reliable, and inexpensive database applications came to the market. Such software, of which MySQL and PostgreSQL are the best examples, gave common users and developers on a budget a practical database choice.

MySQL, fortunately, has left its modest beginnings in the dust, turning into a robust, reliable, and easy-to-manage database application. More astounding, MySQL has managed to retain its open-source roots, continuing to be available for some uses at no expense (although check the licensing for your particular situation). MySQL's capabilities and low cost explain why major operations such as Yahoo!, the United States Census Bureau, and NASA use it within their organizations. But you, too, can incorporate MySQL into your projects. With *MySQL: Visual QuickStart Guide*, you will be doing just that in no time!

What Is MySQL?

MySQL is the world's most popular, and some might argue best, open-source database. In fact, more and more, MySQL is a viable competitor to the pricey goliaths such as Oracle and Microsoft's SQL Server.

MySQL was created and is supported by MySQL AB, a company based in Sweden (www.mysql.com, **Figure i.1**). MySQL is a database management system (DBMS) for relational databases (therefore, MySQL is an RDBMS). A database is simply a collection of (often interrelated) data, be it text, numbers, or binary files, that are stored and kept organized by the DBMS. Technically, MySQL is an *application* that manages files called *databases*, but you will commonly hear the term "database" applied equally to both the files of data and the program itself.

MySQL is an open-source application, like PHP and some variants of Unix, meaning that it is free to run or even modify (the source code itself is downloadable). There are occasions on which you should pay for a MySQL license, though, especially if you are making money from the sales or incorporation of the MySQL product. Check MySQL's licensing policy for more information on this. Any MySQL user may also want to consider subscribing to one of MySQL's Network tiers.

Figure i.1 The MySQL home page, located at www.mysql.com, is where you can obtain the software, view the manual, get support, and more.

Pronunciation Guide

MySQL is technically pronounced "My Ess Que Ell," just as SQL should be said "Ess Que Ell." You will also hear people, although never this author, pronounce it as "My Sequel" and "Sequel." This is technically incorrect. It's a trivial issue, of course, but a common question.

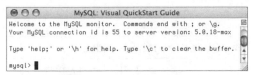

Figure i.2 You'll commonly use the mysql client to communicate with the MySQL server.

Figure i.3 The free, Web-based phpMyAdmin is one of the best tools for working with your MySQL databases.

The MySQL software consists of several pieces, including the MySQL server (*mysqld*, which runs and manages the databases), the MySQL client (*mysql*, which gives you an interface to the server, **Figure i.2**), and numerous utilities for maintenance and other purposes. You can interface with MySQL using most popular programming languages, including PHP, Perl, and Java, all of which will be demonstrated in this book. You can also use C#, C, Ruby, C++, and others. Along with all of these options, there are dozens of third-party applications for interacting with the MySQL server such as phpMyAdmin (**Figure i.3**).

MySQL was written in C and C++, and it functions equally well on several different operating systems. MySQL has been known to handle databases as large as 60,000 tables with more than five billion rows (yes, *billion*). MySQL can work with tables as large as eight million terabytes (since version 3.23) on some operating systems and generally a healthy 4 GB otherwise.

In the next section of this Introduction, I discuss the very important topic of the available MySQL versions. Which version of MySQL you use will greatly impact your experience, particularly what you can and cannot do (as new features are added).

WHAT IS MYSQL?

MySQL Versions

MySQL, at the time of this writing, is on version 5.0.19, with the significant upgrade version 5.1 due out later in 2006. Since the first edition of this book was written (in 2002), there have been several important releases of MySQL: 4.0, 4.1, and 5.0. Each has added new features to the software (**Table i.1**), while changing some functionality in the process. For this reason, I cannot stress this enough: it is *vitally important* that you know and remember what version of MySQL you are using. In this book I will highlight features that are new to, or have changed in, later versions of MySQL. Paying attention to this will help minimize problems and frustrations.

Table i.1 Some of the significant new features, and in which version of MySQL they were added.

MySQL Feature Introductions	
FEATURE	MYSQL VERSION
Full-Text Binary Mode Searches	4.0
Unions	4.0
Subqueries	4.1
Stored Procedures	5.0
Views	5.0
Cursors	5.0
Triggers	5.0 and 5.1

SQL Versions

SQL, which stands for *Structured Query Language* (depending upon whom you ask), is the language used to interact with practically every database application. It is a standardized language, meaning that the terms and syntax it supports depend upon the regulated standard. The current SQL standard was released in 2003.

MySQL, like most database applications, adheres to the standards *for the most part*. MySQL does not support a few features of standardized SQL and has its own particular terminology as well. This is true for most database applications. In this book I focus only on MySQL's implementation of SQL. Almost every SQL command you learn here will be applicable to all database applications, but there may be some minor distinctions. If you ever go from using MySQL to using PostgreSQL or Oracle or SQL Server, you should be fine, but you'll need to do a little research to smooth the transition.

Figure i.4 The online version of the MySQL manual is highly detailed and well organized. You can also download other versions for immediate access from your computer.

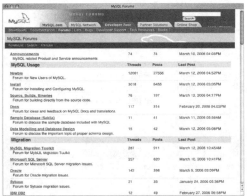

Figure i.5 MySQL's forums are available for troubleshooting or for extending your knowledge.

Primary MySQL Resources

Because MySQL is a free application, most of your questions will need to be answered by members of the MySQL mailing lists rather than by MySQL AB itself. The company is, however, available for contractual support, consulting, and training, which you might want to consider if you are using MySQL on a larger scale or in a corporate environment.

MySQL has a solid online manual (**Figure i.4**), which includes the occasional user-submitted comment. It's searchable, thorough, and able to answer most of the questions you'll come across. Also note that the MySQL manual is available in several different versions, each matching a significant MySQL release. As you look there for help, make sure that you're using the correct corresponding manual.

The MySQL mailing lists (`http://lists.mysql.com`) are populated by users and the MySQL people themselves, who are very informative and responsive. You'll also find specific mailing lists dedicated to the database on Windows and interacting with MySQL from Java, among other topics. Because of the popularity of the mailing lists, there are currently no strong MySQL newsgroups such as you might encounter with other technologies.

Finally, there are also the MySQL forums (`http://forums.mysql.com`, **Figure i.5**). The forums cover MySQL usage, third-party applications, SQL, specific programming languages, and so on.

For links to these and other MySQL references, see Appendix C, "Resources."

PRIMARY MySQL RESOURCES

Technical Requirements

In order to follow the discussions in this book, there are a few, though not too restricting, technical requirements. The first, naturally, would be the MySQL software itself. Fortunately, this is freely available and runs on most operating systems (**Figure i.6**). Chapter 1, "Installing MySQL," will cover the fundamentals of installing MySQL on three popular operating systems: Windows, Linux, and Mac OS X.

The bulk of the chapters involve administering and interacting with the database from a command-line perspective. Whichever application on your operating system gives you this access is acceptable, be it a DOS prompt on Windows (**Figure i.7**), a Linux shell, or the Mac OS X Terminal (**Figure i.8**).

Lastly, the programming chapters covering PHP, Perl, and Java—Chapters 7, 8, 9, and 12—will require a text editor, a Web browser, and so forth. The specific requirements will be discussed in the pertinent chapter.

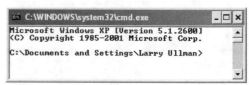

- HP-UX 11.x with the native threads. See Section 2.12.5.2, "HP-UX Version 11 x Notes".
- Linux 2.0+ with LinuxThreads 0.7.1+ or glibc 2.0.7+ for various CPU architectures. See Section 2.12.1, "Linux Notes".
- Mac OS X. See Section 2.12.2, "Mac OS X Notes".
- NetBSD 1.3/1.4 Intel and NetBSD 1.3 Alpha (requires GNU make). See Section 2.12.4.2, "NetBSD Notes".
- Novell NetWare 6.0 and 6.5. See Section 2.8, "Installing MySQL on NetWare".
- OpenBSD 2.5 and with native threads. OpenBSD earlier than 2.5 with the MIT-pthreads package. See Section 2.12.4.3, "OpenBSD 2.5 Notes".
- OS/2 Warp 3, FixPack 29 and OS/2 Warp 4, FixPack 4. See Section 2.12.6, "OS/2 Notes".
- SCO OpenServer 5.0.X with a recent port of the FSU Pthreads package. See Section 2.12.5.8, "SCO UNIX and OpenServer 5.0.x Notes".
- SCO Openserver 6.0.x. See Section 2.12.5.9, "SCO OpenServer 6.0.x Notes".
- SCO UnixWare 7.1.x. See Section 2.12.5.10, "SCO UnixWare 7.1.x and OpenUNIX 8.0.0 Notes".
- SGI Irix 6.x with native threads. See Section 2.12.5.7, "SGI Irix Notes".
- Solaris 2.5 and above with native threads on SPARC and x86. See Section 2.12.3, "Solaris Notes".
- SunOS 4.x with the MIT-pthreads package. See Section 2.12.3, "Solaris Notes".
- Tru64 Unix. See Section 2.12.5.5, "Alpha-DEC-UNIX Notes (Tru64)".
- Windows 9x, Me, NT, 2000, XP, and Windows Server 2003. See Section 2.3, "Installing MySQL on Windows".

Figure i.6 MySQL is available in versions designed to run on almost every operating system, including various types of Unix and Windows.

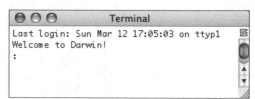

```
C:\WINDOWS\system32\cmd.exe

Microsoft Windows XP [Version 5.1.2600]
(C) Copyright 1985-2001 Microsoft Corp.

C:\Documents and Settings\Larry Ullman>
```

Figure i.7 Windows has a command prompt (or DOS prompt), which will be used in this book.

```
Terminal

Last login: Sun Mar 12 17:05:03 on ttyp1
Welcome to Darwin!
:
```

Figure i.8 Mac OS X comes with the Terminal application, which allows you to interact with the computer on a command-line level.

About This Book

In this book I explain the fundamentals of MySQL, teaching the information that most MySQL users will require. In keeping with the format of the Visual QuickStart series, the information is taught using a step-by-step approach with corresponding images. The demonstrations in the book will be geared toward specific knowledge as opposed to developing in-depth MySQL-based applications (such as a programming text might have).

Many of the examples in the book will be executed from a command-line interface, although the three programming chapters plus Chapter 12, "Techniques for Programming," will function differently. In those chapters, I will go through writing the scripts in detail and then test them using the most applicable technique (be it a Web browser or whatever).

The structure of the book is fairly linear. It begins with basic installation and administration of the software. After that, database design and SQL—elements common to most database applications—will be covered, followed by some MySQL-specific functions. The three programming chapters will come next. The book concludes with newer and more advanced features, some specific database-application techniques, and how to administer the MySQL server and databases. The appendices discuss troubleshooting techniques and provide a reference section along with where to turn for more information.

Is This Book for You?

This book was written for a wide range of people within the beginner to intermediate range. Obviously, this book is for anyone wanting to use MySQL in some capacity, but I specifically had in mind three general types of readers:

◆ Those who have never used any database before

◆ Those who have used other databases and want to know how MySQL specifically operates

◆ Those who are currently using MySQL in a limited capacity and would like to elevate their skills to a more professional level

I should note that I will not teach any programming languages here but rather demonstrate how to use those languages with MySQL.

Companion Web Site

I have developed a companion Web site specifically for this book, which you may reach at www.DMCinsights.com/mysql2. There you will find every script from this book (for the programming chapters), text files containing lengthy SQL commands, and a list of errata that occurred during publication. (If you have a problem with a command or script and are following the book exactly, check the errata to ensure there is not a printing error before driving yourself absolutely mad.) At this Web site you will also find useful Web links, a forum where readers can ask and answer each others' questions (related to the material herein or not), and more!

Questions, Comments, or Suggestions?

If you have any MySQL-specific questions, you can turn to one of the many Web sites, mailing lists, and FAQ repositories already in existence. Appendix C, "Resources," lists the most popular of these options. You can also direct your questions, comments, and suggestions to me directly, via email, at: mysql2@DMCinsights.com. I do try to answer every email I receive, although there is no guarantee as to how quickly I will be able to do so. (Preference and more detailed responses will be given to emails pertaining to the content of this book; more prompt and thoughtful replies with other issues are best sought through the mailing lists or the book's online reader forum.)

INSTALLING MYSQL

Obviously the first thing you'll need to do to begin using MySQL is install the software. But because MySQL is an open-source database application, you have more options when it comes to installation than you would with a commercial application. These choices range from the very simple execution of an installer to customizing and compiling your own installation using MySQL's source files (the actual code MySQL is written in).

In this chapter I will cover basic installation on the Windows, Macintosh, and Linux operating systems. These three platforms cover a large portion of the MySQL audience, but the database is available on many other platforms as well. Between the Windows binary and the Linux source installation instructions, you should have a good sense of the various issues regardless of the operating system you are using.

This chapter covers downloading the software, installing the server, and running the initial setup and configuration. If you have problems with any of the installation steps described here, see Appendix A, "Troubleshooting," or the relevant sections of the MySQL manual.

General Installation Steps

Before going through the actual installation steps, there are some decisions to be made. The first, and most important, two are:

♦ What version of MySQL to install

♦ What installation method to use

At the time of this writing, there are stable releases available of MySQL 4.1 and 5.0, while 5.1 is in its alpha stage (there are also old releases still available of Versions 3.23 and 4.0). Generally I would recommend that you download the current stable version, which is marked as *GA* (Generally Available). The latest version will have the most features available (see the Introduction for a discussion of this). The main reason to install an older version of MySQL would be if you were currently using a different version of MySQL on another computer and wanted to ensure cross-computer consistency with the least amount of effort.

As for the installation method, MySQL is available in a precompiled binary format or as the raw source code. If a binary is available for your platform, you'll want to go with that unless you need to configure the installation (if, for instance, you need to change the default location or add support for other features). The binaries are also available in two formats: Standard (also called *Windows Essentials* as a Windows download) and Max (or just plain *Windows* as a Windows download). The former is smaller and should run faster. The latter has extra features enabled.

MySQL Naming Scheme

When you go to download MySQL, you'll notice that files have their own naming conventions. For example, a release may be called *mysql-5.0.18*. The first number indicates the major version. The second number is the *release level*. The combination of these two numbers is the *release series*, which is the most important thing to remember (4.0, 4.1, 5.0, 5.1, etc.). The third number is the version number within the release series.

Non-production versions will be followed with *-alpha*, *-beta*, or *-rc* (for *release candidate*, which is almost production caliber). I would advise that you avoid these. Finally, if you download the complete binary package, it may also have the word max added to the name.

Before going into the operating-system-specific installation instructions, here is a preview of the general installation steps.

To install MySQL:

1. Confirm that your operating system is supported.

   MySQL is available for a long list of platforms, so it's a safe bet that you can use it. That being said, it's always best to check prior to going through all of the effort. MySQL will run on Windows 9.*x,* Me, NT, 2000, 2003, and XP; Mac OS X; and several variants of Unix and Linux. The full list of supported operating systems appears in the MySQL manual; see section 2.1.1, "Operating Systems Supported by MySQL" (**Figure 1.1**).

2. Select the release series of MySQL you'll want.

   This is where you'll most likely decide to install the most current Generally Available release. MySQL still updates older releases as warranted by bug or security fixes, but you should probably install the current, stable version.

continues on next page

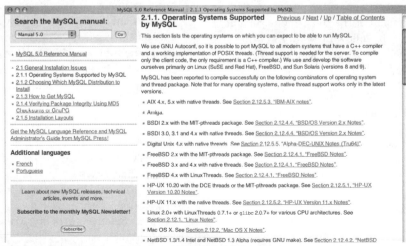

Figure 1.1 MySQL runs on the vast majority of available operating systems.

GENERAL INSTALLATION STEPS

3. Select the distribution format.

   Unless you know you need to create a custom installation, opt for a binary version, if one is available for your operating system. As to the choice between the Standard and Max versions, I leave that up to you. It's really a matter of whether you want a smaller size and faster speed or all of the enabled features.

4. Download the software.

   Just click the link and follow the prompts to get MySQL. There is a form you can optionally fill out to give the MySQL company some information, or you can click the *No thanks...* message to just get the software. You'll probably have to download the software from a mirror site at the end.

5. Make sure you do not have an existing version of MySQL running.

   If you already have a version of MySQL installed and running, see the "Upgrading MySQL" section later in this chapter prior to doing anything else.

6. Install the downloaded software.

   This step will vary the most, as it depends upon what operating system you are using and whether you selected a precompiled binary version or the source code version in Step 3. The following sections of this chapter will focus on this part of the overall process.

7. Set up and start MySQL.

   Some of the setup will be covered in this chapter, and then Chapter 2, "Running MySQL," will take over from there.

✔ Tips

- Use only the latest Generally Available release for mission-critical tasks. The non-stable releases are for the curious, the bug testers, and those with nothing serious to lose.

- The MySQL manual is available in different versions, each corresponding to a MySQL release series. When using the manual, check that it corresponds to the version of MySQL you have.

Verifying the Checksum

For the truly security-conscious, an optional step you can take is to verify the downloaded software to make sure you don't have a Trojan horse (a malicious piece of code disguised as something else). There are a couple of ways to do this, starting by verifying the checksum. A checksum is an MD5 representation of data. So the checksum for the downloadable file should be unique to that download. If what you actually download has a different checksum, it's probably been tampered with.

Alternatively, you can use GnuPG, the GNU Privacy Guard, or (on Linux) RPM's built-in verification mechanism. I don't show or discuss any of these here, but the MySQL manual has instructions for using these tools, as well as where they can be obtained. See the "Installing MySQL" section for specifics.

Table 1.1 After installing MySQL, you'll have these folders (all found within the main MySQL folder).

MySQL Layout on Windows	
SUBFOLDER	CONTAINS
bin	All applications
data	Databases and logs
docs	Documentation
examples	Sample programs and scripts
include	Header files
lib	Code libraries
scripts	Useful scripts
share	Error message files
sql-bench	Benchmark utilities

Installing MySQL on Windows

MySQL will run on most Windows operating systems (specifically those that are at least 32-bit, such as Windows 95, 98, Me, NT, 2000, and XP). If you're using an NT OS such as Windows NT, 2000, or XP (either the Home or Professional version), you can run MySQL as a service, as I'll demonstrate in the next chapter. For my example here, I'll be installing the latest stable release of MySQL on Windows XP Professional.

There are two primary ways of installing the MySQL software on a Windows operating system: using a precompiled distribution or compiling your own binary from the MySQL source files. The former approach is significantly easier than the latter and will be the technique I use here. When you get to the MySQL downloads page, you'll see three items listed for Windows: *Windows Essentials*, which is the Standard binary; just *Windows*, which is the Max version; and, *Without Installer*, which is the source code. The first is the smallest and will work for most people. The second has all the extra bells and whistles.

Once complete, MySQL will be installed in `C:\Program Files\MySQL\MySQL Server` *x.x*, where *x.x* represents the release series installed. This is true as of MySQL 5.0. Prior to that, MySQL was installed in `C:\mysql`, by default. In either case, **Table 1.1** indicates the resulting layout of folders.

Finally, I'll point out that these instructions are correct as of the writing of this book. MySQL has frequently changed the installation process over the years. One release may have an entirely different installation process and result from the next. If you have a problem with these instructions, check the version of the manual that matches the MySQL version you are installing.

To install MySQL on Windows:

1. Download the Zip file from the MySQL Web site.

   Start by pointing your browser to `http://dev.mysql.com/downloads`. Then click the name of the version you'll want. As of the time of this writing, the most current stable release of MySQL is version 5.0.18.

   On the next page, you'll be able to choose which distribution you want (**Figure 1.2**). MySQL recommends the Windows Essentials, but I'd recommend the full version (called just *Windows*) if you want to learn it all.

2. Unzip the downloaded file, if necessary.

   The complete MySQL package comes as a Zip file that must be unzipped (if you don't already have a Zip application, there are free ones available—just search Google or `www.download.com`). It doesn't really matter where you choose to unzip the files in this step.

   At the time of this writing, the Essentials version of the installer is downloaded as a Microsoft Windows Installer (`.msi`) file that does not require unzipping.

3. Run the `setup.exe` or `.msi` application by double-clicking the file.

   Depending upon which file you download, you should now have either an executable (called `setup.exe`) in the unzipped folder or a Microsoft Windows Installer (`.msi`). In either case, just double-click the file to begin the installation process.

   If you are using a version of Windows NT, you must be logged in as an administrator-level user with the permission to install software.

Figure 1.2 Choose between the Essentials or the complete version of MySQL.

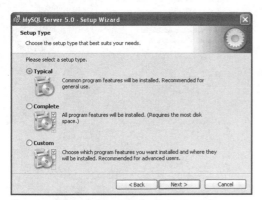

Figure 1.3 Choose an installation type, based upon what best suits your situation and knowledge.

Figure 1.4 You can customize what all is installed, including extra scripts and examples.

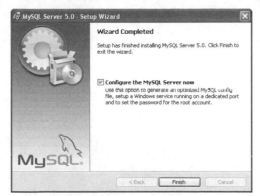

Figure 1.5 After installing MySQL, choose to jump straight into the MySQL configuration wizard.

4. On the second installation page, select the installation type: Typical, Complete, or Custom (**Figure 1.3**).

Naturally, the Typical installation should be fine for most users. If you opt for the Custom Setup, click an item and view the description in the right-hand panel (**Figure 1.4**) to determine if you need that particular item. You absolutely must install the MySQL Server, and you should install the Client Programs.

5. Click your way through the rest of the installation process and, if you want, sign up for a MySQL.com account when prompted.

You don't have to sign up, but doing so has its benefits. For starters, an account lets you post at `http://forums.mysql.com` (a community support forum), subscribe to MySQL newsletters, and the like.

6. Opt for configuring the MySQL Server now when prompted (**Figure 1.5**) and click Finish.

The installation process is now complete, which means you should set up how the MySQL server runs. The installer will take you over to the configuration wizard for this purpose. This topic is discussed in the next section of the chapter, so please read on.

✔ Tips

- The recommendation is that MySQL be run on Windows using the NTFS file system (not FAT or FAT32).

- MySQL suggests a minimum of 200 MB of available disk space, but how much disk space is actually required will depend upon how many databases you have, how much you use indexes, and how much data you store. If space is an issue, download and install the *Essentials* version of MySQL, not the complete.

Configuring MySQL on Windows

Somewhat new to MySQL is the MySQL Server Instance configuration wizard, a graphical tool for customizing how MySQL runs. It's available starting with MySQL 5.0 and only on Windows.

The wizard is fairly simple to use, but it's pretty important, so I'll run through it with you. The end result will be the creation of a my.ini file, which the MySQL server and utilities will use for their settings.

To configure MySQL on Windows:

1. Launch the configuration wizard.

   You can access this immediately after installing MySQL for the first time (see Figure 1.5) or at any point in time later through the Start Menu shortcut (under the MySQL folder, added to the Start menu during installation).

2. Select whether you want to perform a Detailed or Standard configuration (**Figure 1.6**).

   Most users will probably want to go with Standard here (although Detailed is the default). The following steps will go through the Standard configuration.

3. Set the basic MySQL settings (**Figure 1.7**).

   With the Standard configuration, there are just a few choices. You should opt for installing MySQL as a Windows service, and have it launch the server automatically so that it's always running. You should also choose to include MySQL's bin directory in the Windows PATH, which will make it easier to run MySQL applications from the command line.

Figure 1.6 Choose a configuration type: Detailed or Standard.

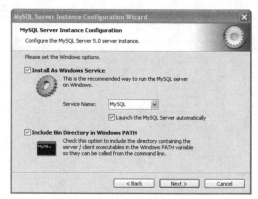

Figure 1.7 I would advise that you go with these settings, for a more trouble-free operation.

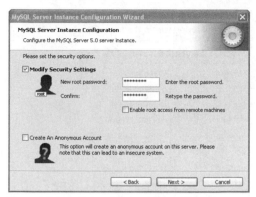

Figure 1.8 Definitely create a secure *root* user password and do not enable remote *root* access!

4. Define the security settings (**Figure 1.8**).

The choices you make here are very important. For starters, enter a good *root* user's password. The *root* user has unlimited access to MySQL, so this password should be secure and one you won't forget.

Besides that, I would recommend that you not enable *root* access from remote machines or create an anonymous account. Both are security risks.

5. Click your way through the rest of the configuration process.

✔ Tips

■ When you install MySQL as a service, it can automatically be started when your computer starts. It can also restart automatically after a system crash.

■ Once you've created the *root* MySQL user, you can create other, day-to-day users, by following the steps outlined in Chapter 2.

■ The MySQL configuration wizard can be used to configure a new installation or to reconfigure an existing MySQL installation. After you've used it once, the next time it runs, you'll be given the option to reconfigure the current instance or remove it entirely. Removing the configuration only stops the MySQL service and deletes the my.ini file; it does not delete the installed files or your databases.

MySQL and Firewalls

If you have a firewall installed and running on your machine, you'll most likely need to tweak it in order for MySQL to run. This is necessary because a firewall, by definition, limits access to your computer. MySQL, by default, uses the port 3306, which may be blocked by the firewall.

If you have problems, which may appear when the configuration wizard attempts to finish doing its thing, try temporarily turning off your firewall to confirm that is the source of the problem. If MySQL works with the firewall disabled, you know the firewall is the issue. The solution then is to adjust the firewall's settings to allow communications through port 3306. How you do this differs from one operating system or firewall program to the next, but a quick search through the applicable firewall help files or Google will turn up useful answers.

Installing MySQL on Macintosh

Mac OS X uses a FreeBSD (Unix) foundation with a Macintosh graphical user interface, meaning that it has the usability and stability of any Unix operating system but the appearance and interface of a Mac. The implication of this is that, now more than ever, there is an Apple operating system that programmers and developers are actively using. Furthermore, most software that installs and runs on a Unix system, such as MySQL, will also work with Mac OS X.

MySQL is available for Mac OS X 10.2 (aka Jaguar) and later in a precompiled binary package. It's quite easy to use, but I'll run through it nonetheless. Note that the server version of Mac OS X comes with MySQL preinstalled, so you will need to perform an update, not an installation, if you are running Mac OS X Server. See later in this chapter for update-specific instructions.

MySQL will be installed in the /usr/local/ mysql-*VERSION* directory, where *VERSION* is the full version name and number (e.g., *max-5.0.18-osx10.4-powerpc*). A symbolic link is then created so that /usr/local/mysql can be used as a shortcut to /usr/local/ mysql-*VERSION*. The folder layout within this directory is represented in **Table 1.2**.

Table 1.2 After installing MySQL, you'll have these folders (all found within the main MySQL folder).

MySQL Layout on Mac OS X	
SUBFOLDER	CONTAINS
bin	All applications
data	Databases and logs
docs	Documentation
include	Header files
lib	Code libraries
man	Unix man pages
scripts	The mysql_install_db script
share/mysql	Error message files
sql-bench	Benchmark utilities

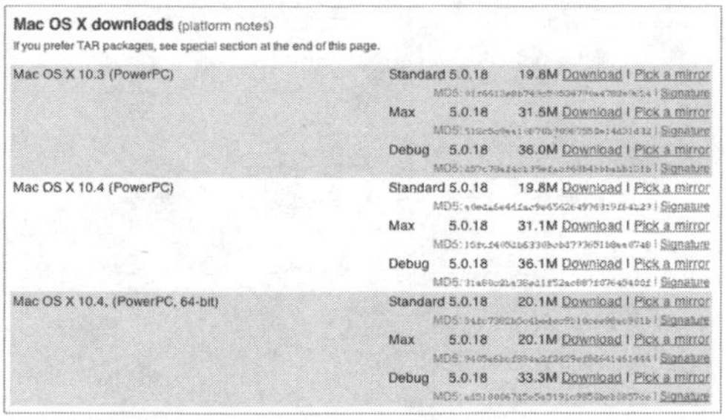

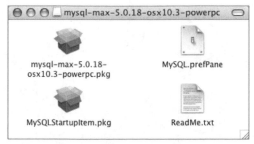

Figure 1.9 Choose the MySQL package you want, matching your version of Mac OS X.

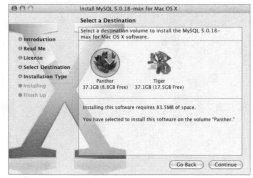

Figure 1.10 The contents of the mounted disk image.

Figure 1.11 If you have multiple hard disks or partitions, install MySQL on the one with the operating system.

To install MySQL on Mac OS X:

1. Download the current package from the MySQL Web site.

   Start by pointing your browser to `http://dev.mysql.com/downloads`. Then click the name of the version you'll want. As of the time of this writing, the most current stable release of MySQL is version 5.0.18.

   On the next page, you'll be able to choose which binary you want (**Figure 1.9**). MySQL recommends the Standard version, but I'd recommend the Max version if you want to learn it all and have the disk space to spare. Make sure you also are picking from the area that matches your version of Mac OS X.

2. Mount the `.dmg` file.

   The downloaded file is of type `.dmg`, a common disk image. Just double-click it to mount the disk so that you may begin the installation process. The result will be a folder of things like that shown in **Figure 1.10**.

3. Install MySQL.

   Double-click the MySQL package—the thing called something like *mysql-version-os-powerpc.pkg*—and follow through its steps. Apart from choosing the destination (**Figure 1.11**), which applies only if you have more than one volume, the installation is mindless.

   continues on next page

INSTALLING MYSQL ON MACINTOSH

4. Install the System Preferences pane by double-clicking the `MySQL.prefPane` item (see Figure 1.10).

The MySQL System Preferences pane is an easy way to control MySQL (**Figure 1.12**). To install it, just double-click the item and your Mac will do the rest.

5. If you want, run the `MySQLStartupItem.pkg` (see Figure 1.10).

By running this installer, a script will be added that automatically starts MySQL every time you start your Mac. This functionality is duplicated by checking the appropriate box in the System Preferences panel (see Figure 1.12).

6. Start MySQL and assign a password to MySQL's *root* user.

You'll learn how to do these two steps in Chapter 2.

✔ Tips

■ The installation of MySQL on the Mac has been greatly simplified. You no longer need to take such steps as creating a separate MySQL user.

■ According to MySQL, there is a bug in the Apple package installer program, which may result in an error that states "You cannot install this software on this disk" on the destination disk selection page (Figure 1.11). If you see this, click Go Back, then click Continue to return to the destination disk selection page, and you should be fine.

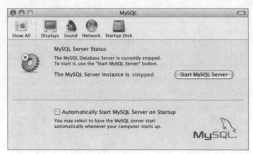

Figure 1.12 MySQL comes with a System Preferences pane that can be used to start and stop the database server.

Table 1.3 After installing MySQL, you'll have these
folders (all found within the main MySQL folder,
/usr/local/mysql).

MySQL Layout on Linux

SUBFOLDER	CONTAINS
bin	All applications
info	Documentation
include/mysql	Header files
lib/mysql	Code libraries
libexec	The mysqld server
man	Unix man pages
share/mysql	Error message files
sql-bench	Benchmark utilities
var	Databases and logs

Being the Root User

Unix-based operating systems, including
Max OS X and Linux, rely on the concept
of users for security purposes. The ulti-
mate user, *root*, can do anything within
the operating system, including destroy
it. For this reason the *root* user should be
handled gingerly, but it is also a necessary
evil when installing new software.

If a *root* user account has already been
established (with a password), you can
become *root* by typing su root within the
Terminal application. You will then be
prompted for the *root* user's password.
Alternatively, you can do everything as
your normal user, but request *root* power
as needed. To do so, preface every command with sudo, like

sudo make install

The first time you do this, and after a
period of inactivity, you will be prompted
for the *root* password. While repeatedly
using sudo may seem tedious, this is less
heavy-handed than to temporarily act as
the *root* user.

Installing MySQL on Linux

According to the manual, the best way to
install MySQL on Linux is to use an RPM (a
package formatted for the Red Hat Package
Manager, an installer which is not limited to
just Red Hat Linux). MySQL provides RPMs
for many different versions of Linux, so if
one is available for the platform you're using,
that's the best and easiest way to go. There
are both server and client RPMs available;
you'll probably want to install both.

Installing an RPM is just a matter of typing

rpm -i MySQL-server-*VERSION*.i386.rpm

in a Terminal (you may need to precede this
with sudo, per the instructions in the sidebar). The RPMs, by default, will install the
applications within the /usr directory with
the data stored in /var/lib/mysql. Further,
the RPM will add the requisite data to the
/etc/rc.d/ directory so that the MySQL
server daemon will be automatically started
when the computer is booted. The RPM also
creates a user called *mysql*, if necessary.
Installing an RPM is straightforward enough
that I will not say more about it, but see the
MySQL manual if you have problems.

Another option, which I will cover here, is to
compile the source code yourself. This isn't
just a Linux thing, you can compile MySQL
yourself on nearly any operating system. All
you need is a compiler like gcc, utilities like
gunzip and tar, plus make. Any number of
problems can occur using this method, so
it's not for the faint of heart, but if you know
what you're doing, this is a great way to get a
version of MySQL that's customized to how
you want it to behave. With this installation
method, the resulting layout will be a little
different (**Table 1.3**), with /usr/local/mysql
as the base directory.

To compile MySQL on Linux:

1. Download the tarball (`tar.gz`) source distribution of MySQL.

   The easiest way to do so is to use your Web browser, saving the file to your home directory. At the time of this writing, the latest Generally Available version is 5.0.18, making the downloaded file `mysql-5.0.18.tar.gz`.

2. Access the server via a command-line interface (**Figure 1.13**).

   In my example here, I will be installing MySQL on Ubuntu 5.10 (Ubuntu is based on the Debian line of Linux). Everything will take place within the Terminal application.

   You will need to have permission to manipulate files and create new directories within the `/usr/local` directory, so you may need to switch to the *root* user or use `sudo`, as I'll do in these steps. See the sidebar "Being the Root User" for more information.

3. Move into the same directory where the downloaded MySQL files are located.

   `cd /path/to/directory`

   Use the preceding command to move into the directory where the source files were saved, changing the path accordingly. In my case, I entered

   `cd ~/Desktop`

   as I saved the download to my desktop.

4. Create a new MySQL user and group (**Figure 1.14**).

   `sudo groupadd mysql`

   `sudo useradd –g mysql mysql`

   This step will allow you to run and manage MySQL as the *mysql* user, rather than *root*. This step adds extra security to your system (it's best not to use *root* unless you absolutely have to).

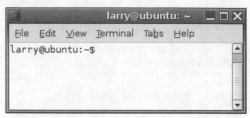

Figure 1.13 On Linux, use the Terminal application to install MySQL.

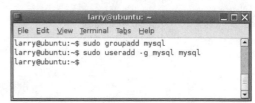

Figure 1.14 Create a new user and group who will own and run MySQL.

Figure 1.15 To create a more optimized MySQL binary, adjust your compiler's behavior to match your processor.

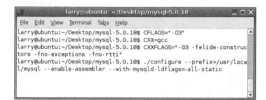

Figure 1.16 If you are using the source files of MySQL, you'll need to configure it yourself. At the very least, be sure to specify the `prefix` in your configuration statement.

5. Unpack the files.

`tar xzvf mysql-5.0.18.tar.gz`

The `tar` command will unpack the downloaded folder. The source versions use a naming convention like `mysql -VERSION.tar.gz`. In this step, and in those following, be sure to change your commands appropriately if you are using a different version than I am here.

6. Move into the new directory.

`cd mysql-5.0.18`

The next couple of steps will take place within the unpacked folder of source code files.

7. Configure gcc's behavior (**Figure 1.15**).

`CFLAGS="-03"`

`CXX=gcc`

`CXXFLAGS="-03 -felide-constructors -fno-exceptions -fno-rtti"`

This is an optional step but may result in a faster, more stable binary. These are also generic settings; ones specific to your processor may be better. Note that those are capital versions of the vowel "o" before each 3. See the MySQL manual or search the Web for more information on what gcc flags to use.

8. Configure the MySQL source files (**Figure 1.16**).

`./configure --prefix=/usr/local/mysql`
`→ --enable-assembler --with-mysqld-`
`→ ldflags=-all-static`

For more information on configuring MySQL, see "Basic Configuration Options" later in this chapter or the pertinent sections of the MySQL manual. The `prefix` option is very important, as it specifies where MySQL, and therefore the actual binary files to be executed, should be placed. The other two options should improve MySQL's performance.

continues on next page

INSTALLING MySQL ON LINUX

9. After the configuration has successfully run (**Figure 1.17**), make and install the files.

```
make
sudo make install
```

These two steps will take some time, depending upon the operating system and processor speed of your server. If you encounter problems with make (you would see error messages and the make would terminate), do not proceed to the sudo make install step. If you continue to have difficulties with this part of the installation, check the MySQL manual or Appendix A, "Troubleshooting," for more information or consider using a binary version instead of the source.

Note that you must run make install as the *root* user, in my case by invoking sudo.

10. Move to the installation directory.

```
cd /usr/local/mysql
```

The next couple of steps will take place from within the installed MySQL folder.

11. Install the default databases.

```
sudo bin/mysql_install_db
→ --user=mysql
```

This step will create the database MySQL needs to function properly (called *mysql*) along with an appropriately named test database (called *test*). Once the script has run, you will see a number of messages regarding the software (**Figure 1.18**).

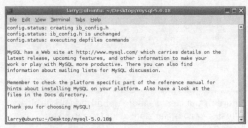

Figure 1.17 If the configuration step (Figure 1.16) worked, you should see a message like this, meaning you are ready to make and install the files.

Figure 1.18 After installing the databases, you will see these lines, telling you what steps to take to run the server.

Figure 1.19 By giving the *mysql* user permissions over your files, you can avoid the security risk of running MySQL as *root*.

12. Change the permissions on the new files (**Figure 1.19**).

```
sudo chown –R root .
sudo chown –R mysql var
sudo chgrp –R mysql .
```

This final step allows the MySQL server to run under the guise of the newly created *mysql* user. All of the files will be marked as owned by the *root* user except for the data directory, var, which will be owned by the same user MySQL will run as.

13. Start MySQL and assign a password to MySQL's *root* user.

You'll learn how to do these two steps in Chapter 2.

✔ Tips

- Depending upon your operating system, you may have to add the *mysql* user and group using different terminology (like adduser and addgroup) than the example here.

- You can also use wget or curl to download MySQL. But since you have to find the full, correct URL of the source files, taking into account which mirror you'll use, I find the browser to be easiest.

- During my configuration, I saw a *No curses/termcap library found* error. To adjust for this, I had to add the --with-named-curses-libs=/lib/ libncurses.so.5 argument to the configuration command.

- If you've already configured MySQL once and need to reconfigure it, first wipe out the previous configuration by running

  make distclean

  within the MySQL source code directory, prior to reconfiguration.

Basic Configuration Options

Because MySQL is open source and very flexible in how it runs, there are numerous ways you can configure the software. By installing MySQL from the source files, as I did on Linux, you can establish certain parameters at the time of installation that affect how the software functions. For starters, you can set the location of the installed files using the `prefix` option (as I did in my Linux example). You can also choose whether or not to install the MySQL server (leaving only the client), and select what language to use. These are just examples; the full listing of options is available by typing `./configure --help` at the command line from within the MySQL source code directory (e.g., `~/Desktop/mysql-5.0.18`) (**Figure 1.20**).

Another way you can affect how MySQL runs is to use a configuration file. On Windows, the easiest way to create and edit such a file is to use the MySQL Server Instance configuration wizard utility, introduced earlier in this chapter. This utility will manage the `my.ini` file, found within the MySQL installation directory.

On any operating system, you can also manually edit a configuration file or even create your own. The installation comes with several configuration samples, which you can tweak. I'll run through how that process would work.

Figure 1.20 The MySQL manual details the most common configuration options, while `./configure --help` gives the entire list.

Script 1.1 This is a sampling of what a basic configuration file looks like.

```
                         Script
1    # Example MySQL config file for medium
     systems.
2    #
3    # This is for a system with little memory
     (32M - 64M) where MySQL plays
4    # an important part, or systems up to
     128M where MySQL is used together with
5    # other programs (such as a web server)
6    #
7    # You can copy this file to
8    # /etc/my.cnf to set global options,
9    # mysql-data-dir/my.cnf to set server-
     specific options (in this
10   # installation this directory is
     /var/mysql) or
11   # ~/.my.cnf to set user-specific options.
12   #
13   # In this file, you can use all long
     options that a program supports.
14   # If you want to know which options a
     program supports, run the program
15   # with the "--help" option.
16
17   # The following options will be passed to
     all MySQL clients
18   [client]
19   #password    = your_password
20   port    = 3306
21   socket      = /var/mysql/mysql.sock
22
23   # Here follows entries for some specific
     programs
24
25   # The MySQL server
26   [mysqld]
27   port    = 3306
28   socket      = /var/mysql/mysql.sock
29   skip-locking
30   key_buffer = 16M
31   max_allowed_packet = 1M
32   table_cache = 64
33   sort_buffer_size = 512K
34   net_buffer_length = 8K
35   read_buffer_size = 256K
36   read_rnd_buffer_size = 512K
37   myisam_sort_buffer_size = 8M
38
39   # Don't listen on a TCP/IP port at all.
     This can be a security enhancement,
40   # if all processes that need to connect
     to mysqld run on the same host.
```

To change MySQL's configuration:

1. Find a MySQL sample configuration file.

   The sample configuration files will be installed when you install MySQL; the only question is where. These should be in the directory where MySQL was placed, but they may turn up somewhere else on Mac OS X and Unix (just do a search in the Terminal to find them).

   The configuration files have the names my-huge.cnf, my-large.cnf, my-medium.cnf, and my-small.cnf. Each file represents a sample configuration for an expected server load. I would start with either my-medium.cnf or my-small.cnf.

2. Make a copy of the file.

   You'll want to make a copy just in case you ever want to use the original version again.

3. Rename the file as my.cnf.

4. Move the file to the correct destination.

   On Windows, this should be either the directory where MySQL was installed (C:\Program Files\MySQL\MySQL Server *x.x*) or the root of the hard drive (C:\my.cnf).

   If you installed on Unix using the source distribution method, you'll want to put the configuration file in /etc.

5. Open the file in any text editor and edit the file as needed.

   The file is pretty easy to understand and contains copious notes (**Script 1.1**). Note that anything after the number symbol (#) is considered a comment and has no effect.

   continues on next page

BASIC CONFIGURATION OPTIONS

6. Save the file.

7. Restart MySQL.

Any changes will take effect the next time you start the MySQL server.

✔ Tips

■ When entering pathnames on Windows in the configuration file, use either forward slashes (/) or two backslashes (\\).

■ In this section I talk about configuration files with respect to how the MySQL server runs. You can also create configuration files for MySQL's client applications and utilities. Such a file would be named and stored as C:\WINDOWS\my.ini or C:\WINNT\my.ini on Windows and ~/.my.cnf on Mac OS X and Unix, where ~ refers to your home directory.

■ You can also adjust how MySQL will run by using configuration settings when you start the MySQL server.

Upgrading MySQL

Eventually you might have the need to upgrade your MySQL installation. When doing so, it's important to consider what type of upgrade you'll be making. If you are staying within the same release series, going from, say, 4.1.12 to 4.1.17 or from 5.0.3 to 5.0.4, that's a relatively safe upgrade. If you are changing the release series, 4.0.9 to 4.1.12 or 4.1.17 to 5.0.18, there's a bit more to it.

The first type of upgrade is best if you want the latest, most stable and secure version, without any hassle. The second type of upgrade is normally for the benefit of adding features but has a higher potential for problems. MySQL recommends jumping only a single release at a time (3.23 to 4.0, 4.0 to 4.1, 4.1 to 5.0, and so on).

The MySQL manual covers the specifics of upgrading from one version of MySQL to another in great detail so that you can be best prepared as to what you might encounter. The directions I give next are more generalized recommendations.

To upgrade MySQL:

1. Back up your existing MySQL data.

   See Chapter 13, "MySQL Administration," for information about how to do this.

2. Stop the currently running MySQL server daemon.

   Technically, this isn't required, especially when upgrading within the same release series (e.g., from 5.0.15 to 5.0.18), but I do think it is a good idea. I will discuss stopping the MySQL application more specifically in Chapter 2.

continues on next page

3. Install the new version of MySQL.

   Follow the directions in this chapter, installing MySQL as you otherwise would. Some steps you can omit here, such as creating a new user and running the `mysql_install_db` script (part of the Linux instructions).

4. Restart MySQL.

5. Update the grant tables, if necessary.

   Sometimes new versions of MySQL will require changes to the *mysql* database. A script called `mysql_fix_privilege_tables` will be installed for this purpose (check your `scripts` directory).

   As a rule of thumb, if upgrading from one major version to another (like from 4.1 to 5.0), you'll have to update the grant tables.

   On Unix and Mac OS X, you can run this script from within the MySQL directory, using this command:

   ```
   ./scripts/mysql_fix_privilege_tables
   → --password=rootUserPassword
   ```

   On Windows, you'll want to run the `mysql_fix_privilege_tables.sql` file in the `mysql` client (which will be discussed in the next chapter). The command would be something like:

   ```
   SOURCE C:/Program Files/MySQL/
   → MySQL Server 5.0/scripts/
   → mysql_fix_privilege_tables.sql
   ```

   On any platform, if you see error warnings about duplicate column names, you can safely ignore those.

   After updating the grant tables, you'll need to stop and restart MySQL one more time.

6. Test, test, test!

   Don't just assume everything went smoothly. Run some queries and check the results to be certain!

✔ **Tips**

■ The Mac MySQL installer does not replace the old version of MySQL. Instead it installs MySQL in a new directory and then changes the symbolic link to point there.

■ Advanced Unix users may also appreciate the benefits of installing MySQL into a version-specific directory, and then updating the symbolic links to make the association to the new installation. This way you'll have the old installation to fall back on, just in case.

RUNNING MySQL

Now that the MySQL software has been successfully installed (presumably), it's time to learn how to start, stop, and basically administer your database server. Assuming that you did not install just the client software (e.g., as a Linux RPM), you now have a database server as well as several different utilities that will aid you in running and maintaining your databases.

In this chapter I will first cover starting and stopping MySQL on different operating systems (Windows XP, Mac OS X, and Ubuntu Linux). After that, I will go into important administrative knowledge that you'll need, regardless of the platform in use. This includes the introduction of two important applications: `mysqladmin` and the `mysql` client. During these discussions you will set a *root* user password, which is vital to security, and learn how to control user access to databases.

Running MySQL on Windows and Windows NT

Unfortunately, you cannot truly know that MySQL has been successfully installed until you've been able to actually start the database server. Starting MySQL is a frequent place of problems and confusion, especially for the beginning or intermediate user. On the bright side, MySQL is very stable and reliable once you have it running, and it can remain up for months at a time without incident. If you run into difficulties in these steps, check the "Starting MySQL" section of Appendix A, "Troubleshooting." Or, as always, search the version of the MySQL manual that corresponds to the version of MySQL that you installed.

When it comes to running MySQL on Windows, the main decision is whether to run it as a *service* or not. If you are using an NT version of Windows, which includes Windows NT, 2000, 2003, and XP (and probably future versions of Windows, too), the recommendation is that you do run MySQL as a service. When you do so, MySQL will automatically start and stop when you turn on and shut down your computer. In fact, if, while running the MySQL Server Instance Configuration Wizard (**Figure 2.1**), you opted to install MySQL as a service and have it launch automatically, MySQL has already been started for you.

If you cannot, or will not, run MySQL as a service, your instructions for controlling MySQL are listed first. Instructions specifically for starting and stopping MySQL as a service will be covered second.

When it comes to starting MySQL, it is very important that the MySQL server not be currently running. This may seem obvious, but trying to start MySQL when it's already running can lead to confusing error messages and is a common problem for MySQL newbies.

Figure 2.1 You may have the option of installing MySQL as a service when you configure the software.

Running MySQL on Windows

Starting MySQL on a Windows operating system is very simple. The only real decision you'll need to make is which version of the MySQL server—called *mysqld*—to start. Depending upon what distribution of MySQL you installed, you will have some combination of the following choices (storage engines, which are referenced in these descriptions, are covered in Chapter 4, "Creating a MySQL Database"):

◆ `mysqld`, the standard server, optimized with support for the InnoDB storage engine

◆ `mysqld-debug`, compiled with full debugging enabled and support for both the InnoDB and BDB storage engines

◆ `mysqld-nt`, similar to `mysqld` except more optimized for the NT family of Windows (NT, 2000, 2003, and XP)

◆ `mysqld-max`, like the `mysqld`, but supporting every feature available

◆ `mysqld-max-nt`, a cross between `mysqld-nt` and `mysqld-max`

As an average user, you may not see a difference when using any of these servers. As you make your decision, I'd recommend starting with the most basic option—`mysqld` or `mysqld-nt`—and then making changes later to fine-tune MySQL's performance. Which MySQL server you use does not affect the reliability of the data stored, which is what matters in the end.

The only trick to manually starting MySQL on Windows is that you'll use a DOS prompt (also called a console window), which you may not previously have encountered. Most of these steps teach how to access a DOS prompt and execute applications from this command-line interface. Stopping MySQL makes use of the `mysqladmin` utility, which I'll also demonstrate.

To start and stop MySQL on Windows:

1. Decide which server you will use.

   Review the preceding list of servers for the possible options. You can confirm which are available to you by looking at the bin directory located within the MySQL default installation folder (just open it in Windows Explorer). You aren't permanently tied to whatever you choose here, so don't sweat it too much, particularly as you're just getting your bearings.

2. Make sure MySQL is not currently running.

   If MySQL is already running, the following steps will result in errors, which may be unintelligible. If you followed the instructions in Chapter 1, "Installing MySQL," MySQL is probably already running. You can stop an active MySQL process using the instructions later in this sequence.

3. Access the Start menu.

4. Select Run.

   The Run window can be used to run any command or program.

5. In the Run window, type cmd (**Figure 2.2**), and press Enter or click OK.

   The code cmd is short for *command*, which is a request for a command window (**Figure 2.3**). Note that your command window may not look quite the same as mine (by default it's white text on a black background, which doesn't look so swell in a book), and the prompt will likely differ.

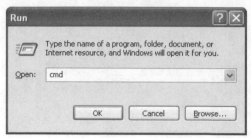

Figure 2.2 Enter cmd in the Run window to access a DOS prompt.

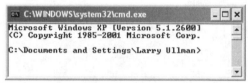

Figure 2.3 A console window, also known as a DOS prompt, or command-line interface.

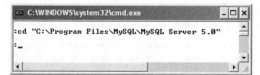

Figure 2.4 Move into the MySQL directory to more easily access its programs.

Figure 2.5 If the MySQL server started properly, you'll see messages like those here (or the like).

6. Move into the MySQL installation directory (**Figure 2.4**).

```
cd C:\"Program Files\MySQL\
→ MySQL Server 5.0"
```

Because you may or may not be able to call the MySQL programs directly (depending upon your PATH, see the first tip), it's best to move into the MySQL directory and call the programs from there. To avoid conflicts with the spaces in the pathname (in *Program Files* and *MySQL Server 5.0*), quotes are used as needed. The easiest way to type all this is to type a few letters and then press Tab, letting the autocomplete feature fill in the rest of each directory's name.

If you installed MySQL in a different location, you'll need to change the path here accordingly.

7. Start the server (**Figure 2.5**).

At the prompt, type the following and press Enter:

```
bin\mysqld --console
```

The important part here is just the mysqld, which is the MySQL server itself. If you want to use a different version of the server (see the earlier list of servers), change that reference.

The --console option means that all results will be displayed in the console window, which is useful, particularly for debugging purposes. You should leave the console window open for the time being (closing the window will attempt to shut down MySQL). If you are running a non-NT version of Windows (something other than Windows NT, 2000, 2003, or XP), mysqld will automatically run in the background and you are free to do whatever with the console window.

continues on next page

RUNNING MySQL ON WINDOWS AND WINDOWS NT

8. Confirm that MySQL is running (**Figure 2.6**).

Repeat Steps 3–6 to bring up a new console window (if necessary) and move into the MySQL directory. Then, at the prompt, type the following and press Enter:

```
bin\mysqlshow -u root -p
```

When prompted, enter the MySQL *root* user password (if you have not yet established a *root* user password, for instance, during server configuration, omit the -p argument).

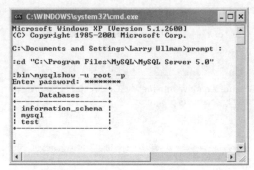

Figure 2.6 The `mysqlshow` utility will show a list of available databases and is also a way to confirm that MySQL is running.

9. Stop the server (**Figure 2.7**).

At the prompt, type the following and press Enter:

```
bin\mysqladmin -u root -p shutdown
```

The `mysqladmin` utility can be used for many things, including stopping a running server. The -u root argument says that `mysqladmin` should perform the command—shutdown—as the MySQL *root* user. When prompted, enter the *root* user password (if you have not yet established a *root* user password, for instance, during server configuration, omit the -p argument).

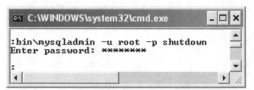

Figure 2.7 Use `mysqladmin` to shut down MySQL. If the MySQL *root* user does not require a password, omit the -p.

10. Start MySQL up again and begin administering your database.

See the remainder of this chapter for information on related MySQL utilities, creating users, and so forth.

✔ Tips

■ If, while running the MySQL Server Instance Configuration Wizard (Figure 2.1), you opted to include the `bin` directory in the Windows `PATH`, then you can start MySQL by just using `mysqld --console`. This will be true no matter what directory you are currently in (within the console window).

■ Technically, on Windows, you could go straight into the `bin` directory and run your commands from there. The syntax demonstrated in the preceding steps is common on other operating systems, so I've used it for consistency's sake.

■ If you don't use the `--console` option when starting MySQL, all output will be written to an error log. This is fine, if not preferred, normally, but it's best to use the `--console` option the first couple times you start the server to make sure there are no problems. The error log would be stored in the data directory (`C:\Program Files\MySQL\MySQL Server 5.0\data`, by default), with a `.err` extension. It is readable in any text editor.

■ You may be able to invoke the `mysqlshow` and `mysqladmin` applications without specifying a user at all, but I think it's best to be explicit.

Running MySQL as a service on Windows

If you are using an NT version of Windows, which covers Windows NT, 2000, 2003, XP, and probably all future versions as well, you can run MySQL as a service. As a service, MySQL can be controlled in two ways: by typing commands in a console window or by using the Windows Service Control Manager. If you would prefer to use the first method, access a DOS prompt (using the Steps 3–5 in the preceding set of instructions) and then enter NET START MySQL to start the service or NET STOP MySQL to stop it (**Figure 2.8**). You can do this no matter what directory you are currently in (in the console window). If MySQL will not start for some reason, you'll need to check the error log, found in the MySQL data directory, with a name ending in .err. This is viewable in any text editor.

The other way you can control the MySQL service is to use Windows' built-in Services utility. I'll run through that process now, but the steps do assume that MySQL has been installed as a service (see the sidebar). The instructions I'll use will apply to Windows XP; you may need to make slight adjustments if you are using a different version of the operating system.

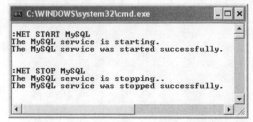

Figure 2.8 Starting and stopping the MySQL service on Windows XP.

Installing MySQL as a Service

The easiest way to install MySQL as a service is to check the right box during the configuration process (see Figure 2.1). If MySQL is not already installed as a service, you'll have to use a console window. Bring one up and move into the MySQL installation directory (using Steps 3–6 in the preceding section of this chapter). At the prompt type

bin\mysqld --install

and press Enter.

If you would like MySQL to be *available* as a service but not have it automatically start and stop, you can use the --install-manual option instead. In such a case, you would use NET START MySQL and NET STOP MySQL to control it. To remove the MySQL service, use mysqld --remove at the DOS prompt.

Figure 2.9 The Windows XP Control Panel, in Classic view. Double-click Administrative Tools here.

Figure 2.10 The Windows XP Control Panel, in Category view. Click Performance and Maintenance here.

Figure 2.11 The Windows list of shortcuts to Administrative Tools like Services.

To start and stop the MySQL service:

1. Click Start to bring up the Start menu.

2. Select Control Panel.

   This brings up the Control Panel window.

3. Double-click the Administrative Tools Control Panel.

   If you are in the Classic view in Windows XP (**Figure 2.9**), the Administrative Tools is immediately available. If you are in the Category view (**Figure 2.10**), you must first click Performance and Maintenance and then click Administrative Tools.

4. In the Administrative Tools window (**Figure 2.11**), double-click Services.

continues on next page

5. In the Services window, click MySQL
(**Figure 2.12**) to select it.

In this window you can see every available service. The current status of each
is listed, along with its startup type
(*Automatic, Manual, Disabled*).

6. Start the service.

You can either click the Start link (found
to the left of the list of services, see
Figure 2.12) or click the right-pointing
triangle at the top of the window (which
looks like a Play button).

7. Stop the service.

With the service started, you can either
click the Stop link (**Figure 2.13**) or use the
square button at the top of the window.

✔ Tips

■ It's recommended that you keep the
Services window closed when installing
MySQL or using NET START MySQL or NET
STOP MYSQL commands.

■ If you right-click the MySQL service and
select Properties from the contextual
menu, you'll be able to tweak the MySQL
service in other ways (**Figure 2.14**). You
can adjust which version of mysqld is
started by the service (see the *Path to
executable* setting), change the Startup
type, and so on.

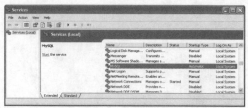

Figure 2.12 You can control the MySQL service using
this Windows tool.

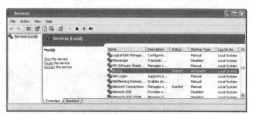

Figure 2.13 The links of options change when a
service is running (compare with Figure 2.12).

Figure 2.14 Each service has a list of properties that
can be adjusted as warranted.

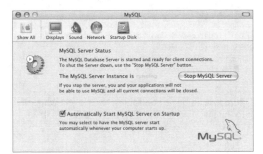

Figure 2.15 MySQL on Mac OS X comes with a System Preferences panel that can be used to stop and start the database server.

Running MySQL on Mac OS X

On Mac OS X, there are a handful of ways to get MySQL running. For starters, there is an optional System Preferences panel (**Figure 2.15**) that handles the task nicely. There is also the choice of having MySQL automatically start when you turn on your computer. You can enable this feature by checking the box in the System Preferences panel or by installing the MySQL Startup Item when you installed MySQL (see the instructions in Chapter 1). With the Startup Item, you can use the information presented in the sidebar to also control MySQL.

Using the Startup Item

The Startup Item is a simple shell script that provides a shortcut for starting and stopping MySQL. In fact, the hardest thing about using the Startup Item is finding where it was installed in the first place. Depending upon your versions of OS X and MySQL, the full path and script name will most likely be one of the following:

◆ /System/Library/MySQL/MySQL

◆ /System/Library/MySQLCOM/MySQLCOM

◆ /Library/MySQL/MySQL

◆ /Library/MySQLCOM/MySQLCOM

Once you confirm its location (just use the Finder to hunt around), you can start and stop MySQL using the proper commands within a Terminal window. These would be simply

sudo /path/to/script start

and

sudo /path/to/script stop

(You have to run them using sudo; you will then be prompted for your Mac OS X administrative password.)

For example, in two test environments I have—MySQL 4.1.13 on Mac OS X 10.4 Server and MySQL 5.0.18 on Mac OS X 10.3 Server—I use

sudo /System/Library/StartupItems/MySQL/MySQL start

If there's a problem, an error message will be displayed, and the Terminal will seem to sit there. In that case, press Enter to get a prompt again. Voilà! That's all there is to it!

Still, knowing how to manually start and stop MySQL is useful, so I'll run through that process. It involves using the Terminal application, with which you may not already be familiar.

To run MySQL on Mac OS X:

1. Open the Terminal application.

   The Terminal is found within your Utilities folder, which itself is inside the Applications folder. Just double-click the icon to open the Terminal.

2. Move to the MySQL directory (**Figure 2.16**).

   ```
   cd /usr/local/mysql
   ```

   To start, you'll want to move yourself into the directory where MySQL was installed. This should be /usr/local/mysql but could be different if you did something special during the installation process. If so, change the path here accordingly.

3. Start MySQL (**Figure 2.17**).

   Type the following at the prompt and press Return:

   ```
   sudo ./bin/mysqld_safe &
   ```

   The mysqld_safe script is used to start the server. It's located in the bin directory and must be run by prepending the command with the period and a slash (it's a Unix requirement). The ampersand at the end of this line tells the script to run in the background.

   Because you must run the script as a superuser (in terms of your operating system), the whole line begins with sudo. You'll then be prompted for your Mac OS X administrative password.

   Press Return to get back to the prompt.

   If MySQL fails to start, make note of the error message displayed and refer to Appendix A, "Troubleshooting," or the MySQL manual for assistance.

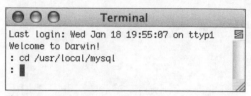

Figure 2.16 To begin controlling MySQL, get yourself into the installation directory, within a Terminal window.

Figure 2.17 Call the mysqld_safe script to start MySQL.

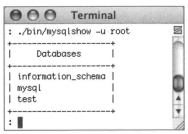

Figure 2.18 The mysqlshow utility will show a list of available databases. It is also an easy way to confirm that MySQL is running.

Figure 2.19 Use mysqladmin to shut down MySQL. If the MySQL *root* user has already been assigned a password, add -p after root.

✔ Tips

- If you are running Mac OS X Server and it came with MySQL preinstalled, make sure you know what version it is. Versions of MySQL prior to 4.0 were started using the safe_mysqld script instead of mysqld_safe. If this is the case, change the preceding commands accordingly.

- The mysqld server (and, therefore, the mysqld_safe script) can take a number of arguments to adjust how it runs. The average user will not need to tinker with these, but the complete listing can be found in the MySQL manual.

4. Confirm that MySQL is running (**Figure 2.18**).

   At the prompt, type the following and press Enter:

   ./bin/mysqlshow -u root

   This quick test should connect to MySQL and reveal the list of databases. If you have already established a MySQL *root* user password, you'll need to add -p at the end of the command to be prompted for that password.

5. Stop MySQL (**Figure 2.19**).

   Type the following at the prompt and press Return:

   ./bin/mysqladmin -u root shutdown

   The mysqladmin utility can be used for many things, including stopping a running server. The -u root argument says that mysqladmin should perform the command—shutdown—as the MySQL *root* user.

   If you have already created a *root* user password, you'll need to add the -p flag, so that it prompts you for that password. In such a case, the full command would be:

   ./bin/mysqladmin -u root -p shutdown

   Keep in mind that the MySQL *root* user is an entirely separate entity than your operating system users.

6. Start MySQL up again and begin administering your database.

   See the remainder of this chapter for information on related MySQL utilities, creating users, and so forth.

RUNNING MySQL ON MAC OS X

Running MySQL on Linux and Unix

On non-Windows systems, the `mysqld` daemon—the process the runs the MySQL server—is started using the `mysqld_safe` script, which ensures that `mysqld` continues to run. This is true for Mac OS X as well as Linux and other flavors of Unix. Calling this script is straightforward and should be pretty simple for those knowledgeable about Unix, so I'll run through it quickly. Stopping MySQL makes use of the `mysqladmin` utility, which I'll also demonstrate.

To start and stop MySQL on Linux and Unix:

1. Log in to your system from a command-line interface.

   For most versions of Unix and Linux, this is a matter of opening the Terminal application.

2. Change to the MySQL directory (**Figure 2.20**).

   `cd /usr/local/mysql`

   Assuming you followed the installation instructions as detailed in Chapter 1, all of the relevant MySQL utilities will now be located within the `bin` subdirectory of the `/usr/local/mysql` directory. Red Hat Linux users may find these utilities in `/usr/bin` instead.

3. Invoke the superuser (**Figure 2.21**).

   `sudo echo`

   This is a little trick I like to do in order to avoid problems with the next step. Enter your administrative password at the prompt. Once you've done that, you can use `sudo` again (in Step 4) without having to reenter the password (which can otherwise cause complications).

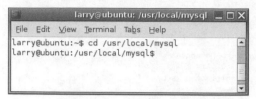

Figure 2.20 To begin controlling MySQL, get yourself into the installation directory, within a Terminal window.

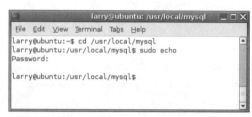

Figure 2.21 To avoid problems using `sudo` when starting MySQL, enter this simple command.

Figure 2.22 Starting MySQL on Linux.

Figure 2.23 The mysqlshow utility will show a list of available databases, which also serves as a confirmation that MySQL is running.

4. Start MySQL (**Figure 2.22**).

    Type the following at the prompt and press Return or Enter:

    `sudo ./bin/mysqld_safe --user=mysql &`

    This line tells the server to keep `mysqld_safe` running constantly. What the `mysqld_safe` script does is check to see if `mysqld` is running and, if it is not, start up the daemon. The very first time you start `mysqld_safe`, it will immediately realize that `mysqld` is not up and will therefore start it.

    If MySQL fails to start, make note of the error message displayed and refer to Appendix A, "Troubleshooting," or the MySQL manual for assistance.

5. Press Enter or Return to get back to the prompt.

6. Confirm that MySQL is running (**Figure 2.23**).

    At the prompt, type the following and press Enter or Return:

    `./bin/mysqlshow -u root`

    This quick test should connect to MySQL and reveal the list of databases. If you have already established a MySQL *root* user password, you'll need to add **-p** at the end of the command to be prompted for the *root* user password.

    continues on next page

7. Stop MySQL (**Figure 2.24**).

Type the following at the prompt and press Enter or Return:

`./bin/mysqladmin -u root shutdown`

The `mysqladmin` utility can be used for many things, including stopping a running server. The `-u root` argument says that `mysqladmin` should perform the command—shutdown—as the MySQL *root* user.

If you have already created a *root* user password, you'll need to add the `-p` flag, so that it prompts you for that password. In such a case, the full command would be:

`./bin/mysqladmin -u root -p shutdown`

8. Again, press Enter or Return to return to the prompt.

✔ Tips

■ MySQL includes a MySQL Instance Manager with version 5.0.4 and later. This tool, which runs on Windows and Unix, can also be used to start and stop the server. See the MySQL manual for details.

■ Some Red Hat users have experienced problems starting MySQL using the preceding directions. If you installed MySQL using an RPM, then it may be already established as a service. If so, you can start `mysqld` using either `service mysqld start` or the linuxconf control panel. A last option would be to use the line `/etc/rc.d/init.d/mysqld start`.

■ On Unix systems (particularly Red Hat Linux), you might also have luck stopping MySQL with `/etc/rc.d/init.d/mysqld stop`.

■ The `mysqld` daemon (and, therefore, the `mysqld_safe` script) can take a number of arguments to adjust how it runs. The average user will not need to tinker with these, but the complete listing can be found in the MySQL manual.

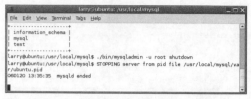

Figure 2.24 Use mysqladmin to shut down MySQL. If the *root* user has already been assigned a password, add -p after root.

Using mysqladmin

The mysqladmin utility, as the name might imply, is used to perform administrative-level tasks on your databases. This includes:

◆ Stopping MySQL (as you saw in the previous sections)

◆ Setting the *root* user's password

◆ Creating databases

◆ Deleting database

◆ And more!

A number of the things you can do with mysqladmin can also be accomplished more directly within the mysql client, which you'll see later in the chapter and in the book. But, in the meantime, another use of mysqladmin—confirming the operation of the server by checking its status—will be demonstrated here. This is a great way to test that MySQL is running, to check that you have the right *root* user password, if necessary, and to confirm the version of MySQL being used.

To demonstrate how most things you do with MySQL, aside from installing, starting, and stopping it, will be essentially the same from one operating system to the next, I'll take images from three different operating systems for these steps. Throughout the rest of the book, you'll also see different operating systems in use, but the functionality and most of the exact commands will be the same regardless of the platform.

To use mysqladmin:

1. Make sure that MySQL is running!

   The MySQL server (mysqld) must be running in order for you to use mysqladmin. If MySQL is not currently running, start it now using the steps outlined earlier.

2. Log in to your system from a command-line interface and move into the MySQL installation directory (**Figure 2.25**).

   Again, refer back to the steps outlined earlier in the chapter for your particular operating system. You'll need to use a DOS console window or the Terminal application, and then use the cd command to change directories.

3. Find out the current version and status of MySQL (**Figure 2.26**).

   At the prompt, type one of the following and press Enter or Return:

   bin\mysqladmin –u root -p version
   → status (Windows)

   or

   ./bin/mysqladmin –u root -p version
   → status (Mac OS X and Unix)

   If you haven't already established a *root* user's password, omit the -p argument. If you have established that password, use the command as shown and enter that password at the prompt.

   If everything worked, you should see how long the MySQL server has been running (in seconds) as well as other statistics.

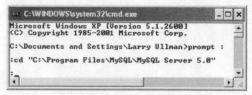

Figure 2.25 Start by accessing the MySQL installation directory from within a command-line interface.

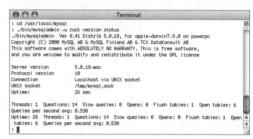

Figure 2.26 The mysqladmin utility can display useful information about your MySQL server.

Figure 2.27 A partial list of the commands that the mysqladmin utility accepts.

4. See what other mysqladmin options are possible (**Figure 2.27**).

At the prompt, type one of the following and press Enter or Return:

bin\mysqladmin -u root -p --help

(Windows)

or

./bin/mysqladmin -u root -p --help

(Mac OS X and Unix)

Again, you'll likely need to change this slightly depending upon whether or not a *root* user password has already been established.

✔ Tips

- Depending upon many combinations of things, you may not have to use -u root when invoking mysqladmin. I think it's best to be explicit, though.

- To check if MySQL is running without viewing all the status details, try just

  mysqladmin -u root -p ping

Setting the Root User Password

One of the most important uses of `mysqladmin` is to assign a password to the *root* user. When MySQL is installed, no such value is established. This is certainly a security risk that ought to be remedied before you begin to use the server.

Just to clarify, your databases can have several users, just as your operating system might. But the MySQL users are different from the operating system users, even if they share a common name. Therefore, the MySQL *root* user is a different entity than the operating system's *root* user (if one exists), having different powers and even different passwords (preferably but not necessarily).

If you used the MySQL Instance Configuration Wizard on Windows (see Chapter 1), you should hopefully have already assigned a password to the *root* user. Otherwise, follow these steps.

To assign a password to the root user:

1. Log in to your system from a command-line interface.

2. Move to the MySQL installation directory. This might be *either*

   `cd /usr/local/mysql` (Mac OS X and Unix)

   or

   `cd C:\"Program Files\MySQL\MySQL`
   → `Server 5.0"` (Windows)

   The full path may also differ for you, so change these commands as necessary.

Figure 2.28 Use `mysqladmin` to establish a password for the *root* user.

Figure 2.29 To change an existing *root* user's password, add the -p option to your `mysqladmin` line (Figure 2.28) so that you'll be prompted for current password.

3. Enter one of the following, replacing *theNEWpassword* with the password you want to use (**Figure 2.28**):

`bin\mysqladmin –u root password` → `'theNEWpassword'` (Windows)

or

`./bin/mysqladmin –u root password` → `'theNEWpassword'` (Mac OS X and Unix)

Keep in mind that passwords within MySQL are case-sensitive, so *Kazan* and *kazan* are not interchangeable. The term `password` that precedes the actual quoted password tells MySQL to encrypt the password that follows.

Once you've established the *root* user's password, it's only slightly more complicated to change it.

To change the root user's password:

1. Log in to your system from a command-line interface.

2. Move to the MySQL installation directory.

3. Enter one of the following, replacing *newNEWpassword* with the password you want to use:

`bin/mysqladmin –u root -p password` → `'newNEWpassword'` (Windows)

or

`./bin/mysqladmin –u root -p password` → `'newNEWpassword'` (Mac OS X and Unix)

Because it has already been established, the *root* user's password is required to use the `mysqladmin` tool from here on out. The -p argument will make `mysqladmin` prompt you for the current password.

4. At the prompt, enter the current (or soon-to-be-old) *root* user password (**Figure 2.29**).

✔ Tip

■ It can, and unfortunately does, happen that you forget or misplace the *root* user password, essentially locking the most important user out of the database. To fix this should it happen, see Appendix A, "Troubleshooting," where I'll walk you through the solution.

Using the mysql Client

Once you have successfully installed and started MySQL, you need some sort of way to interact with it. Whereas mysqld is the MySQL server that manages all the data, you need a client application that will talk to mysqld. The most common way to interface with mysqld—besides using a programming language—is to use the *mysql client* (or *mysql monitor,* as it is also called). This application can be used to connect to mysqld running on the same machine, or even on another. Most of the examples throughout the rest of this book will be accomplished via mysql (the lowercase word *mysql* will refer to the client, as opposed to MySQL, which refers to the software as a whole).

The mysql client can take several arguments up front, including the user name, password, and hostname (computer name). You establish these arguments like so:

```
mysql -u username -p -h hostname
```

The -p option will cause mysql to prompt you for the user's password, just as the mysqladmin tool does. You can specify the password on this line if you prefer, by typing it after the -p prompt, but it will be visible, which is less secure.

Within the mysql client, practically every statement (or SQL command) needs to be terminated by a semicolon. This means that you can continue the same statement over several lines to facilitate typing. With this in mind, you will also see a few different prompts when using the interface, as illustrated in **Figure 2.30** and listed in **Table 2.1**.

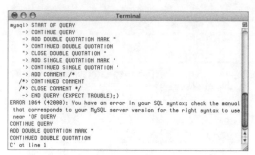

Figure 2.30 The mysql client will indicate what it thinks you are doing by using different prompts.

Table 2.1 These prompts, also represented in Figure 2.30, are used to clue you in as to what the mysql client is expecting.

mysql Client Prompts	
PROMPT	MEANING
mysql>	Ready
->	Continuing a command
'>	Need to finish a single quote
">	Need to finish a double quote
`>	Need to finish a backtick
/*>	Need to finish a comment

Figure 2.31 Invoke the mysql client, which will be the most commonly used method to access databases throughout this book.

As a quick demonstration of working with the mysql client, I will show you how to access mysql, select a database to use, and quit the application. As always, the MySQL server must be running to connect to it from the mysql client.

Before going through the steps, there's an alternative beginning for Windows users. The latest versions of MySQL have created a shortcut to the mysql client. You can access it by selecting Start > All Programs > MySQL > MySQL Server 5.0 > MySQL Command Line Client. This was created during the installation process, but the particulars may differ, depending upon your version of MySQL. If you have this shortcut, you can follow it and skip ahead to Step 4.

To use the mysql client:

1. Log in to your system from a command-line interface.

2. Move to the MySQL installation directory. Steps 1 and 2 should be old hat for you by now.

3. Enter the following text (**Figure 2.31**):

   ./bin/mysql -u root -p

   The -h *hostname* argument described previously is optional, and I tend to leave it off unless I cannot get into mysql otherwise. If you set a password for the *root* user, as detailed earlier in this chapter, you can use the *root* user name and password now.

   continues on next page

4. At the prompt, enter the user's password.

If you used *root* in Step 3 or used the Windows Start menu trick, you would enter the *root* user's password here.

If you ever want to connect to the mysql client using another username, just replace *root* with that username (in Step 3) and enter that user's password at the prompt. On Windows, you'll either need to use a configuration file or manually go through the preceding steps.

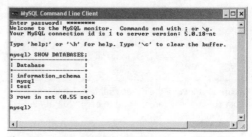

Figure 2.32 The SHOW DATABASES command lists the databases available to the logged-in user.

5. Show all the available databases (**Figure 2.32**).

```
SHOW DATABASES;
```

The SHOW DATABASES command asks MySQL to list every database which you, the logged-in user, can access. The semi-colon that terminates the command is a requirement in the mysql client.

6. Select which database you want to use (**Figure 2.33**).

```
USE test;
```

The USE command tells MySQL which database you want to deal with from here on out (saving typing the database name over and over again later). The mysql_install_db script run during the installation process creates two starter databases—*mysql* and *test*.

If you know in advance which database you will want to use, you can simplify matters by starting mysql with

```
mysql -u username -p databasename
```

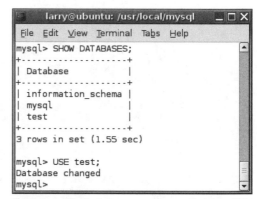

Figure 2.33 The first step you will normally take within the mysql client is to choose the database with which to work.

7. Quit out of mysql.

```
exit
```

You can also use the command quit to leave the client. This step—unlike most other commands you enter—does not require a semicolon at the end.

On Windows, using the Start Menu short-cut, this should also close the window.

Using Other Interfaces

The mysql client (or mysql monitor) is just one of many tools you can use to work with MySQL. Although this will be the application used almost exclusively in this book, you don't have to use the mysql client. There are many other programs available, all of which will provide the same functionality but in a different way.

MySQL also makes two related applications, both of which are free. The first is the MySQL Administrator. The second is the MySQL Query Browser. Both offer a functionality that overlaps with the mysql client and with mysqladmin, but they use a nicer graphical interface.

There are also plenty of third-party tools available. Of these, phpMyAdmin is a popular choice (available from www.phpmyadmin.net). It's a Web-based tool, which requires that you also have a Web server and PHP installed.

If none of these are to your liking, just search the Internet (or your favorite download repository) for MySQL applications for your particular platform.

✔ Tips

- To see what else you can do with the mysql client, type help; at any time (at the mysql prompt, after logging in).

- The mysql client makes use of the Unix readline tool, allowing you to use the up and down arrows to scroll through previously entered commands. This can save you oodles of time later on.

- You can also expedite your work within the mysql client by pressing the Tab key to complete words (type a single # and press Return to see what words can be completed), using Ctrl+A to move your cursor to the beginning of a line, and using Ctrl+E to move the cursor to the end of the line.

- If you are in a long statement and make a mistake, cancel the current operation by typing \c and pressing Return (it must be a lowercase "c"). If mysql thinks a closing single or double quotation mark is missing, you'll need to enter that first.

- Depending upon how MySQL is installed on your system, some Windows users can run the mysql client—and other utilities described in this chapter—simply by double-clicking the executable file found within the mysql/bin folder. You can also directly run the mysql client from the Start > Run menu.

- To be particularly safe when using mysql, start the application using the --i-am-a-dummy argument. And, no, I am not making this up (the argument limits what you can and cannot do).

Users and Privileges

After you have MySQL successfully up and running, and after you've established a password for the *root* user, it's time to begin adding other users. To improve the security of your databases, you should always create new users for accessing your databases, rather than continuing to use the *root* user at all times.

The MySQL privileges system was designed to ensure proper authority for certain commands on specific databases. This technology is how a Web host, for example, can securely have several users accessing several databases, without concern. Each user within the MySQL system can have specific capabilities on specific databases from specific hosts (computers). The *root* user—the MySQL *root* user, not the system's—has the most power and is used for creating subusers, although subusers can be given *root*-like powers (inadvisably so).

When a user attempts to do something with the MySQL server, MySQL will first check to see if the user has the permission to connect to the server at all (based upon the user name and host, the user's password, and the information in the user table of the *mysql* database). Second, MySQL will check to see if the user has the permission to run the specific SQL statement on the specific databases—for example, to select data, insert data, or create a new table. To determine this, MySQL uses the db, host, user, tables_priv, and columns_priv tables, again from the *mysql* database. **Tables 2.2**, **2.3**, and **2.4** list the various privileges that can be set on a user-by-user basis (the groupings are mine for clarification purposes; these are not official MySQL labels).

Table 2.2 This is the list of basic privileges that can be assigned to MySQL users on a case-by-case basis. It is generally safe to assign these to users for a specific database (except for the *mysql* database, which must be kept off-limits).

Basic MySQL Privileges	
PRIVILEGE	ALLOWS
SELECT	Reading of rows from tables
INSERT	Adding new rows of data to tables
UPDATE	Altering existing data in tables
DELETE	Removing existing data in tables
SHOW DATABASES	Listing the available databases
INDEX	Creating and dropping indexes in tables
ALTER	Modifying the structure or properties of a table
CREATE	Creating new tables or databases
CREATE TEMPORARY TABLES	Creating temporary tables
DROP	Deleting existing tables or databases

Table 2.3 These privileges should be given only to administrative users.

Administrative MySQL Privileges	
PRIVILEGE	ALLOWS
RELOAD	Reloading the grant tables (and therefore enact user changes)
SHUTDOWN	Stopping the MySQL server
FILE	Importing data into tables from text files
GRANT OPTION	Creating new users with the same permissions as current user
CREATE USER	Creating new users
REVOKE	Removing the permissions of users
PROCESS	Showing currently running processes
SUPER	Terminating running processes

Table 2.4 These privileges have been added in newer versions of MySQL (mostly 5.0 and up).

Newer MySQL Privileges	
PRIVILEGE	ALLOWS
CREATE VIEW	Creating a view
SHOW VIEW	Using a view
ALTER ROUTINE	Modifying a stored procedure
CREATE ROUTINE	Creating a stored procedure
EXECUTE	Running a stored procedure
LOCK TABLES	Locking tables
REPLICATION CLIENT	Showing replication status
REPLICATION SLAVE	Performing replication

Creating new users

There are a handful of ways to establish users and privileges within MySQL, but the most failsafe is to use the `mysql` client and the GRANT command. The syntax goes like this:

```
GRANT privileges ON database.* TO
→ 'username'@'hostname' IDENTIFIED BY
→ 'password'
```

For the privileges aspect of this statement, you can list specific privileges from those in Tables 2.2, 2.3, and 2.4, or you can allow for all of them using ALL (which is not prudent). The `database.*` part of the statement specifies which database and tables the user can work on. You can name specific tables using `database.tablename` syntax or allow for every database with `*.*` (again, not prudent). Finally, you can specify the user name, the host, and a password.

The user name has a maximum length of 16 characters. When creating a user name, be sure to avoid spaces (use the underscore instead) and note that user names are case-sensitive. The host name is the computer from which the user is allowed to connect. The most secure option is to set the host as `localhost`, meaning that the user can connect only from the same computer on which MySQL is running. The least secure is to use the wildcard character (%), meaning that any host is valid. You can also set the host name to be a specific IP address (192.168.0.1), an IP address within a certain realm (192.168.0.%), or a specific host name (mysite.com). Whatever you decide to do, it is the combination of a username@host that is important. If you create two users—Jessica@apple and Jessica@banana —these are entirely different entities.

The user's password has no length limit but is also case-sensitive. The passwords will be encrypted within the mysql database, meaning they cannot be recovered in a plain text format. Omitting the IDENTIFIED BY 'password' clause results in that user not being required to enter a password (which, once again, should be avoided).

As an example of this process, I will create two new users with specific privileges.

To create new users:

1. Log in to the mysql client.

   You don't necessarily need to log in as the *root* user, but you do need to be a user that has the privilege of creating other users.

2. Create two new databases (**Figure 2.34**).

   CREATE DATABASE alpacas;

   CREATE DATABASE movies;

   Although I have not formally discussed creating databases before now, the syntax is obvious and having two example databases already created will allow for better examples in these steps.

3. Create a user that has management privileges on the *alpacas* database (**Figure 2.35**).

   GRANT SELECT, INSERT, UPDATE, DELETE,
   → CREATE, DROP, ALTER, INDEX ON
   → alpacas.* TO 'llama'@'localhost'
   → IDENTIFIED BY 'camel';

   This user, *llama@localhost*, will be able to create tables, alter tables, insert data, update data, and so forth, on the *alpacas* database. This essentially constitutes every management-type capability aside from creating new users. Be certain to use a password, perhaps one more clever than this.

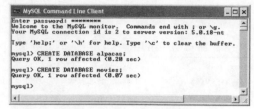

Figure 2.34 Before adding new users, I created a couple of extra databases using the CREATE DATABASE *databasename* SQL command.

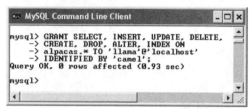

Figure 2.35 The first user I have created will have every requisite privilege for manipulating the *alpacas* database. (It's fine that it shows 0 rows affected.)

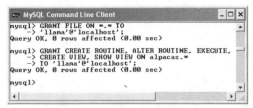

Figure 2.36 The first user has been modified so that they have FILE privileges on every database and MySQL 5.*x* privileges on the *alpacas* database.

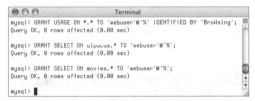

Figure 2.37 The *webuser* created here, who can connect from any host, is a generic and safe user for selecting data from tables.

4. Modify the *llama@localhost* privileges (**Figure 2.36**).

```
GRANT FILE ON *.* TO
→ 'llama'@'localhost';
```

```
GRANT CREATE ROUTINE, ALTER ROUTINE,
→ EXECUTE, CREATE VIEW, SHOW VIEW ON
→ alpacas.* TO 'llama'@'localhost';
```

A couple of interesting things are going on here. First of all, the user has been granted the FILE privilege, which will let them run queries stored in text files. This privilege must be granted globally, not on a specific database. MySQL has a few such privileges that are not database-specific. Others include LOCK_TABLES, RELOAD, and SHOW DATABASES.

Second, I've added a few more privileges, but only on the *alpacas* database. These privileges all relate to MySQL 5.0 and up, so they cannot be granted in earlier versions of the software.

Notice that I don't need to specify the password in these updates, either.

5. Create a user that has browsing-level access to both databases (**Figure 2.37**).

```
GRANT USAGE ON *.* TO 'webuser'@'%'
→ IDENTIFIED BY 'BroWs1ng';
```

```
GRANT SELECT ON alpacas.* TO
→ 'webuser'@'%';
```

```
GRANT SELECT ON movies.* TO
→ 'webuser'@'%';
```

continues on next page

The first line establishes a user—that can connect from any host—and password without granting any privileges at all. The next two lines grant SELECT privileges to two databases. Now the generic *webuser* can browse through records (SELECT from tables) but cannot modify the data therein. A more direct way of creating this user for every database would be to use the command

GRANT SELECT ON *.* TO 'webuser'@'%'
→ IDENTIFIED BY 'BroWs1ng';

except that would also give this user permission to select from the *mysql* database, which is not a good idea. When establishing users and privileges, work your way from the bottom up, allowing the bare minimum of access at all times.

6. Check the new user's privileges (**Figure 2.38**).

SHOW GRANTS FOR 'llama'@'localhost';

The SHOW GRANTS command lists the privileges for a user.

7. Exit out of mysql.

exit

8. Log back in to mysql as one of your new users (**Figure 2.39**).

./bin/mysql -u llama -p alpacas

This command should let you into the mysql client to begin creating the *alpacas* tables. If you're using Windows, you'll need to bring up a console window, then move into the MySQL directory, and then use

bin/mysql -u llama -p alpacas

You cannot use the Start Menu shortcut, as that assumes you are using the *root* user by default.

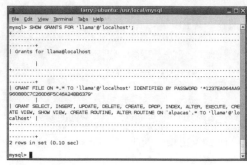

Figure 2.38 The SHOW GRANTS command reveals what specific users are allowed to do. Notice that there are separate entries for the global FILE privilege and the other, *alpacas*-specific ones.

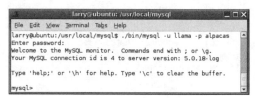

Figure 2.39 Once the new user has been given permission, I can now access the *alpacas* database through the mysql client with that account.

✔ Tips

- Any database whose name begins with *test* can be modified by any user who has permission to connect to MySQL. Therefore, be careful not to create databases with such names unless they are truly experimental.

- There is an even more manual way to create new users: by running INSERT commands on the user and other mysql database tables. This is only for the more experienced users who fully comprehend the relationships among the user, db, and other mysql tables. After running such inserts, you must enact the changes by typing the command FLUSH PRIVILEGES from within the mysql client.

- If you were to grant access to a user with a statement like

  GRANT *privileges* to database.* TO
  → username IDENTIFIED BY 'password'

  that has the effect of granting the privileges to username@'%', which is to say any host is valid for that username.

- New as of MySQL 5.0.2 is the CREATE USER command. It's an alternative way to create a user (without granting privileges).

Changing Passwords

Once a user has been created, changing that user's password could not be more simple. The syntax for the command is:

SET PASSWORD FOR 'username'@'host' =
→ PASSWORD('newPassword')

Obviously you will need to be logged in as a user with the proper privileges in order to execute this. If you want to update your—the currently logged-in user's—password, just use:

SET PASSWORD = PASSWORD('newPassword')

The SET PASSWORD command is available as of MySQL 4.0.

USERS AND PRIVILEGES

Deleting and revoking users

For security purposes it's imperative that you create new users, but it's also often necessary to remove existing users. For starters, MySQL will create, during the installation process, between one and four users from this list (*hostname* is meant to represent the name of the computer on which MySQL is hosted):

◆ root@localhost

◆ root@%

◆ root@*hostname*

◆ @localhost

◆ @%

◆ @*hostname*

Which ones have been created for you depends upon your operating system, version of MySQL, and so on, but you should look into what users exist and get rid of any unnecessary ones. Deleting a user is as simple as running this command, which was added in MySQL 4.1:

`DROP USER username`

If what you'd rather do is just remove some privileges that a user has, you can use the REVOKE command. It works much like GRANT:

```
REVOKE privileges ON database.* FROM
→ 'username'@'host'
```

With respect to securing your initial setup, you may have two anonymous users, meaning that they'll allow connections to MySQL without even using a username and host. There may also be a *root* user that can connect remotely, which is normally not necessary and can be a security risk. Finally, none of these users have passwords at first. Hopefully you've already created the *root* user password, but let's clean up these other users now.

Figure 2.40 This SQL query will show you all of the current users. It also reveals for which ones passwords have been established (although the passwords are encrypted for security purposes).

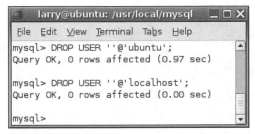

Figure 2.41 Deleting two superfluous users.

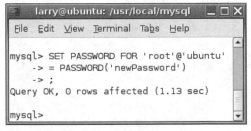

Figure 2.42 Updating a user's password.

To remove existing users:

1. Log in to the `mysql` client as an administrative, preferably *root*, user.

2. Get the list of current users (**Figure 2.40**).

   ```
   SELECT User, Host, Password FROM
   → mysql.user;
   ```

   This query will mean more to you in time, but basically it's a simple way to see all of the listed users and which ones have no passwords.

3. Delete any users that shouldn't exist (**Figure 2.41**).

   ```
   DROP USER ''@'ubuntu';
   DROP USER ''@'localhost';
   ```

   On my Linux box, two anonymous users were created that I no longer want. These commands will remove them.

4. Make sure that all users have passwords (**Figure 2.42**).

   ```
   SET PASSWORD FOR 'root'@'ubuntu' =
   → PASSWORD('newPassword');
   ```

   Again, on my Linux MySQL installation, no password was set for the *root* users. I had already updated the password for *root@localhost*, but *root@ubuntu* (where *ubuntu* is the computer's name) was still lacking this security measure. This command will solve that problem.

   continues on next page

USERS AND PRIVILEGES

5. Revoke privileges as warranted.

   Using the REVOKE command briefly discussed earlier in this section (and more thoroughly covered in the MySQL manual), you can remove specific privileges from a user's arsenal.

6. If you want, repeat Step 2 to confirm the current standing of all users.

   Alternatively, you can use the SHOW GRANTS command to see the privileges allotted to individual users.

7. Exit out of mysql.

   ```
   exit
   ```

Other Security Recommendations

A large part of the security of your MySQL databases is based upon user access. When it comes to your MySQL users, the fundamental rules are:

◆ Grant only the most minimal privileges necessary to each user.

◆ Avoid granting SUPER or PROCESS privileges unless absolutely necessary.

◆ Restrict FILE privilege to administrators.

◆ Always require a password for all users.

◆ Use good, secure passwords (non-dictionary words, incorporating numbers and symbols, mixed-capitalization, etc.).

Besides, those recommendations, you should:

◆ Validate all data used in queries (you'll see this in the programming chapters).

◆ Watch for quotation marks and other problematic characters in queries.

◆ Run the MySQL server as its own user (on Mac OS X and Unix).

As security is such an important topic, best practices and other recommendations will be made throughout the book, as relevant to the topic at hand.

DATABASE DESIGN

Whenever you are working with a relational database management system such as MySQL, the first step in creating and using a database is to establish its structure. Database design, aka *data modeling*, is crucial for successful long-term management of your information. Using a process called *normalization*, you carefully eliminate redundancies and other problems that will undermine the integrity of your data.

The techniques you will learn in this chapter will help to ensure the viability, performance, and reliability of your databases. The example I will use—a record of business transactions such as invoices and expenses—will be referred to in later chapters, but the principles of normalization apply to any database you might create.

Database design is equal parts art and science; learning, and eventually mastering, this skill is necessary to ensure the long-run reliability of the information you store. The technique taught in this chapter will not be MySQL-specific—in fact, you will not use any MySQL tools here at all—but is just as important as anything else covered in the book.

Normalization

Normalization was developed by an IBM researcher named E.F. Codd in the early 1970s (he also invented the relational database). A relational database is merely a collection of data, organized in a particular manner; Dr. Codd created a series of rules called *normal forms* that help define that organization. In this chapter I will discuss the first three of the normal forms, which is sufficient for most database designs.

Before you begin normalizing your database, you must define the role of the application being developed. Whether it means that you thoroughly discuss the subject with a client or figure it out for yourself, understanding how the information will be accessed dictates the modeling. Thus, this chapter will require paper and pen, rather than the MySQL software itself (to be clear, database design is applicable to any relational database, not just MySQL).

Database design texts commonly use examples such as music or book collections (indeed, I use the latter in my book *PHP Advanced for the World Wide Web: Visual QuickPro Guide*), but I will create a more business-oriented accounting database here. The primary purpose of the database will be to track invoices and expenses, but it could easily be expanded to log work hours on projects or whatever. **Table 3.1** reflects a sample record showing the type of data to be stored.

Before designing the database, some basic terminology is required. The next two sections will discuss the notions of *keys* and *relationships*.

Table 3.1 Based on my intended usage of this database, all of the requisite information to be recorded is listed here.

Accounting Data	
ITEM	EXAMPLE
Invoice Number	1
Invoice Date	4/20/2006
Invoice Amount	$30.28
Invoice Description	HTML design
Date Invoice Paid	5/11/2006
Client Information	Acme Industries, 100 Main Street, Anytown, NY, 11111, (800) 555-1234
Expense Amount	$100.00
Expense Category & Description	Web Hosting Fees-Annual contract for hosting www.DMCinsights.com
Expense Date	1/26/2006

✔ Tips

- One of the best ways to determine what information should be stored in a database is to determine what questions will be asked of the database and what data would be included in the answers.

- Although I will demonstrate manual database design, ready-made applications for this express purpose are listed in Appendix C, "Resources."

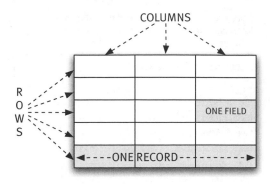

Figure 3.1 The layout of a database table, with labels.

Understanding Keys

Keys are special pieces of data that help to identify a row of information in a table. In database terms, an individual row is also called a *record* and is composed of individual *fields* that correspond to *columns* (**Figure 3.1**).

There are two types of keys you will deal with: *primary* and *foreign*. A primary key is a unique identifier that has to abide by certain rules. They must

◆ Always have a value (they cannot be NULL).

◆ Have a value that remains the same (never changes).

◆ Have a unique value for each record in the table.

The best real-world example of a primary key is the U.S. Social Security number. Although I have heard stories of duplicate numbers being assigned, the principle is that each individual has a unique Social Security number and that the number never changes. Just as the Social Security number is an artificial construct used to identify people, you'll frequently find creating an arbitrary primary key for each table to be the best design practice.

The second type of key is the foreign key. A foreign key is the representation in Table B of the primary key from Table A. If you have a *hollywood* database with a movies table and a directors table, the primary key from directors would be linked as a foreign key in movies. You'll see better how this works as the normalization process continues.

Currently, MySQL only enforces foreign keys when using the InnoDB storage engine (see Chapter 4, "Creating a MySQL Database," for more information on the different storage engines) but generally ignores their existence otherwise. Hence, foreign keys in MySQL are more of a theoretical presence than a binding one, although this should change in later versions of the software. But from a design perspective, you should keep in mind the correlation between primary and foreign keys.

The *accounting* database is just a simple table as it stands, but to start off the normalization process, I'll want to identify or create the primary key (the foreign keys will come in later steps).

To establish a primary key:

1. Look for any fields that meet the three tests for a primary key.

   In this example, the only data that will always be unique, that will have a value, and whose value will never change should be the *Invoice Number*. Mark this field as the primary key using the *(PK)* notation (**Table 3.2**).

2. If no logical primary key exists, invent one.

   Frequently you will need to create a primary key because no good solution presents itself. Even with Social Security numbers and book ISBNs (International Standardized Book Numbers)—which ought to meet the criteria—creating a dummy field expressly to serve as the primary key is a solid idea.

Table 3.2 The first step I take in modeling my database is to identify a primary key—the *Invoice Number.*

Accounting Database	
ITEM	**KEY**
Invoice Number	Primary (PK)
Invoice Date	n/a
Invoice Amount	n/a
Invoice Description	n/a
Date Invoice Paid	n/a
Client Information	n/a
Expense Amount	n/a
Expense Category & Description	n/a
Expense Date	n/a

✔ Tips

■ MySQL allows for only one primary key per table, although you can base a primary key on multiple columns. In such a case, the combination of the values of the multiple columns must abide by the three rules: it can never be NULL, can never change, and must be unique for each record.

■ Ideally, your primary key should always be an integer, which results in better MySQL performance. This is another reason why Social Security numbers and ISBNs, both of which contain hyphens, would not be the best possible primary key (and ISBNs sometimes contain the letter *x*).

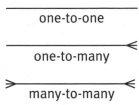

Figure 3.2 These three stick figures (or variations on these) are used in database models to represent the relationships between tables.

Figure 3.3 There is a one-to-one relationship between Social Security numbers and United States citizens.

Figure 3.4 There is a one-to-many relationship between people and gender. Each person only has one gender, but each gender can apply to multiple people.

Understanding Relationships

Pretty much every database consists of multiple tables, where each table stores one segment of the application's data. In a normalized database, some tables will be associated with other tables (not all will, though). For example, going back to a *hollywood* database, there would be a relationship between a table that stores directors and another that stores information about specific movies. The association between two tables is called a *relationship*, of which there are three kinds: *one-to-one*, *one-to-many*, or *many-to-many*. The representative symbols for the three types of relationships are shown in **Figure 3.2**.

The relationship is one-to-one if one and only one item in Table A applies to one and only one item in Table B (e.g., each U.S. citizen has only one Social Security number, and each Social Security number applies to only one U.S. citizen; no citizen can have two Social Security numbers, and no Social Security number can refer to two citizens). **Figure 3.3** shows how this would be diagrammed.

A relationship is one-to-many if one item in Table A can apply to multiple items in Table B. The terms *female* and *male* will apply to many people, but each person can be only one or the other (**Figure 3.4**). A one-to-many relationship is the most common one between tables in a database.

Finally, a relationship is many-to-many if multiple items in Table A can apply to multiple items in Table B. For example, a record album can contain songs by multiple artists, and artists can make multiple albums (**Figure 3.5**). You should try to avoid many-to-many relationships in your design because they lead to data redundancy and integrity problems. They'll be found and fixed during the normalization process.

Relationships and keys work together in that the keys serve as the connection between related tables. The primary key in one table will normally relate to a foreign key in another.

Now that you have the basics of keys and relationships, you can begin to normalize your database.

✔ Tips

- The process of database design results in an ER (entity-relationship) diagram, using boxes for tables and the symbols from Figure 3.2. You'll see this in action over the next several pages.

- The term "relational" in RDBMS actually stems from the tables, which are technically called *relations*.

- As you'll see in time, the normalization process breaks many-to-many relationships, like between artists and albums, down into two one-to-many relationships. To do so, an intermediary table will be invented.

Figure 3.5 There is a many-to-many relationship between albums and artists.

First Normal Form

As a reminder, normalization is the process of applying specific rules, called normal forms, to your database. These rules must be applied in order, starting with the First Normal Form.

For a database to be in First Normal Form (1NF), every table in that database must have the following two properties:

◆ Each column must contain only one value (this is described as being *atomic*).

◆ There cannot be repeating columns of associated data.

Table 3.3 shows how part of a table for storing books might look. The Authors column violates the first of the 1NF standards by storing multiple values. If you were to fix it by turning in into **Table 3.4**, it would still not be 1NF. That structure has repeating columns of associated data (Author1, Author2, and so on).

I'll begin the normalization process by checking the existing structure for 1NF compliance.

Table 3.3 This table is not 1NF compliant because the Authors column is not atomic.

Non-1NF Table	
COLUMN	EXAMPLE
ID	1
Title	C++ Programming
Authors	Larry Ullman and Andreas Signer

Table 3.4 This table is still not 1NF compliant because of the repeating author columns.

Still Non-1NF Table	
COLUMN	EXAMPLE
ID	1
Title	C++ Programming
Author1	Larry Ullman
Author2	Andreas Signer

The Complexity of the Normal Forms

If you do a search online, you can find the *formal rules* of database normalization. They may be the best example of totally obtuse computer-ese you'll ever encounter. Because the rules are so densely written, the question becomes how to translate these into a comprehensible format. The answer is: with a bit of poetic license.

What I'm getting at is this: if you check out five sources that describe the normal forms in layman's terms, you'll see five slightly different explanations. You'll even find the line blurred between where one normal form ends and another begins. This is perfectly fine. What's important is that the spirit of normalization and the end result will be the same, regardless of how these complex rules are simplified.

To make a database 1NF compliant:

1. Identify any field that contains multiple pieces of information.

   Looking back at Table 3.2, two columns are not 1NF compliant: *Client Information* and *Expense Category & Description*. You might think that the two date fields also fail to be atomic (they each contain a day, a month, and a year), but subdividing into separate day, month, and year columns may be taking things too far (see the "Overruling Normalization" sidebar at the end of the chapter).

   As for the second aspect of the 1NF rule, there aren't any reasons for concern with the current structure. Again, you might think that the two date columns break this rule, but while they store the same type of data, the two columns aren't repetitions of each other.

2. Break up any fields found in Step 1 into separate fields (**Table 3.5**).

   To fix this problem, I'll separate *Client Information* into *Client Name*, *Client Street Address*, *Client City*, *Client State*, *Client Zip*, and *Client Phone*. Next, I'll turn *Expense Category & Description* into *Expense Category* and *Expense Description*.

3. Double-check that all new fields created in Step 2 pass the 1NF test.

   Sometimes the changes you make will create new violations of a rule. Repeatedly inspect your data model so that it is perfectly compliant before moving on to the next normal form.

✔ Tip

- The simplest way to think about 1NF is that this rule analyzes a table horizontally. You inspect all of the columns within a single row to guarantee specificity and avoid repetition of similar data.

Table 3.5 After running through the 1NF rules, I've separated two fields—*Client Information* and *Expense Category & Description*, compare with Table 3.2—into atomic subfields.

Accounting Database, 1NF	
ITEM	KEY
Invoice Number	Primary (PK)
Invoice Date	n/a
Invoice Amount	n/a
Invoice Description	n/a
Date Invoice Paid	n/a
Client Name	n/a
Client Street Address	n/a
Client City	n/a
Client State	n/a
Client Zip	n/a
Client Phone	n/a
Expense Amount	n/a
Expense Category	n/a
Expense Description	n/a
Expense Date	n/a

Accounting Database

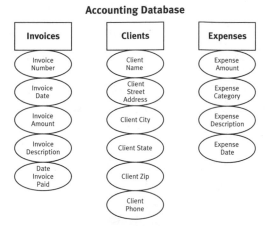

Figure 3.6 To normalize the database, I must move redundant pieces of information—such as the client and expense data—to their own tables.

Second Normal Form

In simplest terms, for a database to be in Second Normal Form (2NF), the database must already be in 1NF (you must normalize in order), and every column in a table that is not a key has to relate only to the primary key. The most obvious indication that a database is not 2NF is if multiple records in a table might have the exact same value for a column. As an example, if you listed an editor along with each book, this value would be repeated in several rows of the books table.

Looking at the *accounting* table (Table 3.5), there are a number of problems. For starters, the client information will not necessarily be particular to any one invoice (a client could be billed several times). Second, the expense information is not tied to the invoices either.

To put this database into 2NF, I'll need to separate out these columns into their own tables, where each value will be represented only once. In fact, normalization could be summarized as the process of creating more and more tables until potential redundancies have been eliminated.

To make a database 2NF compliant:

1. Identify any fields that do not relate directly to the primary key.

   As I stated, all of the client information and expense information are not invoice-particular.

2. Create new tables accordingly (**Figure 3.6**).

   The most logical modification for the existing structure is to make separate *Clients*, *Invoices*, and *Expenses* tables. In my visual representation of the database, I create a box for each table, with the table name as a header and all of its columns (also called its *attributes*) underneath.

continues on next page

3. Assign or create new primary keys (**Figure 3.7**).

Using the techniques described earlier in the chapter, ensure that each new table has a primary key. Because both the *Clients* and *Expenses* tables do not have good unique identifiers, I'll create artificial ones: *Client ID* and *Expense ID*. Arguably, the *Client Name* field could be unique and therefore could be the primary key, but it's always best to use integers for this purpose.

4. Repeat Steps 1–3.

Since I've created new tables with new primary keys, I should double-check to see if there are any 1NF or 2NF problems. In the example (Figure 3.7), there is one glaring issue: the *Expense Category* field may apply to multiple expenses. Therefore, I'll make a new *Expense Categories* table (**Figure 3.8**).

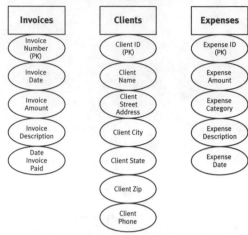

Figure 3.7 Each table in the database should have its own primary key, whether it's a dummy field such as *Client ID* or a necessary one such as *Invoice Number*.

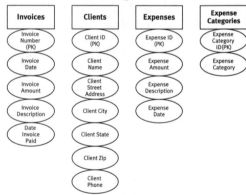

Figure 3.8 The *Expense Category* field, which was part of *Expenses*, should be its own table as well.

Accounting Database

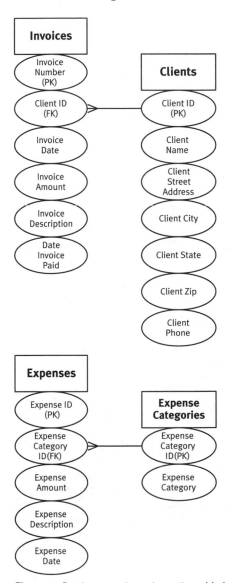

Figure 3.9 For the new primary keys, I've added corresponding foreign keys and indicated the relationships (both one-to-many).

5. Create the requisite foreign keys indicating the relationships (**Figure 3.9**).

The final step in achieving 2NF compliance is to incorporate foreign keys and relationships to identify how all of the data and tables are associated. Remember that a primary key in one table will most likely be a foreign key in another. If you find that the primary key in one table is not represented as a foreign key in another, you may have missed something (but not necessarily).

✔ Tips

■ Another way to test for 2NF is to look at the relationships between tables. The ideal is to create one-to-many situations. Tables that have a many-to-many relationship may need to be restructured.

■ If the 1NF rule calls for a horizontal inspection of your tables, then 2NF calls for a vertical inspection: checking for problematic repetitions within a single column over the course of multiple rows.

Third Normal Form

A database is in Third Normal Form (3NF) if it is in 2NF and every non-key column is independent of every other non-key column. In other words, the fields of a table other than the keys should be mutually independent.

If you followed the first two normalization steps properly, you will not necessarily need to make any changes at this stage. However, if you made a number of changes along the way (as can happen), this could be a last check. For example, say I wanted to record a contact name and email address with each invoice (**Figure 3.10**). The problem is that this information relates not to an invoice but to the client and, therefore, the database would fail the 3NF test.

That example aside, you may frequently find that the 3NF rules do not change your model at all. That's fine and not uncommon. For that matter, in some cases, 3NF may be overkill and would therefore be ignored (see the sidebar for more on that idea).

Accounting Database

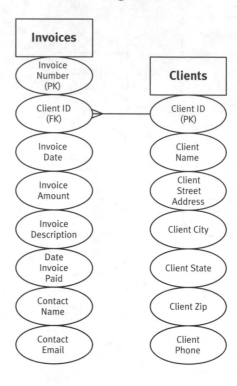

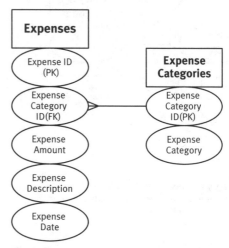

Figure 3.10 Altering the requirements of the database can muddle the design, as it is now no longer normalized with the *Contact Name* and *Email Address* additions (to the *Invoices* table).

Accounting Database

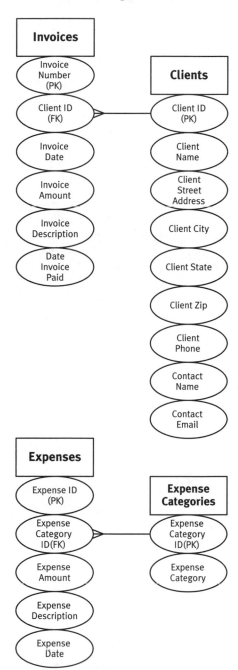

Figure 3.11 To correctly incorporate the new information (Figure 3.10), I've moved it to the *Clients* table.

To make a database 3NF compliant:

1. Identify any fields that violate the 3NF rule.

   As I stated, my additions to the Invoices table are a problem.

2. Create new tables or move fields accordingly (**Figure 3.11**).

   The correct structure would be to add the new contact fields to the *Clients* table.

3. Assign or create new primary and foreign keys, if necessary.

   In this particular example, no further changes are required.

4. Double-check the design for 1NF, 2NF, and 3NF compliance.

   The *Accounting* design is good to go in my opinion. In Chapter 4, you'll learn about choosing MySQL data types, naming rules, and how to actually create the database in MySQL.

✔ Tips

- Once you've sketched out a database on paper, you could create a series of spreadsheets that reflect the design (or use an application specifically tailored to this end). This file can act both as a good reference for the Web developers working on the database as well as a nice thing to give over to the client when the project is completed.

- Once MySQL begins enforcing the implications of foreign keys for all storage engines (in version 5.1 or later), normalizing your database will be even more necessary than it currently is.

Overruling Normalization

As much as ensuring that a database is in 3NF will help guarantee stability and endurance, you won't necessarily normalize every database with which you work. Before undermining the proper methods though, understand that doing so may have devastating long-term consequences.

In the *Accounting* example, I've left my date columns in a debatably non-atomic format (each stores three pieces of information: a day, a month, and a year). I know this won't be a problem because MySQL has a date column type that's easy to work with. As another example, if you have a table listing employees, with a gender column, you'd probably not make a separate gender table, even though the values *Male* and *Female* would be repeated countless times. There are only two gender options, there'll never be a third, and the likelihood of renaming one of these options—changing *Male* to *Fip* or whatever—is very low.

The two primary reasons to overrule normalization are convenience and performance. Fewer tables are easier to manipulate and comprehend. Further, because of their more intricate nature, normalized databases will most likely be slower for updating, retrieving data from, and modifying. Normalization requires that you favor data integrity and scalability over simplicity and speed. On the other hand, there are ways to improve your database's performance but few to remedy corrupted data that can result from poor design.

CREATING A
MySQL DATABASE

4

In Chapter 3, "Database Design," I went through the steps involved in coming up with your database scheme, a process called *normalization*. Those concepts apply to any relational database, whether you're using MySQL or not. In this chapter I cover how to implement a database specifically using MySQL.

This process begins by learning about the various data types that are available and how each of those can be further customized. Then you'll be introduced to indexes, which improve the performance of your database. After that it's time to finalize each table's design, by using proper names and choosing a table type. Finally, you'll get back to working with MySQL's tools by creating, and possibly modifying, your database and tables.

MySQL Data Types

Once you have identified all of the tables and columns that the database will need, you should determine each column's data type. When creating the database, as you will do at the end of this chapter, MySQL requires that you define what sort of information each field will contain. There are three primary categories, as is true for almost every database application:

◆ Numbers

◆ Text

◆ Dates and times

Within each of these, there are a number of variants—some of which are MySQL-specific—you can use. Choosing your column types correctly not only dictates what information can be stored and how but also affects the database's overall performance. Many of the types can take an optional *Length* attribute, limiting their size (in the corresponding tables, the square brackets, [], indicate an optional parameter to be put in parentheses, while parentheses themselves indicate required arguments).

Table 4.1 Here are most of the available numeric column types for use with MySQL databases. For FLOAT, DOUBLE, and DECIMAL, the *Length* argument is the maximum total number of digits and the *Decimals* argument dictates the number of that total to be found after the decimal point. (As of MySQL 5.0.3, the size of DECIMAL column is based upon a formula.)

MySQL Numeric Types

TYPE	SIZE	DESCRIPTION
TINYINT[*Length*]	1 byte	Range of –128 to 127 or 0 to 255 unsigned.
SMALLINT[*Length*]	2 bytes	Range of –32,768 to 32,767 or 0 to 65535 unsigned.
MEDIUMINT[*Length*]	3 bytes	Range of –8,388,608 to 8,388,607 or 0 to 16,777,215 unsigned.
INT[*Length*]	4 bytes	Range of –2,147,483,648 to 2,147,483,647 or 0 to 4,294,967,295 unsigned.
BIGINT[*Length*]	8 bytes	Range of –9,223,372,036,854,775,808 to 9,223,372,036,854,775,807 or 0 to 18,446,744,073,709,551,615 unsigned.
FLOAT[*Length, Decimals*]	4 bytes	A small number with a floating decimal point.
DOUBLE[*Length, Decimals*]	8 bytes	A large number with a floating decimal point.
DECIMAL[*Length, Decimals*]	*Length* + 1 or *Length* + 2 bytes	A DOUBLE with a fixed decimal point.

Table 4.1 lists the numeric types. The biggest distinction is between integer types and real numbers (which contain decimal points). After that it's a matter of the range of possible values (for integers) or what level of precision is necessary (for real numbers).

Table 4.2 lists the text types. Mostly these differ in size, but several allow for storing binary data instead of strings of characters. There are also two extensions of the text types that result in a different behavior—ENUM and SET—which allow you to define a series of acceptable values when creating the table. An ENUM field can have only one of a possible several thousand values, while SET allows for several of up to 64 possible values. There are two caveats with ENUM and SET: These types are not supported by other databases, and their usage undermines normalization.

Table 4.2 Here are the most common column types for storing text in a MySQL database.

MySQL Text Types		
TYPE	SIZE	DESCRIPTION
CHAR[*Length*]	*Length* bytes	A fixed-length field from 0 to 255 characters long.
VARCHAR(*Length*)	String length + 1 or 2 bytes	A fixed-length field from 0 to 255 characters long (65,535 characters long as of MySQL 5.0.3).
TINYTEXT	String length + 1 bytes	A string with a maximum length of 255 characters.
TEXT	String length + 2 bytes	A string with a maximum length of 65,535 characters.
MEDIUMTEXT	String length + 3 bytes	A string with a maximum length of 16,777,215 characters.
LONGTEXT	String length + 4 bytes	A string with a maximum length of 4,294,967,295 characters.
BINARY[*Length*]	*Length* bytes	Similar to CHAR but stores binary data.
VARBINARY[*Length*]	Data length + 1 bytes	Similar to VARCHAR but stores binary data.
TINYBLOB	Data length + 1 bytes	Stores binary data with a maximum length of 255 bytes.
BLOB	Data length + 2 bytes	Stores binary data with a maximum length of 65,535 bytes.
MEDIUMBLOB	Data length + 3 bytes	Stores binary data with a maximum length of 16,777,215 bytes.
LONGDLOB	Data length + 4 bytes	Stores binary data with a maximum length of 4,294,967,295 bytes.
ENUM	1 or 2 bytes	Short for *enumeration*, which means that each column can have one of several possible values.
SET	1, 2, 3, 4, or 8 bytes	Like ENUM except that each column can have more than one of several possible values.

The various date and time types (as listed in **Table 4.3**) have all sorts of unique behaviors, which are documented in the manual and will be discussed throughout the book. You'll primarily use these types without modification, so you need not worry too much about their intricacies.

To choose your data types:

1. Identify whether a column should be a text, number, or date type.

   This is normally an easy and obvious step. If a column will only ever store numeric data, use a number type. If it may contain anything that's not numeric, you'll need to use text.

   You will find that numbers such as dollar amounts could be text fields if you include their corresponding punctuation (dollar signs, commas, and hyphens), but you'll get better results if you store them as numbers and address the formatting elsewhere.

2. Choose the most appropriate subtype for each column.

   For improved performance, keep in mind two considerations:

   ▲ Fixed-length fields (such as CHAR) are generally faster than variable-length fields (such as VARCHAR), but they also take up more disk space. See the sidebar for more information.

   ▲ The size of any field should be restricted to the smallest possible value, based upon what the largest possible input could be. For example, if the longest product name you might store is 20 characters long, then you would set the column as a VARCHAR(20).

   ▲ There is a catch, though: if you insert a string five characters long into a CHAR(2) field, the final three characters will be truncated. This is true for any field: if you exceed the column's range, some data will be lost.

Table 4.3 These are the available date and time column types for MySQL.

MySQL Date and Time Types		
TYPE	SIZE	DESCRIPTION
DATE	3 bytes	In the format of *YYYY-MM-DD*.
DATETIME	8 bytes	In the format of *YYYY-MM-DD HH:MM:SS*.
TIMESTAMP	4 bytes	In the format of *YYYYMMDDHHMMSS*; acceptable range ends in the year 2037.
TIME	3 bytes	In the format of *HH:MM:SS*.
YEAR	1 byte	In the format of *YYYY*, with a range from 1901 to 2155.

Table 4.4 Another aspect of database design is defining the optimal type for each field.

Accounting Data Types		
COLUMN NAME	TABLE	COLUMN TYPE
Invoice Number	Invoices	SMALLINT(4)
Client ID	Invoices	SMALLINT(3)
Invoice Date	Invoices	TIMESTAMP
Invoice Amount	Invoices	DECIMAL(10,2)
Invoice Description	Invoices	TINYTEXT
Date Invoice Paid	Invoices	DATE
Client ID	Clients	SMALLINT(3)
Client Name	Clients	VARCHAR(40)
Client Street Address	Clients	VARCHAR(80)
Client City	Clients	VARCHAR(30)
Client State	Clients	CHAR(2)
Client Zip	Clients	MEDIUMINT(5)
Client Phone	Clients	VARCHAR(14)
Contact Name	Clients	VARCHAR(40)
Contact Email Address	Clients	VARCHAR(60)
Expense ID	Expenses	SMALLINT(4)
Expense Category ID	Expenses	TINYINT(3)
Expense Amount	Expenses	DECIMAL(10,2)
Expense Description	Expenses	TINYTEXT
Expense Date	Expenses	TIMESTAMP
Expense Category ID	Expense Categories	TINYINT(3)
Expense Category	Expense Categories	VARCHAR(30)

With numbers, you'll need to decide whether or not to store a decimal. This breaks your decision into the integer or real number areas. If mathematical precision is important with a real number, use the DECIMAL type, which is more accurate than either FLOAT or DOUBLE.

3. Set the maximum length for text and number columns (**Table 4.4**).

Rather than going over how I defined all 22 columns and why, I've listed the properties I came up with in Table 4.4. Different developers have different preferences, but the most important factor is to tailor each setting to the information at hand rather than using generic (and inefficient) TEXT and INT types at all times.

✔ Tips

■ Many of the data types have synonymous names: INT and INTEGER, DEC and DECIMAL, etc.

■ The TIMESTAMP field is automatically set when an INSERT or UPDATE occurs, even if no value is specified for the field. Depending upon your version of MySQL, there are all sorts of other behaviors for TIMESTAMP columns.

■ The BLOB type is a variant on TEXT that allows for storing binary files in a table. I'll demonstrate this in action in Chapter 12, "Techniques for Programming."

■ An added benefit of the date and time data types is that MySQL will validate that these are real, possible values, when inserting records. Prior to MySQL 5.0.2, this just meant basic validation: no 13 or higher for months, no 32 or higher for days. Since MySQL 5.0.2, this also means the date must exist, so *2006-02-31* would be an invalid date.

■ The size required to store any variable-length string of text will also depend upon the character set being use. For example, accented characters or those in non-English languages may require more space.

CHAR vs. VARCHAR

There is some debate as to the superiority of these two similar types. Both store strings and can be set with a fixed maximum length. One primary difference is that anything stored as a CHAR will always be stored as a string the length of the column (using spaces to pad it). Conversely, VARCHAR strings will be only as long as the stored string.

The two implications of this are

◆ VARCHAR columns tend to take up less disk space.

◆ Unless you are using the InnoDB storage engine (see "Choosing a Storage Engine" later in this chapter), CHAR columns are faster to access than VARCHAR.

Granted, the speed and disk space differences between the two types may be imperceptible in most cases. And you'll also find that you'll define a column using one type but MySQL may automatically use the other type instead, strange as that may seem.

There is also a third, minor difference between these two, prior to MySQL 5.0.3: MySQL trims off extra spaces from CHAR columns when data is retrieved and from VARCHAR when it's inserted. VARCHAR columns no longer have this property as of MySQL 5.0.3, meaning that any extra spaces are kept.

As a rule of thumb, use VARCHAR unless you have a field that will always, or almost always, be the exact same length. This may be a state abbreviation or a product identifier (*SD123*, *PA456*, etc.).

Extra Column Characteristics

When declaring the type for a column, you first select the broad type—number, text, or date—then select a more specific type within these. From there, columns can also be defined with other characteristics. A special characteristic, AUTO_INCREMENT, is discussed in the sidebar, and more common ones are: UNSIGNED, ZEROFILL, NOT NULL, and DEFAULT.

For starters, the number types can be set as UNSIGNED. This means that the column can only store non-negative values. This has a secondary effect with integers of doubling the range of positive numbers that can be stored (the same is not true for real numbers). Number types can also be defined as ZEROFILL, which means that any extra room will be padded on the left with zeros (ZEROFILLs are also automatically UNSIGNED).

Any column type can be defined as NOT NULL. The NULL value in databases is the equivalent of saying that the field has no known value. (This may differ from how you've thought of NULL in other contexts.) Ideally, every record in a database should have a value, but that is rarely the case in practicality. To enforce this limitation on a field, you add the NOT NULL description to its column type.

The AUTO_INCREMENT Designation

One attribute a numeric column can have is AUTO_INCREMENT. When you define a field with this property, you are effectively telling MySQL to set the value of this column to the next logical value in the series. This attribute is normally applied to a table's primary key, like the Invoice Number or Client ID.

Once you've defined your column as such, if you do not set a value for that column when adding a record, the next highest integer will be used. So the first Invoice Number will be 1, the second will be 2, the third will be 3, and so on. MySQL will automatically handle this for you.

Some find it concerning that if you were to later delete Invoice Number 3, there would be a "gap" in the sequence. This is perfectly fine! Your primary key is an arbitrary value. There's no harm in having the Invoice Numbers go 1, 2, 4, 5, 8, ... In fact, the harm would be in trying to "fix" that situation.

When creating a table, you can also specify a default value for any column (except for types TEXT and BLOB). In cases where a large portion of the records will have the same contents, presetting a default will save you from having to specify a value when inserting new rows, unless that value is different from the norm. One example might be

gender ENUM('M','F') DEFAULT 'F'

Table 4.5 lists all of the columns of the *accounting* database, along with their full definitions, after taking the following steps.

Table 4.5 Extra characteristics have been added to each column as appropriate.

Accounting Database, Modified		
COLUMN NAME	TABLE	COLUMN TYPE
Invoice Number	Invoices	SMALLINT(4) UNSIGNED NOT NULL AUTO_INCREMENT
Client ID	Invoices	SMALLINT(3) UNSIGNED NOT NULL
Invoice Date	Invoices	TIMESTAMP NOT NULL
Invoice Amount	Invoices	DECIMAL(10,2) UNSIGNED NOT NULL
Invoice Description	Invoices	TINYTEXT NOT NULL
Date Invoice Paid	Invoices	DATE
Client ID	Clients	SMALLINT(3) UNSIGNED NOT NULL AUTO_INCREMENT
Client Name	Clients	VARCHAR(40) NOT NULL
Client Street Address	Clients	VARCHAR(80) NOT NULL
Client City	Clients	VARCHAR(30) NOT NULL
Client State	Clients	CHAR(2) NOT NULL
Client Zip	Clients	MEDIUMINT(5) UNSIGNED ZEROFILL NOT NULL
Client Phone	Clients	VARCHAR(14)
Contact Name	Clients	VARCHAR(40)
Contact Email Address	Clients	VARCHAR(60)
Expense ID	Expenses	SMALLINT(4) UNSIGNED NOT NULL AUTO_INCREMENT
Expense Category ID	Expenses	TINYINT(3) UNSIGNED NOT NULL
Expense Amount	Expenses	DECIMAL(10,2) UNSIGNED NOT NULL
Expense Description	Expenses	TINYTEXT NOT NULL
Expense Date	Expenses	TIMESTAMP NOT NULL
Expense Category ID	Expense Categories	TINYINT(3) UNSIGNED NOT NULL AUTO_INCREMENT
Expense Category	Expense Categories	VARCHAR(30) NOT NULL

To customize your columns:

1. Identify any column that cannot have a NULL value.

   This is the most important of the extra designations. Any column defined as NOT NULL must always be given a value. As you'll see when you go to add records to a table, failure to give a value to a NOT NULL column results in an error.

   As a rule of thumb, you should define columns as NOT NULL whenever possible. They'll take up slightly less space this way and offer better performance.

2. Identify any number types that should be UNSIGNED.

   This is an easy step to take. If a number must be positive, like the price or quantity of something ordered, it should be UNSIGNED. If it may be negative, like a temperature or a bank balance (d'oh!), do not flag it as such.

3. Identify any number types that should be ZEROFILL.

   The ZEROFILL designation is much less used than UNSIGNED but is necessary in some instances. For example, with the zip code column, some zip codes begin with a *0*, like *02101*. If you were to store this in a non-ZEROFILL integer column, it would be stored as *2101* (because the initial *0* has no meaning to an integer). By defining that column as MEDIUMINT(5) UNSIGNED ZEROFILL, the stored zip codes will retain their initial *0*.

4. Identify any column that should have a default value.

   This step is mostly a matter of personal preference.

✔ Tips

■ Primary keys can never contain NULL values, in accordance with proper database design and with how MySQL functions.

■ If an ENUM column is set as NOT NULL, the default value will automatically be the first of the possible allowed values.

■ Just to clarify what NULL is, understand that NULL has no value and differs from even the number zero, an empty string (''), or a space (' '), which are all *known* values.

■ You should be forewarned that MySQL has an odd "feature" when it comes to UNSIGNED integers. If you perform subtraction with at least one UNSIGNED integer, the result will always be UNSIGNED. So an UNSIGNED column with a value of 2 minus a signed column with a value of 10 will not be −8.

EXTRA COLUMN CHARACTERISTICS

Introduction to Indexes

Indexes are a special system that databases use to improve overall performance. By setting indexes on your tables, you are telling MySQL to pay particular attention to that column or those columns (in layman's terms).

MySQL allows for between 16 and 64 indexes for each table, depending upon the storage engine being used. Each index can be on anywhere from 1 to 15 columns. While a multicolumn index may not seem obvious, it will come in handy for searches frequently performed on the same set of multiple columns (e.g., first and last name, city and state, etc.).

On the other hand, one should not go overboard with indexing. While it does improve the speed of reading from databases, it slows down the process of altering data in a database (because the changes need to be recorded in the index). On the other hand, you'll normally retrieve data from a database much more often than you'll insert new or update existing data.

Indexes are best used on columns

- That are frequently used in the WHERE part of a query

- That are frequently used in an ORDER BY part of a query

- That have many different values (columns with numerous repeating values ought not to be indexed)

- That are frequently used in a JOIN.

MySQL has a few different types of indexes: INDEX, UNIQUE (which requires each row to have a unique value), and PRIMARY KEY (which is just a particular UNIQUE index). There is also a FULLTEXT index, which is discussed in Chapter 10, "Advanced SQL and MySQL." **Table 4.6** lists the indexes I propose for the *accounting* database after these steps.

Table 4.6 To improve the performance of my database, I add a several indexes to help MySQL access the stored information. (This may be an excessive number of indexes, depending upon how the application will be used.)

Accounting Database Indexes		
COLUMN	TABLE	INDEX TYPE
Invoice Number	Invoices	PRIMARY KEY
Client ID	Invoices	INDEX
Invoice Date	Invoices	INDEX
Invoice Amount	Invoices	INDEX
Date Invoice Paid	Invoices	INDEX
Client ID	Clients	PRIMARY KEY
Client Name	Clients	INDEX (or UNIQUE)
Expense ID	Expenses	PRIMARY KEY
Expense Category ID	Expenses	INDEX
Expense Amount	Expenses	INDEX
Expense Date	Expenses	INDEX
Expense Category ID	Expense Categories	PRIMARY KEY
Expense Category	Expense Categories	UNIQUE

To add indexes:

1. Identify any columns that should be marked as the PRIMARY KEY.

   This should be obvious, particularly if you followed the normalization steps taught in the previous chapter. Remember that there will only ever be one primary key per table (although it is possible that the primary key is a composite of multiple columns).

2. Identify any remaining columns whose values must always be UNIQUE.

   The UNIQUE index type is also not used excessively. Most values—dates, numbers, names, cities, zip codes—may repeat, particularly in tables with thousands upon thousands of rows. But depending upon your application, you will find the occasional column that must be UNIQUE, like an email address, a user name (for a registration/login system), or the Expense Category field in the Expense Categories table.

   You would not define a PRIMARY KEY column as also being UNIQUE, because the PRIMARY KEY designation implies uniqueness.

3. Identify any remaining columns that could benefit from an index.

   Use the preceding recommendations for when an index would help and think about what information will be retrieved. If you'll want to see a list of invoices in date or total amount order, those make for logical indexes. If a registration/login table will use the combination of the username and password to verify a login, that should be indexed. You'll also normally want to index your foreign key columns.

✔ **Tip**

■ Indexes are less efficient on variable-length columns, just as MySQL is generally slower dealing with fields that are not of a fixed length. You can compensate for this by indexing only a part of a variable-length column, like the first five or ten characters.

Finalizing a Table's Design

The final step in designing your database is to adhere to certain naming conventions. While MySQL is very flexible on how you name your databases, tables, and columns, here are some good rules to go by (required rules are in bold):

- **Use alphanumeric characters.**

- **Do not use spaces.**

- **Limit yourself to less than 64 characters**.

- Field names should be descriptive.

- Field names should be unique across every table, except for the keys.

- Do not use existing MySQL keywords.

- Use the underscore (_) to separate words.

- Use entirely lowercase words (this is definitely a personal preference rather than a rule).

- Use plural table names (to indicate multiple values stored) and singular column names.

- End primary and foreign key columns with *id* (or *ID*).

- List the primary key first in a table, followed by foreign keys.

These are largely my recommendations and are therefore not absolute, except for limiting yourself to alphanumeric names without spaces. Some developers prefer to use capital letters to break up words (instead of underscores). Some developers like to indicate the column's type in its name. The most important rule is that you remain consistent with the conventions you abide by.

Table 4.7 shows the final database design, after following these next steps.

To finalize your database design:

1. Determine the whole database's name.

   This should be easy to remember and descriptive. The database name must also be unique, so no other database on the same MySQL server can have the same name.

   For the example I've been using in this and the preceding chapter, the actual database name will be *accounting*. You could instead use *Accounting*, but I prefer to always use all-lowercase names.

   continues on next page

Table 4.7 The final database design step incorporates certain naming conventions and orders the columns within each table.

accounting Database, Finalized		
COLUMN NAME	**TABLE**	**COLUMN TYPE**
invoice_id	invoices	SMALLINT(4) UNSIGNED NOT NULL AUTO_INCREMENT
client_id	invoices	SMALLINT(3) UNSIGNED NOT NULL
invoice_date	invoices	TIMESTAMP NOT NULL
invoice_amount	invoices	DECIMAL(10,2) UNSIGNED NOT NULL
invoice_description	invoices	TINYTEXT NOT NULL
date_invoice_paid	invoices	DATE
client_id	clients	SMALLINT(3) UNSIGNED NOT NULL AUTO_INCREMENT
client_name	clients	VARCHAR(40) NOT NULL
client_street	clients	VARCHAR(80) NOT NULL
client_city	clients	VARCHAR(30) NOT NULL
client_state	clients	CHAR(2) NOT NULL
client_zip	clients	MEDIUMINT(5) UNSIGNED ZEROFILL NOT NULL
client_phone	clients	VARCHAR(14)
contact_name	clients	VARCHAR(40)
contact_email	clients	VARCHAR(60)
expense_id	expenses	SMALLINT(4) UNSIGNED NOT NULL AUTO_INCREMENT
expense_category_id	expenses	TINYINT(3) UNSIGNED NOT NULL
expense_amount	expenses	DECIMAL(10,2) UNSIGNED NOT NULL
expense_description	expenses	TINYTEXT NOT NULL
expense_date	expenses	TIMESTAMP NOT NULL
expense_category_id	expense_categories	TINYINT(3) UNSIGNED NOT NULL AUTO_INCREMENT
expense_category	expense_categories	VARCHAR(30) NOT NULL

2. Identify each table's name.

Again, these should be easy to remember and descriptive. Furthermore, no two tables in the same database can have the same name (two tables in two different databases can have the same name, though). I'm going with clients, invoices, expenses, and expense_categories.

3. Label each column within each table.

You'll see a lot of variations here, with everyone having their own style. As I mentioned, I'll add _id_ to any primary or foreign key column. If there is a date field, I tend to put the word _date_ in its name, but for no required reason.

4. Order the columns within each table.

The results of this step are more for your own organization than anything. The order of the columns will have absolutely no impact on the functionality of the table or database. I prefer to put the primary key column first, followed by the foreign keys.

✔ Tips

■ If you give related tables names that begin similarly, they'll appear together when you list all tables in a database. For example, expenses and expense_categories are together in **Figure 4.1**).

■ Database and table names are case-sensitive on Unix systems but insensitive under Windows. Column names are always case-insensitive.

■ By strictly adhering to any set of database design principles, you minimize errors that could occur when programming a database interface, as you will in Chapters 7–9.

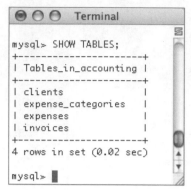

Figure 4.1 Tables are listed in alphabetical order; you can use this to your benefit by giving related tables similar names.

■ You can technically use an existing keyword for a table or column name. But to then refer to that item, you would need to always quote its name using backticks:

SELECT * FROM `table`

Even so, I think it's best not to use existing keywords.

Choosing a Storage Engine

The MySQL database application supports several different types of tables (a table's type is also called its *storage engine*). Although each type supports a different feature set, how you interact with them—in terms of running queries—is generally consistent. I'll quickly gloss over the three main types; as you learn more about MySQL, you may want to read the full MySQL manual pages on these as well.

The most important table type is *MyISAM*. MyISAM tables are great for most applications, handling SELECTs and INSERTs very quickly. But the MyISAM storage engine cannot manage transactions, a feature I talk about in Chapter 10.

After MyISAM, the two most popular storage engines are *InnoDB* and *MEMORY* (which used to be called *HEAP*). InnoDB tables have been part of the default MySQL installation since version 4.0 (if you are using an earlier version, you must enable InnoDB support; see the MySQL manual). InnoDB tables can be used for transactions and perform UPDATEs nicely. But the InnoDB storage engine is generally slower than MyISAM and requires more disk space on the server.

The MEMORY table type is the best performer of the bunch, as such tables store all data in memory, not in files. This comes at a price, as MEMORY tables can only deal with fixed-length column types, have no support for AUTO_INCREMENT, and lose all data in a crash.

To choose a storage engine:

1. Log in to the `mysql` client.

   To choose a storage engine, you should first know what options are available. To do so, you can ask your MySQL server from within the `mysql` client (see Chapter 2, "Running MySQL," for platform-specific instructions).

2. Determine what storage engines are supported by your version of MySQL by running this query (**Figure 4.2**):

   ```
   SHOW ENGINES;
   ```

   The results will differ from one installation of MySQL to the next. This is a good step to take, as there's no point in trying to use a storage engine that's not available.

3. Decide if you need to support transactions.

   Transactions are safer, allowing you to undo some changes and protecting your data in case of a crash. Non-transactional tables are faster, requiring less disk space and memory.

   As a rule of thumb, if you need transactions, go with InnoDB. If not, go with MyISAM.


```
MySQL Command Line Client
mysql> SHOW ENGINES;
+------------+---------+------------------------------------------------------------+
| Engine     | Support | Comment                                                    |
+------------+---------+------------------------------------------------------------+
| MyISAM     | YES     | Default engine as of MySQL 3.23 with great performance     |
| MEMORY     | YES     | Hash based, stored in memory, useful for temporary tables  |
| InnoDB     | DEFAULT | Supports transactions, row-level locking, and foreign keys |
| BerkeleyDB | NO      | Supports transactions and page-level locking               |
| BLACKHOLE  | NO      | /dev/null storage engine (anything you write to it disappears) |
| EXAMPLE    | NO      | Example storage engine                                     |
| ARCHIVE    | YES     | Archive storage engine                                     |
| CSV        | NO      | CSV storage engine                                         |
| ndbcluster | NO      | Clustered, fault-tolerant, memory-based tables             |
| FEDERATED  | NO      | Federated MySQL storage engine                             |
| MRG_MYISAM | YES     | Collection of identical MyISAM tables                      |
| ISAM       | NO      | Obsolete storage engine                                    |
+------------+---------+------------------------------------------------------------+
12 rows in set (0.00 sec)

mysql> _
```

Figure 4.2 The list of available storage engines for this installation of MySQL.

4. Determine if you can trade performance for permanence.

If what the table really requires above all is performance, then MEMORY may be your best bet. Interactions with these tables will be very fast, but all data will be lost in a crash!

✔ Tips

■ The same database can have tables of different types. As an example, an e-commerce database may use MyISAM for storing customer and product data, but use InnoDB for orders (to allow for transactions).

■ Two other popular storage engines are MERGE and BDB (Berkeley Database). The former can treat multiple MyISAM tables as one table. The latter is an alternative to InnoDB, also providing for transactions.

■ The InnoDB storage engine was purchased by Oracle, a rival database company. Oracle also purchased Sleepycat Software, which makes the BDB engine. It is not yet known how this will affect MySQL, but it's entirely possible that both disappear from future versions of the database. This is one reason why it's important to see what storage engines are available by running a SHOW ENGINES query (available as of MySQL 4.0).

■ Each storage engine has different properties: how many indexes are allowed, what kinds of columns can be indexed, how large the table can be (in terms of the size on the server), and so on. If you start using MySQL on this level, read through the associated manual pages for details.

■ If you try to create a table using a storage engine that's not available to that version of MySQL, the server's default storage engine will be used instead.

Character Sets and Collations

Along with the storage engine, another decision you can make when creating tables involves the character set and the collation. Both affect how text is handled by MySQL. These are relatively new features, having become prominent as of MySQL 4.1 (they existed in earlier versions of MySQL but not in this distinct manner).

The *character set* is the body of letters, numbers, and symbols that can be stored in a text column (it only applies to the text types). To specify the character set for an individual column, add the clause `CHARACTER SET` *setname* to your column definition, where *setname* is a specific set. You can find out what sets are available to you by running `SHOW CHARACTER SET` within the `mysql` client. The default character set is *latin1*, which covers English and other Western European languages, but there are also sets for Greek, Russian, Chinese, Korean, and more. At the time of this writing, MySQL supports over 70 character sets!

Related to this is the *collation*, which dictates how characters are compared. For example, a case-insensitive collation treats upper- and lowercase letters as equal. Another collation might address how accented characters in French are ordered. Each character set has a handful of available collations, from the over 30 that MySQL supports. For the default *latin1* character set, *latin1_swedish_ci* is the default collation. Although it may not seem that way, this is a fine combination for handling English and most Western languages.

To choose a character set and collation:

1. Log in to the mysql client.

   As with the storage engine, you should first know what options are available. To do so, you can ask your MySQL server from within the mysql client (see Chapter 2 for platform-specific instructions).

2. Determine what character sets are supported by your version of MySQL by running this query (**Figure 4.3**):

   SHOW CHARACTER SET;

   These results will differ from one installation of MySQL to the next. On my installation of MySQL 5.0.18 on Windows, there were 36 total.

   continues on next page

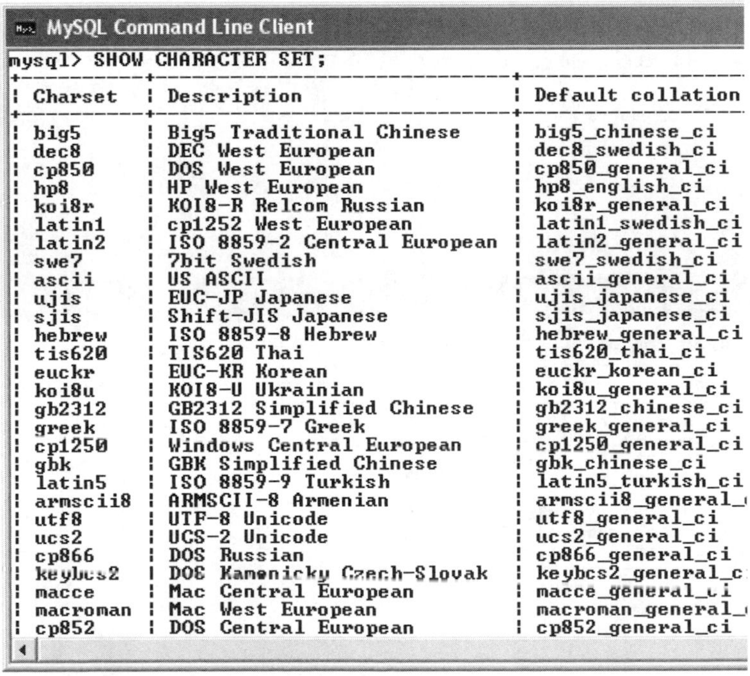

```
MySQL Command Line Client
mysql> SHOW CHARACTER SET;
+----------+-----------------------------+-------------------+
| Charset  | Description                 | Default collation |
+----------+-----------------------------+-------------------+
| big5     | Big5 Traditional Chinese    | big5_chinese_ci   |
| dec8     | DEC West European           | dec8_swedish_ci   |
| cp850    | DOS West European           | cp850_general_ci  |
| hp8      | HP West European            | hp8_english_ci    |
| koi8r    | KOI8-R Relcom Russian       | koi8r_general_ci  |
| latin1   | cp1252 West European        | latin1_swedish_ci |
| latin2   | ISO 8859-2 Central European | latin2_general_ci |
| swe7     | 7bit Swedish                | swe7_swedish_ci   |
| ascii    | US ASCII                    | ascii_general_ci  |
| ujis     | EUC-JP Japanese             | ujis_japanese_ci  |
| sjis     | Shift-JIS Japanese          | sjis_japanese_ci  |
| hebrew   | ISO 8859-8 Hebrew           | hebrew_general_ci |
| tis620   | TIS620 Thai                 | tis620_thai_ci    |
| euckr    | EUC-KR Korean               | euckr_korean_ci   |
| koi8u    | KOI8-U Ukrainian            | koi8u_general_ci  |
| gb2312   | GB2312 Simplified Chinese   | gb2312_chinese_ci |
| greek    | ISO 8859-7 Greek            | greek_general_ci  |
| cp1250   | Windows Central European    | cp1250_general_ci |
| gbk      | GBK Simplified Chinese      | gbk_chinese_ci    |
| latin5   | ISO 8859-9 Turkish          | latin5_turkish_ci |
| armscii8 | ARMSCII-8 Armenian          | armscii8_general_ |
| utf8     | UTF-8 Unicode               | utf8_general_ci   |
| ucs2     | UCS-2 Unicode               | ucs2_general_ci   |
| cp866    | DOS Russian                 | cp866_general_ci  |
| keybcs2  | DOS Kamenicky Czech-Slovak  | keybcs2_general_c |
| macce    | Mac Central European        | macce_general_ci  |
| macroman | Mac West European           | macroman_general_ |
| cp852    | DOS Central European        | cp852_general_ci  |
```

Figure 4.3 Part of the list of available character sets.

CHARACTER SETS AND COLLATIONS

3. Decide which character set to use.

The character set will correspond to the languages and types of characters being stored in your database. You can pick a different character set for each column, if necessary, so one column could have some text in English while another has a translation of that same text in Thai.

4. See which collations are available for that character set by running the following query (**Figure 4.4**):

SHOW COLLATION LIKE 'latin1%'

To find the possible collations for the chosen character set, run this query. Change *latin1* to whatever character set you are using.

5. Pick your collation.

From the list provided by MySQL (Figure 4.4), first note the default collation and which ones are compiled (meaning they are supported). Then, if you think you might need other than the default, read up on the other collations in the MySQL manual and choose accordingly.

✔ Tips

■ Both the character set and the collation can be established on a server, database, table, or column level. If you don't specify the character set or collation for a column, the table's default set and collation will be used. The same applies to a table (which would use the database's defaults) and a database (which would use the server's defaults).

■ You can also set the character set for interactions when connecting to a MySQL database (e.g., when using the mysql client). See the MySQL manual for instructions.

■ The collation can be adjusted within a single SQL query. This will affect the ordering and grouping of your results for just that query.

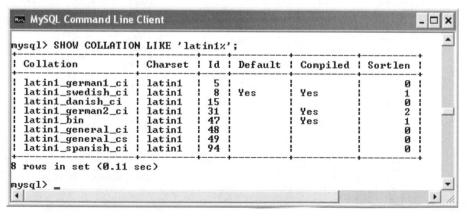

Figure 4.4 The list of available collations for one particular character set.

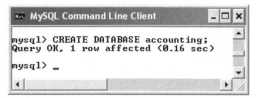

Figure 4.5 Creating the new database.

Creating Databases

Once you've run through all of the steps for designing and finalizing a database (a surprising amount of work), it's time to actually create the database within MySQL. To create both the database and the tables, you'll use the mysql client and some basic SQL.

In Chapter 2, "Running MySQL," I quickly defined two databases to help demonstrate how to add users. As you may recall, the syntax for creating a new database is

CREATE DATABASE *dbname*

To specify a character set or collation for the entire database, add another clause to the end of the CREATE query:

CREATE DATABASE *dbname* CHARACTER SET *setname* COLLATE *collationname*

To demonstrate the CREATE statement, I'll establish the *accounting* database.

To create a database:

1. Log in to the mysql client.

    If you don't know how to do this yet, you'll need to see the instructions in Chapter 2. You will also need to be logged in as a user with permission to create new databases.

2. Create the new database (**Figure 4.5**).

    CREATE DATABASE accounting;

    This first line, as you've already seen, creates the database (assuming that you are logged in to mysql as a user with permission to create new databases).

    Also, although SQL is case insensitive, I will make it a habit to capitalize the SQL words, helping to separate them from the database, table, and column names. If you would rather not capitalize these terms, you have that option.

    continues on next page

3. Confirm the existence of the database (**Figure 4.6**).

SHOW DATABASES;

The SHOW command, which does not need to be discussed in detail, reveals the list of databases that the logged-in user can access.

✔ Tips

■ You can also create databases, but not tables, using the mysqladmin application.

mysqladmin –u root –p create
→ *databasename*

■ You can always see how an existing database was created by using a SHOW CREATE command (**Figure 4.7**):

SHOW CREATE DATABASE *dbname*

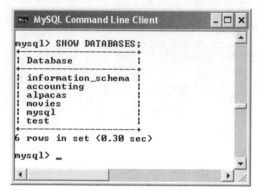

Figure 4.6 The newly created *accounting* database appears in the full list.

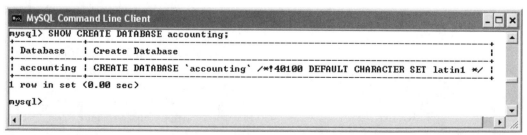

Figure 4.7 A SHOW CREATE query indicates how a database or table was made. Notice in this example that there's also a comment for version 4.01.00 (and greater) regarding the default character set.

Creating Tables

Once you have a database, you can begin making the tables, also using the CREATE term:

```
CREATE TABLE tablename (
columnname description,
column2name description…
)
```

As you can see from the preceding syntax, after naming the table, you define each column—in order—within parentheses. Each column and description should be separated by a comma. Should you choose to create indexes at this time, you can add those at the end of the creation statement (you can add indexes at a later time, as well).

```
CREATE TABLE tablename (
columnname description,
column2name description,
indextype (columns)
)
```

If you want to name any of the indexes, change that part of the query to

```
indexname (columns)
```

To specify the storage engine when you define a table, add a clause to the end of the creation statement:

```
CREATE TABLE tablename (
columnname description,
column2name description…
) ENGINE = INNODB
```

(Prior to MySQL 4.0.18, you have to use the word TYPE instead of ENGINE). If you don't specify a storage engine when creating tables, MySQL will use the default type (InnoDB on Windows, MyISAM otherwise).

To specify a character set or collation for the entire table, add another clause to the end of the CREATE query:

CREATE TABLE *tablename* (

column1name description,

column2name description...

) ENGINE = MyISAM CHARACTER SET *setname*

→ COLLATE *collationname*

I'll now create the four tables that compose the *accounting* database.

To create tables:

1. Access the mysql client and select the *accounting* database (**Figure 4.8**).

    USE accounting;

    It'll be easier to create the tables if you select the database first. You will need to be logged in as a user that has permission to create tables on this database.

2. Create the invoices table (**Figure 4.9**).

    CREATE TABLE invoices (

    invoice_id SMALLINT(4) UNSIGNED NOT
    → NULL AUTO_INCREMENT,

    client_id SMALLINT(3) UNSIGNED NOT
    → NULL,

    invoice_date TIMESTAMP NOT NULL,

    invoice_amount DECIMAL(10,2) UNSIGNED
    → NOT NULL,

    invoice_description TINYTEXT NOT
    → NULL,

    date_invoice_paid DATE,

    PRIMARY KEY (invoice_id),

    INDEX (client_id),

    INDEX (invoice_date),

    INDEX (invoice_amount),

    INDEX (date_invoice_paid)

    );

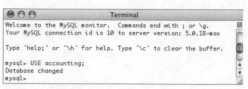

Figure 4.8 The first steps I take are to log in to mysql and select the *accounting* database.

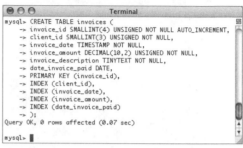

Figure 4.9 The mysql client allows you to enter commands over multiple lines, making long SQL statements more readable.

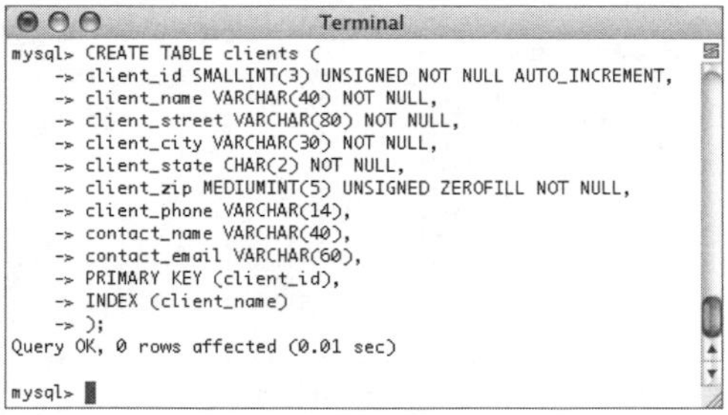

Figure 4.10 MySQL will report if a command worked, using the Query OK statement as indicated here.

This step takes the information about the invoices table I established earlier and integrates that within the CREATE table syntax. The order in which you enter the columns here will dictate the order the columns appear in the table. You'll also need to specify any indexes last so that they are enacted after the column itself has been created.

Because the mysql client will not run a query until it encounters a semicolon, you can enter statements over multiple lines as I do in Figure 4.9.

3. Create the clients table (**Figure 4.10**).

   CREATE TABLE clients (

   client_id SMALLINT(3) UNSIGNED NOT
   → NULL AUTO_INCREMENT,

   client_name VARCHAR(40) NOT NULL,

   client_street VARCHAR(80) NOT NULL,

   client_city VARCHAR(30) NOT NULL,

   client_state CHAR(2) NOT NULL,

   client_zip MEDIUMINT(5) UNSIGNED
   → ZEROFILL NOT NULL,

   client_phone VARCHAR(14),

   contact_name VARCHAR(40),

   contact_email VARCHAR(60),

   PRIMARY KEY (client_id),

   INDEX (client_name)

   );

   This table has the most columns but only two indexes.

   continues on next page

CREATING TABLES

4. Create the expenses table (**Figure 4.11**).

CREATE TABLE expenses (

expense_id SMALLINT(4) UNSIGNED NOT
→ NULL AUTO_INCREMENT,

expense_category_id TINYINT(3)
→ UNSIGNED NOT NULL,

expense_amount DECIMAL(10,2)
→ UNSIGNED NOT NULL,

expense_description TINYTEXT NOT
→ NULL,

expense_date TIMESTAMP NOT NULL,

PRIMARY KEY (expense_id),

INDEX (expense_category_id),

INDEX (expense_amount),

INDEX (expense_date)

);

5. Finally, create the expense_categories
table (**Figure 4.12**).

CREATE TABLE expense_categories (

expense_category_id TINYINT(3)
→ UNSIGNED NOT NULL AUTO_INCREMENT,

expense_category VARCHAR(30) NOT
→ NULL,

PRIMARY KEY (expense_category_id),

UNIQUE (expense_category)

);

This is the simplest of the four tables,
with only two columns and two indexes.

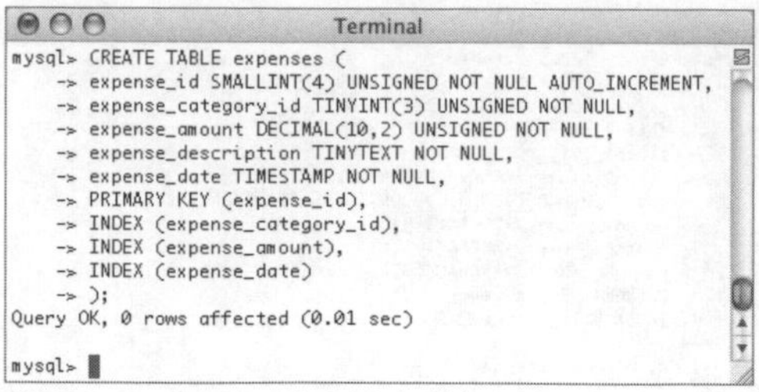

Figure 4.11 Creating the third table.

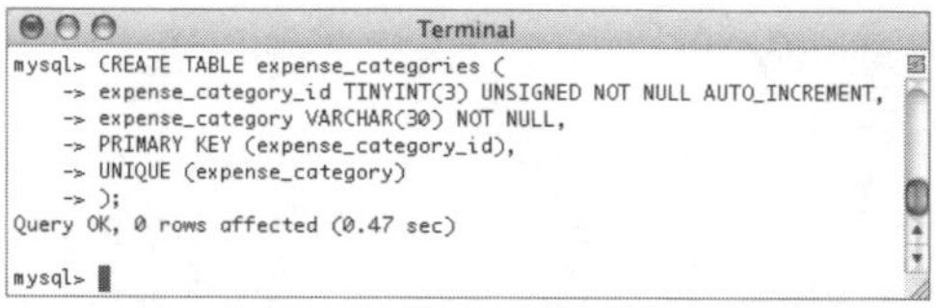

Figure 4.12 Creating the fourth and final table.

6. Confirm the existence of the tables (**Figure 4.13**).

SHOW TABLES;

SHOW COLUMNS FROM invoices;

The SHOW command can reveal the tables in a database or the column names and types in a table.

✔ Tips

- DESCRIBE tablename, which you might see in other resources, is the same statement as SHOW COLUMNS FROM tablename.

- You can also run a SHOW CREATE TABLE tablename query to see how an existing table was created.

- If you run a SHOW CREATE TABLE tablename query after making a table, you'll see how MySQL implements your creation. Doing so will help you see how MySQL may change column types for its own performance purposes.

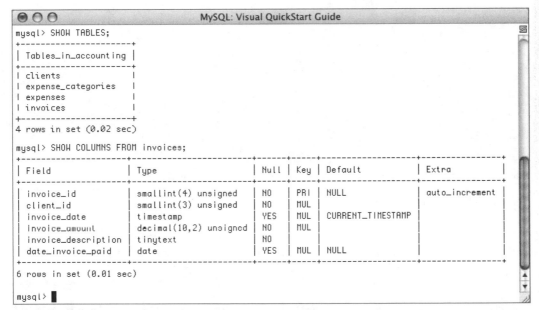

Figure 4.13 You can confirm the existence and structure of databases and tables using the SHOW command. Don't be alarmed by the results of the SHOW COLUMNS command. MySQL has its own way of describing a table that might differ from how you created it.

Modifying Tables

The final topic to discuss in this chapter is how to modify an existing table. You might need to do so for any reason, but keep in mind all the rules about normalization, indexes, naming conventions, and the like before you make changes. It's easy to undermine all of the planning you put into a database by making a "quick fix."

The ALTER SQL keyword is primarily used to modify the structure of a table in your database. Commonly this refers to adding, deleting, or changing the columns therein. It also applies to renaming the table as a whole and altering the indexes. The basic syntax of ALTER is:

```
ALTER TABLE tablename CLAUSE
```

Because there are so many possible clauses, I've listed the common ones in **Table 4.8**. A more complete listing is included in Appendix B, "SQL and MySQL References."

Table 4.8 The ALTER SQL command can be used to modify tables in numerous ways.

ALTER TABLE Clauses		
CLAUSE	USAGE	MEANING
ADD COLUMN	ALTER TABLE tblname ADD COLUMN colname coltype	Adds a new column to the end of the table.
CHANGE COLUMN	ALTER TABLE tblname CHANGE COLUMN colname newcolname newcoltype	Allows you to change the data type and properties.
DROP COLUMN	ALTER TABLE tblname DROP COLUMN colname	Removes a column from a table, including all of its data.
ADD INDEX	ALTER TABLE tblname ADD INDEX indexname (columns)	Adds a new index on the listed column(s).
DROP INDEX	ALTER TABLE tblname DROP INDEX indexname	Removes an existing index.
RENAME AS	ALTER TABLE tblname RENAME AS newtblname	Changes the name of a table.

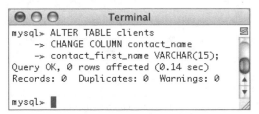

Figure 4.14 To rename or redefine a column, use the ALTER TABLE *tablename* CHANGE COLUMN syntax.

To demonstrate using the ALTER command, I'll modify the clients table to separate the contact_name field into the more normalized contact_first_name and contact_last_name columns. In this example, I'm assuming that there's no data in the table yet. If there was, I would need to account for that (perhaps by adding the new columns, moving the data over, and then deleting the original column). Because an ALTER command could have serious repercussions on a table, you should always back up the table before execution (see Chapter 13).

To alter a table's structure:

1. Access the mysql client and select the *accounting* database, if you have not already.

   USE accounting;

2. Rename the contact_name field (**Figure 4.14**).

   ALTER TABLE clients

   CHANGE COLUMN contact_name

   contact_first_name VARCHAR(15);

   This command merely changes the name and data type definition of the contact_name column. Instead of being a VARCHAR(40), the column is now called contact_first_name and is a VARCHAR(15). If any data was in this column, it would remain but be truncated to 15 characters long.

   continues on next page

Deleting Tables and Databases

In order to delete a table or database, you use the DROP command. This is as simple as

DROP DATABASE *dbname*

DROP TABLE *tablename*

Obviously once you've deleted a table, all of that table's data is gone for good. Once you've deleted a database, all of its tables and data are history.

MODIFYING TABLES

3. Create a new contact_last_name column (**Figure 4.15**).

ALTER TABLE clients

ADD COLUMN contact_last_name
→ VARCHAR(25)

AFTER contact_first_name;

Now the table contains a new column, although there are currently no values in it. When adding a new column to a table, you can use the AFTER *columname* description to indicate where in the table the new column should be placed.

4. Confirm the table's structure (**Figure 4.16**).

SHOW COLUMNS FROM clients;

✔ Tips

■ To change the type of an existing table—which is perfectly acceptable—use an ALTER command:

ALTER TABLE *tablename* ENGINE = MYISAM

■ You can also confirm the structure of a table after making alterations using SHOW CREATE TABLE *tablename*. As you would see from running this query, it would not show the original CREATE statement but rather what CREATE statement would need to be executed in order to recreate the table as it currently is.

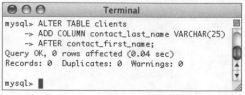

Figure 4.15 To add a new column to a table, use ALTER TABLE *tablename* ADD COLUMN.

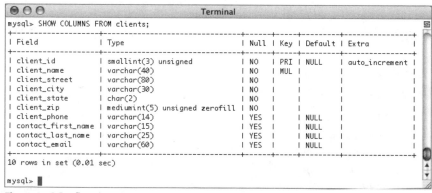

Figure 4.16 Confirm the table's structure by running a SHOW COLUMNS command.

BASIC SQL

SQL, short for Structured Query Language (although this is sometimes debated), is a group of special words used exclusively for interacting with databases. Every major database uses SQL, and MySQL is no exception.

SQL was created shortly after E.F. Codd came up with the theory of a relational database (along with normalization). Decades later, in 1989, the American National Standards Institute (ANSI)—the organization responsible for maintaining the language—released the first SQL standard, referred to now as SQL 89. SQL2 was released in 1992. In 1999, SQL 3 was released, although it has not been completely supported as yet. And in 2003, a new standard was defined, with increased XML support.

Using the *accounting* database created in Chapter 4, "Creating a MySQL Database," this chapter will discuss and demonstrate all of the major SQL terms. Since you must use SQL to communicate with MySQL, the remainder of the book will, in part, rely upon the information presented here. The entire chapter assumes that you have created the *accounting* database, per the instructions in the last chapter, and that you are logged in to the mysql client as a user with permission to interact with that database.

Using Values in Queries

Before you begin actually using SQL to interact with MySQL, you should have an understanding of how values must be used in your queries. I want to be explicit as to how you should treat the different data types in your SQL commands. Always abide by these rules:

♦ Numeric values shouldn't be quoted.

♦ Numeric values must not contain commas.

♦ String values (for CHAR, VARCHAR, and TEXT column types) must always be quoted.

♦ Date and time values must always be quoted.

♦ Functions, introduced in Chapter 6, "MySQL Functions," cannot be quoted.

♦ The world NULL must not be quoted.

Along with those rules, you have to watch out for certain characters in strings that could break your queries. For example, if you quote some text using single quotes, a single quote (an apostrophe) within that text will ruin the query. To avoid problems in these instances, you can escape the apostrophe in the string by preceding it with a backslash: \'. **Table 5.1** lists the characters that must be escaped in your strings.

With the date formats, not only do you have to quote the value used, but it also has to be in the right format. The standard format is *YYYY-MM-DD HH:MM:SS*. You can also use a two-digit year in this format, but I'd advise against ever doing so (remember that whole "Y2K" thing?). In fact, you can also get away with using a single digit for the day or month, when applicable, but I think it's best to always use two digits there (so January is 01, not 1).

Table 5.1 These characters all have special meanings when used in queries. The letters are all case-sensitive! The percentage character and the underscore are necessary because these characters, when not escaped, can be used as wildcards in searches.

Escape Characters

CHARACTER	MEANING
\'	Single quotation mark
\"	Double quotation mark
\b	Backspace
\n	Newline
\r	Carriage return
\t	Tab
\\	Backslash
\%	Percentage character
_	Underscore character

Alternatively, you could use other punctuation as your delimiters: *YYYY/MM/DD HH:MM:SS* or *YYYY.MM.DD HH.MM.SS*. You can even forgo delimiters entirely, but it's important to use four digits for the year and two for everything else in that case: *YYYYMMDDHHMMSS*.

Finally, I'll point out that SQL keywords—INSERT, SELECT, FROM, WHERE, and so on—are case-insensitive. I tend to capitalize these words so that they stand out, but this is not required. If you'd rather type your SQL in all lowercase, that's fine. As for the database, table, and column names, these are case-sensitive on Unix and case-insensitive on Windows and Mac OS X.

✔ Tips

- If you use an invalid date in a query, it will be treated as a "zero" value for that type: 0000-00-00 00:00:00 (DATETIME) or 0000-00-00 (DATE).

- If you use double quotation marks to encapsulate a string, a single quotation mark within that string is not a problem, and vice versa. You only need to escape a quotation mark within a string if that string is encapsulated by the same type of quotation mark.

- The Boolean values of true and false can be written using any case—*TRUE*, *True*, *true*—but are not quoted. MySQL will evaluate the Boolean true as 1 and the false as 0.

- If you escape a character that's not listed in Table 5.1, the escape will be ignored. Thus \m is the same as just *m*.

DDL and DML

SQL is broken down into two broad categories: *Data Definition Language (DDL)* and *Data Manipulation Language (DML)*. The first group of SQL commands are used to create, alter, and delete databases, tables, and indexes. All of these are discussed in Chapter 4. The second group of SQL commands relate to the data stored in a table. That's what's covered in this chapter.

Knowing about these two labels isn't mandatory, nor will it impact how you use a database. Still, you'll see these terms elsewhere, so you might want to be familiar with them.

Inserting Data

After your database and tables have been created, you can start populating them with data using the INSERT command. There are two formats for inserting data. With the first, you specify the columns to be used.

```
INSERT INTO mytable (col1, col2 …)
→ VALUES ('value1', 56, …)
```

```
INSERT INTO mytable (col4, col8)
→ VALUES (8.2156, 'valueY')
```

Using this structure, you can add rows of records, populating only the columns that matter. The result will be that any columns not given a value will be treated as NULL (or given a default value, if one was established). However, if a column cannot have a NULL value (it was defined as NOT NULL), not specifying a value will cause an error.

The second format for inserting records is not to list the columns but to include a value for every one.

```
INSERT INTO mytable VALUES
→ ('value1', NULL, 20.6, 'value3', …)
```

If you use this second method, you must specify a value, even a NULL value, for every column. If there are six columns in the table, you must list six values. Failure to match the values or number of values to the columns (or number of columns) will also cause an error. For this reason, the first format of inserting records is generally preferable. Secondarily, if you add columns to a table at a later time, the first kind of INSERT will still work, whereas this second kind would fail.

Semicolons and Queries

In the mysql client, the semicolon is used to indicate the end of a command or query, letting mysql know when to try to execute a statement. This can be confusing, as people tend to think that the semicolon is part of the SQL query, when it is not.

For this reason, in this book I do not use a semicolon when discussing or demonstrating SQL queries in general. However, if a step expects that you are entering a query in the mysql client, then I *will* use a semicolon, as is required by mysql.

When running queries from a programming language or another interface like phpMyAdmin, the semicolon is most likely not necessary.

As you'll also see later in the chapter, you can terminate a query in mysql using \G instead of a semicolon. This alteration also tells mysql to return the results in a vertical listing, instead of the default horizontal table. I use this alternative command terminator where the query results are less legible in their default (horizontal) view.

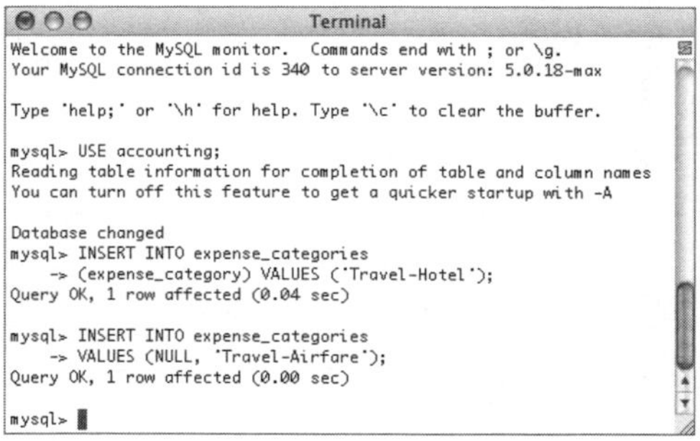

Figure 5.1 Here are the two ways you can insert data into a table.

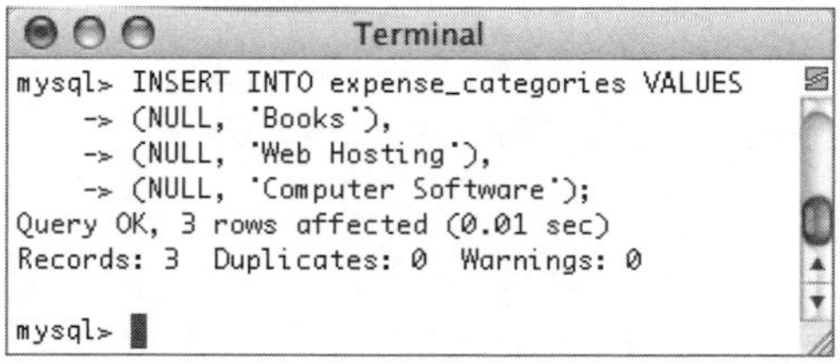

Figure 5.2 With MySQL, I can enter as many values into a table as I want in one command.

MySQL also allows you to insert multiple rows at one time, separating each record from the next by a comma.

```
INSERT INTO mytable (col1, col4)
→ VALUES ('valueA', 234),
→ ('valueC', 4946), ('valueE', 2)
```

While you can do this with MySQL, it is not acceptable within the ANSI SQL standard (and therefore is not something that can be done with all database applications).

To insert data into a table:

1. Insert a new row of data into the expense_categories table (**Figure 5.1**).

   Your syntax would be one of the following:

   ▲ INSERT INTO expense_categories
     → (expense_category) VALUES
     → ('Travel-Hotel');

   ▲ INSERT INTO expense_categories
     → VALUES (NULL, 'Travel-Airfare');

   Since this table contains only two columns, one of which is automatically incremented, there's little difference between the two methods.

   The NULL value works because the expense_category_id column is defined as AUTO_INCREMENT. When MySQL sees NULL being used here, it will automatically choose the next highest integer value for that column.

2. Insert several more values into the expense_categories table (**Figure 5.2**).

   INSERT INTO expense_categories VALUES

   (NULL, 'Books'),

   (NULL, 'Web Hosting'),

   (NULL, 'Computer Software');

   Since MySQL allows you to insert multiple values at once, you can take advantage of this and fill up the table with records.

   continues on next page

INSERTING DATA

3. Insert a record into the clients table
(**Figure 5.3**).

Your query can be structured in many
ways. Just three examples are:

```
INSERT INTO clients VALUES
(NULL, 'Acme Industries', '100 Main
→ Street',
'Anytown', 'NY', 11111, '(888) 555-
→ 1234',
'Jane', 'Doe',
→ 'Jane@acme_industries.com');
INSERT INTO clients (client_name,
→ contact_first_name,
→ contact_last_name) VALUES
('Winesburg Press', 'Sherwood',
→ 'Anderson');
INSERT INTO clients VALUES
(NULL, 'Galt on the Hill', '1000
→ Tuttle Drive',
'Brazilia', 'IL', 60000, NULL, NULL,
NULL, 'jimmy.johns@example.com');
```

Just be absolutely certain that the number of values you have correspond to the
number of columns, either in the table or
named in the query.

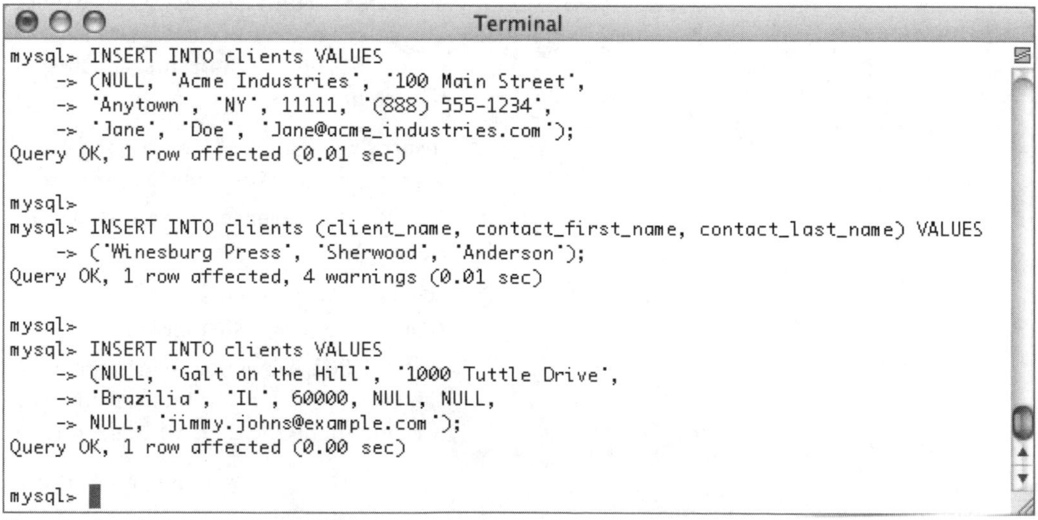

```
● ● ●                          Terminal
mysql> INSERT INTO clients VALUES
    -> (NULL, 'Acme Industries', '100 Main Street',
    -> 'Anytown', 'NY', 11111, '(888) 555-1234',
    -> 'Jane', 'Doe', 'Jane@acme_industries.com');
Query OK, 1 row affected (0.01 sec)

mysql>
mysql> INSERT INTO clients (client_name, contact_first_name, contact_last_name) VALUES
    -> ('Winesburg Press', 'Sherwood', 'Anderson');
Query OK, 1 row affected, 4 warnings (0.01 sec)

mysql>
mysql> INSERT INTO clients VALUES
    -> (NULL, 'Galt on the Hill', '1000 Tuttle Drive',
    -> 'Brazilia', 'IL', 60000, NULL, NULL,
    -> NULL, 'jimmy.johns@example.com');
Query OK, 1 row affected (0.00 sec)

mysql> █
```

Figure 5.3 Populating the clients table.

4. Continue Steps 2 and 3 until you've thoroughly populated the `expense_categories` and `clients` tables.

At this point, because of the more complicated nature of a relational database, I am not going to add records to either the `invoices` or `expenses` tables, as these rely on information in the `clients` and `expense_categories` tables. You'll see later in the chapter how to insert records into them.

✔ Tips

■ The term `INTO` in `INSERT` statements is optional in current versions of MySQL.

■ The SQL commands I used to populate my tables are available for download from the book's corresponding Web site: `www.DMCInsights.com/mysql2`. You don't have to use them yourself, but if you don't, your results in the rest of the chapter may differ from mine.

Selecting Data

Now that the database has some records in it, you can begin to retrieve the information with the most used of all SQL terms, SELECT. This term is used to return rows of records that meet certain criteria. A SELECT query looks like so:

SELECT *whatcolumns* FROM *whattable*

You just ask MySQL to return whichever columns you want (the data stored in them, that is) for a particular table. For the columns, one option is to list them individually, with each separated from the next by a comma:

SELECT user_id, first_name, last_name
→ FROM users

Another option is to use an asterisk, meaning that you want to view every column:

SELECT * FROM users

There are a few benefits to being explicit about which columns are selected. The first is performance: there's no reason to fetch columns that you will not be using. The second is order: you can return columns in an order other than their layout in the table. The third—and you'll see this in Chapter 6— is accessibility: it allows you to manipulate the values in those columns using functions.

To select data from a table:

1. Retrieve all the data from the expense_categories table (**Figure 5.4**).

    SELECT * FROM expense_categories;

    This very basic SQL command will retrieve every column of every row stored within that table and present them.

Figure 5.4 This is a simple SELECT query, returning all of the table's records and columns.

INSERT...SELECT

Another way you can populate one table is by selecting data from another table. To do so, use an INSERT...SELECT query. The syntax is

INSERT INTO *tablename* (*col1*, *col2*, …)
→ SELECT *colA*, *colB*, … FROM *othertable*

As with any INSERT query, the important consideration is that one value is supplied for each column (listed or in the table).

This query isn't frequently used, but it can be quite the time saver in the right circumstances.

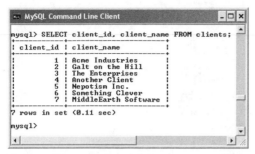

Figure 5.5 You can limit the information returned by a SELECT query by specifying the columns to include.

2. Retrieve just the client_id and client_name fields from clients (**Figure 5.5**).

   SELECT client_id, client_name FROM
   → clients;

   Instead of showing the data from every field in the clients table, you can use the SELECT statement to limit yourself to only the pertinent information.

3. Using the information retrieved in Steps 1 and 2, populate the expenses table (**Figure 5.6**).

   INSERT INTO expenses VALUES

   (NULL, 3, 19.99, 'Larry Ullman\'s
   → "MySQL: Visual QuickStart Guide"',
   → '2002-04-20'),

   (NULL, 1, 105.50, 'Palmer House
   → Hotel, Chicago', '2002-1-26'),

   (NULL, 2, 689.00, 'Flight to
   → Chicago', '2002-01-26'),

   (NULL, 5, 99.99, 'Mmmm...software',
   → NULL);

   continues on next page

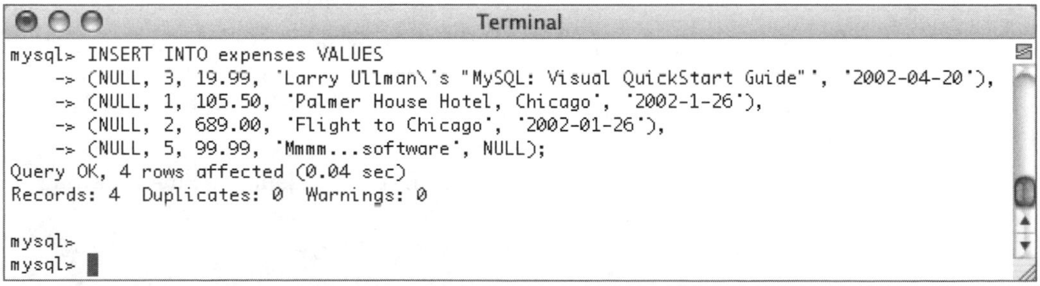

SELECTING DATA

```
mysql> INSERT INTO expenses VALUES
    -> (NULL, 3, 19.99, 'Larry Ullman\'s "MySQL: Visual QuickStart Guide"', '2002-04-20'),
    -> (NULL, 1, 105.50, 'Palmer House Hotel, Chicago', '2002-1-26'),
    -> (NULL, 2, 689.00, 'Flight to Chicago', '2002-01-26'),
    -> (NULL, 5, 99.99, 'Mmmm...software', NULL);
Query OK, 4 rows affected (0.04 sec)
Records: 4  Duplicates: 0  Warnings: 0

mysql>
mysql>
```

Figure 5.6 Now that my expense_category_id foreign keys have been established, I can populate the expenses table.

Now that you can view the primary keys from the `expense_categories` and `clients` tables (`expense_category_id` and `client_id`, respectively), it's possible to insert data into the other two tables. Because the database is relational, it's important to align records, matching up primary keys in one table with foreign keys in another. Thus, to indicate that an expense is a *Book*, you enter the expense using 3 as the `expense_category_id`. Maintaining these relationships is at the heart of a normalized database and requires use of both `SELECT` and `INSERT` commands.

4. Populate the `invoices` table.

For the `invoices` records, you'll need to match the `client_id` in the `invoices` table with the `client_id` in the `clients` table. Your queries might look like this:

```
INSERT INTO invoices VALUES
→ (NULL,4,'2006-04-24','1902.34',
→ 'Conjugation: verbs, nouns,
→ adjectives.', NULL);

INSERT INTO invoices (client_id,
→ invoice_date, invoice_amount,
→ invoice_description) VALUES
→ (4,'2008-07-20','942.00','Technical
→ writing.');
```

5. Continue with this process until the database has oodles of information in it, in every table.

Throughout the rest of this chapter I will be performing queries based upon the records I enter into my database. Should your database not have the same specific records (clients, expense categories, etc.) as mine, change the particulars accordingly. That being said, the fundamental thinking behind the following queries should still apply regardless of the data, since the *accounting* database has a set column and table structure.

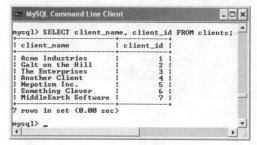

Figure 5.7 Changing the order of the columns in your SELECT query alters the order of the retrieved data.

✔ Tips

■ Strange as it may sound, you can actually use `SELECT` without naming tables or columns. You'll see this in action in the next chapter.

■ The order in which you list columns in your `SELECT` statement (assuming you are not retrieving everything) dictates the order in which the values are returned. Compare Figure 5.5 with **Figure 5.7**.

■ With `SELECT`, you can even retrieve the same column multiple times, allowing you to manipulate the column in many different ways.

Table 5.2 These are the most common MySQL operators. Appendix B, "SQL & MySQL References," will contain the exhaustive list.

MySQL Operators

Operator	Meaning
=	equals
<	less than
>	greater than
<=	less than or equal to
>=	greater than or equal to
!= (also <>)	not equal to
IS NOT NULL	has a value
IS NULL	does not have a value
IN	value found within a list
BETWEEN	within a range
NOT BETWEEN	outside of a range
OR (also ||)	where one of two conditionals is true
AND (also &&)	where both conditionals are true
NOT (also !)	where the condition is not true

Using Conditionals

The problem with the SELECT statement as used in the preceding section is that it will automatically retrieve every record. While this isn't a problem when dealing with a few rows of information, it will greatly hinder the performance of your database as the number of records grows. To improve the efficiency of your SELECT statements, there are different conditionals you can use in almost limitless combinations. These conditionals utilize the SQL term WHERE and are written much as you'd write a conditional in any programming language.

SELECT *whatcolumns* FROM *tablename* WHERE
→ *conditions*

The conditions are normally a combination of column names, literal values (numbers or strings), and operators. **Table 5.2** lists the most common operators you would use within a WHERE conditional. Example queries are:

SELECT expense_amount FROM expenses
→ WHERE expense_amount >= 10.00
SELECT client_id FROM clients WHERE
→ client_name = 'Acme Industries'

These operators can be used together, along with parentheses, to create more complex conditionals.

SELECT expense_amount FROM expenses
→ WHERE (expense_amount >= 10.00) AND
→ (expense_amount <= 20.00)
SELECT client_id FROM clients WHERE
→ (client_name = 'Acme Industries') OR
→ (client_name = 'Something Clever')

To demonstrate using conditionals, I'll retrieve more specific data from the *accounting* database. The examples that follow will show just a few of the possibilities. Over the course of this chapter and the entire book you will see any number of variants on SELECT conditionals.

To select particular data from a table:

1. Select the `expense_description` for every *Books* expense type (**Figure 5.8**).

   SELECT expense_description FROM
   → expenses

   WHERE expense_category_id = 3;

   Since I know that *Books* in the `expense_categories` table has an `expense_category_id` of 3, I can create this SQL query. It will return the `expense_description` for each record that has an `expense_category_id` foreign key of 3. Note that numbers should not be placed within quotation marks in your conditionals (or anywhere else in your query).

   If you did not enter a *Books* expense type, change your query accordingly.

2. Select the invoice ID, amount, and date of every invoice entered since March 1, 2006 (**Figure 5.9**).

   SELECT invoice_id, invoice_amount,
   → invoice_date

   FROM invoices

   WHERE invoice_date >= '2006-03-01';

   You can perform greater than and less than (or greater than or equal to, less than or equal to) calculations using dates, as I've done here.

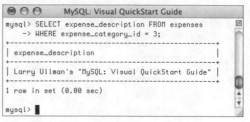

Figure 5.8 The conditional in this query uses the expenses table's expense_category_id foreign key to select a particular record.

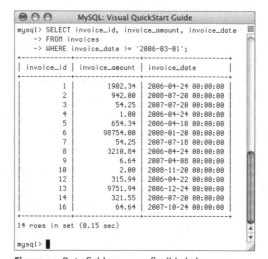

Figure 5.9 Date fields are very flexible in how you access the information, including being able to relatively select dates.

USING CONDITIONALS

mysql> SELECT * FROM expenses
    -> WHERE expense_date IS NULL;
Empty set (0.00 sec)

mysql>

Figure 5.10 Because NULL is a special value in databases, the IS NULL and IS NOT NULL operators are used for these cases. No records were returned because every expense has an expense_date value.

3. Select everything from every record in the expenses table that does not have a date (**Figure 5.10**).

SELECT * FROM expenses
WHERE expense_date IS NULL;

The IS NULL conditional is the same as saying "does not have a value." Keep in mind that an empty string is the same thing as a value, in NULL terms, and therefore would not match this condition. Such a case would match

SELECT * FROM expenses WHERE
→ expense_date = '';

✔ Tips

■ Strange as it may seem, you do not have to select a column on which you are performing a WHERE.

SELECT invoice_id FROM invoices WHERE
→ client_id = 4

The reason for this is that the columns listed after SELECT only determine what *columns* to return. Conversely, a WHERE clause determines which *rows* to return.

■ You can perform mathematical calculations within your queries using the numeric addition (+), subtraction (-), multiplication (*), and division (/) characters.

■ It's important that you never try to compare a NULL value to anything, as NULL is special and the results you'll see can be esoteric. For example, the conditionals NULL > 1, NULL < 1 and NULL = 1 all have the same result. For NULL comparisons, always use IS NULL and IS NOT NULL instead.

Using LIKE and NOT LIKE

Using numbers, dates, and NULLs in conditionals is a straightforward process, but strings can be trickier. You can check for string equality with a query such as

```
SELECT * FROM users WHERE user_name =
→ 'trout'
```

However, comparing strings in a more liberal manner requires extra operators and characters. If, for example, you wanted to match a person's last name that could be *Smith* or *Smiths* or *Smithson*, you would need a more flexible query. This is where the LIKE and NOT LIKE conditionals come in. These are used—primarily with strings—in conjunction with two wildcard characters: the underscore (_), which matches a single character, and the percentage sign (%), which matches zero or more characters. In my last name example, the query I would write would be

```
SELECT * FROM users WHERE last_name LIKE
→ 'Smith%'
```

This query will perform a search on all columns whose last_name value begins with *Smith*. Because it's a case-insensitive search by default, it would also apply to names that begin with *smith*.

The \G Terminator in mysql

As I alluded to earlier in this chapter (see the sidebar "Semicolons and Queries"), you can terminate your queries in the mysql client using \G instead of a semicolon. The benefit of this is that your results will be displayed as a vertical list of records instead of a horizontal one. When selecting many columns or an entire table, this is often a more legible way to view the results. For this reason, I'll occasionally use \G throughout the book. Remember that this is just a way to change the *look* of the output and also means that no semicolon is required. Also, this is a mysql client feature, not an aspect of SQL.

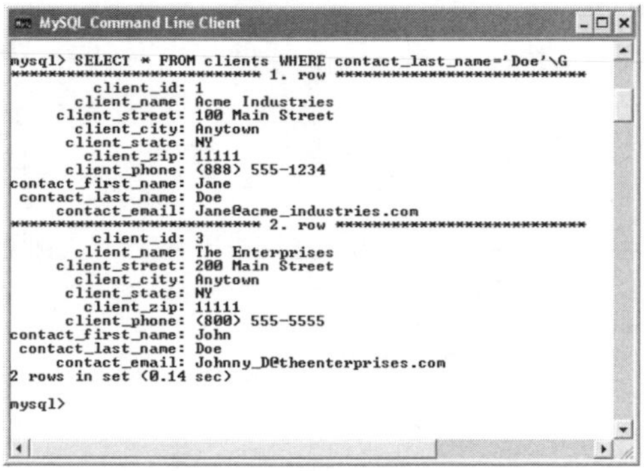

Figure 5.11 Simple, case-sensitive equality tests can be accomplished using the equality operator. The \G at the end of the query tells mysql to show the results as a vertical list of records.

Figure 5.12 Using LIKE allows me to perform a case-insensitive search on a text column.

To use LIKE:

1. Select all of the client information in which the client's contact has a last name of *Doe* (**Figure 5.11**).

   SELECT * FROM clients WHERE
   → contact_last_name='Doe'\G

   If you're hoping to match a literal string, do not use LIKE, use the equality comparison operator instead.

   If you're paying attention, you're probably wondering what that \G is doing at the end of the query. This is for aesthetic purposes and is explained in the sidebar.

2. Select all of the client information in which the client's contact has a last name of *Doe*, case-insensitive (**Figure 5.12**).

   SELECT * FROM clients WHERE last_name
   → LIKE 'Doe'\G

   Because LIKE is case-insensitive, I can use it to find a literal string regardless of capitalization. No wildcard character is needed in this situation.

   continues on next page

3. Select the client and contact names for every record whose contact's first name is not John, Joe, Joey, etc. (**Figure 5.13**).

SELECT client_name, contact_first_name,
→ contact_last_name

FROM clients WHERE

contact_first_name NOT LIKE 'Jo%';

If I want to rule out certain possibilities, I can use NOT LIKE with the wildcard.

✔ Tips

■ The wildcard characters can be used at the front and/or the back of a string in your queries.

SELECT * FROM users WHERE user_name =
→ '_smith%'

■ Queries with a LIKE conditional are generally slow, so use this format sparingly. Conditionals such as LIKE 'some%' can still make use of indexes, which improves their speed, but conditionals with an initial wildcard (LIKE '%some%' or LIKE '%some') cannot, making them much less efficient.

■ Although LIKE and NOT LIKE are normally used with strings, they can also be applied to numeric columns, should the need arise. That being said, there are normally more efficient ways to do searches on numeric columns.

■ To use either the underscore or the percentage sign in a LIKE or NOT LIKE query, you will need to escape them (by preceding the character with a backslash) so that they are not confused as wildcards.

■ The underscore can be used in combination with itself, so, as an example, LIKE '__' would find any two-letter combination.

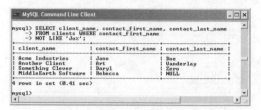

Figure 5.13 The NOT LIKE operator allows you to eliminate certain records based upon loose definitions (such as *Jo*%).

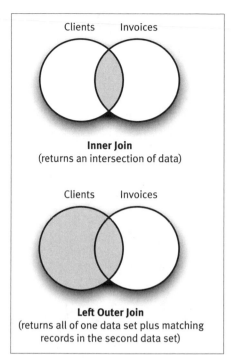

Inner Join
(returns an intersection of data)

Left Outer Join
(returns all of one data set plus matching records in the second data set)

Figure 5.14 These Venn diagrams represent the two primary ways the data in two tables can be retrieved using joins.

Performing Joins

Because relational databases are more complexly structured, they sometimes require special query statements to retrieve the information you need most. *Joins*—SQL queries performed by cross-referencing tables— are used to extract more usable data from relational databases. As you can see from **Figure 5.14**, the returned data can be the intersection of two sets of records (see the top image) or all of one data set plus the intersection of the other.

Several types of joins are conceivable according to SQL, each returning a different set of data. Beginning to intermediate users will find that the two most basic joins (which I'll teach in this chapter) will satisfy almost every need. The most used join is called an *inner* join. For example, if you want to match up all the clients with their invoices, this could be done using two syntaxes:

```
SELECT * FROM invoices, clients WHERE
→ invoices.client_id = clients.client_id
SELECT * FROM invoices INNER JOIN
→ clients ON invoices.client_id =
→ clients.client_id
```

This join will retrieve all of the information from both the `invoices` and `clients` tables wherever an `invoices.client_id` is the same as the `clients.client_id`. In other words, the query will replace the `client_id` foreign key in the `invoices` table with all of the information for that client in the `clients` table. An inner join like this will only return records wherein a match is made (so if a client record did not match an existing invoice, that client's information would not be returned).

When selecting from multiple tables and columns, you must use the dot syntax (*table.column*) if there are columns with the same name. This is normally the case when dealing with relational databases because a primary key from one table will have the same name as a foreign key from another.

The second type of join I'll discuss—an *outer* join—differs from an inner join in that it could return records not matched by a conditional. It comes in both *left outer join* and *right outer join* varieties (also just called a *left join* or *right join*). For example:

```
SELECT * FROM clients LEFT JOIN
→ invoices ON invoices.client_id =
→ clients.client_id
```

With that query, all of the `clients` records will be returned, and if a client has any corresponding invoice records, those will be returned as well. This differs from the inner join in that all the data from the first listed table will be returned whether or not a match is made to the second table.

The right outer join just gives precedence to the second table listed instead of the first. These two queries have the same result:

```
SELECT * FROM invoices RIGHT JOIN
→ clients ON invoices.client_id =
→ clients.client_id
SELECT * FROM clients LEFT JOIN
→ invoices ON invoices.client_id =
→ clients.client_id
```

If both tables in an outer join have the same column name, you can simplify your query with

```
SELECT * FROM invoices LEFT JOIN
→ clients USING (client_id)
```

Joins are complicated stuff, so hopefully these next examples will help to clarify these points.

To use joins:

1. Retrieve the invoice amount, the invoice date, and the client names for every invoice (**Figure 5.15**).

   ```
   SELECT invoice_amount, invoice_date,
   → client_name FROM invoices, clients
   WHERE invoices.client_id =
   → clients.client_id;
   ```

   This query, which includes an inner join, will return each client's name, invoice amount, and invoice date, if they have been invoiced. As you can see in the figure, the result is one record, with all three pieces of information, for each matching client and invoice. If a client has not been invoiced, they would not be included in the results.

```
MySQL: Visual QuickStart Guide
mysql> SELECT invoice_amount, invoice_date,
    -> client_name FROM invoices, clients
    -> WHERE invoices.client_id = clients.client_id;

+----------------+---------------------+------------------+
| invoice_amount | invoice_date        | client_name      |
+----------------+---------------------+------------------+
|        1902.34 | 2006-04-24 00:00:00 | The Enterprises  |
|         942.00 | 2008-07-20 00:00:00 | The Enterprises  |
|          54.25 | 2007-07-20 00:00:00 | Winesburg Press  |
|           1.00 | 2006-04-24 00:00:00 | Galt on the Hill |
|         654.34 | 2006-04-10 00:00:00 | Acme Industries  |
|       98754.00 | 2008-01-20 00:00:00 | Acme Industries  |
|          54.25 | 2007-07-18 00:00:00 | Winesburg Press  |
|        3210.84 | 2006-04-24 00:00:00 | Galt on the Hill |
|           6.64 | 2007-04-08 00:00:00 | The Enterprises  |
|           2.00 | 2008-11-20 00:00:00 | The Enterprises  |
|           9.96 | 2001-07-03 00:00:00 | The Enterprises  |
|         315.94 | 2006-04-22 00:00:00 | Winesburg Press  |
|        9751.94 | 2006-12-24 00:00:00 | Galt on the Hill |
|         321.55 | 2006-07-20 00:00:00 | The Enterprises  |
|           2.55 | 2001-07-27 00:00:00 | Another Client   |
|          64.64 | 2007-10-24 00:00:00 | Nepotism Inc.    |
+----------------+---------------------+------------------+
16 rows in set (0.91 sec)

mysql>
```

Figure 5.15 The basic inner join, albeit wordy, returns more usable information from your database than would a standard query.

2. Retrieve the expense category, expense date, and expense amount for every expense (**Figure 5.16**).

   ```
   SELECT expense_category,
   → expense_amount, expense_date FROM
   → expense_categories, expenses WHERE
   → expense_categories.
   → expense_category_id = expenses.
   → expense_category_id;
   ```

   This query is another application of the same principle as that in Step 1. Because I am again performing an inner join, the order of the tables will not matter (the end result will be the same if you reverse the table listings).

```
MySQL: Visual QuickStart Guide
mysql> SELECT expense_category, expense_amount, expense_date
 FROM expense_categories, expenses WHERE expense_categories.
 expense_category_id = expenses. expense_category_id;
+-------------------+----------------+---------------------+
| expense_category  | expense_amount | expense_date        |
+-------------------+----------------+---------------------+
| Books             |          19.99 | 2002-04-20 00:00:00 |
| Travel-Hotel      |         105.50 | 2002-01-26 00:00:00 |
| Travel-Airfare    |         689.00 | 2002-01-26 00:00:00 |
| Computer Software |          99.99 | 2006-02-02 23:01:31 |
+-------------------+----------------+---------------------+
4 rows in set (0.04 sec)

mysql>
```

Figure 5.16 Inner joins are usable wherever you have a primary key–foreign key relationship, as I do here between `expenses` and `expense_categories`.

continues on next page

3. Retrieve all of the client names and all of the invoices for those clients (**Figure 5.17**).

```
SELECT client_name, invoice_id,
→ invoice_amount, invoice_date,
→ invoice_description FROM clients
→ LEFT JOIN invoices USING
→ (client_id);
```

This query—an outer join—will retrieve every client name and then associate the appropriate invoices with each. Even if a client has no invoices (see *Something Clever* at bottom), the client will be listed. If I had used an inner join, *Something Clever* would be omitted from the returned results (see Figure 5.15).

```
● ● ●                          MySQL: Visual QuickStart Guide
mysql> SELECT client_name, invoice_id, invoice_amount, invoice_date, invoice_description FROM clients LEFT JOIN invoices
USING (client_id);
+----------------------+------------+----------------+---------------------+------------------------------------------+
| client_name          | invoice_id | invoice_amount | invoice_date        | invoice_description                      |
+----------------------+------------+----------------+---------------------+------------------------------------------+
| Acme Industries      |          5 |         654.34 | 2006-04-10 00:00:00 | Work, work, work.                        |
| Acme Industries      |          6 |       98754.00 | 2008-01-20 00:00:00 | Technical writing.                       |
| Winesburg Press      |          3 |          54.25 | 2007-07-20 00:00:00 | Hand wringing                            |
| Winesburg Press      |          7 |          54.25 | 2007-07-18 00:00:00 | Pacing.                                  |
| Winesburg Press      |         12 |         315.94 | 2006-04-22 00:00:00 | Miscellaneous Services                   |
| Galt on the Hill     |          4 |           1.00 | 2006-04-24 00:00:00 | Miscellaneous Services                   |
| Galt on the Hill     |          8 |        3210.84 | 2006-04-24 00:00:00 | Pondering                                |
| Galt on the Hill     |         13 |        9751.94 | 2006-12-24 00:00:00 | Reading.                                 |
| The Enterprises      |          1 |        1902.34 | 2006-04-24 00:00:00 | Conjugation: verbs, nouns, adjectives.   |
| The Enterprises      |          2 |         942.00 | 2007-07-20 00:00:00 | Technical writing.                       |
| The Enterprises      |          9 |           6.64 | 2007-04-08 00:00:00 | Shady dealings.                          |
| The Enterprises      |         10 |           2.00 | 2008-11-20 00:00:00 | Brilliance.                              |
| The Enterprises      |         14 |         321.55 | 2006-07-20 00:00:00 | HTML, PHP, MySQL Web development.        |
| The Enterprises      |         11 |           9.96 | 2001-07-03 00:00:00 | Don't ask.                               |
| Another Client       |         15 |           2.55 | 2001-07-27 00:00:00 | Hand wringing                            |
| Nepotism Inc.        |         16 |          64.64 | 2007-10-24 00:00:00 | Miscellaneous Services                   |
| Something Clever     |       NULL |           NULL |                NULL | NULL                                     |
| MiddleEarth Software |       NULL |           NULL |                NULL | NULL                                     |
+----------------------+------------+----------------+---------------------+------------------------------------------+
18 rows in set (0.05 sec)
```

Figure 5.17 Left joins are more particular in their wording than inner joins and do not require matches to return records. Compare this result with that in Figure 5.18.

4. Retrieve all of the invoice IDs, amounts, dates, and descriptions, along with the corresponding client names (**Figure 5.18**).

```
SELECT client_name, invoice_id,
→ invoice_amount, invoice_date,
→ invoice_description FROM invoices
→ LEFT JOIN clients USING (client_id);
```

This query only differs from that in Step 3 in that here I am left-joining invoices to clients rather than the other way around. The end result is that two fewer records are returned, as there are no invoices associated with two clients.

```
mysql> SELECT client_name, invoice_id, invoice_amount, invoice_date, invoice_description FROM invoices LEFT JOIN
clients USING (client_id);
+----------------+------------+----------------+---------------------+---------------------------------------+
| client_name    | invoice_id | invoice_amount | invoice_date        | invoice_description                   |
+----------------+------------+----------------+---------------------+---------------------------------------+
| The Enterprises |          1 |        1902.34 | 2006-04-24 00:00:00 | Conjugation: verbs, nouns, adjectives.|
| The Enterprises |          2 |         942.00 | 2008-07-20 00:00:00 | Technical writing.                    |
| Winesburg Press |          3 |          54.25 | 2007-07-20 00:00:00 | Hand wringing                         |
| Galt on the Hill |         4 |           1.00 | 2006-04-24 00:00:00 | Miscellaneous Services                |
| Acme Industries |          5 |         654.34 | 2006-04-10 00:00:00 | Work, work, work.                     |
| Acme Industries |          6 |       98754.00 | 2008-01-20 00:00:00 | Technical writing.                    |
| Winesburg Press |          7 |          54.25 | 2007-07-18 00:00:00 | Pacing.                               |
| Galt on the Hill |         8 |        3210.84 | 2006-04-24 00:00:00 | Pondering                             |
| The Enterprises |          9 |           6.64 | 2007-04-08 00:00:00 | Shady dealings.                       |
| The Enterprises |         10 |           2.00 | 2008-11-20 00:00:00 | Brilliance.                           |
| The Enterprises |         11 |           9.96 | 2001-07-03 00:00:00 | Don't ask.                            |
| Winesburg Press |         12 |         315.94 | 2006-04-22 00:00:00 | Miscellaneous Services                |
| Galt on the Hill |        13 |        9751.94 | 2006-12-24 00:00:00 | Reading.                              |
| The Enterprises |         14 |         321.55 | 2006-07-20 00:00:00 | HTML, PHP, MySQL Web development.      |
| Another Client  |         15 |           2.55 | 2001-07-27 00:00:00 | Hand wringing                         |
| Nepotism Inc.   |         16 |          64.64 | 2007-10-24 00:00:00 | Miscellaneous Services                |
+----------------+------------+----------------+---------------------+---------------------------------------+
16 rows in set (0.00 sec)

mysql>
```

Figure 5.18 The order of the tables in a left join will affect the results returned. Every record from the first table will always be retrieved, regardless of the conditional.

✔ Tips

- MySQL differs from standard SQL in how it refers to joins. I've simplified this discussion here, focusing on the two most important types of joins, and stuck to the MySQL implementation.

- You can perform joins on more than two tables. You can even join a table with itself!

- Joins can be created using conditionals involving any columns, not just the primary and foreign keys, as I have done here.

- Joins that do not include a WHERE clause (e.g., SELECT * FROM invoices, clients) are called *full* joins and will return a Cartesian product: every record from Table A combined with every record from Table B. This construct can have unwieldy results with larger tables.

Figure 5.19 This ORDER BY returns the fields alphabetically by expense_category.

Sorting Query Results

Whereas the WHERE conditional places restrictions on what records are returned, the ORDER BY clause will affect how that data is returned. Much as listing the columns of a table arranges the returned order (compare Figures 5.5 and 5.7), ORDER BY structures the entire list. You use this phrase like so:

SELECT * FROM *tablename* ORDER BY *column*

SELECT invoice_amount, invoice_date FROM
→ invoices ORDER BY invoice_date

The default order when using ORDER BY is ascending, meaning that numbers increase from small to large and dates go from oldest to most recent. You can reverse this order by specifying DESC.

SELECT expense_description, expense_date
→ FROM expenses ORDER BY expense_date DESC

You can even order the returned values by multiple columns, as I'll demonstrate.

Note that the order in which records are stored in a table is entirely meaningless. For this reason, when you do not dictate the order of the returned data, it will be presented to you in somewhat unpredictable ways. If the order of the records in important, use an ORDER BY clause.

To sort data:

1. Show all of the expense categories in alphabetical order (**Figure 5.19**).

   SELECT * FROM expense_categories
   → ORDER BY expense_category;

   Since the expenses table has two columns, there are four ways of viewing the records in it: sorted by each column descending and ascending. This query will give an alphabetical presentation of the expenses table, based upon the expense_category.

   continues on next page

2. Order the invoices by both client and invoice date (**Figure 5.20**).

```
SELECT client_id, invoice_date,
→ invoice_amount FROM invoices ORDER
→ BY client_id ASC, invoice_date DESC;
```

In this query, the effect would be that every column and row is returned, first ordered by the client_id, and then by the invoice_date within the client_ids.

✔ Tips

- Because MySQL works naturally with any number of languages, the ORDER BY will be based upon the character set and collation being used. Both topics are discussed in Chapter 4.

- If the column that you chose to sort on contains NULL values, those will appear first in ascending order and last in descending order.

- The sorting is case-insensitive by default. You can make a text column sort in a case-sensitive fashion using the keyword BINARY:

```
SELECT * FROM table ORDER BY BINARY col
```

Technically this tells MySQL not to use a collation, but that normally has the effect of a case-sensitive search.

- You can, and frequently will, use ORDER BY in conjunction with WHERE, joins, or other clauses. When doing so, place the ORDER BY after the other conditions.

```
SELECT invoice_id, invoice_amount,
→ invoice_date FROM invoices WHERE
→ invoice_date >= '2006-03-01' ORDER
→ BY invoice_date DESC
```

- It is up to the database application to determine how results are returned when you do not use an ORDER BY clause. With MySQL, this is currently likely to be on the primary key ascending, but that could always change. As a rule of thumb, remember that the order in which records are stored and retrieved is entirely meaningless. Use ORDER BY to create meaning.

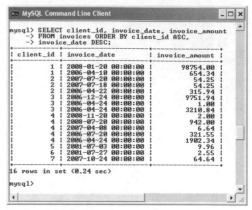

Figure 5.20 A double ORDER BY will sort the list by the first clause and then re-sort within that listing by the second clause.

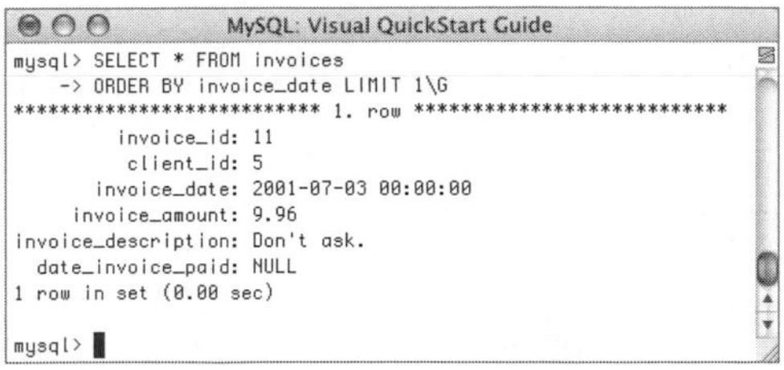

```
● ○ ○          MySQL: Visual QuickStart Guide
mysql> SELECT * FROM invoices
    -> ORDER BY invoice_date LIMIT 1\G
*************************** 1. row ***************************
       invoice_id: 11
        client_id: 5
     invoice_date: 2001-07-03 00:00:00
   invoice_amount: 9.96
invoice_description: Don't ask.
 date_invoice_paid: NULL
1 row in set (0.00 sec)

mysql>
```

Figure 5.21 The LIMIT 1 clause will ensure that only one record is ever returned, saving me the hassle of viewing unnecessary rows of information.

Limiting Query Results

Another SQL term you can add to your SELECT statement is LIMIT. Unlike WHERE, which affects which records to return, or ORDER BY, which decides how those records are sorted, LIMIT states how many records to return. It is used like so:

SELECT *whatcolumns* FROM *tablename* LIMIT
→ *howmany*

SELECT *whatcolumns* FROM *tablename* LIMIT
→ *startingwhere, howmany*

SELECT * FROM *tablename* LIMIT 10

SELECT * FROM *tablename* LIMIT 10, 20

In the third example, only the initial 10 records from the query will be returned. In the fourth, 20 records will be returned, starting with the tenth.

You can use LIMIT with WHERE and/or ORDER BY, appending it to the end of your query.

SELECT * FROM invoices WHERE
→ invoice_amount > 100.00 ORDER BY
→ invoice_amount ASC LIMIT 10

Even though LIMIT does not reduce the strain of a query on the database (since it has to assemble every record, and then cut down the list), it will minimize overhead when it comes to the client or programming interface. As a rule, when writing queries, there is never any reason to return columns or rows that you will not need.

To limit the amount of data returned:

1. Select the earliest invoice (**Figure 5.21**).

   SELECT * FROM invoices

   ORDER BY invoice_date LIMIT 1\G

   To return the earliest anything, I must sort the data by a date, in ascending order. Then, to see just one invoice, I apply a LIMIT 1 to the query.

   continues on next page

2. Select the two most expensive sand paper expenditures (**Figure 5.22**).

```
SELECT expense_amount,
→ expense_description FROM expenses,
expense_categories WHERE
→ expenses.expense_category_id =
expense_categories.expense_category_id
→ AND
expense_category = 'Sand Paper'
ORDER BY expense_amount DESC LIMIT 2;
```

This may look like a complex query, but it's just a good application of the information learned so far. First, I determine what columns to return, specifically naming the `expense_amount` and `expense_description` columns. Second, I list both tables to be used, since I'll be performing a join. Third, I establish my conditionals, which establish the join (`expenses.expense_category_id = expense_categories.expense_category_id`) and identify which category I want to use (`expense_category = 'Sand Paper'`). Finally, I sort the qualifying records so that the most expensive expenditures are listed first and then I limit it down to two records. If your database does not contain a sand paper expense category, alter this query using another example.

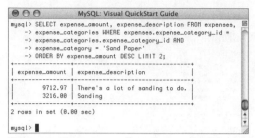

Figure 5.22 The very complicated query shown here distills the information stored in the *accounting* database into a supremely usable form.

✔ Tips

- You'll almost always want to use a `LIMIT` with an `ORDER BY` clause. Without the `ORDER BY`, there's no guarantee as to the order in which the records are returned. Therefore, there would be no guarantee as to what records are affected by the `LIMIT`.

- In the next chapter, "MySQL Functions," you'll learn one last clause, `GROUP BY`, to use with your `SELECT` statements.

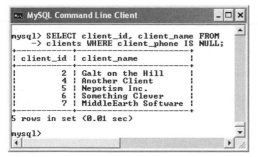

Figure 5.23 Prior to updating a record, you must know what the primary key is for that record. Then you'll have a reference point for your UPDATE query (Figure 5.24).

Updating Data

Once your tables contain some data, you have the option of changing existing records. The most frequent reason for doing this is if information has been entered incorrectly. Or, in the case of user information, if data gets changed (such as a last name or email address) and that needs to be reflected in the database.

The syntax for updating columns is

UPDATE *tablename* SET *column=value*

You can adjust multiple columns at one time, separating each from the next by a comma.

UPDATE *tablename* SET *column1='value'*,
→ *column2='value2'*…

Normally you will want to use a WHERE clause to specify what rows to affect; otherwise, the change would be applied to every row.

UPDATE *tablename* SET *column1='value'*
→ WHERE *column2='value2'*

Updates, along with deletions, are one of the most important reasons to use a primary key. This number, which should never change, can be a reference point in WHERE clauses, even if every other field needs to be altered.

To update records:

1. Find the client ID and name of any client without a phone number listed (**Figure 5.23**).

   SELECT client_id, client_name FROM
   → clients WHERE client_phone IS NULL;

   In order to perform the update, I'll need to know the primary key of the record.

   continues on next page

UPDATING DATA

2. Update the phone number for a specific client (**Figure 5.24**).

UPDATE clients SET client_phone =
→ '(800) 123-4567' WHERE client_id = 2;

When I originally entered this client, I did not include this information. Using UPDATE, I can always go back in and assign this value later.

3. Confirm that the update worked (**Figure 5.25**).

SELECT * FROM clients WHERE
→ client_id=2 \G

✔ Tips

■ Be extra certain to use a WHERE conditional whenever you use UPDATE unless you want the changes to affect every row.

■ You should never have to perform an UPDATE on the primary key column, because this value should never change. Altering a primary key in one table could destroy the integrity of a relationship with another table.

■ You can apply a LIMIT clause to an update to make sure it doesn't erroneously update too many records:

UPDATE clients SET client_phone =
→ '(800) 123-4567' WHERE client_id =
→ 2 LIMIT 1

With this query it's unlikely or impossible that more than one record would be updated, but the extra insurance is nice.

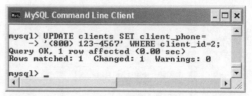

Figure 5.24 The UPDATE SQL command is an easy way to alter existing data in your tables.

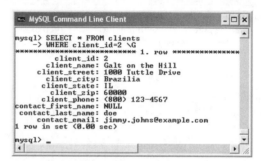

Figure 5.25 A comparable SELECT query reflects the updated information.

Deleting Data

Another step you can easily take on existing data is to entirely remove it from the database. To do this, you use the DELETE command.

DELETE FROM *tablename* WHERE *column=value*

Note that once you have deleted a record, there is no way of retrieving it, so you may want to back up your database before performing any deletes (see Chapter 13, "MySQL Administration"). Also, you should get in the habit of using WHERE when deleting data, or else you will delete all of the data in a table. The query DELETE FROM *tablename* will empty out a table, while still retaining its structure. Similarly, the command TRUNCATE TABLE *tablename* will delete an entire table (both the records and the structure) and recreate the structure. The end result is the same, but this method is faster and safer.

Another issue with deleting records has to do with the integrity of a relational database. In the *accounting* example, since the invoices table has a client_id field, if a client is deleted you might create phantom records because certain invoices, which kept that client_id reference, are now linked to a nonexistent client. Until MySQL formally supports foreign key relationships, this will be an issue to watch out for. In short, do not delete any records without altering the corresponding related records.

I'll go through an example of this by explaining the steps I would take if I decided to combine all of the *Travel* expense categories into one.

To delete data:

1. View the current expense categories (**Figure 5.26**).

```
SELECT * FROM expense_categories
ORDER BY expense_category ASC;
```

To determine which fields I am combining, I'll look at the contents of the table one last time. I should also make note of what expense_category_ids are represented by travel categories, which are 1 and 2.

2. Delete the two records from the table (**Figure 5.27**).

```
DELETE FROM expense_categories WHERE
expense_category_id IN (1, 2);
```

To be sure that I am deleting the right rows, I make use of the primary keys. I could have also used a query like DELETE FROM expense_categories WHERE expense_category LIKE 'Travel-%', although that would have been less precise.

3. Create a new *Travel* category.

```
INSERT INTO expense_categories VALUES
→ (NULL, 'Travel');
```

4. Retrieve the Travel category's *expense_category_id* (**Figure 5.28**).

```
SELECT expense_category_id FROM
expense_categories WHERE
expense_category='Travel';
```

You'll notice that deleting records from tables leaves gaps in your primary keys (in terms of auto-incrementation). Although expense_categories is currently missing numbers 1 and 2, the next record is inserted at 24. This is perfectly fine, as the primary key value is arbitrary.

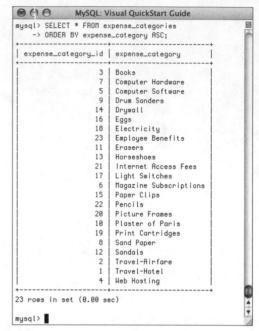

Figure 5.26 To delete all of the travel expense categories, I'll list them in alphabetical order first.

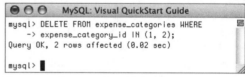

Figure 5.27 Two records are deleted using the primary key to refer to them.

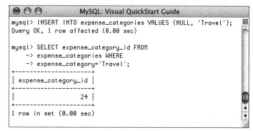

Figure 5.28 The next step in the process is to insert and select a new category.

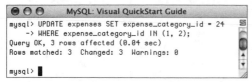

Figure 5.29 Finally, I should update the related expenses table to incorporate the new changes.

5. Update the expenses table to reflect these changes (**Figure 5.29**).

```
UPDATE expenses SET
→ expense_category_id = 24
WHERE expense_category_id IN (1, 2);
```

Because the expense_categories table relates to the expenses table, I must apply the changes made to the one to the other.

✔ Tips

■ To delete all of the data in a table, as well as the table itself, use DROP.

```
DROP TABLE tablename
```

■ To delete an entire database, including every table therein and all of its data, use

```
DROP DATABASE databasename
```

■ Remember that if you log in to the mysql client with the --i-am-a-dummy parameter, mysql will not allow you to run UPDATE or DELETE queries without a WHERE conditional.

■ Beginning with MySQL version 4.0, you can run a DELETE query across multiple tables at the same time.

DELETING DATA

6

MySQL Functions

MySQL has dozens of built-in functions that are designed to simplify common tasks. I'll cover the most useful ones here, but don't be surprised if you find that MySQL has added others in newer versions of the software. In my personal opinion, it's the functions that make querying a database so useful (SQL by itself is too vanilla).

Most of the functions you'll learn in this chapter are used in conjunction with SQL queries to format and alter the returned data. As in the preceding chapter, every example will be demonstrated from within the mysql client. Each example will be based upon the existing *accounting* database and be used to illustrate common database techniques.

Text Functions

The first group of functions I will demonstrate are those meant for manipulating the various text and character columns. Most of the functions in this category are listed in **Table 6.1**.

To use any function, you need to modify your query so that you specify to which column or columns the function should be applied.

```
SELECT FUNCTION(column) FROM tablename
```

To specify multiple columns, you can write a query like either of these:

◆ SELECT *, FUNCTION(column) FROM
  → tablename

◆ SELECT column1, FUNCTION(column2),
  → column3 FROM tablename

While the function names themselves are case-insensitive, I will continue to write them in an all-capitalized format, to help distinguish them from table and column names (as I do with SQL terms). One important rule with functions is that you cannot have spaces between the function name and the opening parenthesis for that function, although spaces within the parentheses are acceptable.

I'll repeat this last bit because it's a common cause of problems: *do not have a space between a function's name and its opening parenthesis!*

Table 6.1 These are some, but not all, of the functions you can use on text columns in MySQL.

Text Functions	
FUNCTION AND USAGE	**PURPOSE**
LENGTH(*text*)	Returns the length of the string stored in the column.
LEFT(*text*, *x*)	Returns the leftmost *x* characters from a column.
RIGHT(*text*, *x*)	Returns the rightmost *x* characters from a column.
TRIM(*text*)	Trims excess spaces from the beginning and end of the stored string.
UPPER(*text*)	Capitalizes the entire stored string.
LOWER(*text*)	Turns the stored string into an all-lowercase format.
SUBSTRING(*text*, *start*, *length*)	Returns *length* characters from *column* beginning with *start* (indexed from 1).
FIND_IN_SET (*str*, *set*)	Returns a positive number if *str* is found in *set*; returns 0 otherwise.

Figure 6.1 Once again, the mysql client and the *accounting* database will be the basis of all examples in this chapter.

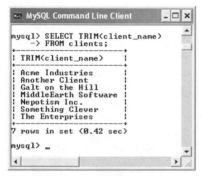

Figure 6.2 The TRIM() function eliminates superfluous spaces from the beginnings and ends of returned values.

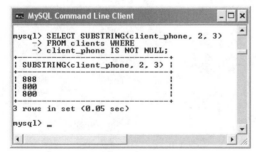

Figure 6.3 This application of the SUBSTRING() function returns only the second through fifth characters of a stored value.

To format text:

1. Open the mysql client and select the *accounting* database (**Figure 6.1**).

   USE accounting;

   As in the preceding chapter, from here on I will assume you are already using the *accounting* database within the mysql client.

2. Remove all extraneous white spaces from the client names (**Figure 6.2**).

   SELECT TRIM(client_name) FROM
   → clients;

   The TRIM() function will automatically strip white spaces (spaces, tabs, and returns) from both the beginning and end of a string.

3. View just the area codes for all client phone numbers (**Figure 6.3**).

   SELECT SUBSTRING(client_phone, 2, 3)
   → FROM clients WHERE client_phone IS
   → NOT NULL;

   The SUBSTRING() function returns part of a string. Its first argument is the literal string or column name. Its second argument is where to begin in that string, counting from 1. Since the first character in a phone number should be the opening parenthesis, I want to begin at the second character. The third argument, which is optional, dictates how many characters should be returned (all of the remaining characters are returned if this argument is omitted).

   continues on next page

4. Find the longest expense category name (**Figure 6.4**).

```
SELECT LENGTH(expense_category),
→ expense_category FROM
expense_categories ORDER BY
LENGTH(expense_category) DESC
LIMIT 1;
```

This query first gathers all of the expense categories, along with their length. Then it sorts this data from the longest category on down. Finally, only the first (i.e., the longest) record is returned.

✔ Tips

■ A query like that in Step 4 (also Figure 6.4) may be useful for helping to fine-tune your column lengths once your database has some records in it.

■ You can use most of the MySQL functions while running queries other than SELECT. Most frequently you might use a function to format data used in an INSERT.

■ Two other useful functions are not mentioned here because of the complexity of their syntax and use. The first is LOCATE(), which returns the starting position of one character or string found within another. The second is REPLACE(), which returns a string after replacing some characters or text with other characters and text. Both are detailed in the manual, of course.

■ Functions can be equally applied to both columns and literal strings. For example, the following is perfectly acceptable:

```
SELECT UPPER('makemebig')
```

■ New in MySQL 4.1 is the ability to convert some text from one character set to another. To do so, use the CONVERT() function. Mind you, this won't translate text from one language to another; it just changes the characters used.

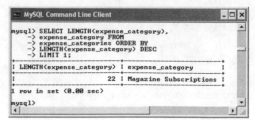

Figure 6.4 You can even use a function within an ORDER BY clause.

Concatenation and Aliases

CONCAT(), perhaps the most useful of the text functions, deserves its own discussion, along with its frequent SQL companion, the alias. The CONCAT() function accomplishes *concatenation*, which is a fancy word that refers to appending multiple values together. The syntax for concatenation requires you to place, within parentheses, the various values you want assembled, in order and separated by commas:

```
CONCAT(column1, column2)
```

While you can—and normally will—apply CONCAT() to columns, you can also incorporate strings, entered within single quotation marks. To format a person's name as *Surname, First* from two columns, you would use

```
CONCAT(last_name, ', ', first_name)
```

Because concatenation is used to create a new value, you'll want a new way to refer to the returned result. This is where the SQL concept of *aliases* comes in. An alias is merely a symbolic renaming. It works using the term AS:

```
SELECT CONCAT(last_name, ', ',
→ first_name) AS name FROM users
```

The result of this query would be that all users in the table would have their name formatted as you might want it displayed, and the returned column would be called *name*.

You can, in your queries, make an alias of any column or table. That general syntax is:

```
SELECT column AS alias_name FROM table
→ AS tbl_alias
```

To use concatenation and aliases:

1. Display all of the client address information as one value (**Figure 6.5**).

   ```
   SELECT client_name,
   → CONCAT(client_street, ', ',
   → client_city, ', ', client_state,
   → ' ', client_zip) AS address
   → FROM clients;
   ```

   This first use of the CONCAT() function assembles all of the address information into one neat column, renamed *address* (see the figure). If you wanted, you could add WHERE client_street IS NOT NULL and client_city IS NOT NULL and client_state IS NOT NULL to the query to rule out incomplete addresses. (Or you could just add one of those three clauses.)

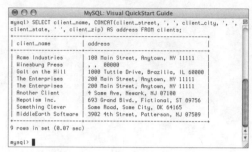

Figure 6.5 The CONCAT() function is one of the most useful tools for refining your query results. Remember that there cannot be any spaces between any function's name and its opening parenthesis!

2. Select every expense, along with its description and category (**Figure 6.6**).

```
SELECT expense_amount, expense_date,
CONCAT(expense_category, ': ',
→ expense_description) FROM expenses,
expense_categories WHERE
expenses.expense_category_id =
→ expense_categories.expense_
→ category_id;
```

In this query, I have performed a join so that I can display both expense and expense category information at the same time. The concatenation takes place over two columns from two different tables.

If you look at the column names in the image, you'll see the result of using functions without aliases.

continues on next page

continues on next page

```
mysql> SELECT expense_amount, expense_date,
    -> CONCAT(expense_category, ': ', expense_description) FROM expenses,
    -> expense_categories WHERE
    -> expenses.expense_category_id = expense_categories.expense_category_id;
+----------------+---------------------+-----------------------------------------------------------------------------+
| expense_amount | expense_date        | CONCAT(expense_category, ': ', expense_description)                          |
+----------------+---------------------+-----------------------------------------------------------------------------+
|          19.99 | 2002-04-20 00:00:00 | Books: Larry Ullman's "MySQL: Visual QuickStart Guide"                       |
|         105.50 | 2006-02-03 14:51:17 | Travel: Palmer House Hotel, Chicago                                          |
|         689.00 | 2006-02-03 14:51:17 | Travel: Flight to Chicago                                                    |
|          99.99 | 2006-02-02 23:01:31 | Computer Software: Mmmm...software                                           |
|          64.99 | 2006-02-03 14:51:17 | Travel: Flight from Chicago                                                  |
|          64.50 | 0000-00-00 00:00:00 | Computer Hardware: Apple PowerBook                                           |
|        6464.00 | 2006-01-26 00:00:00 | Plaster of Paris: Sculpting                                                  |
|          67.94 | 2006-04-20 00:00:00 | Pencils: Writing implements needed to fill in little bubbles on tests.       |
|           1.97 | 2006-04-20 00:00:00 | Drywall: Reconstruction                                                      |
|        3216.00 | 2006-01-26 00:00:00 | Sand Paper: Sanding                                                          |
|        9712.97 | 2006-01-26 00:00:00 | Sand Paper: There's a lot of sanding to do.                                  |
|         312.64 | 2006-02-03 14:14:11 | Computer Software: Software upgrade.                                         |
|          25.00 | 2006-05-09 00:00:00 | Picture Frames: Frame to display Jess' diploma.                             |
|          39.99 | 2006-05-09 00:00:00 | Internet Access Fees: Monthly expense for cable modem Internet access.       |
|          19.99 | 2006-05-09 00:00:00 | Books: Larry Ullman's "PHP for the World Wide Web: Visual QuickStart Guide". |
|          29.99 | 2006-05-24 00:00:00 | Books: Larry Ullman's "PHP Advanced for the World Wide Web: Visual QuickPro Guide" |
|         129.00 | 2006-05-24 00:00:00 | Computer Software: Software to create visual representations of databases.   |
|          29.99 | 2006-05-24 00:00:00 | Books: Larry Ullman's "PHP Advanced for the World Wide Web: Visual QuickPro Guide" |
+----------------+---------------------+-----------------------------------------------------------------------------+
18 rows in set (0.00 sec)

mysql>
```

Figure 6.6 Functions can be applied in different ways, including across multiple tables.

3. Show the three most-expensive invoices, along with the client name and identification number (**Figure 6.7**).

```
SELECT invoices.*,
CONCAT(client_name, ' - ',
→ clients.client_id) AS client_info
FROM invoices LEFT JOIN clients
USING (client_id)
ORDER BY invoice_amount DESC
LIMIT 3\G
```

To perform this query, I use a left join, order the results by the `invoice_amount`, and limit the results to just three records. The `CONCAT()` function is applied to the client's name and ID.

So that the results are easier to peruse, I use the `\G` modifier to terminate the query (this is a feature of `mysql` that I discuss in Chapter 5, "Basic SQL").

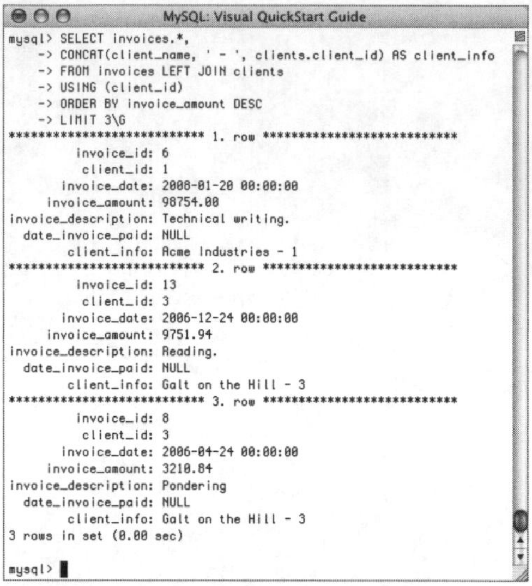


```
mysql> SELECT invoices.*,
    -> CONCAT(client_name, ' - ', clients.client_id) AS client_info
    -> FROM invoices LEFT JOIN clients
    -> USING (client_id)
    -> ORDER BY invoice_amount DESC
    -> LIMIT 3\G
*************************** 1. row ***************************
         invoice_id: 6
          client_id: 1
       invoice_date: 2008-01-20 00:00:00
     invoice_amount: 98754.00
invoice_description: Technical writing.
  date_invoice_paid: NULL
        client_info: Acme Industries - 1
*************************** 2. row ***************************
         invoice_id: 13
          client_id: 3
       invoice_date: 2006-12-24 00:00:00
     invoice_amount: 9751.94
invoice_description: Reading.
  date_invoice_paid: NULL
        client_info: Galt on the Hill - 3
*************************** 3. row ***************************
         invoice_id: 8
          client_id: 3
       invoice_date: 2006-04-24 00:00:00
     invoice_amount: 3210.84
invoice_description: Pondering
  date_invoice_paid: NULL
        client_info: Galt on the Hill - 3
3 rows in set (0.00 sec)

mysql>
```

Figure 6.7 The `CONCAT()` and alias techniques can be applied to any query, including joins.

4. Simplify the query from Step 2 using aliases for table names (**Figure 6.8**).

```
SELECT expense_amount, expense_date,
→ CONCAT(expense_category, ': ',
→ expense_description) FROM
expenses AS e,
expense_categories AS e_c
WHERE e.expense_category_id =
→ e_c.expense_category_id;
```

The query itself is the same as it was in Step 2 except that I have simplified typing it by using aliases for the table names. In wordy queries and joins, this is a nice shorthand to use.

✔ Tips

- CONCAT() has a corollary function called CONCAT_WS(), which stands for *with separator*. The syntax is:

  ```
  CONCAT_WS(separator, column1,
  → column2, …).
  ```

  The separator will be inserted between each of the columns listed. A nice feature of this function is that it skips any NULL values.

- An alias can be up to 255 characters long and is always case-sensitive.

- The AS term used to create an alias is optional. You could write a query more simply as

  ```
  SELECT column alias_name FROM table
  ```

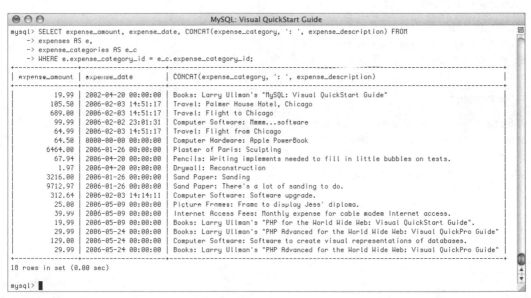

Figure 6.8 I've simplified my queries, without affecting the end result, by using aliases for my table names (compare with Figure 6.6).

Numeric Functions

Besides the standard math operators that MySQL uses (for addition, subtraction, multiplication, and division), there are about two dozen functions dedicated to formatting and performing calculations on number columns. **Table 6.2** lists the most common of these, some of which I will demonstrate shortly.

I want to highlight three of these functions: FORMAT(), ROUND(), and RAND(). The first—which is not technically number-specific—turns any number into a more conventionally formatted layout. For example, if you stored the cost of a car as 20198.2, FORMAT(car_cost, 2) would turn that number into the more common 20,198.20.

ROUND() will take one value, presumably from a column, and round that to a specified number of decimal places. If no decimal places are indicated, it will round the number to the nearest integer. If more decimal places are indicated than exist in the original number, the remaining spaces are padded with zeros (to the right of the decimal point).

The RAND() function, as you might infer, is used for returning random numbers. Specifically, it returns a value between 0 and 1.0.

```
SELECT RAND()
```

A further benefit to the RAND() function is that it can be used with your queries to return the result in a random order.

```
SELECT * FROM tablename ORDER BY RAND()
```

Table 6.2 Here are the most-used number functions, omitting the various trigonometric and exponential ones.

Numeric Functions	
FUNCTION AND USAGE	**PURPOSE**
ABS(*num*)	Returns the absolute value of *num*.
CEILING(*num*)	Returns the next-highest integer based upon the value of *num*.
FLOOR(*num*)	Returns the integer value of *num*.
FORMAT(*num*, *y*)	Returns *num* formatted as a number with *y* decimal places and commas inserted every three digits.
MOD(*x*, *y*)	Returns the remainder of dividing *x* by *y* (either or both can be a column).
POW(*x*, *y*)	Returns the value of *x* to the *y* power.
RAND()	Returns a random number between 0 and 1.0.
ROUND(*x*, *y*)	Returns the number *x* rounded to *y* decimal places.
SIGN(*num*)	Returns a value indicating whether *num* is negative (–1), zero (0), or positive (+1).
SQRT(*num*)	Calculates the square root of *num*.

To use numeric functions:

1. Display the invoices by date, formatting the amounts as dollars (**Figure 6.9**).

```
SELECT *, CONCAT('$', FORMAT
→ (invoice_amount, 2)) AS amount FROM
→ invoices ORDER BY invoice_date ASC\G
```

Using the FORMAT() function, as just described, in conjunction with CONCAT(), you can turn any number into a currency format as you might display it in a Web page or application.

Notice in the figure how the invoice amount is actually returned twice: once as part of all columns (*) and the second time in its formatted shape.

continues on next page

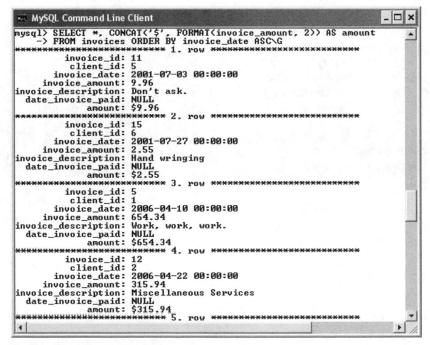

Figure 6.9 Applying two functions and the right formatting to the invoice_amount column generates the better amount values.

2. Round each expense amount to the nearest dollar (**Figure 6.10**).

SELECT ROUND(expense_amount),
→ expense_amount FROM expenses;

The ROUND() function, when you do not specify a decimal argument, simply rounds every value to the nearest integer.

3. Retrieve all of the client names in a random order twice (**Figure 6.11**).

SELECT client_id, client_name FROM
→ clients ORDER BY RAND();

SELECT client_id, client_name FROM
→ clients ORDER BY RAND();

Although this may not be the most practical use of the ORDER BY RAND() clause, it does give you an idea of how it works. While the RAND() function is not absolutely random, it is effective enough for most cases. Notice that you do not specify to which column RAND() is applied.

✔ Tips

■ Along with the mathematical functions listed here, a number of trigonometry, exponential, and other types of functions are available. Of course you can also use any of the mathematical operators: +, -, *, and /.

■ The MOD() function is the same as using the percentage sign:

SELECT MOD(9,2)

SELECT 9%2

■ Once again, remember that functions can be applied to columns or to hard-coded values. The following queries are perfectly acceptable:

SELECT ROUND(34.089, 1)

SELECT SQRT(81)

SELECT ABS(-8)

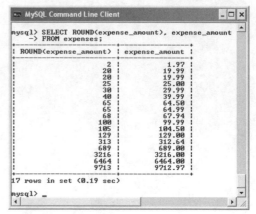

Figure 6.10 The ROUND() function is useful in situations where decimal values do not matter.

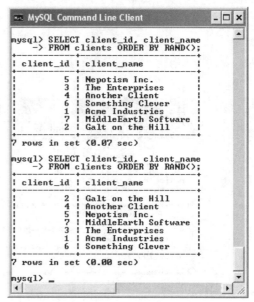

Figure 6.11 Running the same query twice with the ORDER BY RAND() clause returns the same results but in different order.

Date and Time Functions

The date and time column types in MySQL are particularly flexible and useful. But because many database users are not familiar with all of the available date and time functions, these options are frequently underused.

Whether you want to make calculations based upon a date or to return only the month name from a stored value, MySQL has a function for that purpose. **Table 6.3** lists most of these functions.

As you can tell, the many date and time functions range from those returning portions of a date column to those that return the current date or time. These are all best taught by example.

Table 6.3 MySQL uses several different functions for working with dates and times in your databases. In the usage examples, *dt* could represent a date, a time, or a datetime.

Date and Time Functions	
FUNCTION AND USAGE	PURPOSE
HOUR(*dt*)	Returns just the hour value of *dt*.
MINUTE(*dt*)	Returns just the minute value of *dt*.
SECOND(*dt*)	Returns just the second value of *dt*.
DATE(*dt*)	Returns just the date value of *dt*.
DAYNAME(*dt*)	Returns the name of the day of *dt*.
DAYOFMONTH(*dt*)	Returns just the numerical day of *dt*.
MONTHNAME(*dt*)	Returns the name of the month of *dt*.
MONTH(*dt*)	Returns just the numerical month value of *dt*.
YEAR(*dt*)	Returns just the year value of *dt*.
DATE_ADD(*dt*, INTERVAL *x type*)	Returns the value of *x* units added to *dt* (see the sidebar).
DATE_SUB(*dt*, INTERVAL *x type*)	Returns the value of *x* units subtracted from *dt* (see the sidebar).
CONVERT_TZ(*dt*, *from_zone*, *to_zone*)	Converts *dt* from one time zone to another.
CURDATE()	Returns the current date.
CURTIME()	Returns the current time.
NOW()	Returns the current date and time.
UNIX_TIMESTAMP(*dt*)	Returns the number of seconds since the epoch or since the date specified.

To use date and time functions:

1. Display every invoice billed in April (**Figure 6.12**).

   `SELECT * FROM invoices WHERE`

   `MONTH(invoice_date) = 4\G`

   Because April is the fourth month, this query will return only those invoices billed then. Another way of writing it would be to use `WHERE MONTHNAME(invoice_date) = 'April'` (although it's best to use numbers instead of strings wherever possible).

2. Show the current date and time, according to MySQL (**Figure 6.13**).

   `SELECT CURDATE(), CURTIME();`

   To show what date and time MySQL currently thinks it is, you can select the `CURDATE()` and `CURTIME()` functions, which return these values. This is an example of a query that can be run without referring to a particular table name (or without even selecting a database).

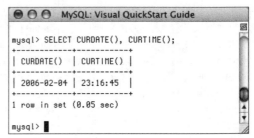

```
mysql> SELECT * FROM invoices WHERE
    -> MONTH(invoice_date) = 4\G
*************************** 1. row ***************************
       invoice_id: 1
        client_id: 4
     invoice_date: 2006-04-24 00:00:00
   invoice_amount: 1982.34
invoice_description: Conjugation: verbs, nouns, adjectives.
date_invoice_paid: NULL
*************************** 2. row ***************************
       invoice_id: 4
        client_id: 3
     invoice_date: 2006-04-24 00:00:00
   invoice_amount: 1.00
invoice_description: Miscellaneous Services
date_invoice_paid: NULL
*************************** 3. row ***************************
       invoice_id: 5
        client_id: 1
     invoice_date: 2006-04-10 00:00:00
   invoice_amount: 654.34
invoice_description: Work, work, work.
date_invoice_paid: NULL
*************************** 4. row ***************************
       invoice_id: 8
        client_id: 3
     invoice_date: 2006-04-24 00:00:00
   invoice_amount: 3210.84
invoice_description: Pondering
date_invoice_paid: NULL
*************************** 5. row ***************************
       invoice_id: 9
        client_id: 4
     invoice_date: 2007-04-08 00:00:00
   invoice_amount: 6.64
invoice_description: Shady dealings.
date_invoice_paid: NULL
*************************** 6. row ***************************
       invoice_id: 12
        client_id: 2
     invoice_date: 2006-04-22 00:00:00
   invoice_amount: 315.94
invoice_description: Miscellaneous Services
date_invoice_paid: NULL
6 rows in set (0.01 sec)

mysql>
```

Figure 6.12 Using the MONTH() function, I can narrow down my search results based upon the values in a date column.

```
mysql> SELECT CURDATE(), CURTIME();
+------------+-----------+
| CURDATE()  | CURTIME() |
+------------+-----------+
| 2006-02-04 | 23:16:45  |
+------------+-----------+
1 row in set (0.05 sec)

mysql>
```

Figure 6.13 The CURDATE() and CURTIME() functions return the current date and time. The same can be accomplished with NOW().

3. Display every expense filed in the past two months (**Figure 6.14**).

```
SELECT CONCAT('$', FORMAT
→ (expense_amount, 2)) AS amount,
expense_date, expense_category,
expense_description
FROM expenses AS e,
expense_categories AS e_c
WHERE (e.expense_category_id =
→ e_c.expense_category_id)
AND (expense_date BETWEEN
SUBDATE(CURDATE(), INTERVAL 2 MONTH)
AND CURDATE());
```

continues on next page

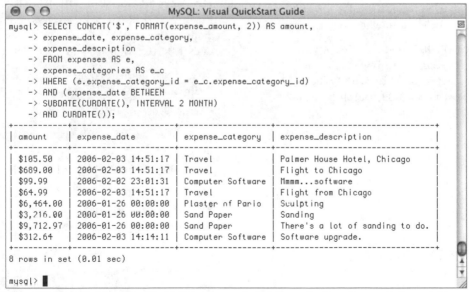

```
mysql> SELECT CONCAT('$', FORMAT(expense_amount, 2)) AS amount,
    -> expense_date, expense_category,
    -> expense_description
    -> FROM expenses AS e,
    -> expense_categories AS e_c
    -> WHERE (e.expense_category_id = e_c.expense_category_id)
    -> AND (expense_date BETWEEN
    -> SUBDATE(CURDATE(), INTERVAL 2 MONTH)
    -> AND CURDATE());
+-----------+---------------------+-------------------+-------------------------------+
| amount    | expense_date        | expense_category  | expense_description           |
+-----------+---------------------+-------------------+-------------------------------+
| $105.50   | 2006-02-03 14:51:17 | Travel            | Palmer House Hotel, Chicago   |
| $689.00   | 2006-02-03 14:51:17 | Travel            | Flight to Chicago             |
| $99.99    | 2006-02-02 23:01:31 | Computer Software | Mmmm...software               |
| $64.99    | 2006-02-03 14:51:17 | Travel            | Flight from Chicago           |
| $6,464.00 | 2006-01-26 00:00:00 | Plaster of Paris  | Sculpting                     |
| $3,216.00 | 2006-01-26 00:00:00 | Sand Paper        | Sanding                       |
| $9,712.97 | 2006-01-26 00:00:00 | Sand Paper        | There's a lot of sanding to do. |
| $312.64   | 2006-02-03 14:14:11 | Computer Software | Software upgrade.             |
+-----------+---------------------+-------------------+-------------------------------+
8 rows in set (0.01 sec)

mysql>
```

Figure 6.14 Here I've used the CURDATE() function again (see Figure 6.13) to set a range of acceptable dates for selecting expenses.

This query uses a lot of different techniques covered to this point. For starters, it's a simple join to incorporate the expense category along with the expense information. Second, I've converted the expense amount into a more readable format. Third, there are two conditions set in the `WHERE` clause: one for the join and another limiting results to the previous six months. The `BETWEEN` term is used to specify a range from two months ago, `SUBDATE(CURDATE(), INTERVAL 2 MONTH)`, and today, `CURDATE()`, which rules out expenses that may have been prebilled (i.e., are in the future).

✔ Tips

■ Because MySQL is such a fast and powerful application, you should try to let it handle most of the formatting of values. Beginning programmers will commonly retrieve values from MySQL and then use the programming language to format the data, which is less efficient.

■ The `NOW()` and `CURDATE()` functions are often used to set the value for a date or datetime column when inserting records:

```
INSERT INTO invoices (client_id,
→ invoice_date, invoice_amount,
→ invoice_description) VALUES (23,
→ NOW(), 3049.39, 'blah blah')
```

DATE_ADD() and DATE_SUB()

The `DATE_ADD()` and `DATE_SUB()` functions, which are synonyms for `ADDDATE()` and `SUBDATE()`, perform calculations upon date values. The syntax for using them is

`FUNCTION(date, INTERVAL x type)`

In the example, *date* can be either an entered date or a value retrieved from a column. The *x* value varies, depending upon which *type* you specify. The available types are `SECOND`, `MINUTE`, `HOUR`, `DAY`, `MONTH`, and `YEAR`. There are even combinations of these: `MINUTE_SECOND`, `HOUR_MINUTE`, `DAY_HOUR`, and `YEAR_MONTH`.

To add two hours to a date, you would write

`DATE_ADD(date, INTERVAL 2 HOUR)`

To add two weeks from December 31, 2006:

`DATE_ADD('2006-12-31', INTERVAL 14`
`→ DAY)`

To subtract 15 months from a date:

`DATE_SUB(date, INTERVAL '1-3'`
`→ YEAR_MONTH)`

This last query tells MySQL that you want to subtract 1 year and 3 months from the value stored in the *date* column.

Table 6.4 The terms for date and time formatting are not obvious, but this table lists the most important ones.

DATE_FORMAT() and TIME_FORMAT() Parameters

TERM	MEANING	EXAMPLE
%e	Day of the month	1–31
%d	Day of the month, two digit	01–31
%D	Day with suffix	1st–31st
%W	Weekday name	Sunday–Saturday
%a	Abbreviated weekday name	Sun–Sat
%c	Month number	1–12
%m	Month number, two digit	01–12
%M	Month name	January–December
%b	Month name, abbreviated	Jan–Dec
%Y	Year	2002
%y	Year	02
%l	Hour	1–12
%h	Hour, two digit	01–12
%k	Hour, 24-hour clock	0–23
%H	Hour, 24-hour clock, two digit	00–23
%i	Minutes	00–59
%S	Seconds	00–59
%r	Time	8:17:02 PM
%T	Time, 24-hour clock	20:17:02
%p	AM or PM	AM or PM

Formatting the Date and Time

There are two additional date and time functions that you might find yourself using more than all of the others combined. These are DATE_FORMAT() and TIME_FORMAT(). There is some overlap between the two in that DATE_FORMAT() can be used to format both the date and the time, whereas TIME_FORMAT() can format only a time value. The syntax is

```
SELECT DATE_FORMAT(date_column,
→ 'formatting') FROM tablename
```

The *formatting* relies upon combinations of key codes and the percentage sign to indicate what values you want returned. **Table 6.4** lists the available date and time formatting parameters. You can use these in any combination, along with textual additions such as punctuation to return a date and time in a more presentable form.

Assuming that a column called dt has the date and time of *2006-04-30 23:07:45* stored in it, common formatting tasks and results would be

◆ Time (*11:07:02 PM*)
   DATE_FORMAT(dt, '%r')

◆ Time without seconds (*11:07 PM*)
   DATE_FORMAT(dt, '%l:%i %p')

◆ Date (*April 30th, 2006*)
   DATE_FORMAT(dt, '%M %D, %Y')

To format the date and time:

1. Return the current date and time as *Month DD, YYYY - HH:MM* (**Figure 6.15**).

   SELECT DATE_FORMAT(NOW(),'%M %e,
   → %Y - %l:%i');

   Using the NOW() function, which returns the current date and time, I can practice my formatting to see what results are returned.

2. Display the current time, using 24-hour notation (**Figure 6.16**).

   SELECT TIME_FORMAT(CURTIME(),'%T');

   Although the DATE_FORMAT() function can be used to format both the date and the time (or just the date), if you want to format just the time, you must use the TIME_FORMAT() function. This can be applied to a time value (such as CURTIME() returns) or a date-time value (from NOW()).

3. Select every expense, ordered by date and amount, formatting the date as *Weekday (abbreviated) Day Month (abbreviated) Year* (**Figure 6.17**).

   SELECT DATE_FORMAT(expense_date,
   → '%a %b %e %Y') AS the_date,

   CONCAT('$', FORMAT(expense_amount, 2))
   → AS amount

   FROM expenses

   ORDER BY expense_date ASC,

   expense_amount DESC;

   This is just one more example of how you can use these formatting functions to alter the output of a SQL query.

✔ Tip

- The STR_TO_DATE() function is the opposite of DATE_FORMAT(). It uses the same parameters but takes a submitted string and formats it as a date.

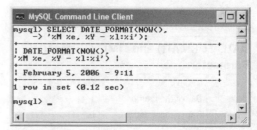

Figure 6.15 The DATE_FORMAT() function uses combinations of parameters to return a formatted date.

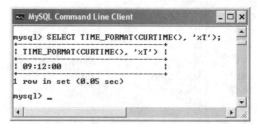

Figure 6.16 If you are formatting just the time, you must use the TIME_FORMAT() function.

Figure 6.17 DATE_FORMAT() will apply only to stored date values; NULL values will not be affected (see the first record).

Table 6.5 Different encryption functions are available as of new releases of MySQL, so know what version you are using!

Encryption Functions		
FUNCTION	ADDED	NOTES
MD5()	3.23.2	Returns a 32-digit hash.
SHA1()	4.0.2	Returns a 40-digit hash.
AES_ENCRYPT()	4.0.2	Encrypts data using AES algorithm.
AES_DECRYPT ()	4.0.2	Decrypts AES_ENCRYPT() data.
ENCODE()	3.x	Older encryption function.
DECODE()	3.x	Decrypts ENCODE() data.
DES_ENCRYPT()	4.0.1	Encrypts data using DES algorithm, requires SSL.
DES_DECRYPT ()	4.0.1	Decrypts DES_ENCRYPT() data.
ENCRYPT()	3.x	May not be available on Windows, no decryption possible.

Encryption Functions

MySQL has several different encryption and decryption functions built into the software (**Table 6.5**). You may have already seen one of these, PASSWORD(), since it's used to encrypt the various user passwords for MySQL access. MySQL advises against using this one in your own tables, and it can be a cause of problems (see Appendix A, "Troubleshooting," for more).

Two functions, MD5() and SHA1(), create what's called a *hash*: a fixed-length mathematical representation of data. So the MD5() of the word *rabbit* is *a51e47f646375ab6bf5dd2c42d3e6181*. If you store the hash of some data in your database, you can never retrieve the actual data back out (because the data itself was never stored). What you can do is later compare the stored value against the calculated hash of a submitted value. For example, you store the hash of a password and then, when a user logs in, calculate the hash of the login password and see if the two values are equal. These two functions are fine for low-security situations, but both are crackable, meaning they don't provide guaranteed security.

If you want true encryption, you'll need to use one of several functions also listed in the table. Each of these takes two arguments: the data to be encrypted or decrypted, and a *salt* argument. The salt is any random value that will make the encryption more unique and more secure. The same salt must be used to encode and decode data, though, so the salt must be stored or memorized somehow. Also, these encryption functions return binary data, which must be stored in a BLOB column type.

Of the true encryption functions, the most secure at the time of this writing are AES_ENCRYPT() and AES_DECRYPT(). An example of how you would use them in a query is:

```
INSERT INTO users (username, user_pass)
→ VALUES ('trout', AES_ENCRYPT
→ ('myPass1', 'NaCL#'))
```

To retrieve that stored data, you could use this query:

```
SELECT username, AES_DECRYPT(user_pass,
→ 'NaCL#') FROM users
```

To encrypt and decrypt data:

1. Create a new logins table (**Figure 6.18**).

```
CREATE TABLE logins (
login_id INT UNSIGNED NOT NULL
→ AUTO_INCREMENT,
client_id SMALLINT UNSIGNED NOT NULL,
login_name TINYBLOB,
login_pass CHAR(40),
PRIMARY KEY (login_id),
INDEX (client_id)
);
```

Because none of the current tables would logically use encryption, I'm creating a new one. The premise behind this table is that each client can have any number of logins in order to access their account information. The table will contain a login_id, a login_pass, and a login_name. To associate each login with a client, the client_id is a foreign key here (relating to the primary key with the same name in the clients table).

For extra security, the login_name will be encrypted and decrypted and must therefore be a BLOB type (I've chosen TINYBLOB). The password will be stored using the SHA1() function, which always returns a string 40 characters long. Hence, that column is defined as a CHAR(40).

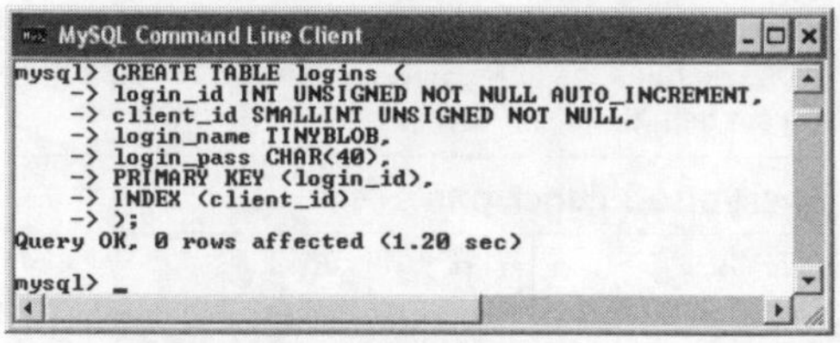

Figure 6.18 The logins table will be used to demonstrate encryption and decryption.

Figure 6.19 I encrypt values when storing them...

Figure 6.20 ...and decrypt them for retrieval.

Figure 6.21 These functions are case-sensitive, so entering a password incorrectly will return no results.

The primary key index and an index on the client_id (since it's a foreign key and will be used in joins and WHERE clauses) are added as well.

2. Insert a new login record (**Figure 6.19**).

   INSERT INTO logins

   (client_id, login_name, login_pass)
   → VALUES

   (4, AES_ENCRYPT('larryeullman',
   → 'w1cKet'), SHA1('larryPASS'));

   Here I am adding a new record to the table, using the SHA1() function to encrypt the password (*larrypass*) and AES_ENCRYPT() with a salt of *w1cKet* to encrypt the user name (*larryeullman*). If you are not using at least version 4.0.2 of MySQL, you'll need to change this query to use the MD5() and ENCODE() functions instead.

3. Retrieve the user's information (**Figure 6.20**).

   SELECT client_id FROM logins WHERE
   → (login_pass = SHA1('larryPASS') AND
   → AES_DECRYPT(login_name, 'w1cKet') =
   → 'larryeullman');

   Whenever you store a SHA1() or MD5() encrypted string, to make a comparison match, you simply use the same function again. If these match, the right password was entered; otherwise, no value will be returned by this query (**Figure 6.21**).

   Any value stored using an encryption function can be retrieved (and matched) using the corresponding decryption function, as long as the same salt is used (here, *w1cKet*).

ENCRYPTION FUNCTIONS

Grouping Functions

The theory of grouping query results is similar to ordering and limiting query results in that it uses a GROUP BY clause. However, this is significantly different from the other clauses because it works by grouping the returned data into similar blocks of information. For example, to group all of the invoices by client, you would use

SELECT * FROM invoices GROUP BY client_id

The returned data is altered in that you've now aggregated the information instead of returning just the specific itemized records. So where the database might have seven invoices for one client, the GROUP BY would return all seven of those records as one. I did not discuss the idea in the preceding chapter because you will normally use one of several grouping (or aggregate) functions in conjunction with GROUP BY. **Table 6.6** lists these.

You can apply combinations of WHERE, ORDER BY, and LIMIT conditions to a GROUP BY, normally structuring your query like this:

SELECT *columns* FROM *tablename* WHERE
→ *clause* GROUP BY *columnname* ORDER BY
→ *columnname* LIMIT *x*

To group data:

1. Find the largest invoice amount
   (**Figure 6.22**).

   SELECT MAX(invoice_amount) FROM
   → invoices;

   Since the MAX() function returns the largest value for a column, this is the easiest way to return the desired result. Another option would be to write

   SELECT invoice_amount FROM invoices
   → ORDER BY invoice_amount DESC LIMIT 1

Table 6.6 The grouping, or *aggregate*, functions are normally used with the GROUP BY clause in a SQL query.

Grouping Functions	
FUNCTION AND USAGE	PURPOSE
MIN(*column*)	Returns the smallest value from the column.
MAX(*column*)	Returns the largest value from the column.
SUM(*column*)	Returns the sum of all of the values in the column.
COUNT(*column*)	Counts the number of rows.
GROUP_CONCAT(*values*)	Returns a concatenation of the grouped values.

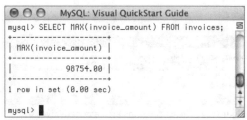

```
mysql> SELECT MAX(invoice_amount) FROM invoices;
+---------------------+
| MAX(invoice_amount) |
+---------------------+
|            98754.00 |
+---------------------+
1 row in set (0.00 sec)

mysql>
```

Figure 6.22 The MAX() function performs a type of grouping, even if the GROUP BY clause is not formally stated.

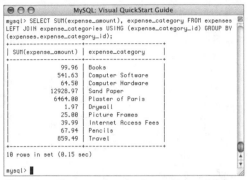

Figure 6.23 The SUM() function is used here with a GROUP BY clause to total up fields with similar expense_category_ids.

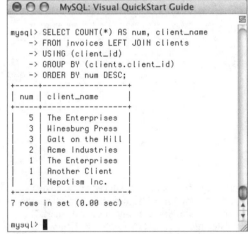

Figure 6.24 The COUNT() function returns the number of records that apply to the GROUP BY criteria (here, client_id).

2. Determine how much has been spent under each expense category (**Figure 6.23**).

```
SELECT SUM(expense_amount),
→ expense_category FROM expenses LEFT
→ JOIN expense_categories USING
→ (expense_category_id) GROUP BY
→ (expenses.expense_category_id);
```

To accomplish this task, I first use a left join to incorporate the name of the expense category into the results. Then I simply group all of the expenses together by category ID and summarize their respective amounts. MySQL will return a table of two columns: the total and the category.

3. See how many invoices have been billed to each client (**Figure 6.24**).

```
SELECT COUNT(*) AS num, client_name
FROM invoices LEFT JOIN clients
USING (client_id)
GROUP BY (clients.client_id)
ORDER BY num DESC;
```

Whenever you need to determine how many records fall into a certain category, a combination of COUNT() and GROUP BY will get the desired result. With grouping, you can order the results as you would with any other query.

continues on next page

GROUPING FUNCTIONS

4. Alter the query in Step 2 so that it reflects how many invoices are tied into each total amount (**Figure 6.25**).

SELECT COUNT(*), SUM(expense_amount),

expense_category FROM expenses LEFT

→ JOIN expense_categories

USING (expense_category_id)

GROUP BY (expenses.expense_

→ category_id);

Here I've used the COUNT() function again, along with an alias, to count each record in each grouping. You can apply multiple aggregate functions within the same query, although that syntax can get tricky.

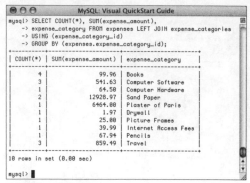

Figure 6.25 By adding COUNT() to the query in Figure 6.23, I can also show how many expenses are included in each SUM() column.

✔ Tips

- NULL is a peculiar value, as you've seen, and it's interesting to know that GROUP BY will group NULL values together, since they have the same nonvalue.

- When used as COUNT(*columnname*), only non-null values will be counted. When you use COUNT(*), all rows will be counted.

- The GROUP BY clause, and the functions listed here, take some time to figure out, and MySQL will report an error whenever your syntax is inapplicable. Experiment within the mysql client to determine the exact wording of any query you might want to run in an application.

- You can optionally use a WITH ROLLUP modifier in a GROUP BY query. It will summarize grouped columns for you (**Figure 6.26**).

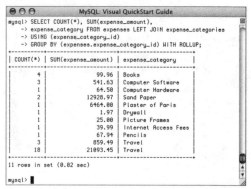

Figure 6.26 If you add WITH ROLLUP to the query in Figure 6.25, MySQL will summarize the total number of expenses and the total amount of expenses. The last listed record reflects these totals. (The word *Travel* under expense_category is actually meaningless on that line.)

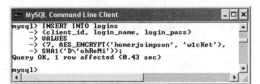

Figure 6.27 To test LAST_INSERT_ID() (Figure 6.28), I'll add another record to the logins table.

Other Functions

To conclude this chapter, I'll discuss two final functions that do not fit neatly into any of the earlier categories. The first, LAST_INSERT_ID(), is critical for working within a relational database. The second, DISTINCT(), assists you in adjusting what results to return from a table.

Using LAST_INSERT_ID

LAST_INSERT_ID() is a function that returns the value set by the last INSERT statement for a column that's automatically incremented. For example, in the *accounting* database example, the expense_categories table uses an expense_category_id column that was defined as a not-null, unsigned integer that was the primary key and would be auto-incremented. This meant that every time a NULL value was entered for that column, MySQL would automatically use the next logical value. LAST_INSERT_ID() will return that value. You can use it like so:

SELECT LAST_INSERT_ID()

To use LAST_INSERT_ID():

1. Insert another user into the logins table (**Figure 6.27**).

   INSERT INTO logins

   (client_id, login_name, login_pass)
   → VALUES

   (4, AES_ENCRYPT('homerjsimpson',
   → 'w1cKet'), SHA1('D\'ohReMi'));

   Make sure when working with encryption that you use the same encryption function and salt for every record in the table, or else you will have difficulty accurately retrieving data later.

   continues on next page

2. Retrieve that record's `login_id` (**Figure 6.28**).

`SELECT LAST_INSERT_ID();`

This command returns just one value in one column, which reflects the primary key inserted in Step 1. When using relational databases, use `LAST_INSERT_ID()` to ensure proper primary key–to–foreign key integrity.

✔ Tips

■ The `LAST_INSERT_ID()` function is the same as PHP's `mysql_insert_id()`.

■ The `LAST_INSERT_ID()` function will return the first ID created if you insert several records at one time.

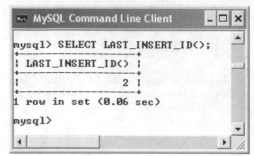

Figure 6.28 `LAST_INSERT_ID()` is a specific function that returns only the number corresponding to the previous insert.

LAST_INSERT_ID() Confusion

A common misunderstanding about `LAST_INSERT_ID()` is that it will return the last inserted value into the table, regardless of where it comes from. This is not true. The function will return only the last inserted ID for a query made by the current connection. Therefore, if ten scripts and three `mysql` clients are all connected to a database at the same time, and each inserts a value into a table and then recalls this value, each script or client will return only the ID correlating to that session's previous insert.

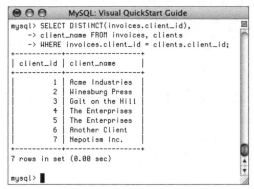

Figure 6.29 DISTINCT() is somewhat like the aggregate functions in that it helps to group the returned records.

Using DISTINCT

The DISTINCT() function is used to weed out duplicate values and is normally applied to a column.

SELECT DISTINCT(*columnname*) FROM
→ *tablename*

This is frequently used in conjunction with GROUP BY so that the number of unique records, based upon a category, can be retrieved and possibly counted.

To use DISTINCT():

1. List the different clients that have been billed (**Figure 6.29**).

   SELECT DISTINCT(invoices.client_id),

   client_name FROM invoices, clients

   WHERE invoices.client_id =
   → clients.client_id;

   Instead of listing every client for every invoice, this query will list only each unique client. It also rules out any clients that have not yet been billed (the join accomplishes that).

   continues on next page

2. Count how many different clients have been billed (**Figure 6.30**).

```
SELECT COUNT(DISTINCT(client_id))
FROM invoices;
```

The combination of the COUNT() and DISTINCT() functions returns just the one number, rather than every applicable record.

✔ Tips

■ There are many other miscellaneous MySQL functions, such as DATABASE(). If you were to run the query SELECT DATABASE(), it would tell you which database is currently being used.

■ The USER() function will tell you which user is currently being used. This is a combination of *username@host*.

■ If you're familiar with the concept of casting—forcibly changing the type of a piece of data, possibly changing the value of the data in the process—rest assured that MySQL has several casting functions available. See the manual for specifics.

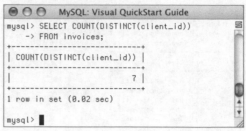

Figure 6.30 Using DISTINCT() along with COUNT() returns the number of unique values in a table.

MySQL and PHP

PHP and MySQL have been used together for years, and the combination has improved the popularity of both technologies. PHP now supports two different sets of MySQL functions. The original, *mysql*, is meant for working with versions of MySQL up to 4.1. The newer functions, *mysqli* (MySQL Improved), are available as of PHP 5 and take advantage of added MySQL features. These functions also offer speed and security benefits. For these reasons, this chapter will use the newer *mysqli* functions, which means that you must be using at least PHP 5 with MySQL 4.1.1 (with support for *mysqli* built into PHP). If you are using an older version of either PHP or MySQL, you'll need to use the original *mysql* extension. Documentation for those functions is available in the PHP manual, in my other books, and in oodles of places online.

This chapter provides the basic tools for PHP-MySQL interactions. I do not discuss the fundamentals of PHP at all. Chapter 12, "Techniques for Programming," expands upon the information discussed here, showing more advanced applications of these ideas.

In this chapter I will use the existing *accounting* database, creating a PHP interface for managing the expenses side of the application. Using the knowledge taught here, you should find it easy to make the corresponding scripts for the invoices half of the database.

Connecting to MySQL and Selecting a Database

The first step when dealing with MySQL—connecting to the server—requires the appropriately named `mysqli_connect()` function:

```
$database_connection = mysqli_connect
→ ('host', 'user', 'password');
```

The values you use in place of *host*, *user*, and *password* are determined from the users and privileges set up within the *mysql* database (see Chapter 2, "Running MySQL," for more information). Normally, the host will be *localhost*, but not necessarily. In any case, the most important rule about connecting to MySQL from PHP is this: use the same username/hostname/password combination that you would to connect using the `mysql` client.

The `$database_connection` variable is a reference point that PHP will use to the newly created connection (you can use another name for this variable, like just `$dbc`). Many of the other PHP functions for interacting with MySQL will take this variable as an argument.

Once you have connected to MySQL, you will need to select the database with which you want to work. This is the equivalent of saying USE *databasename* within the `mysql` client and is accomplished with the `mysqli_select_db()` function:

```
mysqli_select_db($dbc, 'databasename');
```

Alternatively, you can connect to MySQL and select the database in one fell swoop:

```
$dbc = mysqli_connect ('host', 'user',
→ 'password', 'databasename');
```

I'll start the demonstration of connecting to MySQL by creating a special file just for that purpose. Every PHP script that requires a MySQL connection can then include this file.

MySQL's PHP Connector

Because PHP and MySQL go so well together, the good people at MySQL provide updated versions of the *mysql* and *mysqli* libraries for PHP. The connector package is just a build of the MySQL-related PHP functions, but using the latest versions of the MySQL client libraries (which PHP itself may or may not contain).

The connector will contain all bug fixes and support the latest MySQL features. You can download the latest connector package from the MySQL Web site. Note that it is only available for Windows and that installation instructions are included on the connector's download page.

Script 7.1 The `mysqli_connect.inc.php` script will be used by every other script in this application. In this script, a connection to the database is established.

```
1    <?php
2
3    // ***** mysqli_connect.inc.php *****
4    // ***** Script 7.1 *****
5    // Developed by Larry E. Ullman
6    // MySQL: Visual QuickStart Guide
7    // SECOND EDITION
8    // Contact: mysql2@DMCinsights.com
9    // Created: February 15, 2006
10   // Last modified: February 15, 2006
11   // This file contains the database access
     information
12   // for the accounting database.
13   // This file also establishes a connec-
     tion to MySQL
14   // and selects the accounting database.
15
16   // Database-specific information:
17   DEFINE ('DB_USER', 'username');
18   DEFINE ('DB_PASSWORD', 'password');
19   DEFINE ('DB_HOST', 'localhost');
20   DEFINE ('DB_NAME', 'accounting');
21
22   // Connect to MySQL and select the data-
     base:
23   $dbc = mysqli_connect(DB_HOST, DB_USER,
     DB_PASSWORD, DB_NAME);
24   ?>
```

To connect to and select a database:

1. Begin a new PHP document in your text editor (**Script 7.1**).

   `<?php`

2. Add the appropriate comments.

   ```
   // ***** mysql_connect.inc.php *****
   // ***** Script 7.1 *****
   // Developed by Larry E. Ullman
   // MySQL: Visual QuickStart Guide
   // SECOND EDITION
   // Contact: mysql2@DMCinsights.com
   // Created: February 15, 2006
   // Last modified: February 15, 2006
   // This file contains the database
   → access information
   // for the accounting database.
   // This file also establishes a
   → connection to MySQL
   // and selects the accounting
   → database.
   ```

   For the most part, I will refrain from including prodigious comments within the steps, but I did want to pinpoint these lines to give you a sense of how I might document a configuration file. Also, as a matter of convenience, I'll include the filename and script name as a comment in every script in this book (for easier reference).

   continues on next page

3. Set the database host, username, password, and database name as constants.

```
DEFINE ('DB_USER', 'username');
DEFINE ('DB_PASSWORD', 'password');
DEFINE ('DB_HOST', 'localhost');
DEFINE ('DB_NAME', 'accounting');
```

I prefer to establish these variables as constants for security reasons (they cannot be changed this way), but that isn't required. Setting these values as some sort of variable makes sense so that you can separate the configuration parameters from the functions that use them, but again, this is not required.

The only truly important consideration is that you use a username/hostname/password combination that has privileges in MySQL to interact with the *accounting* database.

4. Connect to MySQL and select the database to be used.

```
$dbc = mysqli_connect(DB_HOST,
→ DB_USER, DB_PASSWORD, DB_NAME);
```

The mysqli_connect() function, if it successfully connects to MySQL, will return a resource link that corresponds to the open connection. This link will be assigned to the $dbc variable.

While connecting, I'm also selecting the database (since this application will interact with only one database). Failure to select the database will create problems in later scripts, although if an application uses multiple databases, you might not want to globally select one here.

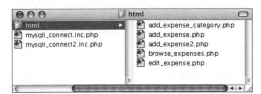

Figure 7.1 Assuming that html is the root directory of my Web documents (e.g., www.dmcinsights.com or http://localhost would lead there), the configuration files should be stored outside of it. This image was taken on Mac OS X.

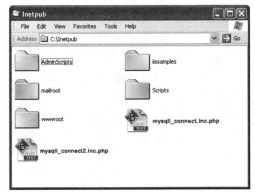

Figure 7.2 Assuming that wwwroot is the root directory of my Web documents (e.g., www.dmcinsights.com or http://localhost would lead there), the configuration files should be stored outside of it. This image was taken on Windows.

5. Close the PHP and save the file as `mysqli_connect.inc.php`.

```
?>
```

I chose to name the file with an `.inc.php` extension. This indicates to me that the file is used as an inclusion in other PHP scripts.

6. Upload the file to your server, above the Web document root (**Figures 7.1** and **7.2**).

Because the file contains sensitive MySQL access information, it ought to be stored securely. If you can, place it in the directory immediately above or otherwise outside of the Web directory. This isn't required, but it's a nice bit of extra security.

✔ Tips

- If you place the connection script in the Web directory, then you can run it in a Web browser. If there are *no problems*, the result will be a blank page. If a connection problem occurs, you'll see error messages.

- In this chapter I discuss the most important of PHP's *mysqli* functions. All of these, and many, many more, are well documented in the PHP manual (*not* the MySQL manual). You'll also find plenty of sample usage code there.

- Once you've written one `mysqli_connect.inc.php` file, you can easily make changes to the `DEFINE()` lines to use the script for other projects.

Executing Simple Queries

Once you have successfully connected to and selected a database, you can start executing queries. These queries can be as simple as inserts, updates, and deletions—as I'll demonstrate here—or as involved as complex joins returning numerous rows, as you'll see later in the chapter. In any case, the PHP function for executing a query is mysqli_query(). It takes the database connection as its first argument and the actual query to be run as its second. You'll normally want to assign the returned result to a variable:

```
$query_result = mysqli_query ($dbc,
→ $query);
```

The $query_result variable will, in layman's terms, contain reference information for the result of a query. In other words, $query_result will be a pointer to the data being returned by MySQL and can be used to determine the successful execution of a query.

With simple queries that do not return records, you can check their effectiveness by invoking the mysqli_affected_rows() function. For example:

```
echo '# of affected rows: ' .
→ mysqli_affected_rows($dbc);
```

This function returns the number of rows that were affected by INSERT, UPDATE, DELETE, and similar queries. This corresponds to what MySQL reports when running such queries within the mysql client (**Figure 7.3**).

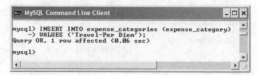

Figure 7.3 MySQL reports upon how many records were affected by certain types of queries. You can mimic this in PHP by using mysqli_affected_rows().

EXECUTING SIMPLE QUERIES

One final, albeit optional, step in your script would be to close the existing MySQL connection:

```
mysqli_close($dbc);
```

This line closes the database connection established by the `mysqli_connect()` function. It is not required, because PHP will automatically close the connection when a script terminates, but using it does make for good programming form.

To demonstrate this process, I'll make a PHP page that displays and handles a form. The express purpose will be to add different expense categories to the database.

Troubleshooting PHP and MySQL

When using PHP and MySQL together, there are many reasons why problems might occur. For starters, if you receive an error that claims `mysqli_connect()` is an *undefined function*, it means that PHP has not been installed with MySQL support. If you see an error that says *Client does not support authentication protocol*, this means that you're using an older version of the PHP MySQL libraries with a newer version of MySQL. The solution is discussed in Appendix A, "Troubleshooting." If you cannot connect to MySQL and aren't seeing these problems, the most likely cause is that you are not using a username/hostname/password combination that's been established in MySQL. See Chapter 2 for instructions on creating users.

Once you have PHP and MySQL working together and once you can connect to a database, most errors stem from your SQL queries. Later in the chapter you'll learn how to make use of MySQL's error messages, but the best debugging technique is this:

1. Print, using PHP, the query that is being executed.

2. Run that same query using another interface like the `mysql` client or phpMyAdmin.

The first step verifies what exact query PHP is running in MySQL. This is particularly important with PHP, as many queries will be dynamically generated and could actually be other than you would think. The second step will show you what result that query gives. The result could be an error or not. In any case, these two simple steps will reveal whether you have a PHP, MySQL, or SQL problem occurring. And identifying the problem is the first step in solving it!

To execute simple queries:

1. Create a new PHP document in your text editor (**Script 7.2**).

2. Begin with the standard HTML code.

```
<!DOCTYPE html PUBLIC "-//W3C//DTD
→ XHTML 1.0 Transitional//EN"
"http://www.w3.org/TR/xhtml1/DTD/xhtm
→ l1-transitional.dtd">
<html xmlns="http://www.w3.org/1999/
→ xhtml" xml:lang="en" lang="en">
<head>
    <meta http-equiv="content-type"
    → content="text/html; charset=
    → iso-8859-1" />
    <title>Add An Expense
    Category</title>
</head>
<body>
```

EXECUTING SIMPLE QUERIES

Script 7.2 This PHP page makes it possible to add records to the database—specifically the expense_categories table—via your Web browser.

```
1    <!DOCTYPE html PUBLIC "-//W3C//DTD XHTML 1.0 Transitional//EN"
2            "http://www.w3.org/TR/xhtml1/DTD/xhtml1-transitional.dtd">
3    <html xmlns="http://www.w3.org/1999/xhtml" xml:lang="en" lang="en">
4    <head>
5        <meta http-equiv="content-type" content="text/html; charset=iso-8859-1" />
6        <title>Add An Expense Category</title>
7    </head>
8    <body>
9    <?php
10
11   // ***** add_expense_category.php *****
12   // ***** Script 7.2 *****
13   // This page displays and handles a form
14   // for inserting records into the expense_categories table.
15
16   if (isset($_POST['submitted'])) { // If the form has been submitted, handle it.
17
18       // Check the required form fields.
19       if (!empty($_POST['expense_category'])) {
20
21           // Include the MySQL information:
22           require_once ('../mysqli_connect.inc.php');
23
```

Script continues on next page

In this book I will be following XHTML guidelines, so my code may look slightly different from what you are accustomed to. This is a minor point and immaterial to the topic at hand.

3. Start the PHP section of the page.

```
<?php
```

4. Write a conditional that checks if the form has been submitted.

```
if (isset($_POST['submitted'])) {
```

continues on next page

Script 7.2 *continued*

```
24       // Create the query:
25       $q = "INSERT INTO expense_categories (expense_category) VALUES ('{$_POST['expense_catego-
         ry']}')";
26
27       // Execute the query:
28       $r = mysqli_query ($dbc, $q);
29
30       // Print a message indicating success or not:
31       if (mysqli_affected_rows($dbc) == 1) {
32           echo '<b><font color="green">The category has been added!</font></b>';
33       } else {
34           echo '<b><font color="red">The category could not be added!</font></b>';
35       }
36
37       // Close the database connection:
38       mysqli_close($dbc);
39
40   } else { // Print a message if they failed to enter a category.
41       echo '<b><font color="red">You forgot to enter the category!</font></b>';
42   }
43
44 } else { // If the form has not been submitted, display it.
45
46 // Close out of the PHP for ease of coding.
47 ?>
48       Add a new category to the expense_categories table:<br />
49       <form action="add_expense_category.php" method="post">
50       <input type="text" name="expense_category" size="30" maxlength="30" /><br />
51       <input type="hidden" name="submitted" value="true" />
52       <input type="submit" name="submit" value="Submit!" />
53       </form>
54 <?php
55 } // Finish the main "submit" conditional.
56 ?>
57 </body>
58 </html>
```

This page will both display an HTML form and handle its submission. Therefore I'll create one large conditional that determines which step to take (display or handle) based upon whether or not the submit variable has a value. You'll see this pattern repeated in other scripts in this chapter.

To check if the form has been submitted, I'll refer to a hidden input that will act as a flag.

5. Verify that all of the required fields were filled out.

```
if (!empty($_POST
→ ['expense_category'])) {
```

Because I do not want the script inserting blank expense categories into the table, I first make sure that text was entered into this field before proceeding. As a rule, any field that cannot be NULL in the database, aside from primary keys, ought to be checked by your scripts for values. Validating form-submitted data is critical; checking that the field isn't empty provides a minimal amount of security.

6. Include the MySQL connection page.

```
require_once ('../mysql_connect.
→ inc.php');
```

This one line of code will insert the contents of mysqli_connect.inc.php into this script, thereby creating a connection to MySQL and selecting the database. You may need to change the reference to the location of the file as it is on your server.

7. Write and run the query.

```
$q = "INSERT INTO expense_categories
→ (expense_category) VALUES
→ ('{$_POST['expense_category']}')";
$r = mysqli_query ($dbc, $q);
```

This query itself is similar to those demonstrated in Chapter 5, "Basic SQL." After assigning the query to a variable, it is run through the mysqli_query() function, which sends the SQL to MySQL.

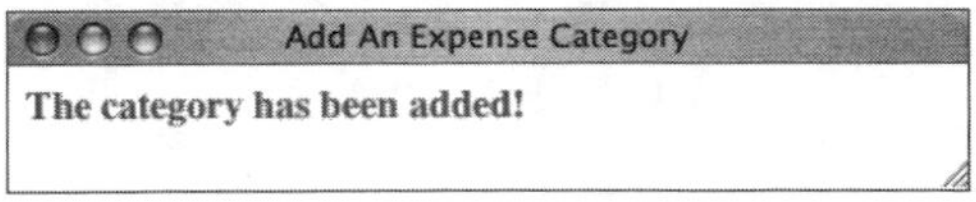

The category has been added!

Figure 7.4 The script will display a message indicating successful insertion of a new category.

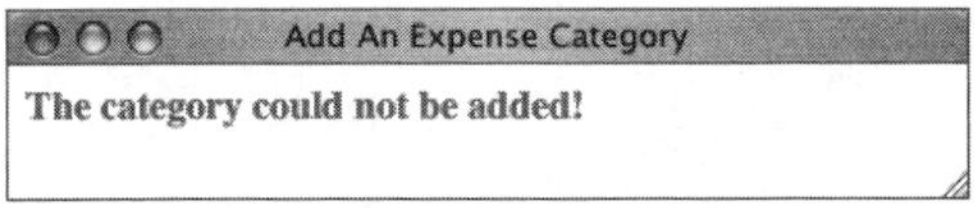

The category could not be added!

Figure 7.5 A message like this normally means there was a problem with the query. The "Error Handling" section later in the chapter discusses some useful debugging techniques.

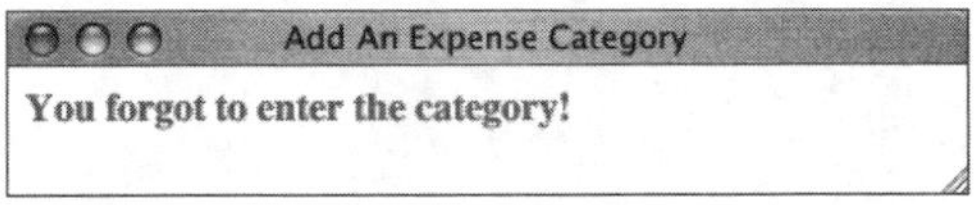

You forgot to enter the category!

Figure 7.6 Failure to fill out the form properly results in this message.

8. Print out the appropriate messages (**Figures 7.4** and **7.5**).

```
if (mysqli_affected_rows($dbc) == 1) {
    echo '<b><font color="green">The
    → category has been added!
    → </font></b>';
} else {
    echo '<b><font color="red">The
    → category could not be added!
    → </font></b>';
}
```

The `mysqli_affected_rows()` function will return the number of rows in the database affected by the previous query. In this case, the INSERT query should create one new row.

9. Close the database connection.

```
mysqli_close($dbc);
```

While closing the database connection is not required, it's always a good idea (assuming the connection is no longer required).

10. Finish up the first part of the conditional and display the second part.

```
    } else {
        echo '<b><font color=
        → "red">You forgot to enter
        → the category!</font></b>';
    }
} else {
```

This completes the "handle" part of the script. The message will be printed if the form is not filled out (**Figure 7.6**). The rest of this page will be used for displaying the form.

continues on next page

EXECUTING SIMPLE QUERIES

11. Create the HTML form.

```
?>
Add a new category to the
→ expense_categories table:<br />
<form action="add_expense_
→ category.php" method="post">
<input type="text" name="expense_
→ category" size="30" maxlength="30"
→ /><br />
<input type="hidden" name=
→ "submitted" value="true" />
<input type="submit" name=
→ "submit" value="Submit!" />
</form>
```

I've kept the form and HTML as simple as possible. Here you should notice that I use an HTML input name (*expense_category*) that corresponds exactly to what the MySQL column name is. The maximum size of the input box also corresponds exactly to the maximum size of the column in the table. Neither of these settings is required, but both make for fewer mistakes. Also, since this page both displays and handles the form, the action attribute refers to this script.

One change you could make would be to offer up multiple text boxes for inserting expense categories. Then you could change your query on the handle side to perform multiple inserts.

12. Complete the script.

```
<?php
}
?>
</body>
</html>
```

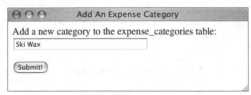

Figure 7.7 The simple HTML form first displayed by add_expense_category.php allows you to add records to the expense_categories table.

```
●○○        MySQL: Visual QuickStart Guide
mysql> SELECT * FROM expense_categories;
+---------------------+----------------------+
| expense_category_id | expense_category     |
+---------------------+----------------------+
|                  25 | Ski Wax              |
|                  24 | Travel               |
|                   3 | Books                |
|                   4 | Web Hosting          |
|                   5 | Computer Software    |
|                   6 | Magazine Subscriptions |
|                   7 | Computer Hardware    |
|                   8 | Sand Paper           |
|                   9 | Drum Sanders         |
|                  10 | Plaster of Paris     |
|                  11 | Erasers              |
|                  12 | Sandals              |
|                  13 | Horseshoes           |
|                  14 | Drywall              |
|                  15 | Paper Clips          |
|                  16 | Eggs                 |
|                  17 | Light Switches       |
|                  18 | Electricity          |
|                  19 | Print Cartridges     |
|                  20 | Picture Frames       |
|                  21 | Internet Access Fees |
|                  22 | Pencils              |
|                  23 | Employee Benefits    |
+---------------------+----------------------+
23 rows in set (0.00 sec)

mysql>
```

Figure 7.8 Use the mysql client (or another interface) to confirm that the operations of your PHP script did work.

13. Save the file as

    add_expense_category.php.

    I prefer longer, more descriptive filenames, but if you would like to use something different, be sure to also change the initial <form> tag accordingly.

14. Test the file by running the script in your Web browser (**Figure 7.7**).

    After running the script, you can always ensure that it worked by using the mysql client to view the values in the table (**Figure 7.8**).

✔ Tips

- You should not end your queries with a semicolon in PHP, as you did when using the mysql client. This is a common, albeit harmless, mistake to make. (Lines of PHP code do conclude with a semicolon, of course.)

- If, in the form, you submit text that contains a single quotation mark, the character will need to be escaped (preceded by a backslash) before the string is inserted into the database. Otherwise, the quotation mark will interfere with those delineating column values. For more information, see the sidebar "Magic Quotes" under "Security Considerations" later in this chapter.

- You are not always obligated to create a $q (or $query) variable as I tend to do. Instead, you could directly insert your query text into mysqli_query():

  $r = mysqli_query($dbc, 'SELECT *
  → FROM tablename');

  However, as the construction of your queries becomes more complex, using a variable will be the only option.

Retrieving Query Results

In the preceding section of this chapter I discuss and demonstrate how to execute simple queries on a MySQL database. A simple query, as I'm calling it, could be defined as one that begins with `INSERT`, `UPDATE`, `DELETE`, or `ALTER`. What all four of these have in common is that they return no data, just an indication of their success. Conversely, a `SELECT` query generates information (i.e., it will return rows of records) that has to be handled by other PHP functions.

The primary tool for handling `SELECT` query results is `mysqli_fetch_array()`. This function returns one row of data at a time, as an array. You'll want to use this function within a loop that will continue to access every returned row as long as there are more to be read. The basic construction for reading every record from a query is

```
while ($row = mysqli_fetch_array
→ ($query_result)) {
    // Do something with $row.
}
```

This function takes an optional parameter dictating what type of array is returned: associative, indexed, or both. An associative array allows you to refer to column values by name, whereas an indexed array requires you to use only numbers (starting at 0 for the first column). Each parameter is defined by a constant listed in **Table 7.1**.

To see how many records were returned by a query, use `mysqli_num_rows()`:

```
$num = mysqi_num_rows($query_result);
```

Table 7.1 Adding one of these constants as an optional parameter to the `mysqli_fetch_array()` function dictates how you can access the values returned.

mysqli_fetch_array() Constants	
CONSTANT	EXAMPLE
MYSQLI_ASSOC	`$row['column']`
MYSQLI_NUM	`$row[0]`
MYSQLI_BOTH	`$row[0]` or `$row['column']`

Once you are done with a query result set, you can release the memory used by that result with

```
mysqli_free_result($query_result);
```

Like using `mysqli_close()`, this isn't required but is more professional.

To demonstrate how to handle results returned by a query, I will create a script for adding an expense to the database. In the script, a pull-down menu will be created based upon the values in the `expense_categories` table. The overall structure of the script will be very similar to `add_expense_category.php`.

To retrieve query results:

1. Create a new PHP document in your text editor (**Script 7.3**).

continues on next page

Script 7.3 The `add_expense.php` script retrieves the values from the `expense_categories` table to create a pull-down menu. This pull-down menu is part of a form used to add expenses to the database.

```
1    <!DOCTYPE html PUBLIC "-//W3C//DTD XHTML 1.0 Transitional//EN"
2            "http://www.w3.org/TR/xhtml1/DTD/xhtml1-transitional.dtd">
3    <html xmlns="http://www.w3.org/1999/xhtml" xml:lang="en" lang="en">
4    <head>
5        <meta http-equiv="content-type" content="text/html; charset=iso-8859-1" />
6        <title>Enter An Expense</title>
7    </head>
8    <body>
9    <?php
10
11   // ***** add_expense.php *****
12   // ***** Script 7.3 *****
13   // This page displays and handles a form for
14   // inserting records into the expenses table.
15
16   // Include the MySQL information:
17   require_once ('../mysqli_connect.inc.php');
18
19   if (isset($_POST['submitted'])) { // If the form has been submitted, handle it.
20
21       // Check the required form fields:
22       if (isset($_POST['expense_category_id']) AND (!empty($_POST['expense_amount'])) AND
             (!empty($_POST['expense_description'])) ) {
```

Script continues on next page

2. Begin with the standard HTML code.

```
<!DOCTYPE html PUBLIC "-//W3C//DTD
→ XHTML 1.0 Transitional//EN"
"http://www.w3.org/TR/xhtml1/DTD/
→ xhtml1-transitional.dtd">
<html xmlns="http://www.w3.org/1999/
→ xhtml" xml:lang="en" lang="en">
<head>
    <meta http-equiv="content-type"
    → content="text/html; charset=
    → iso-8859-1" />
    <title>Enter An Expense</title>
</head>
<body>
```

Script 7.3 *continued*

```
23
24          // Create the query:
25          $q = "INSERT INTO expenses VALUES (NULL, {$_POST['expense_category_id']}, '" . addslash-
            es($_POST['expense_amount']) . "', '" . addslashes($_POST['expense_description']) . "',
            NOW())";
26
27          // Execute the query:
28          $r = mysqli_query ($dbc, $q);
29
30          // Print a message indicating success or not:
31          if (mysqli_affected_rows($dbc) == 1) {
32              echo '<b><font color="green">The expense has been added!</font></b>';
33          } else {
34              echo '<b><font color="red">The expense was not entered into the table!</font></b>';
35          }
36
37      } else { // Print a message if they failed to enter a required field:
38          echo '<b><font color="red">You missed a required field!</font></b>';
39      }
40
41  } else { // If the form has not been submitted, display it.
42
43      echo 'Enter an expense:<br />
44      <form action="add_expense.php" method="post">
45      <p>Expense Category: <select name="expense_category_id">';
46
47      // Display the expense categories:
48      $r = mysqli_query ($dbc, 'SELECT * FROM expense_categories ORDER BY expense_category');
49      while ($row = mysqli_fetch_array ($r, MYSQLI_NUM)) {
```

Script continues on next page

3. Begin the PHP section and include the MySQL connection script.

```php
<?php
require_once ('../mysql_connect.inc.
→ php');
```

Because both steps of this script (displaying and handling the form) require database access, I'll need to include this file immediately within the PHP, rather than within the conditional, as I had done previously (see Script 7.2).

4. Create the main conditional.

```php
if (isset($_POST['submitted'])) {
```

Once again, this conditional will determine which role (handle or display the form) the script will be playing.

continues on next page

Script 7.3 *continued*

```
50          echo "<option value=\"$row[0]\">$row[1]</option>\n";
51       }
52
53       // Tidy up (not required):
54       mysqli_free_result($r);
55
56       // Finish the form:
57       echo '</select></p>
58       <p>Expense Amount: <input type="text" name="expense_amount" size="10" maxlength="10" /></p>
59       <p>Expense Description: <textarea name="expense_description" rows="5"
         cols="40"></textarea></p>
60       <input type="hidden" name="submitted" value="true" />
61       <input type="submit" name="submit" value="Submit!" />
62       </form>';
63
64    } // Finish the main "submit" conditional.
65
66    // Close the connection (not required):
67    mysqli_close($dbc);
68
69    ?>
70    </body>
71    </html>
```

5. Check all of the required form fields.

```
if (isset($_POST['expense_category_
→ id']) AND (!empty($_POST['expense_
→ amount'])) AND (!empty($_POST
→ ['expense_description'])) ) {
```

For this script, I'm checking three fields: the *expense_category_id*, the *expense_amount*, and the *expense_description*.

6. Create the appropriate MySQL query.

```
$q = "INSERT INTO expenses VALUES
→ (NULL, {$_POST['expense_category_
→ id']}, '" . addslashes($_POST
→ ['expense_amount']) . "', '" .
→ addslashes($_POST['expense_
→ description']) . "', NOW())";
```

This query differs slightly from that in Script 7.2 because I have incorporated the addslashes() function. This function will automatically escape any problem characters. You will learn more about this issue later in the chapter, but I'm going to start using this technique from here on.

7. Run the query and report upon the results (**Figure 7.9**).

```
$r = mysqli_query ($dbc, $q);
if (mysqli_affected_rows($dbc) == 1) {
    echo '<b><font color="green">The
    → expense has been added!
    → </font></b>';
} else {
    echo '<b><font color="red">The
    → expense was not entered into the
    → table!</font></b>';
}
```

As with the previous script, the error message would normally be due to a problem with the SQL query.

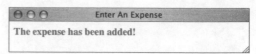

Figure 7.9 If there were no problems adding the expense to the database, a basic message is displayed.

Figure 7.10 If any of the three required fields are not filled out, the user sees this message and the query is not run on the database.

8. Complete the first part of the main conditional.

```
} else {
    echo '<b><font color="red">You
    → missed a required field!
    → </font></b>';
}
} else {
```

If you wanted to make the script more professional, you could add conditionals here to specify which field or fields in particular were omitted. As it stands (**Figure 7.10**), a minimal amount of form validation is performed.

9. Start the HTML form.

```
echo 'Enter an expense:<br />
<form action="add_expense.php" method=
→ "post">
<p>Expense Category: <select name=
→ "expense_category_id">';
```

The *expense_category_id* pull-down menu will be created by PHP using the stored values in the database. The first step in making this happen is to create the initial SELECT tag in the HTML form.

10. Generate a pull-down menu based upon the expense_categories table.

```
$r = mysqli_query ($dbc, 'SELECT *
→ FROM expense_categories ORDER BY
→ expense_category');
while ($row = mysqli_fetch_array
→ ($r, MYSQLI_NUM)) {
    echo "<option value=\"$row[0]\">
    → $row[1]</option>\n";
}
```

continues on next page

RETRIEVING QUERY RESULTS

Turning a table into a pull-down menu is a three-step process:

▲ Create the query and run it.

▲ Retrieve the results using `mysqli_fetch_array()` within a loop.

▲ Print out the `<option>` HTML values for each returned row.

For my query—which I directly run in the `mysqli_query()` function without the use of a `$q` or `$query` variable—I have decided to select everything from the table, ordering it by the `expense_category`. The `ORDER BY` aspect of the query will dictate the order of the pull-down menu. The `mysqli_fetch_array()` function is fed the `MYSQLI_NUM` parameter so that I can only refer to the returned values using indexes (which isn't difficult since there are only two columns).

11. Free up the MySQL resources.

```
mysqli_free_result($r);
```

Since the query returned several rows of data, I'm going to run the `mysqli_free_result()` function after fetching all the results. This isn't required but is a good technique.

12. Complete the HTML form.

```
echo '</select></p>

<p>Expense Amount: <input type=
→ "text" name="expense_amount" size=
→ "10" maxlength="10" /></p>

<p>Expense Description: <textarea
→ name="expense_description" rows=
→ "5" cols="40"></textarea></p>

<input type="hidden" name=
→ "submitted" value="true" />

<input type="submit" name="submit"
→ value="Submit!" />

</form>';
```

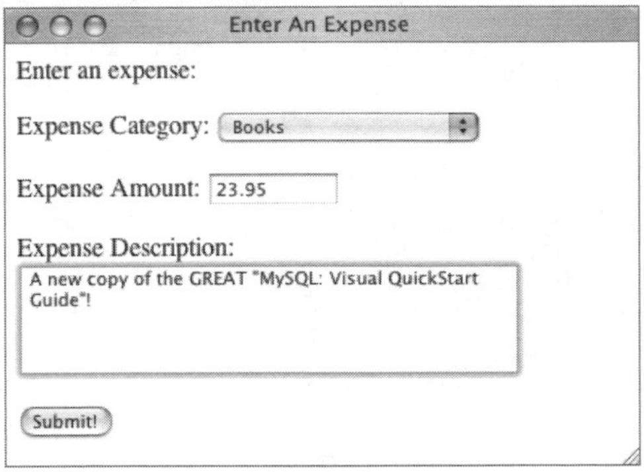

Figure 7.11 This script brings in the values of the `expense_categories` table as a pull-down menu that can be used when a user adds an expense.

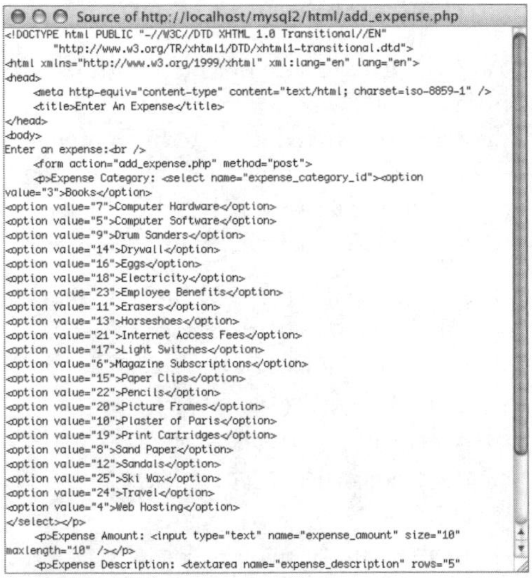


```
<!DOCTYPE html PUBLIC "-//W3C//DTD XHTML 1.0 Transitional//EN"
        "http://www.w3.org/TR/xhtml1/DTD/xhtml1-transitional.dtd">
<html xmlns="http://www.w3.org/1999/xhtml" xml:lang="en" lang="en">
<head>
    <meta http-equiv="content-type" content="text/html; charset=iso-8859-1" />
    <title>Enter An Expense</title>
</head>
<body>
Enter an expense:<br />
    <form action="add_expense.php" method="post">
    <p>Expense Category: <select name="expense_category_id"><option
value="3">Books</option>
<option value="7">Computer Hardware</option>
<option value="5">Computer Software</option>
<option value="9">Drum Sanders</option>
<option value="14">Drywall</option>
<option value="16">Eggs</option>
<option value="18">Electricity</option>
<option value="23">Employee Benefits</option>
<option value="11">Erasers</option>
<option value="13">Horseshoes</option>
<option value="21">Internet Access Fees</option>
<option value="17">Light Switches</option>
<option value="6">Magazine Subscriptions</option>
<option value="15">Paper Clips</option>
<option value="22">Pencils</option>
<option value="20">Picture Frames</option>
<option value="10">Plaster of Paris</option>
<option value="19">Print Cartridges</option>
<option value="8">Sand Paper</option>
<option value="12">Sandals</option>
<option value="25">Ski Wax</option>
<option value="24">Travel</option>
<option value="4">Web Hosting</option>
</select></p>
    <p>Expense Amount: <input type="text" name="expense_amount" size="10"
maxlength="10" /></p>
    <p>Expense Description: <textarea name="expense_description" rows="5"
```

Figure 7.12 Viewing the HTML source of the page (Figure 7.11) reveals the pull-down menu code created by PHP.

The form finishes the HTML for the pull-down menu and displays the last two input boxes. Make sure that the name of your `submitted` hidden input is the same (capitalization included) as it is in the script's main conditional.

13. Finish the script.

```
}
mysqli_close($dbc);
?>
</body>
</html>
```

As the MySQL connection was established prior to the main `IF` conditional, it needs to be closed after this conditional.

14. Save the file as `add_expense.php`, upload it to your Web server, and test in your browser (**Figure 7.11**).

To see the result of the `mysqli_fetch_array()` function, in conjunction with a `while` loop, also check out the HTML source (**Figure 7.12**).

✓ Tips

- The function `mysqli_fetch_row()` (which you might run across) is the equivalent of
  ```
  mysqli_fetch_array($query_result,
  → MYSQLI_NUM);
  ```
- The function `mysqli_fetch_assoc()` is the equivalent of
  ```
  mysqli_fetch_array($query_result,
  → MYSQLI_ASSOC);
  ```
- The `mysqli_multi_query()` function allows you to execute multiple queries at once. To do so, each query needs to be separated by a semicolon. If these queries return records, you'll need to handle them differently than you would a single `SELECT` query result. See the PHP manual for code examples.

Using mysqli_insert_id()

Relational databases can be tricky when it comes to using primary and foreign keys. To maintain the integrity of this relationship, a primary key must be created in one table (e.g., expense_categories) before being used as a foreign key in another (expenses). As you witnessed in Chapter 6, "MySQL Functions," the LAST_INSERT_ID() function returns the previously created primary key (auto-incremented number). In PHP, there is the similar mysqli_insert_id() function.

```
$id = mysqli_insert_id($dbc);
```

When making an application based upon a relational database, you'll frequently create scripts like add_expense.php, which ties in the primary key of one table (expense_categories) as a foreign key in another (expenses). However, if, when adding an expense, you'd like to choose an expense category that has not yet been created, you'll need to establish a new primary key (i.e., a new expense_category_id) before using it as a foreign key (in the new expense record). Such situations can be a challenge when using relational databases.

To demonstrate the mysqli_insert_id() function, I'll modify the PHP page that displays and handles a form for entering expenses. A pull-down menu of existing expense categories will still be created, but the user will have the option of adding a new expense category on the spot. If a new expense category is entered, it will be added and its primary key will be used as the foreign key within the expenses table.

Procedural vs. OOP

The *mysqli* extension of functions differs from the older *mysql* set in another way: they can be invoked using either a procedural or object-oriented syntax. Which you use is entirely up to you, but I've stuck with the procedural syntax in this book.

If you want to use the OOP version, that's straightforward enough. A sample section of code might look like this:

```
$db = new mysqli ('host', 'user',
→ 'password', 'databasename');
$r = $db->query('SELECT * FROM
→ tablename');
while ($row = $r->fetch_array
→ (MYSQLI_NUM)) {
    // Use $row.
}
$r->close();
$db->close();
```

There are three classes defined in this extension: mysqli, which manages the connection itself; mysqli_result, which is used for handling query results like in the preceding code; and mysqli_stmt, for working with prepared statements.

To use mysqli_insert_id():

1. Open add_expense.php (Script 7.3) in your text editor.

2. Change the validation conditional (Script 7.3, line 22) to read (**Script 7.4**).

```
if ( (isset($_POST['expense_
→ category_id']) or !empty($_POST
→ ['expense_category'])) AND
→ (strlen($_POST['expense_amount']) >
→ 0) AND (strlen($_POST['expense_
→ description']) > 0) ) {
```

continues on next page

Script 7.4 The more complex add_expense2.php script (as I've called it) can use either a pull-down menu or a new entry for determining the expense category.

```
1   <!DOCTYPE html PUBLIC "-//W3C//DTD XHTML 1.0 Transitional//EN"
2           "http://www.w3.org/TR/xhtml1/DTD/xhtml1-transitional.dtd">
3   <html xmlns="http://www.w3.org/1999/xhtml" xml:lang="en" lang="en">
4   <head>
5       <meta http-equiv="content-type" content="text/html; charset=iso-8859-1" />
6       <title>Enter An Expense</title>
7   </head>
8   <body>
9   <?php
10
11  // ***** add_expense2.php *****
12  // ***** Script 7.4 *****
13  // This page displays and handles a form for
14  // inserting records into the expenses table.
15
16  // Include the MySQL information:
17  require_once ('../mysqli_connect.inc.php');
18
19  if (isset($_POST['submitted'])) { // If the form has been submitted, handle it.
20
21      // Check the required form fields:
22      if ( (isset($_POST['expense_category_id']) or !empty($_POST['expense_category'])) AND
        (strlen($_POST['expense_amount']) > 0) AND (strlen($_POST['expense_description']) > 0) ) {
23
24          // Start the main query:
25          $q = "INSERT INTO expenses VALUES (NULL, ";
26
27          // Determine if a new expense category was entered:
28          if (!empty($_POST['expense_category'])) {
29
```

Script continues on next page

The change is in the first part of the conditional. Instead of just checking the $_POST['expense_category_id'] value, the script checks it and $_POST['expense_category']. As long as either is valid—the first for an existing expense category or the second for a new expense category—that part of the conditional will be true.

3. Begin rewriting the main query.

```
$q = "INSERT INTO expenses VALUES
→ (NULL, ";
```

The query in this script will, in the end, be similar to that in Script 7.3, but it will be built differently to take into account the possibility of a new expense category being entered. On this line I have begun the query.

Script 7.4 *continued*

```
                                                    Script
30          // Create a second query:
31          $q2 = "INSERT INTO expense_categories (expense_category) VALUES ('" .
            addslashes($_POST['expense_category']) . "')";
32
33          // Execute the second query and react accordingly:
34          if (mysqli_query ($dbc, $q2)) {
35              echo '<b><font color="green">The new expense category has been
                added!</font></b><br />';
36              $q .= mysqli_insert_id($dbc) . ", ";
37          } else {
38              echo '<b><font color="red">The new expense category was not entered into the
                table!</font></b><br />';
39              $problem = TRUE;
40          }
41
42      } else { // Finish the expense_category conditional.
43          $q .= "{$_POST['expense_category_id']}, ";
44      }
45
46      // Finish the main query:
47      $q .= "'" . addslashes($_POST['expense_amount']) . "', '" .
        addslashes($_POST['expense_description']) . "', NOW())";
48
49      // Check to see if there was a problem:
50      if (!$problem) {
51
52          // Print a message indicating success or not:
53          if (mysqli_query ($dbc, $q)) {
54              echo '<b><font color="green">The expense has been added!</font></b>';
55          } else {
56              echo '<b><font color="red">The expense was not entered into the
                table!</font></b>';
57          }
58
```

Script continues on next page

Script 7.4 *continued*

```
59          } else { // If there was a problem:
60              echo '<b><font color="red">The expense was not entered into the table because the
                expense_category could not be added!</font></b>';
61          }
62
63      } else { // Print a message if they failed to enter a required field:
64          echo '<b><font color="red">You missed a required field!</font></b>';
65      }
66
67  } else { // If the form has not been submitted, display it.
68
69      echo 'Enter an expense:<br />
70      <form action="add_expense2.php" method="post">
71      <ul>
72      <li>Expense Category: <select name="expense_category_id">';
73
74      // Display the expense categories:
75      $r = mysqli_query ($dbc, 'SELECT * FROM expense_categories ORDER BY expense_category');
76      while ($row = mysqli_fetch_array ($r, MYSQLI_NUM)) {
77          echo "<option value=\"$row[0]\">$row[1]</option>\n";
78      }
79
80      // Tidy up (not required):
81      mysqli_free_result($r);
82
83      // Finish the form:
84      echo '</select></li>
85      or<br />
86      <li>Enter a new expense category: <input type="text" name="expense_category" size="30"
          maxlength="30" /></li>
87      </ul>
88      <p>Expense Amount: <input type="text" name="expense_amount" size="10" maxlength="10" /></p>
89      <p>Expense Description: <textarea name="expense_description" rows="5"
          cols="40"></textarea></p>
90      <input type="hidden" name="submitted" value="true" />
91      <input type="submit" name="submit" value="Submit!" />
92      </form>';
93
94  } // Finish the main "submit" conditional.
95
96  // Close the connection (not required):
97  mysqli_close($dbc);
98
99  ?>
100 </body>
101 </html>
```

4. Add a new expense category if one was entered.

```
if (!empty($_POST['expense_category'])) {
    $q2 = "INSERT INTO expense_
    → categories (expense_category)
    → VALUES ('" . addslashes($_POST
    → ['expense_category']) . "')";
    if (mysqli_query ($dbc, $q2)) {
        echo '<b><font color="green">
        → The new expense category has
        → been added!</font></b><br />';
        $q .= mysqli_insert_id($dbc) . ", ";
    } else {
        echo '<b><font color="red">The
        → new expense category was not
        → entered into the table!
        → </font></b><br />';
        $problem = TRUE;
    }
}
```

This code is an application of that in add_expense_category.php (Script 7.2). First it checks if an expense category was entered. If so, it will add that record to the expense_categories table and use the mysqli_insert_id() function to add that expense category's primary key value to the main query. Messages are printed indicating the successful running of the query (**Figure 7.13**).

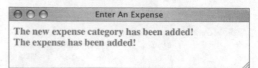

Figure 7.13 Dual messages reveal how the script successfully completed each database insertion.

5. Complete the main query.

```
} else {
    $q .= "{$_POST['expense_
    → category_id']}, ";
}
$q .= "'" . addslashes($_POST
→ ['expense_amount']) . "', '" .
→ addslashes($_POST['expense_
→ description']) . "', NOW())";
```

If no expense category was entered, the main query will be appended with the *expense_category_id* value, which is set by the pull-down menu based upon existing categories.

6. Check for problems and run the query.

```
if (!$problem) {
    if (mysqli_query ($dbc, $q)) {
        echo '<b><font color="green">
        → The expense has been added!
        → </font></b>';
    } else {
        echo '<b><font color="red">The
        → expense was not entered into
        → the table!</font></b>';
    }
} else {
    echo '<b><font color="red">The
    → expense was not entered into the
    → table because the expense_
    → category could not be added!
    → </font></b>';
}
```

The $problem variable, established in Step 4, is true if the script was not able to add the new expense category (in which case, the expense itself should not entered). Otherwise, this part of the script behaves as it previously had.

continues on next page

Both here and in Step 4, I just check that the query runs okay rather than invoke the `mysqli_affected_rows()` function. This is only to simplify the code; you can certainly use that function in a conditional instead.

7. Add an `expense_category` input to the form.

```
<li>Enter a new expense category:
→ <input type="text"
→ name="expense_category" size="30"
→ maxlength="30" /></li>
```

In addition to adding this field, I've changed the HTML slightly by adding a bullet list so that the user sees the two possible options as selecting an expense category or adding a new one.

8. Save the file, upload it to your Web server, and test in a Web browser (**Figures 7.14, 7.15,** and **7.16**).

For ease of demonstration, I've chosen to rename this script `add_expense2.php` to distinguish it from its predecessor. With that in mind, I also changed the form's `action` attribute. This is an optional change.

✔ Tips

■ You must call `mysqli_insert_id()` immediately after an `INSERT` query and before running any other queries.

■ The `mysqli_insert_id()` function will return 0 if no `AUTO_INCREMENT` value was created.

■ Remember that when you are dealing with numbers in SQL, they need not be enclosed by quotation marks (in fact, they really shouldn't). For this reason, the *expense_category_id* values are not enclosed. I do enclose the *expense_amount* values, though, because they are coming from a text field and could possibly not be numeric, due to user error.

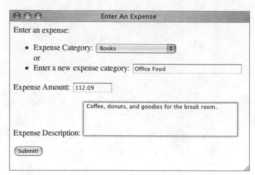

Figure 7.14 The form is more user-friendly now because it no longer requires the user to create an expense category before entering an expense.

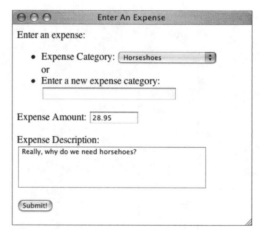

Figure 7.15 If no new expense category is entered...

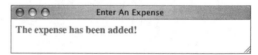

Figure 7.16 ...the script will function as it had before.

Error Handling

Error handling, which is important in any script, is even more of an issue when dealing with databases, since the probability for errors will increase dramatically. Common errors you will encounter are

- Failure in connecting to a database
- Failure in selecting a database
- Inability to run a query
- No results being returned by a query
- Unexpected results being returned by a query

Experience will teach you why these errors normally occur, but immediately seeing what the problem is in your scripts can save you much debugging time. Depending upon your PHP installation, if you have a problem with MySQL, the result may be a blank page, which is no help at all!

To have your scripts give informative reports about errors that occur, you make use of the `mysqli_error()` and `mysqli_errno()` functions. The former will print a textual version of the error that MySQL returned, and the latter will return the corresponding number. Both take the database connection as their only argument.

Connection errors are handled differently, though. To report on these use `mysqli_connect_error()`.

Along with these functions are two PHP terms you can use for error handling: @ and `die()`. The @, when used preceding a function name, will suppress any error messages or warnings the function might invoke, while `die()` will terminate the execution of a script and send any message within the parentheses to the Web browser.

Errors and PHP's display_errors Setting

PHP's *display_errors* setting dictates whether or not errors, when they occur, are shown in the Web browser. The current default is that they *not* be shown, which means that any error results in a blank or partially blank screen. In such cases, if you use any of the *mysqli* functions to report a MySQL error, you'll then see the information you need.

However, if *display_errors* is on, then you'll see PHP's error message *and* the message created by the *mysqli* error function. In theses cases, you might want to prepend any potentially problematic function calls with @, which will suppress the PHP error. You'll see this in action in the `edit_expense.php` script.

As a rule of thumb, use die() with any function whose successful execution is mandated by the remainder of the script (such as connecting to MySQL and selecting the database). Use @ with functions that might be problematic but would not necessitate stopping the script.

To use error handling:

1. Open mysqli_connect.inc.php (Script 7.1) in your text editor.

2. Change the connection code (line 23) to include die() and mysqli_connect_error() (**Script 7.5**).

   $dbc = @mysqli_connect(DB_HOST,
   → DB_USER, DB_PASSWORD, DB_NAME) or
   → die ('Could not connect to MySQL:
   → ' . mysqli_connect_error());

   This code will first attempt to connect to MySQL. If it fails to do so, any errors that might otherwise be displayed are suppressed by the @. In such a case, the or die() section will kick in, where the error will be handled more gracefully.

   Since the die() function can take any string within its parentheses, you can make your error messages as descriptive or customized as you'd like. Here I'm using mysqli_connect_error() along with a text string, but I could also add HTML formatting to the code.

3. Save the file and upload it to your Web server.

   Once again, for ease of reference, I'll be renaming my script as mysqli_connect2.inc.

Script 7.5 In the new version of mysqli_connect.inc. php, I've added different error-handling techniques for a more professional result.

```
1    <?php
2
3    // ***** mysqli_connect2.inc.php *****
4    // ***** Script 7.5 *****
5    // Developed by Larry E. Ullman
6    // MySQL: Visual QuickStart Guide
7    // SECOND EDITION
8    // Contact: mysql2@DMCinsights.com
9    // Created: February 15, 2006
10   // Last modified: February 15, 2006
11   // This file contains the database access
     information
12   // for the accounting database.
13   // This file also establishes a connec-
     tion to MySQL
14   // and selects the accounting database.
15
16   // Database-specific information:
17   DEFINE ('DB_USER', 'username');
18   DEFINE ('DB_PASSWORD', 'password');
19   DEFINE ('DB_HOST', 'localhost');
20   DEFINE ('DB_NAME', 'accounting');
21
22   // Connect to MySQL and select the data-
     base:
23   $dbc = @mysqli_connect(DB_HOST, DB_USER,
     DB_PASSWORD, DB_NAME) or die ('Could not
     connect to MySQL: ' .
     mysqli_connect_error());
24
25   ?>
```

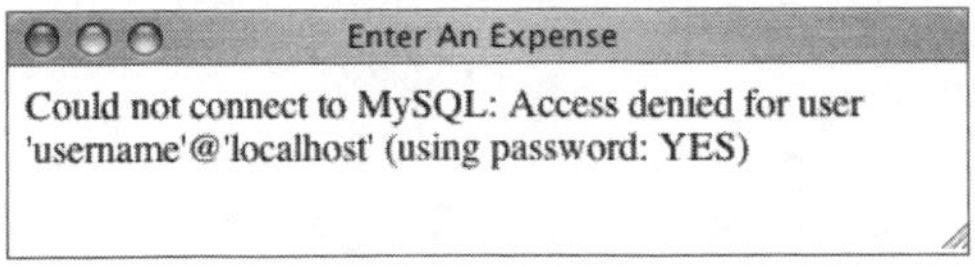

Figure 7.17 The or die() construct terminates a script if no database connection can be made and reports upon the error.

```
╒ ╕
  ⊝ ⊝ ⊝         Enter An Expense
  Could not connect to MySQL: Unknown database 'oy vay'
```

Figure 7.18 If the script could not select the proper database, a plain message is stated and the script's execution is halted.

4. Test how these changes affect the execution of your scripts by altering the DB_USER, DB_PASSWORD, DB_HOST, or DB_NAME value to purposefully create errors (**Figures 7.17** and **7.18**).

✔ Tips

- Appendix A, "Troubleshooting," covers common MySQL errors in more detail, along with common causes.

- As mentioned in a sidebar earlier in the chapter, the best method of debugging PHP scripts that interact with MySQL is to use the mysql clients to confirm what results you should be seeing.

- Another common problem with PHP and MySQL comes from not referring to the returned results properly. If you refer to columns by name, you have to do so in an exact, case-sensitive manner. If you use an alias in your query, you must use that alias in PHP.

ERROR HANDLING

Security Considerations

Database security with respect to PHP comes down to two broad issues:

◆ Protecting the database access information

◆ Inspecting the information being stored in the database

You can accomplish the first objective by securing the MySQL connection script. I discussed some of the options for safeguarding the `mysqli_connect.inc.php` file earlier in this chapter. The best, although not always possible, method is to store the file outside of the Web document root (Figures 7.1 and Figure 7.2) so that it is never viewable from a Web browser.

For the second objective, there are numerous options. One, as I've been doing in this chapter, is to use the `$_POST` array (or `$_GET`) instead of global variables. Second, and this is beyond the scope of this book, is to use regular expressions to make sure that submitted data matches what you would expect it to be. I also recommend that numeric values be type cast (forcibly converted) before use in a query.

With strings, you need to protect against problematic characters. Thus far I've done so using the `addslashes()` function on submitted data to escape problematic characters. (The same benefit could be achieved by using PHP's Magic Quotes feature, as mentioned in the sidebar.) Alternatively, you could use the specific `mysqli_real_escape_string()` function:

```
$str = mysqli_real_escape_string ($dbc,
→ $str);
```

This function acts like `addslashes()`—and should be used with any text—but is more database-specific. It also takes into account the character set being used, which is a great advantage in multilingual and non-English applications.

To demonstrate this function, and also to show one last PHP/MySQL technique, I will write a script that allows a user to edit an expense record.

To use mysqli_real_escape_string():

1. Create a new PHP document in your text editor, beginning with the HTML (**Script 7.6**).

   ```
   <!DOCTYPE html PUBLIC "-//W3C//DTD
   → XHTML 1.0 Transitional//EN"
   "http://www.w3.org/TR/xhtml1/DTD/
   → xhtml1-transitional.dtd">
   <html xmlns="http://www.w3.org/1999/
   → xhtml" xml:lang="en" lang="en">
   <head>
       <meta http-equiv="content-type"
       → content="text/html; charset=
       → iso-8859-1" />
       <title>Edit An Expense</title>
   </head>
   <body>
   ```

   continues on next page

continues on next page

Script 7.6 The final script in this chapter incorporates better security by way of the `mysqli_real_escape_string()` function. It also demonstrates how to run an UPDATE query from a PHP script.

```
1   <!DOCTYPE html PUBLIC "-//W3C//DTD XHTML 1.0 Transitional//EN"
2           "http://www.w3.org/TR/xhtml1/DTD/xhtml1-transitional.dtd">
3   <html xmlns="http://www.w3.org/1999/xhtml" xml:lang="en" lang="en">
4   <head>
5       <meta http-equiv="content-type" content="text/html; charset=iso-8859-1" />
6       <title>Edit An Expense</title>
7   </head>
8   <body>
9   <?php
10
11  // ***** edit_expense.php *****
12  // ***** Script 7.6 *****
13  // This page displays and handles a form for
14  // editing records in the expenses table.
15  // This page requires receipt of an eid (expense_id).
16
17  // Include the MySQL information:
18  require_once ('../mysqli_connect2.inc.php');
```

Script continues on next page

Script continues on next page

2. Start the PHP section, including the MySQL information.

```php
<?php
require_once ('../mysqli_connect2.
→ inc.php');
```

If you didn't rename the mysqli_ connect.inc.php script in the previous section, be sure to use the correct (original) script name here.

3. Create the conditional for displaying or handling the form.

```php
if (isset($_POST['submitted'])) {
```

Script 7.6 *continued*

```
19
20    if (isset($_POST['submitted'])) { // If the form has been submitted, handle it.
21
22        // Check the required form fields:
23        if ( (isset($_POST['expense_category_id']) OR !empty($_POST['expense_category'])) AND
              !empty($_POST['expense_amount']) AND !empty($_POST['expense_description']) ) {
24
25            // Start the query:
26            $q = "UPDATE expenses SET ";
27
28            // Determine if a new expense category was entered:
29            if (!empty($_POST['expense_category'])) {
30
31                // Create a second query:
32                $q2 = "INSERT INTO expense_categories VALUES (NULL, '" . mysqli_real_escape_string
                      ($dbc, $_POST['expense_category']) . "')";
33
34                // Execute the second query and react accordingly:
35                $r = @mysqli_query ($dbc, $q2);
36                if (@mysqli_affected_rows($r) == 1) {
37                    echo '<b><font color="green">The new expense category has been
                          added!</font></b><br />';
38                    $q .= "expense_category_id=" . mysqli_insert_id($dbc) . ", ";
```

Script continues on next page

4. Check the required form fields.

```
if ( (isset($_POST['expense_
→ category_id']) OR !empty($_POST
→ ['expense_category'])) AND
→ !empty($_POST['expense_amount'])
→ AND !empty($_POST['expense_
→ description']) ) {
```

This code is similar to that in add_expense2.php. The form will allow the user to select from the list of current expense categories or to enter a new one.

5. Begin the main query.

```
$q = "UPDATE expenses SET ";
```

Since this form will be for editing existing records, the query will be an UPDATE rather than an INSERT. Otherwise, this section (and the next) of the script is familiar territory.

continues on next page

Script 7.6 *continued*

```
39        } else {
40            echo '<b><font color="red">The new expense category was not entered into the
             table!</font></b><br />';
41            echo '<b><font color="red">MySQL reported: '. mysqli_error($dbc) .'</font></b><br
             />';
42            $problem = TRUE;
43        }
44
45    } else { // Finish the expense_category conditional.
46        $q .= "expense_category_id=" . (int) $_POST['expense_category_id'] . ', ';
47    }
48
49    // Finish the query:
50    $q .= "expense_amount=" . (float) $_POST['expense_amount'] . ", expense_description='" .
         mysqli_real_escape_string($dbc, $_POST['expense_description']) . "', expense_date='" .
         mysqli_real_escape_string($dbc, $_POST['expense_date']) . "' WHERE expense_id=" . (int)
         $_POST['expense_id'];
51
52    // Check to see if there was a problem:
53    if (!$problem) {
54
55        // Execute the query:
56        $r = @mysqli_query ($dbc, $q);
57
```

Script continues on next page

195

6. Check for a new expense category and handle it accordingly.

```
if (!empty($_POST['expense_
→ category'])) {
   $q2 = "INSERT INTO expense_
   → categories VALUES (NULL, '" .
   → mysqli_real_escape_string ($dbc,
   → $_POST['expense_category']) .
   → "')";
   $r = @mysqli_query ($dbc, $q2);
   if (@mysqli_affected_rows($r) ==
   → 1) {
      echo '<b><font color="green">
      → The new expense category has
      → been added!</font></b><br />';
      $q .= "expense_category_id=" .
      → mysqli_insert_id($dbc) . ", ";
```

Script 7.6 *continued*

```
58            // Print a message indicating success or not:
59            if (@mysqli_affected_rows($dbc) == 1) {
60                echo '<b><font color="green">The expense has been edited!</font></b>';
61            } else {
62                echo '<b><font color="red">The expense was not edited!</font></b>';
63                echo '<b><font color="red">MySQL reported: '. mysqli_error($dbc) .'</font></b><br
                  />';
64            }
65        } else { // If there was a problem:
66            echo '<b><font color="red">The expense was not edited because the new expense cate-
              gory could not be added!</font></b>';
67        }
68
69     } else { // Print a message if they failed to enter a required field:
70        echo '<b><font color="red">You missed a required field!</font></b>';
71     }
72
73 } else { // If the form has not been submitted, display it.
74
75     // Create the query:
76     $q = 'SELECT * FROM expenses WHERE expense_id = ' . (int) $_GET['eid'] . ' LIMIT 1';
77
78     // Execute the query:
79     $r = @mysqli_query ($dbc, $q);
```

Script continues on next page

```
} else {
    echo '<b><font color="red">
    → The new expense category was
    → not entered into the table!
    → </font></b><br />';
    echo '<b><font color="red">
    → MySQL reported: '.
    → mysqli_error($dbc)
    → .'</font></b><br />';
    $problem = TRUE;
}
```

One change you'll need to make when using an UPDATE is that instead of a query being of the form INSERT INTO *tablename* VALUES ('*value*', '*value2*'…), it will now be UPDATE *tablename* SET *column*='*value*', *column2*='*value2*', …. In this part of the script, if the *expense_category_id* is changed, it will be updated by the query.

continues on next page

Script 7.6 *continued*

```
80
81      // See if an expense was returned:
82      if (@mysqli_num_rows($r) == 1) {
83
84          // Retrieve and print the results:
85          $row = mysqli_fetch_array ($r, MYSQLI_ASSOC);
86          mysqli_free_result($r);
87
88          echo 'Edit this expense:<br />
89          <form action="edit_expense.php" method="post">
90          <ul>
91          <li>Expense Category: <select name="expense_category_id">';
92
93          // Display the expense categories:
94          $r2 = mysqli_query ($dbc, 'SELECT * FROM expense_categories ORDER BY expense_category');
95          while ($row2 = mysqli_fetch_array ($r2, MYSQLI_NUM)) {
96              if ($row2[0] == $row['expense_category_id']) {
97                  echo "<option value=\"$row2[0]\" selected=\"selected\">$row2[1]</option>\n";
98              } else {
99                  echo "<option value=\"$row2[0]\">$row2[1]</option>\n";
100             }
101         }
102
103         mysqli_free_result($r2);
```

Script continues on next page

Note that for security purposes, I send the new expense category through the `mysqli_real_escape_string()` function. For debugging purposes, I invoke the `mysqli_error()` function, in case the query doesn't work for some reason (**Figure 7.19**). I might also want to print the query that was executed if I need more help debugging the problem.

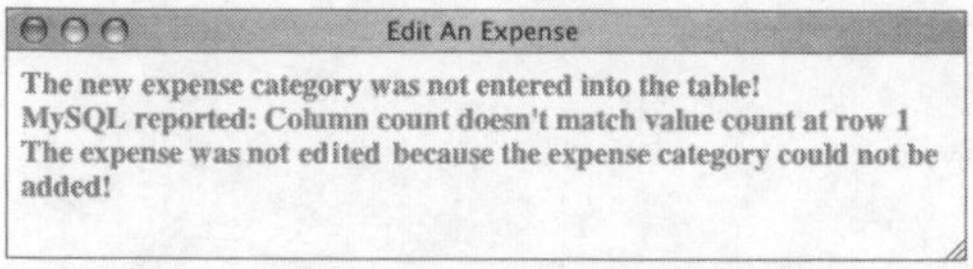

Figure 7.19 If the new expense category could not be added, the MySQL error is reported (for debugging purposes).

Script 7.6 *continued*

```
104
105         // Finish the form:
106         echo '</select></li>
107         or<br />
108         <li>Enter a new expense category: <input type="text" name="expense_category" size="30"
            maxlength="30" /></li>
109         </ul>
110         <p>Expense Amount: <input type="text" name="expense_amount" value="' .
            $row['expense_amount'] . '" size="10" maxlength="10" /></p>
111         <p>Expense Date: <input type="text" name="expense_date" value="' . $row['expense_date']
            . '" size="10" maxlength="10" /></p>
112         <p>Expense Description: <textarea name="expense_description" rows="5" cols="40">' .
            $row['expense_description'] . '</textarea></p>
113         <input type="hidden" name="submitted" value="true" />
114         <input type="submit" name="submit" value="Submit!" />
115         <input type="hidden" name="expense_id" value="' . $_GET['eid'] . '" />
116         </form>';
117
118     } else { // No record returned!
119         echo '<b><font color="red">This page must receive a valid expense ID!</font></b>';
120     }
121
122 } // Finish the main "submit" conditional.
123
```

Script continues on next page

Script 7.6 *continued*

```
           📄 Script
124  // Close the connection (not required):
125  mysqli_close($dbc);
126
127  ?>
128  </body>
129  </html>
```

Edit An Expense

The expense has been edited!

Figure 7.20 As with the other scripts in this chapter, a standard message indicates successful execution of the script.

7. Complete the main query.

```
} else {
    $q .= "expense_category_id=" . (int)
    → $_POST['expense_category_id'] .
    → ', ';
}
$q .= "expense_amount=" . (float)
→ $_POST['expense_amount'] . ",
→ expense_description='" . mysqli_
→ real_escape_string($dbc, $_POST
→ ['expense_description']) . "',
→ expense_date='" . mysqli_real_
→ escape_string($dbc, $_POST
→ ['expense_date']) . "' WHERE
→ expense_id=" . (int) $_POST
→ ['expense_id'];
```

The first part of this code completes the expense category conditional. If a current expense category is used, that value is type cast to an integer and added to the query. Two other numbers—the expense amount and the expense ID—are also type cast. If you wanted, you could validate that each of these values is greater than 0 as well.

For the strings in the query, each is run through the mysqli_real_escape_string() function.

8. Execute the query and report upon the results (**Figure 7.20**).

```
if (!$problem) {
    $r = @mysqli_query ($dbc, $q);
    if (@mysqli_affected_rows($dbc) ==
    → 1) {
        echo '<b><font color=
        → "green">The expense has been
        → edited!</font></b>';
    } else {
        echo '<b><font color="red">The
        → expense was not edited!
        → </font></b>';
```

continues on next page

```
    echo '<b><font color="red">
    → MySQL reported: '.
    → mysqli_error($dbc)
    → .'</font></b><br />';
    }
} else {
    echo '<b><font color="red">The
    → expense was not edited because
    → the expense category could not
    → be added!</font></b>';
}
```

In this example, I've decided to use the `mysqli_affected_rows()` function, which returns the number of rows affected by the previous query. It's usable whenever you run an UPDATE, ALTER, DELETE, or INSERT.

9. Complete the conditionals.

```
    } else {
        echo '<b><font color="red">
        → The expense was not edited
        → because the new expense
        → category could not be
        → added!</font></b>';
    }
} else {
    echo '<b><font color="red">You
    → missed a required field!
    → </font></b>';
}
} else {
```

This completes the "handling" section of the form, which updates the record. The rest of the form will display the record, within an HTML form, for editing purposes.

10. Select the current record from the database.

```
$q = 'SELECT * FROM expenses WHERE
→ expense_id = ' . (int)
→ $_GET['eid'] . ' LIMIT 1';
$r = @mysqli_query ($dbc, $q);
if (@mysqli_num_rows($r) == 1) {
    $row = mysqli_fetch_array ($r,
    → MYSQLI_ASSOC);
    mysqli_free_result($r);
```

To edit a record, I'll need to retrieve it from the database. The best way of doing so is to refer to the record's primary key (`expense_id`). This script assumes that it will receive the `expense_id` as a variable in the URL called *eid*. This value is type cast for sake of security.

To confirm that the expense ID is valid, I use `mysqli_num_rows()`. Then I fetch that one row (since I am retrieving only one record, there's no need for a `while` loop). At the end of this section of code, the `$row` associative array will contain all of the information related to one expense.

11. Start the HTML form.

```
echo 'Edit this expense:<br />
<form action="edit_expense.php"
→ method="post">
<ul>
<li>Expense Category: <select
→ name="expense_category_id">';
```

The form will be very much like the `add_expense.php` form, although with preset values.

continues on next page

12. Create the pull-down menu.

```
$r2 = mysqli_query ($dbc, 'SELECT *
→ FROM expense_categories ORDER BY
→ expense_category');
while ($row2 = mysqli_fetch_array
→ ($r2, MYSQLI_NUM)) {
    if ($row2[0] == $row
    → ['expense_category_id']) {
        echo "<option value=\"$row2[0]\"
        → selected=\"selected\">$row2
        → [1]</option>\n";
    } else {
        echo "<option value=\
        → "$row2[0]\">$row2[1]
        → </option>\n";
    }
}
mysqli_free_result($r2);
```

This pull-down menu is more involved than the similar one used in **add_expense. php** because I want to match up the current *expense_category_id* value with that in the pull-down menu so that the current category is automatically displayed. This can be accomplished with a basic **if-else** conditional and the **selected="selected"** HTML code.

13. Finish the rest of the HTML form.

```
echo '</select></li>
or<br />
<li>Enter a new expense category:
→ <input type="text" name=
→ "expense_category" size="30"
→ maxlength="30" /></li>
</ul>
<p>Expense Amount: <input
→ type="text" name="expense_amount"
→ value="' . $row['expense_amount']
→ . '" size="10" maxlength="10"
→ /></p>
```

```
<p>Expense Date: <input type="text"
→ name="expense_date" value="' .
→ $row['expense_date'] . '"
→ size="10" maxlength="10" /></p>

<p>Expense Description: <textarea
→ name="expense_description"
→ rows="5" cols="40">' .
→ $row['expense_description'] .
→ '</textarea></p>

<input type="hidden" name=
→ "submitted" value="true" />

<input type="submit" name="submit"
→ value="Submit!" />

<input type="hidden" name=
→ "expense_id" value="' .
→ $_GET['eid'] . '" />

</form>';
```

For standard text inputs and text areas, you can preset a value based upon stored information by using the value attribute for text boxes or simply entering the stored information between the text area tags. The record's primary key must be stored as a hidden variable so that the script knows on which record to run the UPDATE query.

14. Complete the PHP script and the HTML code.

```
    } else {
        echo '<b><font color="red">This
        → page must receive a valid
        → expense ID!</font></b>';
    }
}
mysqli_close($dbc);
?>
</body>
</html>
```

continues on next page

Magic Quotes

Magic Quotes—PHP's ability to automatically escape problem characters—has changed significantly over PHP's development. As a convenience, Magic Quotes handles single and double quotation marks submitted by an HTML form, retrieved from a database, and so forth. But, to encourage more security-conscious programming, PHP now comes with Magic Quotes disabled. If this is the case with your server, you must use either the addslashes() or mysqli_real_escape_string() function instead.

You can easily determine what you need to do by running some of the scripts in this chapter using strings with single quotation marks in them as examples. If the queries are not being entered, Magic Quotes is turned off and you must escape these characters. If data is being entered with multiple backslashes, this means that you have Magic Quotes turned on and are also using addslashes() or mysqli_real_escape_string() and you should therefore eliminate one of these features.

15. Save the file as `edit_expense.php`, upload it to your server, and test in your Web browser (**Figures 7.21** and **7.22**).

As it stands, to test this script, you'll need to append the URL with code like `?eid=x`, where *x* refers to an `expense_id` of a record in the database.

✔ Tips

■ The information discussed in this and the previous section can easily be applied to the earlier scripts as well to improve their security and error management.

■ On the book's Web site, you can download a `browse_expenses.php` page that links to this `edit_expense.php` script.

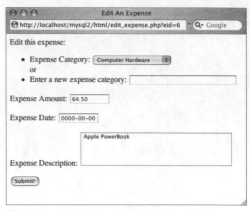

Figure 7.21 Since this record was entered without a date value, I can update that item using this form.

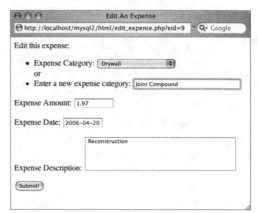

Figure 7.22 The `edit_expense.php` script, like `add_expense.php`, also allows you to enter a new category for an item.

MYSQL AND PERL

Long before PHP came along as a major player in Web development, programmers were using Perl (Practical Extraction and Report Language) for system management and Web applications alike. Perl was developed by Larry Wall over 20 years ago and since then has become a popular language for writing CGI (Common Gateway Interface) scripts for dynamically handling Web content.

This chapter is for several different types of users. The first would be the Perl user who has not yet worked with MySQL. The second is the Perl user who has worked with MySQL but needs a refresher on the basics. Finally, this chapter could be read by non-Perl developers who would like to see how readily Perl interacts with MySQL (especially compared with, say, PHP or Java).

Perl can be used on nearly any operating system, including Unix, Windows, and Macintosh. While you can create CGI scripts with Perl, all of the examples in the chapter will be run as simple Perl scripts on the computer, without using a Web server. I will demonstrate how to install the extra Perl modules to support MySQL, but it will be assumed that you have at least version 5.6.1 or higher of Perl already.

Installing Perl with MySQL Support on Windows

Although Perl was not created with Windows in mind, to program in Perl on your Windows computer is remarkably easy thanks to a product called ActivePerl. ActivePerl is freely distributed by ActiveState, which you can find at www.activestate.com. ActivePerl is a complete Perl package, easy to install and run on any Windows platform.

Along with Perl, you will need the DBI and DBD modules to write scripts that interact with MySQL. On Windows, with ActivePerl, you can use the Perl Package Manager (PPM) to add the extra DBI and DBD modules. The PPM comes with ActivePerl and simplifies the task of installing CPAN modules. (CPAN, short for Comprehensive Perl Archive Network, is a library of shared code that simplifies common programming tasks.) Despite all of these different tools, the only requirement of the following installation instructions is that you are connected to the Internet as you proceed through them.

To install Perl with MySQL support on Windows:

1. Download the most current version of ActivePerl from www.activestate.com.

   If you are installing ActivePerl on Windows 2000 or XP, you need to download only the Windows Installer Package (an MSI file). Otherwise, you'll see the other requirements for installation when you go through the download steps. At the time of this writing the current version of ActivePerl was 5.8.7.815.

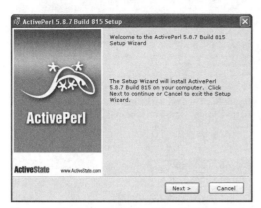

Figure 8.1 The ActivePerl Setup Wizard will take you through the installation of Perl on Windows.

Figure 8.2 The PPM (Perl Package Manager) must be installed in order to easily add Perl support for MySQL.

2. Run the downloaded executable by double-clicking the file (**Figure 8.1**).

The installer will take you through a few steps, giving you prompts at certain points to help customize the installation. Accepting the default settings will best ensure problem-free operation of ActivePerl.

Do make sure that you install the PPM (Perl Package Manager) on the Setup page (**Figure 8.2**).

This concludes the installation of ActivePerl on your system. Now you'll need to install the database modules.

3. Access a DOS prompt.

There are many ways of doing this, including clicking the Start menu, selecting Run, and entering cmd in the box that appears (then pressing Enter).

4. Test that Perl was successfully installed by entering the following and pressing Enter (**Figure 8.3**):

perl -v

The command perl -v will report on the version of Perl currently installed and running on your system, along with any other pertinent information. This is a simple test of the installation.

continues on next page

Figure 8.3 If ActivePerl was installed correctly, you should see a message like this after running perl -v.

INSTALLING PERL WITH MySQL SUPPORT

5. At the prompt, type `ppm` and press Enter (**Figure 8.4**).

This command should start up the ActivePerl Perl Package Manager. You'll see a `ppm>` prompt once you are within the application.

6. Install the DBI module by typing this at the prompt and pressing Enter:

`install DBI`

PPM will download and install all of the necessary files, reporting on its success (**Figure 8.5**).

7. Install the MySQL module for Perl (**Figure 8.6**).

`install DBD-MySQL`

Once the DBI package has been installed, you'll need to install the database-specific modules, such as DBD-MySQL. The Perl scripts will use DBI and DBD-MySQL together to connect to the databases.

8. Exit out of PPM by typing `quit` and pressing Enter.

✔ Tips

- ActivePerl is also available in versions for other operating systems, although it's most frequently used as a Windows solution for Perl.

- To learn more about Perl and CPAN, see www.perl.com and www.cpan.org, respectively.

- If you intend to use Perl to write CGI scripts, run `install CGI` within PPM.

- Within PPM you can check what modules have been installed by entering `query term` within the application (after Step 5). For example, `query mysql` should reveal that DBD-mysql is installed.

- You might see PPM referred to as either the Perl Package Manager or the Programmer's Package Manager.

Figure 8.4 The Perl Package Manager simplifies the installation of extra Perl modules.

Figure 8.5 Using PPM, you should first install the DBI module for general database interactions.

Figure 8.6 To use Perl with the MySQL database in particular, you'll need to install the DBD-MySQL package.

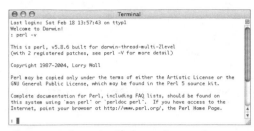

Figure 8.7 Before going further, make sure that you have a good installation of Perl.

Installing Perl Support for MySQL on Unix and Mac OS X

Like PHP, Perl is automatically installed on most Unix operating systems, including Mac OS X. Along with Perl you will need several modules to access MySQL, primarily DBI and DBD::mysql. A third, called Data-Dumper, is also necessary but may already be installed on your setup.

You have two options for installation:

◆ Use CPAN.

◆ Build and install each module manually.

The former is much easier than the latter and is what I will do in the following steps. There are a couple of assumptions involved, though, so see the sidebar on CPAN.

To install Perl support for MySQL:

1. Open a Terminal window.

2. Test that Perl is installed by entering the following and pressing Return (**Figure 8.7**).

   ```
   perl -v
   ```

   The command perl -v will report on the version of Perl currently installed and running on your system, along with any other pertinent information. This is a simple test of the installation.

   continues on next page

Using CPAN

CPAN was created to provide a regulated system of code for performing certain tasks. CPAN itself is also able to install modules you might need (in other words, CPAN can upgrade its own capabilities).

To access CPAN, use the Terminal application and enter the following (pressing Return afterward):

```
perl -MCPAN -e shell
```

The first time you use CPAN, you'll need to answer a slew of questions, most of which will work with the default settings. Once you are in CPAN, you should install several packages, starting with Bundle::libnet, followed by DBI and DBD::mysql. To install any package with CPAN, enter install *packagename*.

For CPAN to build and install modules, it does require some common Unix utilities, like gcc and make. If you are using Mac OS X, you should install the Developer Tools prior to running CPAN, so that your computer has these utilities.

3. Access CPAN as a superuser (**Figure 8.8**).

   `sudo perl -MCPAN -e shell`

   For a problem-free installation, you should run CPAN as an administrative user (accomplished by sudo). Enter your system's administrative password at the prompt.

4. Install the Data::Dumper module by typing this at the prompt and pressing Return:

   `install Data::Dumper`

   If CPAN reports that Data::Dumper is up to date already, then you are good to continue.

5. Install the DBI module by typing this at the prompt and pressing Return:

   `install DBI`

   PPM will download and install all of the necessary files, reporting on its success (**Figure 8.9**).

6. Install the MySQL module by typing this at the prompt and pressing Return:

   `force install DBD::mysql`

   Once the DBI package has been installed, you'll need to install the database-specific modules, such as DBD::mysql. The Perl scripts will use DBI and DBD::mysql together to connect to the databases.

   The installation is preceded by force because some of the tests will fail if you've already established a *root* user password for MySQL (which you hopefully have). To ignore those failures, force the installation.

7. Type quit and press Return to leave CPAN.

✔ Tips

■ To see if your Perl system is already configured to interact with MySQL, enter `perldoc DBD::mysql` at a command prompt (**Figure 8.10**).

■ You should update the DBD::mysql package any time you install a new version of MySQL. To do so, just repeat Step 3 and Step 6.

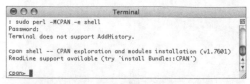

Figure 8.8 Perl support for MySQL will be installed using CPAN. Invoke CPAN as a superuser.

Figure 8.9 If CPAN reports that the make install is OK, the package was successfully installed.

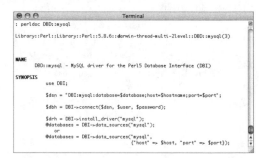

Figure 8.10 The documentation for DBD::mysql gives you the syntax for using the package.

Script 8.1 This simple Perl script tests for the presence of the MySQL driver.

```
        ○ ○ ○              Script
1    #!/usr/bin/perl -w
2
3    # Script 8.1 - test.pl
4    # This script just reveals
5    # what drivers are installed.
6
7    # Use what needs to be used.
8    use strict;
9    use DBI;
10
11   # Print a header message.
12   print "The following drivers are
     installed:\n";
13
14   # Create the @drivers array.
15   my @drivers = DBI->available_drivers();
16
17   # Print each driver.
18   foreach (@drivers) {
19       print "$_ \n";
20   }
```

Testing Perl and MySQL

Before I go into detail on how to use Perl to connect to and interact with MySQL, I'll go through a quick exercise first. This script will demonstrate how I will be writing Perl scripts throughout the chapter. Further, it will test that MySQL support is available before you start writing the remaining Perl scripts.

While this chapter will in no way replace a solid Perl book or tutorial, I'll quickly go over the steps of a basic Perl script. Even those programmers coming from other languages (such as PHP) ought to be able to follow these guidelines to write basic Perl documents. Also, most of the steps will be explained in some detail here, and knowledge of them will be assumed (and therefore not explained) in later sections.

To write a simple Perl script:

1. Create a new document in your text editor (**Script 8.1**).

   Since Perl scripts are just text files, it will not matter what text editor you use as long as it can save a file as plain text (not RTF).

2. Include the shebang line (unless you are using ActivePerl on Windows).

   `#!/usr/bin/perl -w`

   This line tells the computer to use the Perl application to process this text file. You'll need to change this line to match the location of the **perl** file on your system. Another common variant on this line would be `#!/usr/local/bin/perl -w`. On Windows with ActivePerl, you can omit this line entirely, although it does not hurt to use it.

   The -w flag enables many useful warnings when executing the code. This is recommended for debugging purposes.

   continues on next page

3. Enforce strict programming.

```
use strict;
```

The `use strict` command ensures a safer form of programming without adding too much overhead to your scripts. I'll be using it throughout this chapter, with the main result being that I need to declare variables before using them (see Step 5).

For non-Perl programmers, I'll also mention that every line in Perl, aside from the shebang and control structures, must end in a semicolon. Single-line comments can be preceded by a number (or pound) sign.

4. Include the DBI module and print an introductory message.

```
use DBI;

print "The following drivers are
→ installed:\n";
```

This first line will be required in all of the scripts throughout this chapter. It tells the script to make use of the DBI module that is necessary for interacting with MySQL. The second line tells the user what is to follow.

5. Declare and initialize an array.

```
my @drivers = DBI->
→ available_drivers();
```

The `@drivers` array will contain all of the drivers that are available to the DBI in this particular installation of Perl. Those values are automatically determined by the `available_drivers()` method of the `DBI` class. The `my` statement is required when doing strict programming, and you'll see an error if it is omitted.

Figure 8.11 To make a file executable on Unix operating systems (which means it can be run by entering ./filename.pl), you need to change its permissions.

6. Loop through and print each driver.

```
foreach (@drivers) {
    print "$_ \n";
}
```

The construct here will loop through the @drivers array, accessing each element one at a time. The elements, now referred to by the special $_ variable, will be printed, followed by a new line (\n).

7. Save the file as test.pl.

I'll be using the .pl extension throughout this chapter (which ActivePerl on Windows will recognize automatically).

You must make sure that your text editor does not add another hidden extension (like Notepad, which may try to add .txt to the end of the file's name).

8. Change the permissions of the file using the command line, if required (**Figure 8.11**).

```
chmod u+x test.pl
```

On Unix and Mac OS X operating systems, you need to tell the OS that this file should be executable. To do so, you use the chmod command to add executable status (x) to the file for the file's user (u). Again, this step is not necessary for Windows users.

You will need to be within the directory where test.pl was saved in order to run this command.

continues on next page

TESTING PERL AND MYSQL

9. Run the file.

On Windows systems, *either*

▲ Enter `perl C:\`*path*`\to\test.pl` at the command prompt and press Enter.

or

▲ Enter just `C:\`*path*`\to\test.pl` at the command prompt and press Enter.

Windows users can also `cd` to the directory where `test.pl` is and type `test.pl` or `perl test.pl` (**Figure 8.12**).

Unix and Mac OS X users can *do one of two things:*

▲ Move into the directory where you saved the script, type `./test.pl` at the command prompt, and press Return (**Figure 8.13**).

or

▲ Enter `perl /`*path*`/to/test.pl` at the command prompt and press Return.

If you use the `./test.pl` method, include the shebang line and change the file's permissions. Otherwise, skip those two steps.

In all of these examples, replace *path/to/* with the actual path to your script.

However you run the file, you should see the word *mysql* included in the list of drivers printed out (Figures 8.12 and 8.13). This confirms that you can connect to MySQL from a Perl script.

✔ Tips

■ To check a script for problems without executing it, use `perl -c /path/to/`*filename*`.pl`.

■ When specifically using Perl for Web development, you have the option of using the mod_perl Apache module, in which case you would use Apache::DBI rather than just DBI. You'll also need the CGI module.

■ If you are interacting with MySQL 4.1 or greater, you need at least version 2.9003 of DBD::mysql.

Figure 8.12 Running `test.pl` (here, on Windows) confirms that you can run a Perl script and that the MySQL support has been established.

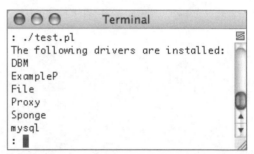

Figure 8.13 Running the script prints out a list of every DBI driver that your Perl installation can now use.

Connecting to MySQL

Once you know that you can successfully get a Perl script to work and that the mysql DBI module is present, you can start writing scripts that interact with the database. The first step in doing so is to connect to the server. For this you use the `DBI->connect()` method. Its first argument is a string of text in the form of *DBI:mysql:database:host:port*. The host and port are optional. The next two arguments are the username and the password. A full connection attempt might look like this:

```
$dbh = DBI->connect('DBI:mysql:
→ accounting:localhost', 'username',
→ 'password');
```

The first argument in the preceding line, `DBI:mysql:accounting:localhost`, referred to as the *data source name*, is sometimes assigned to a `$dsn` variable and then incorporated into this function:

```
my $dsn = 'DBI:mysql:accounting:
→ localhost';
$dbh = DBI->connect($dsn, 'username',
→ 'password');
```

The *username, hostname*, and *password* values are those you need to connect to MySQL from any application. These values should be the same as those used to connect through the `mysql` client.

I'll discuss error management later in the chapter, but another, optional, argument should be used in calling the function. By setting the *RaiseError* flag to *true* (give it a value of *1*), any MySQL errors will be reported:

```
$dbh = DBI->connect('DBI:mysql:accounting:
→ localhost, 'username', 'password',
→ {RaiseError => 1})
```

The result of the DBI->connect() line is assigned to a $dbh (database handle) variable that the rest of the script will refer to. Whenever you use the DBI->connect() method, you also need to use disconnect() when the script has concluded using the database:

$dbh->disconnect();

For the first MySQL-Perl script, I'll use these techniques to simply connect to and disconnect from the database. Once you have this working, you can begin to execute queries.

To connect to MySQL:

1. Create a new text document in your text editor.

2. Start with the shebang line, if necessary (**Script 8.2**).

   #!/usr/bin/perl -w

3. Enforce strict programming and incorporate the DBI module.

   use strict;

   use DBI;

4. Connect to MySQL.

   my $dbh = DBI->connect('DBI:mysql:
   → accounting:localhost', 'username',
   → 'password', {RaiseError => 1});

   For this example, I will be using the *accounting* database that has been discussed throughout the book. Change the *username* and *password* values to whatever has permission to access this database on your server.

Script 8.2 The mysql_connect.pl script merely checks for a successful connection to the MySQL server.

```
1   #!/usr/bin/perl -w
2
3   # Script 8.2 - mysql_connect.pl
4   # This script attempts to connect
5   # to the database and reports
6   # upon the results.
7
8   # Use what needs to be used.
9   use strict;
10  use DBI;
11
12  # Connect to the database.
13  my $dbh = DBI->connect('DBI:mysql:
    accounting:localhost', 'username',
    'password', {RaiseError => 1});
14
15  # Report on the success of the connection
    attempt.
16  if ($dbh) {
17
18      print "Successfully connected to the
        database! \n";
19
20  }
21
22  # Disconnect.
23  $dbh->disconnect;
```

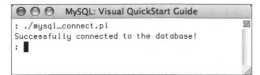

Figure 8.14 If you have the proper permissions to access the database, you'll see this message; otherwise...

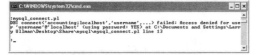

Figure 8.15 ...you'll see an error message and the script will stop running.

5. Print a message indicating success.

```
if ($dbh) {
    print "Successfully connected to
    → the database! \n";
}
```

The $dbh variable, which is a reference to the database connection, can be used to test whether or not the connection went through. Because I am using *RaiseError*, an inability to establish a connection will kill the script, so a "Could not connect to the database!" message (the potential else part of this conditional) is unnecessary.

6. Close the connection.

```
$dbh->disconnect;
```

This is an important step because it clears up resources used by both MySQL and Perl.

7. Save the file as mysql_connect.pl, change the permissions (if necessary), and run the script (**Figures 8.14** and **8.15**).

This script—assuming you have successfully run the test.pl script—should work or not work solely on the basis of the permissions of the username, host name, and password you use. If you have problems connecting to the database, check those parameters first.

✔ Tips

- In Perl you cannot make persistent connections to MySQL, unless you use mod_perl.

- In the data source name (DSN), mysql must be lowercase, and the host can be omitted if it is localhost.

Retrieving Query Results

Once you know how to connect to MySQL, you can start querying the database. There are two general types of queries: those that return records (i.e., SELECT queries) and those that do not (ALTER, CREATE, UPDATE, and DELETE). Queries of the first type are slightly more complicated, but I'll go ahead and demonstrate one of those first. Executing queries that return results is a two-step process just to send the query to the database. It requires both the prepare() and execute() methods.

Assuming you have connected to the database and assigned that result to $dbh, you would then do this:

```
$sth = $dbh->prepare("SQL QUERY
→ STATEMENT");
$sth->execute();
```

The result returned by the prepare() call is assigned to a variable that I'll call $sth (short for *statement handle*). Normally, before you execute the query, you'll want to make sure that prepare() returned a good result. The easiest way to do so is to use the defined() function.

```
if (defined($sth)) {
   $sth->execute();
} else {
   print "Could not execute the
   → query!\n";
}
```

After executing the query, you can retrieve all of the returned values using the fetchrow_array() function. It returns each record as an indexed array, beginning with 0. (See the accompanying sidebar, "Referring to Columns by Name," for other options.)

```
while (@row = $sth->fetchrow_array()) {
   print "$row[0] $row[1]…\n";
}
```

Referring to Columns by Name

The fetchrow_array() method is the most efficient and common way to retrieve values from the database, but it does have one significant drawback: You cannot refer to the columns by name to get their values. There are other, more complex, options, though.

The first and easiest is to use fetchrow_hashref(). It works like fetchrow_array() but allows you to name the columns to retrieve their values.

```
while ($row = $sth->fetchrow_hashref()) {
   print $row->{'column'};
}
```

Unfortunately, this method is significantly slower than fetchrow_array().

Second, if you know exactly how many columns will be returned, and in what order, you can assign these values to variables when you use fetchrow_array():

```
while ( ($col1, $col2, $col3) = $sth->
→ fetchrow_array()) ) {…
```

The third option is to use the bind_col() method to preassign column numbers to variable names. This system requires significantly more programming, so see the MySQL and Perl documentation for examples.

Script 8.3 The `browse_tables.pl` script is a simple interface to show the list of tables in a given database.

```
 ⦿ ⦿ ⦿                    📄 Script
1   #!/usr/bin/perl -w
2
3   # Script 8.3, 'show_tables.pl'
4   # This script takes a database name as
5   # a command line argument and shows
6   # the tables in that database.
7
8   # Use what needs to be used.
9   use strict;
10  use DBI;
11
12  # This script takes one argument when
    invoked.
13  # The argument is a database name.
14  my $database = $ARGV[0];
15
16  if (defined($database)) {
17
18      # Connect to the database.
19      my $dbh = DBI->connect("DBI:mysql:
        $database:localhost", 'username',
        'password', {RaiseError => 1});
20
21      # Query the database.
22      my $sth = $dbh->prepare('SHOW TABLES');
23
24      if (defined($sth)) {
25          $sth->execute();
26          my @row;
27          while (@row = $sth->
            fetchrow_array()) {
28              print "$row[0]\n";
29          }
30      }
31      $sth->finish();
32
33      # Disconnect.
34      $dbh->disconnect;
35
36  } else {
37      print "Please enter a database name
        when calling this script! \n";
38  }
```

Once you have finished retrieving the values, you conclude the query process.

```
$sth->finish();
```

As a simple example of using this information, I'll write a Perl script that takes the name of a database as an argument and displays all of the tables in that database.

To retrieve query results:

1. Create a new Perl script (**Script 8.3**).

   ```
   #!/usr/bin/perl -w
   use strict;
   use DBI;
   ```

2. Determine which database to use and check that one was entered.

   ```
   my $database = $ARGV[0];
   if (defined($database)) {
   ```

   This script will take one argument, the database name, which will be accessed via the @ARGV array and assigned to the $database variable. If the variable has a value, it's safe to proceed with the script.

3. Connect to MySQL and prepare the query.

   ```
   my $dbh = DBI->connect("DBI:mysql:
   → $database:localhost", 'username',
   → 'password', {RaiseError => 1});
   my $sth = $dbh->prepare('SHOW
   → TABLES');
   ```

   The connection line in this script is slightly different from its predecessors in that it now uses a variable for the database name. To do this, I had to change the quotation marks from single to double, so that the script would insert the value of $database (*interpolate* the variable).

   As for the query itself, it's quite simple: SHOW TABLES will return a list of tables in the current database.

   continues on next page

4. Execute the query.

```
if (defined($sth)) {
    $sth->execute();
```

If the `prepare()` statement worked, `$sth` has a good value and the query can be executed.

5. Retrieve and print every record.

```
my @row;
while (@row = $sth->fetchrow_array())
{
    print "$row[0]\n";
}
```

The most foolproof method to access every column returned for every row is to use this construct here. It will print out each element, one line at a time. With the `SHOW TABLES` query, each element will be a single table name. You can confirm what results the Perl script receives by running that same query using the `mysql` client (**Figure 8.16**).

6. Finish the query and close the database connection.

```
$sth->finish();
$dbh->disconnect;
```

7. Finish the main conditional.

```
} else {
    print "Please enter a database
    → name when calling this script!
    → \n";
}
```

If the script's user failed to enter a database name, a message will be printed saying so.

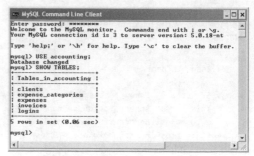

Figure 8.16 Know what results your scripts will receive by running the same query using another interface.

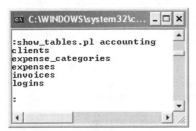

Figure 8.17 The show_tables.pl script will list every table in the database named, such as *accounting* here.

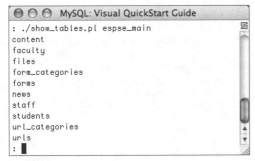

Figure 8.18 As long as the script has permission to access a database, it will list its tables without further modification. (This database is not discussed in this book.)

8. Save the script as show_tables.pl, change the permissions (if necessary), and run the script using the syntax ./show_tables.pl *databasename* or perl show_tables.pl *databasename* (**Figures 8.17** and **8.18**).

Remember that your script will still need the proper permissions to access any database you enter here. With that in mind, you'll have the easiest time if you use the *root* username and password to connect, although that is less secure.

✔ Tips

■ Perl will return the value undef if the column's value is NULL, so it's a good idea to use defined() again to check the value of the column before using it. The defined() function will not catch empty strings, however.

■ The term undef means NULL as well as no result returned.

■ Do not end your SQL queries with a semicolon as you would within the mysql monitor.

■ To see how many records were returned by a query, use code like this:

```
$nr = ($sth->execute());
```

■ If a query returns only a single row with a single value, you can do this:

```
$r = $sth->fetchrow_array();
print $r;
```

Executing Simple Queries

Now that you know how to handle queries that return results, let's go back a step and perform the simpler task of executing simple queries. In this section, I'll show how to execute simple queries using the do() method.

$sth = $dbh->do("*QUERY STATEMENT*");

The do() function is run using the database handler created when connecting to the database (e.g., $dbh). It will normally return the number of rows affected by a query, if applicable.

To demonstrate this function, I'll write a Perl script that will add a new login account to the *accounting* database's logins table. This table was added to this database in Chapter 6, "MySQL Functions," for the purpose of assigning login accounts to clients. It makes use of both the SHA1() and AES_ENCRYPT() functions. See Chapter 6 or the MySQL manual for more on these and their syntax.

To execute simple queries:

1. Create a new Perl script in your text editor with the standard beginning lines of code (**Script 8.4**).
   ```
   #!/usr/bin/perl -w
   use strict;
   use DBI;
   ```

2. Print some introductory text.
   ```
   print "Use this program to add a new
   → login account.\n\n";
   print "Client Name (Client ID):\n";
   ```

3. Establish a connection to the database.
   ```
   my $dbh = DBI->connect("DBI:mysql:
   → accounting:localhost", 'username',
   → 'password', {RaiseError => 1});
   ```
   In this script the database, *accounting*, is hard-coded, not taken from user input.

Script 8.4 This script add_user.pl takes inputted information to add records to the database.

```
1    #!/usr/bin/perl -w
2
3    # Script 8.4 - add_user.pl
4    # This script adds a user to the logins
     table.
5    # It relies upon user input.
6
7    # Use what needs to be used.
8    use strict;
9    use DBI;
10
11   # Print a message.
12   print "Use this program to add a new
     login account.\n\n";
13   print "Client Name (Client ID):\n";
14
15   # Connect to the database.
16   my $dbh = DBI->connect("DBI:mysql:
     accounting:localhost", 'username',
     'password', {RaiseError => 1});
17
18   # Show the current clients with their
     IDs.
19   my $sql = "SELECT client_name, client_id
     FROM clients ORDER BY client_name ASC";
20
21   # Query the database.
22   my $sth = $dbh->prepare($sql);
23
24   if (defined($sth)) {
25       $sth->execute();
26       my @row;
27       while (@row = $sth->fetchrow_array())
         {
28           print "$row[0] ($row[1])\n";
29       }
30   }
31   $sth->finish();
32
33   # Get the information from the user.
34   print "Enter the client ID: ";
35   my $client_id = <STDIN>;
36   print "Enter the login username: ";
37   my $name = <STDIN>;
38   print "Enter the login password: ";
39   my $pass1 = <STDIN>;
40   print "Confirm the login password: ";
41   my $pass2 = <STDIN>;
42
43   # Make sure the passwords match.
```

Script continues on next page

Script 8.4 *continued*

```
44    while ($pass1 ne $pass2) {
45        print "The passwords you entered did
          not match! Try again!\n";
46
47        # Re-request the password.
48        print "Enter the login password: ";
49        $pass1 = <STDIN>;
50        print "Confirm the login password: ";
51        $pass2 = <STDIN>;
52
53    } # End of WHILE loop.
54
55    # Query the database.
56    $sql = "INSERT INTO logins (client_id,
          login_name, login_pass) VALUES ($client_id,
          AES_ENCRYPT('$name', 'w1cKet'),
          SHA1('$pass1'))";
57    my $affected= $dbh->do($sql);
58
59    # Report on the success of the query
          attempt.
60    if ($affected== 1) {
61        print "The login account has been
          added! \n";
62    } else {
63        print "The login account could not be
          added! \n";
64    }
65
66    # Disconnect.
67    $dbh->disconnect;
```

4. List the current clients with their client IDs.

```
my $sql = "SELECT client_name,
→ client_id FROM clients ORDER BY
→ client_name ASC";
my $sth = $dbh->prepare($sql);
if (defined($sth)) {
    $sth->execute();
    my @row;
    while (@row = $sth->
→ fetchrow_array()) {
        print "$row[0] ($row[1])\n";
    }
}
$sth->finish();
```

Because one of the pieces of information needed to create a login account is the client ID, that information needs to be presented to the user. To do so, a simple query is run and the results are printed (**Figure 8.19**). Most of this syntax matches what was taught in the preceding section of this chapter.

continues on next page

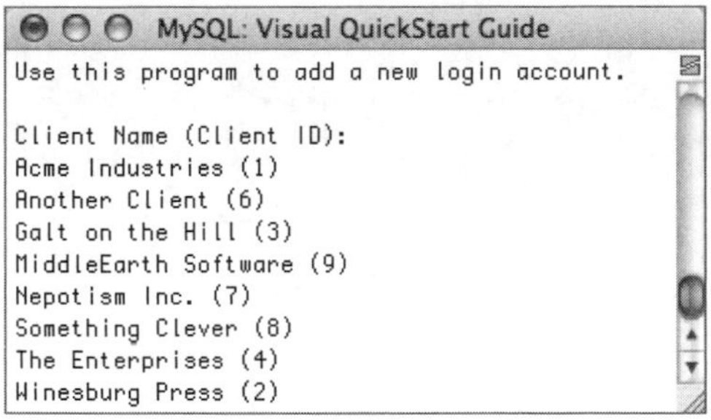

Figure 8.19 The script begins by listing the clients along with their respective ID numbers.

5. Prompt for the client's ID.

```
print "Enter the client ID: ";
my $client_id = <STDIN>;
```

This script will prompt for three things (**Figure 8.20**): the client's ID, the username, and the password. These correspond to the fields in the `clients` table. The value keyed in at this first prompt will be assigned to the `$client_id` variable.

6. Prompt for the username and password.

```
print "Enter the login username: ";
my $name = <STDIN>;

print "Enter the login password: ";
my $pass1 = <STDIN>;

print "Confirm the login password: ";
my $pass2 = <STDIN>;
```

To make sure there are no errors in the inputted password, it will be requested twice and then compared.

7. Confirm that the passwords match.

```
while ($pass1 ne $pass2) {
    print "The passwords you entered
    → did not match! Try again!\n";
    print "Enter the login password: ";
    $pass1 = <STDIN>;
    print "Confirm the login password: ";
    $pass2 = <STDIN>;
}
```

This loop checks to see if the first entered password matches the second, confirmed one. If it does not, it will print an error message and give another chance to re-enter both (**Figure 8.21**). This process will be repeated until the passwords match.

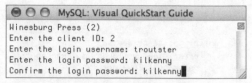

Figure 8.20 When you run the script, you will be prompted three times for information (plus a confirmation of the password), which will then be added to the database to make a new user.

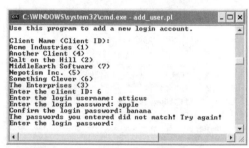

Figure 8.21 If the two passwords entered do not match, you'll be prompted to re-enter these values.

8. Create the INSERT query and send it to the database.

```
$sql = "INSERT INTO logins
→ (client_id, login_name, login_pass)
→ VALUES ($client_id, AES_ENCRYPT|
→ ('$name', 'w1cKet'), SHA1
→ ('$pass1'))";

my $affected= $dbh->do($sql);
```

This query is nearly identical to that from Chapter 6 except that it uses the values submitted by a user rather than hard-coded ones. The final query will be something like

```
INSERT INTO logins (client_id,
→ login_name, login_pass) VALUES (7,
→ AES_ENCRYPT('sophie', 'w1cKet'),
→ SHA1('isabella'))
```

Once the query has been created, it is run through the do() function.

9. Print a message indicating the success of the query.

```
if ($affected== 1) {
    print "The login account has been
    → added! \n";
} else {
    print "The login account could not
    → be added! \n";
}
```

The do() function in Step 8 will return the number of affected rows for queries such as ALTER, UPDATE, and DELETE. The number of affected rows was assigned to the $sth variable, so if it is equal to 1, the query worked.

continues on next page

10. Close the database connection.

$dbh->disconnect;

11. Save the file as add_user.pl, change the permissions (if necessary), and run the script (**Figure 8.22**).

✔ **Tips**

■ To increase the security of this script, you could use regular expressions to check the values entered by the script's user.

■ At the end of the chapter you'll learn how to improve the security and error reporting when executing queries. As it stands, one problem is that apostrophes in the submitted values will break the query (**Figure 8.23**).

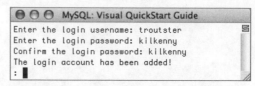

Figure 8.22 A login account has been created by this Perl script.

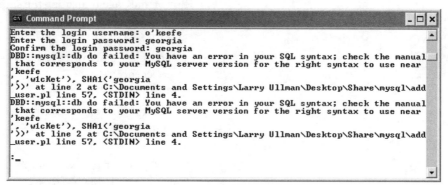

Figure 8.23 This version of the Perl script does not safeguard against apostrophes in the user-submitted data. This could lead to problems and will be remedied in time.

Script 8.5 This script retrieves the last automatically incremented value from the invoices table.

```
1    #!/usr/bin/perl -w
2
3    # Script 8.5 - add_invoice.pl
4    # This script adds an invoice to the
     invoices table.
5    # It relies upon user input.
6
7    # Use what needs to be used.
8    use strict;
9    use DBI;
10
11   # Print a message.
12   print "Use this program to add an
     invoice.\n\n";
13   print "Client Name (Client ID):\n";
14
15   # Connect to the database.
16   my $dbh = DBI->connect("DBI:mysql:
     accounting:localhost", 'username',
     'password', {RaiseError => 1});
17
18   # Show the current clients with their
     IDs.
19   my $sql = "SELECT client_name, client_id
     FROM clients ORDER BY client_name ASC";
20
21   # Query the database.
22   my $sth = $dbh->prepare($sql);
23
24   if (defined($sth)) {
25       $sth->execute();
26       my @row;
27       while (@row = $sth->fetchrow_array())
     {
28           print "$row[0] ($row[1])\n";
29       }
30   }
31   $sth->finish();
32
33   # Get the information from the user.
34   print "Enter the client ID: ";
35   my $client_id = <STDIN>;
36   print "Enter the invoice amount: ";
37   my $amount = <STDIN>;
38   print "Enter the invoice description: ";
39   my $desc = <STDIN>;
40
41   # Query the database.
```

Script continues on next page

Retrieving the Insert ID

In Chapter 6, I cover the LAST_INSERT_ID() function, which is a MySQL-specific tool for retrieving the value inserted into an auto-incremented field. In Chapter 7, "MySQL and PHP," I demonstrate PHP's mysql_insert_id() function, which serves the same purpose. With Perl, you would use a construct like this:

```
$sth = $dbh->do ("INSERT INTO tablename
→ (table_id, column) VALUES (NULL,
→ 'value') ");

$insert_id = $dbh->{'mysql_insertid'}
```

With this in mind, I'll create a new script, similar to add_user.pl, that lets a user create an invoice and reports the new invoice number back to them.

To retrieve an insert ID:

1. Create a new Perl script in your text editor with the standard beginning lines of code (**Script 8.5**).

   ```
   #!/usr/bin/perl -w
   use strict;
   use DBI;
   ```

2. Print some introductory text.

   ```
   print "Use this program to add an
   → invoice.\n\n";
   print "Client Name (Client ID):\n";
   ```

3. Establish a connection to the database.

   ```
   my $dbh = DBI->connect("DBI:mysql:
   → accounting:localhost", 'username',
   → 'password', {RaiseError => 1});
   ```

continues on next page

4. List the current clients with their client IDs.

```perl
my $sql = "SELECT client_name,
→ client_id FROM clients ORDER BY
→ client_name ASC";
my $sth = $dbh->prepare($sql);
if (defined($sth)) {
   $sth->execute();
   my @row;
   while (@row = $sth->
→ fetchrow_array()) {
      print "$row[0] ($row[1])\n";
   }
}
$sth->finish();
```

The code to this point is exactly like that in add_user.pl.

5. Prompt for the client's ID, the invoice amount, and the invoice description.

```perl
print "Enter the client ID: ";
my $client_id = <STDIN>;
print "Enter the invoice amount: ";
my $amount = <STDIN>;
print "Enter the invoice description: ";
my $desc = <STDIN>;
```

This script will prompt for three things (**Figure 8.24**): the client's ID, the invoice amount, and the invoice description. These correspond to the fields in the invoices table. Along with these fields, the table also has an invoice ID, which will be automatically generated, an invoice date, which will be automatically set as the current date (because it's a TIMESTAMP type), and the date_invoice_paid date.

Script 8.5 *continued*

```perl
42    $sql = "INSERT INTO invoices (client_id,
         invoice_amount, invoice_description)
         VALUES ($client_id, $amount, '$desc')";
43    my $affected= $dbh->do($sql);
44
45    # Report on the success of the query
         attempt.
46    if ($affected== 1) {
47        print "Invoice #" . $dbh->
             {'mysql_insertid'} . " has been
             created.\n";
48    } else {
49        print "The invoice could not be
             created! \n";
50    }
51
52    # Disconnect.
53    $dbh->disconnect;
```

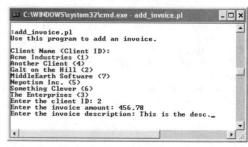

Figure 8.24 The script requests three pieces of information from the user.

RETRIEVING THE INSERT ID

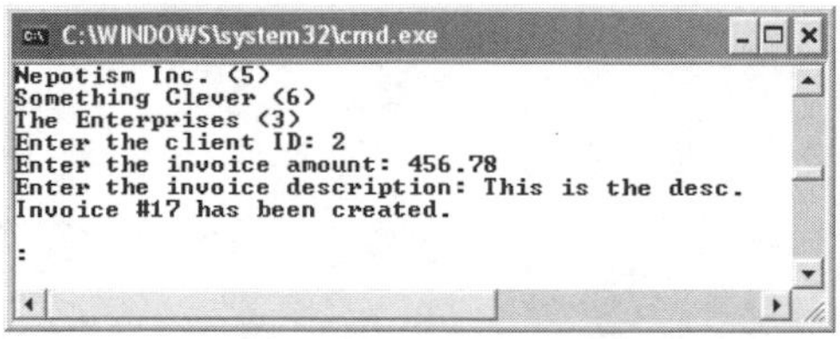

Figure 8.25 The invoice number is revealed to the user.

6. Create the INSERT query and send it to the database.

```
$sql = "INSERT INTO invoices
→ (client_id, invoice_amount,
→ invoice_description) VALUES
→ ($client_id, $amount, '$desc')";
my $affected= $dbh->do($sql);
```

Nothing new here. You could do some validation on the submitted data before using it in a query, though.

7. Print a message indicating the success of the query.

```
if ($affected== 1) {
    print "Invoice #" . $dbh->
    → {'mysql_insertid'} . " has been
    → created.\n";
} else {
    print "The invoice could not be
    → created! \n";
}
```

Now, if the invoice is created in the database, the invoice ID is returned by calling $dbh->{'mysql_insertid'}.

8. Close the database connection.

```
$dbh->disconnect;
```

9. Save the file as add_invoice.pl, change the permissions (if necessary), and run the script (**Figure 8.25**).

✔ Tips

- Another option for obtaining the last MySQL insert ID is to use the format $query->{'insertid'}. Or you could run a SELECT LAST_INSERT_ID() query and fetch the results.

- You may want to add code that chops the extra spaces off of the user-submitted invoice description. Otherwise, the newline character that's appended to the end of each string will also be stored in the database.

Error Handling

To this point I've only used a minimum of error handling. Specifically, I've turned on *RaiseError* when connecting to MySQL. By doing so, if a connection error occurs, the die() function will be invoked, printing an error message and stopping the script. You may have already witnessed this. An alternative is to use *PrintError*. It prints any error messages but does not stop the script. To use *PrintError*, code

```
my $dbh = DBI->connect('DBI:mysql:
→ accounting:localhost', 'username',
→ 'password', {PrintError => 1});
```

To take error management even further, you can use the err() function. It returns a true/false value indicating if an error occurred. To reference the specific error, use the errstr() function.

```
my $dbh = DBI->connect('DBI:mysql:
→ accounting:localhost', 'username',
→ 'password');
if (DBI->err()) {
    print "Could not connect. MySQL said:
    → " . DBI->errstr();
}
```

If you encounter an error after preparing, executing, or doing a query, you would then refer to the statement handler:

```
if ($sth->err()) {
    print "Error running the query. MySQL
    → said: " . $sth ->errstr();
}
```

Practice is better than theory, so I'll create a new show_tables.pl script that implements error management.

Script 8.6 This modified version of show_tables.pl takes error handling to a detailed level.

```
1    #!/usr/bin/perl -w
2
3    # Script 8.6, 'show_tables2.pl'
4    # This script takes a database name as
5    # a command line argument and shows
6    # the tables in that database.
7
8    # Use what needs to be used.
9    use strict;
10   use DBI;
11
12   # This script takes one argument when
     invoked.
13   # The argument is a database name.
14   my $database = $ARGV[0];
15
16   if (defined($database)) {
17
18       # Connect to the database.
19       my $dbh = DBI->connect("DBI:mysql:
         $database:localhost", 'username',
         'password', {PrintError => 0,
         RaiseError => 0});
20
21       # Check for errors.
22       if (DBI->err()) {
23           print "Could not connect to the
             database! MySQL reported: " .
             DBI->errstr() . "\n";
24           exit(1);
25       }
26
```

Script continues on next page

To handle errors:

1. Create a new Perl script (**Script 8.6**).

   ```
   #!/usr/bin/perl -w
   use strict;
   use DBI;
   ```

2. Determine which database to use and check that one was entered.

   ```
   my $database = $ARGV[0];
   if (defined($database)) {
   ```

   This code is exactly as it is in the original version of the script.

3. Connect to MySQL.

   ```
   my $dbh = DBI->connect("DBI:mysql:
   → $database:localhost", 'username',
   → 'password', {PrintError => 0,
   → RaiseError => 0});
   ```

   Since I'll be handling errors more specifically within the script, I'm turning off both *PrintError* and *RaiseError*.

4. Check for, and report on, any errors.

   ```
   if (DBI->err()) {
       print "Could not connect to the
       → database! MySQL reported: " .
       → DBI->errstr() . "\n";
       exit(1);
   }
   ```

   The conditional first checks for the presence of an error. If one exists, then a message is printed, including the actual error (**Figure 8.26**). Finally the script is terminated using exit().

continues on next page

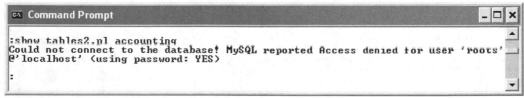

Figure 8.26 How connection errors are now handled by the script.

ERROR HANDLING

5. Prepare and execute the query.

```
my $sth = $dbh->prepare('SHOW
→ TABLES');
if (defined($sth)) {
    $sth->execute();
```

This code is also unchanged from the other version of the script.

6. Check for errors, and then retrieve and print every record.

```
if ($sth->err()) {
    print "Could not execute the
    → query! MySQL reported: " . $sth-
    → >errstr() . "\n";
} else {
    my @row;
    while (@row = $sth->
    → fetchrow_array()) {
        print "$row[0]\n";
    }
    $sth->finish();
}
```

If there was an execution problem, `$sth->err()` will be true and that error needs to be reported (**Figure 8.27**). Otherwise, the data is fetched and printed like before.

Script 8.6 *continued*

```
○ ○ ○                        Script
27    # Query the database.
28    my $sth = $dbh->prepare('SHOW
      TABLES');
29
30    if (defined($sth)) {
31        $sth->execute();
32
33        # Check for errors.
34        if ($sth->err()) {
35            print "Could not execute the
              query! MySQL reported: " .
              $sth->errstr() . "\n";
36        } else {
37            my @row;
38            while (@row = $sth->
              fetchrow_array()) {
39                print "$row[0]\n";
40            }
41            $sth->finish();
42        }
43    } else {
44        print "Could not prepare the
          query! MySQL reported: " .
          $dbh->errstr() . "\n";
45    }
46
47    # Disconnect.
48    $dbh->disconnect;
49
50 } else {
51    print "Please enter a database name
      when calling this script! \n";
52 }
```

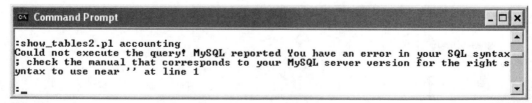

Figure 8.27 Query errors are also handled specifically by the script.

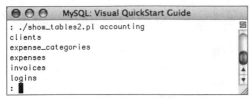

Figure 8.28 If there aren't any problems, you'll see no errors.

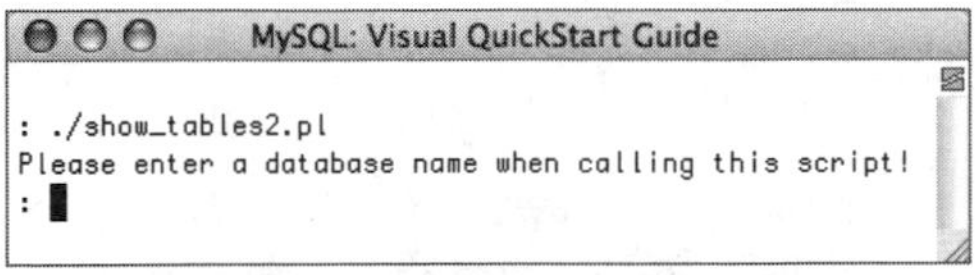

```
: ./show_tables2.pl
Please enter a database name when calling this script!
: 
```

Figure 8.29 Don't forget to reference a specific database when running this script!

7. Complete the `defined($sth)` conditional.

```
} else {
    print "Could not prepare the
→ query! MySQL reported: " . $dbh-
→ >errstr() . "\n";
}
```

If the conditional is false, an error likely occurred and that should also be printed.

8. Close the database connection and finish the main conditional.

```
$dbh->disconnect;
} else {
    print "Please enter a database
→ name when calling this script!
→ \n";
}
```

9. Save the script as `show_tables2.pl`, change the permissions (if necessary), and run the script using the syntax `./show_tables.pl` *databasename* or `perl show_tables.pl` *databasename* (**Figures 8.28** and **8.29**).

✔ Tip

- Another very useful debugging technique, besides printing the MySQL error, is to print out the actual query that was run. This is even more true with dynamically generated queries. It's important that you confirm exactly what query is being run.

ERROR HANDLING

Security Considerations

To this point in the chapter I have not delved too much into the security implications when it comes to using Perl to interact with MySQL. Security considerations are important but also diverse, so I'll highlight a few of the most important techniques here.

First up, the most important step to take is to validate the user input in some way, especially if that input will be used in a query. You can check for specific values when appropriate, use regular expressions to compare input to patterns, and so on. For numeric values, you can also cast them for protection.

After validation, with strings in particular it's a good idea to prevent errors that might occur if apostrophes or other problematic characters appear in user-submitted data. The quote() method will accomplish this nicely:

```perl
my $string = "Apostrophes aren't good.";
my $safe_string = $dbh->quote($string);
```

I'll implement some security techniques by rewriting the add_invoice.pl script.

To improve Perl script security:

1. Open add_invoice.pl (Script 8.5) in your text editor.

2. Replace the way the client's ID is read with this code (**Script 8.7**):

```perl
my $client_id = 0;
while ($client_id <= 0) {
    print "Enter the client ID: ";
    $client_id = <STDIN>;
}
```

continues on next page

Script 8.7 I've added some validation routines and applied quote() to the description string to improve the security of this script.

```perl
1   #!/usr/bin/perl -w
2
3   # Script 8.7 - add_invoice2.pl
4   # This script adds an invoice to the
    invoices table.
5   # It relies upon user input.
6
7   # Use what needs to be used.
8   use strict;
9   use DBI;
10
11  # Print a message.
12  print "Use this program to add an
    invoice.\n\n";
13  print "Client Name (Client ID):\n";
14
15  # Connect to the database.
16  my $dbh = DBI->connect("DBI:mysql:
    accounting:localhost", 'username',
    'password', {RaiseError => 1});
17
18  # Show the current clients with their
    IDs.
19  my $sql = "SELECT client_name, client_id
    FROM clients ORDER BY client_name ASC";
20
21  # Query the database.
22  my $sth = $dbh->prepare($sql);
23
24  if (defined($sth)) {
25
26      $sth->execute();
27      my @row;
28      while (@row = $sth->fetchrow_array())
    {
29          print "$row[0] ($row[1])\n";
30      }
31      $sth->finish();
32
33  } else { # Print the error.
34      print "Error! MySQL said: " . $sth-
    >errstr() . "\n";
35  }
36
37  # Get the information from the user.
38  my $client_id = 0;
39  while ($client_id <= 0) {
40      print "Enter the client ID: ";
41      $client_id = <STDIN>;
42  }
```

Script continues on next page

Script 8.7 *continued*

```
43
44   my $amount = 0;
45   while ($amount <= 0) {
46       print "Enter the invoice amount: ";
47       $amount = <STDIN>;
48   }
49
50   print "Enter the invoice description: ";
51   my $desc = <STDIN>;
52
53   # Watch for quotes.
54   $desc = $dbh->quote($desc);
55
56   # Query the database.
57   $sql = "INSERT INTO invoices (client_id,
         invoice_amount, invoice_description)
         VALUES ($client_id, $amount, $desc)";
58   my $affected = $dbh->do($sql);
59
60   # Report on the success of the query
         attempt.
61   if ($affected == 1) {
62       print "Invoice #" . $dbh->
         {'mysql_insertid'} . " has been
         created.\n";
63   } else {
64       print "The invoice could not be
         created! \n";
65       print "Error! MySQL said: " .
         $sth->errstr() . "\n";
66   }
67
68   # Disconnect.
69   $dbh->disconnect;
```

This is a simple technique. First it initializes `$client_id` with an invalid value of 0. Then it checks to see if `$client_id` has an invalid value. If so, the user will be prompted. The loop will check the user input to see if it's invalid, in which case the user will be reprompted (**Figure 8.30**). This continues until a client ID with a value greater than 0 is entered.

3. Replace the way the invoice amount is read with this code:

   ```
   my $amount = 0;
   while ($amount <= 0) {
       print "Enter the invoice amount: ";
       $amount = <STDIN>;
   }
   ```

   This is just a repeat of the system used to validate the client ID.

4. After reading in the description, add this line:

   ```
   $desc = $dbh->quote($desc);
   ```

   The quote() method does two things: first it escapes apostrophes within the string itself. It also wraps the string within its own single quotes, meaning that single quotes are not necessary for this input in the query.

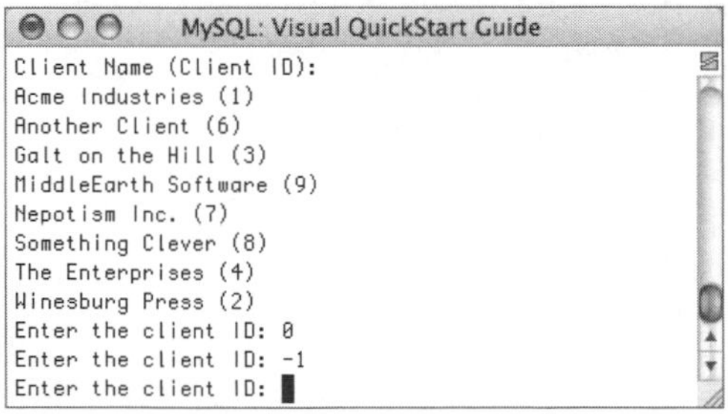

Figure 8.30 The script now waits until a client ID greater than 0 is entered.

5. Change the query to read:

```
$sql = "INSERT INTO invoices
→ (client_id, invoice_amount,
→ invoice_description) VALUES
→ ($client_id, $amount, $desc)";
```

The only difference is that $desc is no longer within quotes because wrapping single quotation marks have been added by $dbh->quote().

6. Save the script as add_invoice2.pl, change the permissions (if necessary), and run the script (**Figures 8.31** and **8.32**).

Make sure that you use some apostrophes and erroneous input to really test the script.

✔ Tips

- With the -w flag, this Perl script will complain if a user enters a string or character for the client ID or invoice amount. More important, though, the script will not attempt to run a query using those values.

- If you wanted to be really sophisticated, you could confirm that the client ID entered by the user is actually a valid client ID (by querying the database).

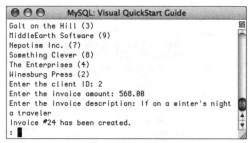

Figure 8.31 Invalid input and apostrophes are no longer a problem for this script.

Figure 8.32 If the user enters valid information, they are only prompted once for each piece.

Using Prepared Statements

The last topic I'll discuss with respect to Perl is the *prepared statement*. Prepared statements offer many benefits. First, they are often a faster method of running queries, particularly in applications where the same query is run multiple times, using different values for each. The second benefit is that you do not need to worry about escaping problematic characters like apostrophes. They'll automatically be handled by the process. A minor plus as well is that they separate the query from the data used in the query, which can make for more readable code.

To start, you prepare a query as you already have been, but you use question marks to act as placeholders where the actual data will later go:

```
my $sth = $dbh->prepare("INSERT INTO
→ tablename (col1, col2) VALUES (?, ?)");
```

The question mark represents the data that will be added to the query. Note that no quotation marks go around a placeholder, even if it may represent string data (which otherwise has to be quoted in queries). Once you've prepared the query, you can then associate data with that placeholder when you execute the query:

```
$sth->execute("some value", 235);
```

This has the effect of replacing the first placeholder in the query with the text *some value*. The second placeholder will be replaced with 235. The result will be the execution of the query

```
INSERT INTO tablename (col1, col2)
→ VALUES ('some value', 235)
```

If you want to run the query again using new values, just repeat the execute() line. You only need to prepare the statement once.

To demonstrate this, I'll write a script that lets a user enter multiple expense categories. This will mostly be an adaptation of the early script that let a user enter a single expense category.

To use prepared statements:

1. Create a new Perl script (**Script 8.8**).

   ```
   #!/usr/bin/perl -w
   use strict;
   use DBI;
   ```

Script 8.8 Prepared statements provide a faster and more secure way to run similar queries multiple times.

```
1   #!/usr/bin/perl -w
2
3   # Script 8.8 - add_categories.pl
4   # This script adds categories to the expense_categories table.
5   # It relies upon user input.
6
7   # Use what needs to be used.
8   use strict;
9   use DBI;
10
11  # Print a message.
12  print "Use this program to add expense categories.\n\n";
13
14  # Connect to the database.
15  my $dbh = DBI->connect("DBI:mysql:accounting:localhost", 'username', 'password',
    {RaiseError => 1});
16
17  # Prepare the query.
18  my $sth = $dbh->prepare("INSERT INTO expense_categories (expense_category) VALUES (?)");
19
20  if (defined($sth)) {
21
22      # Get the first category.
23      print "Enter an expense category or enter 'q' to quit: ";
24      chop (my $cat = <STDIN>);
25
26      while ($cat ne "q") {
27
28          # Execute the query.
29          $sth->execute($cat);
30          if ($sth->err()) {
```

Script continues on next page

2. Print an introductory message and connect to the database.

```
print "Use this program to add
→ expense categories.\n\n";

my $dbh = DBI->connect
→ ("DBI:mysql:accounting:localhost",
→ 'username', 'password', {RaiseError
→ => 1});
```

This code is exactly as it is in the original version of the script.

3. Prepare the query.

```
my $sth = $dbh->prepare("INSERT INTO
→ expense_categories
→ (expense_category) VALUES (?)");
```

This is the first step in the prepared query process. The query is defined, using one placeholder for the actual expense_category value.

continues on next page

Script 8.8 *continued*

```
31              print "The expense category could not be added.\n\n";
32              # Print MySQL error, if desired.
33              # exit() ?
34          } else {
35              print "The expense category has been added.\n\n";
36          }
37
38          # Reprompt.
39          print "Enter an expense category or enter 'q' to quit: ";
40          chop ($cat = <STDIN>);
41
42      }
43
44  }
45
46  # Disconnect.
47  $dbh->disconnect;
```

4. Get the category from the user.

```
if (defined($sth)) {
    print "Enter an expense category
    → or enter 'q' to quit: ";
    chop (my $cat = <STDIN>);
```

The user is prompted to enter an expense category. They are also given a way to terminate the script, when the time is right (**Figure 8.33**). This is more important later in the script, when a loop is used to continually take the user input.

I'm also chopping off the extraneous spaces so that they aren't added to the database (and so that my `while` loop condition will work).

5. Check that a category has been entered and execute the query.

```
while ($cat ne "q") {
    $sth->execute($cat);
```

Because the user has been provided with an "out" (entering the letter *q* to quit), the loop has to check for that. If `$cat` does not equal *q*, then the query will be executed using the submitted value.

6. Check for errors, then reprompt.

```
if ($sth->err()) {
    print "The expense category could
    → not be added.\n\n";
} else {
    print "The expense category has
    → been added.\n\n";
}
print "Enter an expense category or
→ enter 'q' to quit: ";
chop ($cat = <STDIN>);
```

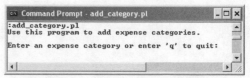

Figure 8.33 The initial prompt with instructions for quitting.

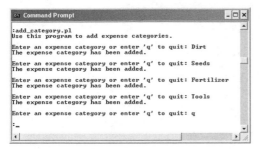

Figure 8.34 The user can enter multiple categories and quit the application when they are done.

If there was an execution problem, `$sth->err()` will be true. Otherwise, it's safe to assume that the query worked. The user is reprompted and the next category is read in. After this, the loop will check the condition again. This whole process will be repeated until the user enters just *q*.

For debugging purposes, you may also want to print the MySQL error message, should one exist, and maybe terminate the script using `exit()`.

7. Complete the `defined($sth)` conditional and disconnect from the database.

```
}
$dbh->disconnect;
```

8. Save the script as `add_category.pl`, change the permissions (if necessary), and run the script (**Figure 8.34**).

✔ Tips

- Prepared statements can be used with any type of query, not just `INSERTs`. The greatest performance benefit comes from queries that are run multiple times with only modifications in the data used.

- The process demonstrated here is also referred to as *bound variables*. Specifically, this is binding input variables. You can also bound output variables (assigning the values returned by a `SELECT` query to Perl variables).

- To assign the value `NULL` to a placeholder, use `undef` (without quotes).

- Do not use `quote()` with your prepared statement values or else your strings will be over-quoted.

MySQL and Java

Over the past several years, Java has emerged as a very popular programming language, thanks largely to its platform independence. You can use Java to create applets that run on Web pages, to write JavaServer Pages (JSPs), or to develop stand-alone applications.

Because Java always uses JDBC (Java Database Connectivity) to connect to a database, if you write your code properly and adhere to SQL standards, your Java applications can be easily ported from platform to platform and database application to database application. When it comes to using Java with MySQL, there is MySQL's own special JDBC interface, called *MySQL Connector/J*.

Like the preceding two chapters, this one will not actually teach Java, though I will explain some basic Java stuff as the scripts are created. Beginning users should be able to write simple Java applications from these instructions. For the most part, the focus will be on using JDBC and the MySQL Connector/J to interact with a MySQL database.

Installing Java Support for MySQL

To be able to access a MySQL database from a Java application, you will need two things (aside from MySQL itself):

◆ Java Development Kit (JDK) version 1.4 or higher (which includes JDBC)

◆ MySQL Connector/J

Installing Java itself is beyond the scope of this book but fortunately not a daunting task for the average user. Most developers will be satisfied with using the Java 2 Platform, Standard Edition (J2SE), which can be downloaded from http://java.sun.com. Mac OS X users benefit from Apple's tight integration of Java into the operating system (Mac OS X version 10.4 comes with version 1.4.2 of J2SE), whereas Windows has intermittently supported the technology over its evolution (you may have a version of the JDK already installed).

In this section, I will demonstrate how to make the MySQL Connector/J driver usable with your already-installed Java. As the most common source of difficulty involves your Java CLASSPATH (see the sidebar), these instructions will attempt to squash those problems in advance.

Java and the CLASSPATH

Simply put, the CLASSPATH is a list of directories where Java will search when compiling or running applications. If, like the scripts in this chapter, your Java application references an external class, then Java has to be able to find that class. So it'll look within the CLASSPATH directories for it. If Java finds the referenced class in one of those directories, great. If it doesn't, that's a problem, and a common one at that.

When using a third-party class like MySQL Connector/J, you have two options: install it within the CLASSPATH or modify the CLASSPATH to include the location of MySQL Connector/J. The first method is the most foolproof, which is what I describe in the accompanying instructions. As for the second method, this is something you can do:

◆ Permanently

◆ For the current session only

◆ When you compile a Java application

◆ When you run a Java application

How you adjust the CLASSPATH depends upon which of these cases you prefer and the operating system being used. If you'd rather add MySQL Connector/J to your CLASSPATH (instead of the easy installation method I describe), search the Web for instructions particular to your operating system.

To install the MySQL Connector/J:

1. Make sure you've installed the JDK.

This is available from Sun, although it may already be installed on your operating system. You can test if Java is installed, as well as see the version installed, by running `java -version` (**Figure 9.1**) at the command line.

2. Find Java's `lib/ext` directory.

This is the most important step but, unfortunately, one for which I cannot offer universally specific instructions. It depends upon your operating system, your version of the JDK, and how it was installed. What you'll ultimately need to find is a folder called `ext`, which itself is located within a folder called `lib`, which is located within the Java installation folder. Use your operating system's find or search feature to hunt for it. On my Windows XP installation, this was `C:\Sun\AppServer\jdk\jre\lib\ext`. I also had a `C:\Program Files\Java\jre1.5.0_06\lib\ext` directory, so I placed a copy of MySQL Connector/J there as well. On my Mac OS X installation, this was `/System/Library/Frameworks/JavaVM.framework/Versions/1.4.2/Home/lib/ext`. On Unix and Linux, this may be `/usr/lib/jvm/<version>/lib/ext`.

continues on next page

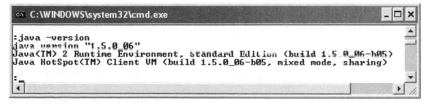

Figure 9.1 Confirm that Java is installed by having it report on its currently installed version.

3. Download the current version of the MySQL Connector/J from www.mysql.com.

On MySQL's downloads page, you'll find links to this product under the *Drivers and Connectors* heading. You'll want to download the latest Generally Available (GA) release, marked as *recommended*. At the time of this writing, that was version 3.1, with version 5 in development.

4. Expand the downloaded file.

The file is available in either a .tar.gz or .zip format. Once you've expanded the downloaded file, you will have a folder containing many things, including the actual driver, which is a .jar file called something like *mysql-connector-java-X.X.X-bin.jar*.

5. Move the driver to its new location.

Use Windows Explorer, the Finder, or whatever, to move the driver file (from Step 4) to the directory identified in Step 2.

✔ Tips

■ For a deployed Web application, place the JDBC driver (the .jar file) in the WEB-INF/lib directory.

■ Be careful with all of your commands, class names, and filenames, as Java is case-sensitive.

Connecting to the Database

Before I demonstrate how to use JDBC in more detail, it's best to confirm that you can successfully connect to the database. This implies that Java can access the JDBC driver and that you're using the right connection information for MySQL. Frequently this can be the most taxing step in the whole process. It starts with stating that you want to use the SQL classes:

```
import java.sql.*;
```

Then, you specify which `java.sql.Driver` class to use. In this case, it will be the MySQL Connector/J:

```
Class.forName("com.mysql.jdbc.Driver");
```

On some systems that code can be problematic. A more foolproof version is:

```
Class.forName("com.mysql.jdbc.Driver").
→ newInstance();
```

Next, you can establish a connection to the database using the DriverManager:

```
Connection con = DriverManager.
→ getConnection(url, "username",
→ "password");
```

The `url` value is a string that indicates the database, hostname, and more, in the format *jdbc:protocol:dsn*, where *protocol* (in this case) would be `mysql`, and *dsn* would include the hostname, the port, and the database name, like so (the square brackets indicate optional parameters):

```
jdbc:mysql://[hostname][:port]/
→ databasename
```

As an example, to connect to the *test* database, without specifying a host, your url would be

jdbc:mysql:///test

To specify the host and the port, use

jdbc:mysql://localhost:3306/test

At the end of the script, after all of the MySQL interaction has been completed, you should close the database connection and free up its resources using the connection's close() method:

con.close();

To connect to MySQL:

1. Create a new Java class in your text editor or Java development tool (**Script 9.1**).

   As long as you have Java installed, you can write the scripts in nearly any text editor. If you have a particular program for coding, compiling, and running Java, so much the better.

Script 9.1 This simple Java class establishes a connection to a MySQL database.

```
1    import java.sql.*;
2
3    // Script 9.1 'Connect.java'
4
5    public class Connect {
6
7        public static void main(String argv[]) throws Exception {
8
9            // Initialize variables.
10           Connection con = null;
11
12           try {
13
14               // Set the connection URL.
15               String url = "jdbc:mysql:///test";
16
17               Class.forName("com.mysql.jdbc.Driver").newInstance();
18
19               // Connect.
20               con = DriverManager.getConnection(url);
21
```

Script continues on next page

2. Use the `sql` classes and define the class.

```
import java.sql.*;
public class Connect {
    public static void main(String
    → argv[]) throws Exception {
```

The first application I will write will be called **Connect** and have just one main block of code to be executed. I'll use this basic format throughout the chapter.

3. Initialize the connection variable.

```
Connection con = null;
```

The con variable will be of type `java.sql.Connection`, as defined by the `java.sql.*` classes. Here I'm setting its initial value to `null`.

continues on next page

Script 9.1 *continued*

```
22              // Report on the results.
23              if (con != null) {
24                  System.out.println("A database connection has been established!");
25              }
26
27         } catch (Exception e) {
28
29              System.out.println("Problem: " + e.toString());
30
31         }
32
33         // Clean up.
34         finally {
35
36              if (con != null) {
37
38                  try {
39                      con.close();
40                  } catch (Exception e) {
41                      System.out.println(e.toString());
42                  }
43                  con = null;
44              }
45         }
46
47     } // End of main().
48
49 } // End of class Connect.
```

4. Establish a connection to the *test* database.

```
try {
    String url = "jdbc:mysql:///test";
    Class.forName("com.mysql.
    → jdbc.Driver").newInstance();
    con = DriverManager.
    → getConnection(url);
```

The second line of this group defines the JDBC `url` variable (the address for connecting to the database). The third line dictates which driver should be loaded, and the final line attempts to make a connection, assigning the connection to the previously established con variable.

In this example I am not using a specific hostname, username, or password. This is fine as long as the permissions on your MySQL database allow for an unnamed user without a password from any host to connect to the *test* database. If the permissions would not allow for this, the Java application will fail here (**Figure 9.2**) and you should change the settings accordingly. As with any time you interact with MySQL, using the proper username, password, and host is critical to the success of your Java applications.

5. Print a message if the connection was made.

```
if (con != null) {
    System.out.println("A database
    → connection has been
    → established!");
}
```

To a degree, this code is not really necessary, because a failure to connect to the database will throw an error. On the other hand, should the connection be made, I'd like to indicate its success somehow.

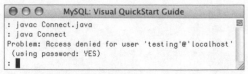

Figure 9.2 Any MySQL connection issues are reported just as they would be when trying to access a database using the mysql client.

6. Complete the try clause.

```
} catch (Exception e) {
    System.out.println("Problem: " +
    → e.toString());
}
```

Any exceptions caused by the try code will be caught here. For simplicity's sake, the exception message is just printed. The most common problem would be a failure to find the driver (**Figure 9.3**).

7. Perform any cleanup.

```
finally {
    if (con != null) {
        try {
            con.close();
        } catch (Exception e) {

            System.out.println(e.toString());
        }
    }
    con = null;
}
```

From the perspective of MySQL, the only relevant line here is `try { con.close(); }`, which closes an open database connection. If, for some reason, it cannot close the connection, the error message will be reported.

continues on next page

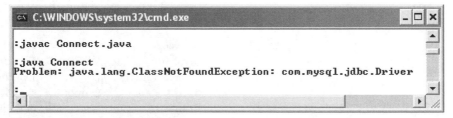

Figure 9.3 If Java cannot find the MySQL Connector/J driver, you'll see an error message like this. See the installation instructions and the sidebar for troubleshooting information.

CONNECTING TO THE DATABASE

8. Complete the class.

```
    } // End of main().
} // End of class Connect.
```

I've added comments to help avoid confusion with all of the closing curly braces at the end of the script.

9. Save the file as `Connect.java`.

Per Java's syntax, you will need to make sure you name the file using the same spelling and capitalization as the name of the class.

10. Compile `Connect.java`.

There are two primary options for doing this:

▲ Type `javac /path/to/Connect.java` at a command prompt (or just move into the same directory as `Connect.java` and use `javac Connect.java`).

or

▲ Use your Java IDE to compile the class.

If you don't know how to compile a Java application, refer to any of the available tutorials online.

Troubleshooting

Java can be more than a little difficult, particularly as you first try to get everything running. If, when compiling your first Java application, the computer complains that it doesn't recognize `javac`, you should first check that it is installed. You can do a simple search for it or make sure you installed a Java Development Kit (JDK). If you can find it on your computer, then it's probably not in your system `PATH`: the realm of places your computer looks for applications. There are tutorials online for altering your `PATH`; see one pertaining to your operating system.

If `javac` and `java` work but you see any errors involving *java.lang.NoClassDefFoundError* or the *com.mysql.jdbc.Driver*, this is most likely because Java cannot find the MySQL Connector/J. This is a `CLASSPATH` issue, discussed in the first section of this chapter.

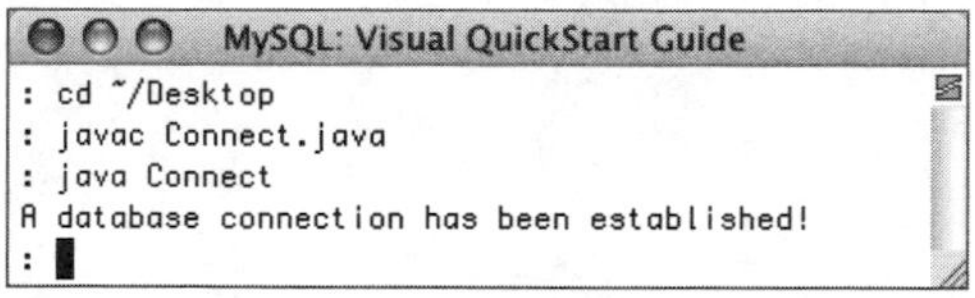

Figure 9.4 Successfully running the application creates this message.

11. Run Connect (**Figure 9.4**).

Again, two choices:

▲ Type `java Connect` at a command prompt from within the same directory as the `Connect.java` file.

or

▲ Use your Java development application to run the class.

If you have not already added the MySQL Connector/J driver to the default `CLASSPATH` or stored the driver in the existing `CLASSPATH`, you'll need to tell Java the driver's location when you run the file. To do so, at the command prompt you would instead type

```
java -classpath /path/to/
→ mysql-connector-java-X.X.X-bin.
→ jar Connect
```

✔ Tips

■ Sometimes if you specify `localhost` as the host, Java will replace this value with the IP address of the host (e.g., *192.169.1.1* or *127.0.0.1*), which may interfere with the permissions as established in the MySQL database. If you have a problem connecting and are definitely using the right username and password combination, set the host value explicitly in your Java code.

■ You can add extra parameters to your url string by using this format:

```
jdbc:mysql:///test?name=value&name2=
→ value2
```

For example, an alternative way to establish a connection is to put the username and password in the url:

```
jdbc:mysql:///test?user=
→ Marc&password=Javaman
```

Executing Simple Queries

Once you've been able to successfully connect to the database, you start interacting with it. For beginners, the easiest first thing to do is to execute a simple query—one that alters a database without returning any results. Queries that begin with INSERT, ALTER, CREATE, DELETE, or UPDATE fall into this category.

Running a simple query is a two-step process. First you create a statement variable that will be used to run the query, and then you execute a query using the statement variable. Commonly your code might look like this:

```
Statement stmt;
stmt = con.createStatement();
stmt.executeUpdate("DELETE FROM
→ tablename WHERE column='value'");
stmt.close();
```

The createStatement() method creates an open channel through which queries can be run. The executeUpdate() method actually runs the query on the database, and then the close() method will free up the resources assigned to the open connection. Note that executeUpdate() is not used for just UPDATE queries. It's used for any query that doesn't return results (other than a numeric value indicating rows affected or the like). This function also returns the number of affected rows, which can be used to verify the results.

As a basic example of this, I'll write an application that takes command-line arguments for populating the clients table in the *accounting* database.

To execute a simple query:

1. Create a new Java application in your text editor or Java development tool (**Script 9.2**).

```
import java.sql.*;
public class Insert {
    public static void main(String
    → args[]) throws Exception {
```

The beginning part of this script differs from Script 9.1 only in the name of the class, changing *Connect* to *Insert*.

continues on next page

Script 9.2 The Insert Java class takes five command-line arguments and adds them as the client's name and address in the clients table.

```
1    import java.sql.*;
2
3    // Script 9.2 'Insert.java'
4
5    public class Insert {
6
7        public static void main(String args[]) throws Exception {
8
9            // Initialize variables.
10           Connection con = null;
11           Statement stmt = null;
12           int affected = 0;
13
14           try {
15
16               // Connect to MySQL.
17               String url = "jdbc:mysql:///accounting";
18               Class.forName("com.mysql.jdbc.Driver").newInstance();
19               con = DriverManager.getConnection(url, "username", "password");
20
21               // Run the query.
22               stmt = con.createStatement();
23               affected = stmt.executeUpdate("INSERT INTO clients (client_name, client_street,
                 client_city, client_state, client_zip) VALUES ('" + args[0] + "', '" + args[1] + "',
                 '" + args[2] + "', '" + args[3] + "', '" + args[4] + "')");
24
25               // Print a message.
26               if (affected == 1) {
27                   System.out.println("The client was added to the database!");
28               } else {
29                   System.out.println("The client could not be added to the database!");
30               }
```

Script continues on next page

2. Initialize the variables.

```
Connection con = null;
Statement stmt = null;
int affected = 0;
```

Along with a connection variable, simple queries will require a variable of type Statement. I'm also declaring an integer, which will be used to reflect the number of affected rows.

3. Establish a connection to the *accounting* database.

```
try {
    String url = "jdbc:mysql:///
    → accounting";
    Class.forName("com.mysql.jdbc.
    → Driver").newInstance();
    con = DriverManager.getConnection
    → (url, "username", "password");
```

Script 9.2 *continued*

```
31              }
32
33          // Catch exceptions.
34          catch (SQLException e) {
35              System.out.println("Problem: " + e.toString());
36          }
37
38          // Clean up.
39          finally {
40              if (stmt != null) {
41                  try {
42                      stmt.close();
43                  } catch (Exception e) {
44                      System.out.println(e.toString());
45                  }
46                  stmt = null;
47              }
48              if (con != null) {
49                  try {
50                      con.close();
51                  } catch (Exception e) {
52                      System.out.println(e.toString());
53                  }
54                  con = null;
55              }
```

Script continues on next page

Script 9.2 *continued*

```
56              }
57
58          } // End of main().
59
60      } // End of class Insert.
```

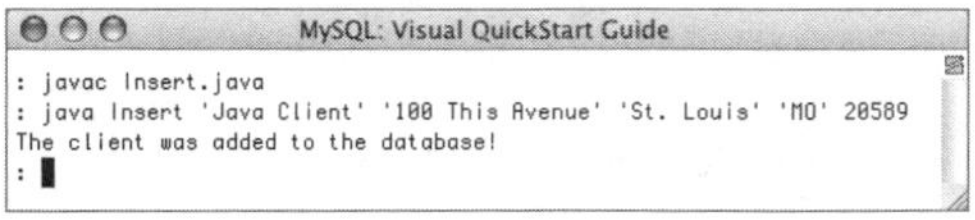

Figure 9.5 I can use Java to add records to a database by typing new values on the command line as I run the application.

There are three very significant changes you'll need to make in this script compared with the previous one: the database name (from *test* to *accounting*), the username, and the password. Be certain to use a user/hostname/password combination that has permission to connect to and modify the *accounting* database.

Remember that if you need to use the hostname (because *localhost* won't work), that value gets placed between `mysql://` and the database name.

4. Execute an INSERT query.

```
stmt = con.createStatement();

affected = stmt.executeUpdate
→ ("INSERT INTO clients (client_name,
→ client_street, client_city,
→ client_state, client_zip) VALUES
→ ('" + args[0] + "', '" + args[1] +
→ "', '" + args[2] + "', '" + args[3]
→ + "', '" + args[4] + "')");
```

The first step is to establish the `stmt` variable based upon the `createStatement()` method of the con connection variable. Then the query is fed as an argument to the `executeUpdate()` method. In this example, I'll be adding a client's name along with their address. These values will be retrieved as command-line arguments typed when the application is run (**Figure 9.5**). To access their values, I refer to `args[0]` through `args[4]`, which is established in the initial class line. The resulting query will be something like

```
INSERT INTO clients (client_name,
→ client_street, client_city,
→ client_state, client_zip) VALUES
→ ('Name', 'Street', 'City',
→ 'State', 12345)
```

continues on next page

EXECUTING SIMPLE QUERIES

Note that I haven't done any data validation or checking here, which you'll likely want to do using standard Java methods. You could also create a more interactive application, one that actually prompts the user for specific pieces of data.

5. Report on the success.

```
if (affected == 1) {
    System.out.println("The client was
    → added to the database!");
} else {
    System.out.println("The client
    → could not be added to the
    → database!");
}
```

Since executeUpdate() returns the number of affected rows, I can use that value to confirm whether or not the query worked. If the query didn't work, you might want to also print out the query for debugging purposes.

6. Complete the try clause and catch any errors that might have occurred.

```
}
catch (SQLException e) {
    System.out.println("Problem: " +
    → e.toString());
}
```

The catch block of code will report on any errors caught by MySQL when executing the query (**Figure 9.6**). It's similar in usage and result to the catch used in the Connect class, although it's catching an exception of type SQLException.

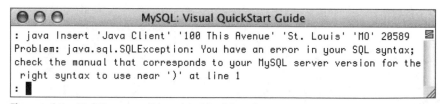

Figure 9.6 Any MySQL errors will be printed for debugging purposes.

7. Wrap up the class.

```
finally {
    if (stmt != null) {
        try {
            stmt.close();
        } catch (Exception e) {
            → System.out.println(e.toString
            → ());
        }
        stmt = null;
    }
    if (con != null) {
        try {
            con.close();
        } catch (Exception e) {
System.out.println(e.toString());
        }
        con = null;
    }
}
} // End of main().
} // End of class Insert.
```

One addition to this script is that I now formally close the stmt variable as well as con. Closing these frees up the resources required while the application is running.

8. Save the file as Insert.java.

9. Compile Insert.java.

continues on next page

10. Run `Insert` (**Figure 9.7**).

    To run the application, follow the steps as explained in the previous section of this chapter, but be sure to add the five requisite arguments (for the client's name, street address, city, state, and zip code):

    ```
    java Insert client street city state
    → zip
    ```

    To insert any strings with spaces in them, quote the entire string (as in Figures 9.6 and 9.7).

MySQL: Visual QuickStart Guide
: java Insert 'Fishmongers, Inc.' '6 Coffee Way, Suite 2B' 'Seattle' 'WA' 12345
The client was added to the database!
:

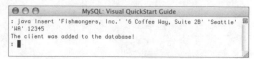

Figure 9.7 Another client is added to the database.

✔ Tips

- Besides lacking data validation, this script will also fail if the user enters data containing apostrophes (**Figure 9.8**). One solution for this would be to use prepared statements, discussed at the end of the chapter.
- If you want to run multiple non-`SELECT` queries, you can reuse the `stmt` object without recalling `createStatement()`:

  ```
  stmt = con.createStatement();
  stmt.executeUpdate("INSERT INTO
  → expense_categories (expense_
  → category) VALUES ('Office
  → Furniture')");
  stmt.executeUpdate("INSERT INTO
  → expense_categories (expense_
  → category) VALUES ('Parking')");
  ```

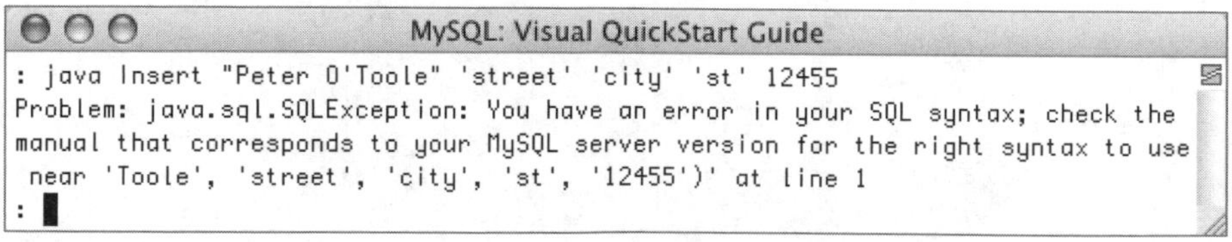
MySQL: Visual QuickStart Guide
: java Insert "Peter O'Toole" 'street' 'city' 'st' 12455
Problem: java.sql.SQLException: You have an error in your SQL syntax; check the manual that corresponds to your MySQL server version for the right syntax to use near 'Toole', 'street', 'city', 'st', '12455')' at line 1
:

Figure 9.8 Apostrophes in submitted data will break the query.

Table 9.1 These functions are used to fetch query results into variables. The right function should be used that matches the type of value returned (i.e., the MySQL data type of that column).

The getXXX() Functions

FUNCTION	RECOMMENDED FOR
getShort()	Small integers
getInt()	Integers
getLong()	Big integers
getFloat()	Floats
getDouble()	Floats and doubles
getBigDecimal()	Decimals
getString()	Char, varchar, and text types
getDate()	Dates
getTime()	Time values
getTimestamp()	Timestamps

Retrieving Query Results

While a simple query is easy to execute (as in the preceding example), the more complicated queries that select records from a database will require slightly more involved Java applications.

First of all, instead of using the executeUpdate() function, you'll need to run the query through the executeQuery() method. This function returns a ResultSet object, which will be used to access each returned row. The easiest way to do so is to use a while loop and the next() method:

```
ResultSet rs = stmt.executeQuery
→ ("SELECT * FROM tablename");
while (rs.next()) {
    // Do something with the results.
}
```

One way of using the results is to assign the column values to variables. You'll need to use one of the getXXX() functions, listed in **Table 9.1**, corresponding to the type of value being retrieved. These functions will accept either the column name or number (indexed starting at 1) as an argument. For example:

```
while (rs.next()) {
    int key = rs.getInt(1);
    String value = rs.getString
    → ("stringcolumnname");
}
```

As an application of this, this next script will show a few of the clients in the database.

To retrieve query results:

1. Create a new Java application in your
text editor or Java development tool
(**Script 9.3**).

```
import java.sql.*;
public class Select {
    public static void main(String
    → args[]) throws Exception {
```

2. Initialize the variables.

```
Connection con = null;
Statement stmt = null;
ResultSet rs = null;
int id = 0;
String name = null;
```

The application will introduce a new
variable called rs of type ResultSet. This
variable will be used to access the results
of the query. Also, I've initialized an integer, which will be used to temporarily store
the client's ID number, and a string, which
will temporarily store the client's name.

Script 9.3 The Select class runs a basic query on a table and displays the results.

```
1    import java.sql.*;
2
3    // Script 9.3 'Select.java'
4
5    public class Select {
6
7        public static void main(String args[]) throws Exception {
8
9            // Initialize variables.
10           Connection con = null;
11           Statement stmt = null;
12           ResultSet rs = null;
13           int id = 0;
14           String name = null;
15
16           try {
17
18               // Connect to MySQL.
19               String url = "jdbc:mysql:///accounting";
```

Script continues on next page

3. Establish a connection to the *accounting* database.

```
try {
    String url = "jdbc:mysql:///
    → accounting";
    Class.forName("com.mysql.jdbc.
    → Driver").newInstance();
    con = DriverManager.getConnection
    → (url, "username", "password");
```

Again, be certain to use a user/host/password combination that has permission to connect to and select from the *accounting* database.

continues on next page

Script 9.3 *continued*

```
20          Class.forName("com.mysql.jdbc.Driver").newInstance();
21          con = DriverManager.getConnection(url, "username", "password");
22
23          // Run the query.
24          stmt = con.createStatement();
25          rs = stmt.executeQuery("SELECT client_id, client_name FROM clients ORDER BY
            client_name ASC LIMIT 5");
26
27          // Fetch the results.
28          while (rs.next()) {
29              id = rs.getInt(1);
30              name = rs.getString("client_name");
31
32              System.out.println(id + ": " + name);
33          }
34      }
35
36      // Catch exceptions.
37      catch (SQLException e) {
38          System.out.println("Problem: " + e.toString());
39      }
40
41      // Clean up.
42      finally {
```

Script continues on next page

RETRIEVING QUERY RESULTS

4. Execute a SELECT query.

```
stmt = con.createStatement();
rs = stmt.executeQuery("SELECT
→ client_id, client_name FROM clients
→ ORDER BY client_name ASC LIMIT 5");
```

Like before, the first step is to establish the stmt variable based upon the createStatement() method of the con connection variable. Then the query is fed as an argument to the executeQuery() method, rather than the executeUpdate() used previously. For demonstration purposes, this query will display five records of client information. Naturally, you can run any sort of SELECT query from Java, as long as it is SQL compliant.

Script 9.3 *continued*

```
43              if (rs != null) {
44                  try {
45                      rs.close();
46                  } catch (SQLException e) {
47                      // Do nothing with exception.
48                  }
49                  rs = null;
50              }
51              if (stmt != null) {
52                  try {
53                      stmt.close();
54                  } catch (SQLException e) {
55                      // Do nothing with exception.
56                  }
57                  stmt = null;
58              }
59              if (con != null) {
60                  try {
61                      con.close();
62                  } catch (SQLException e) {
63                      // Do nothing with exception.
64                  }
65              }
66          }
67
68      } // End of main().
69
70  } // End of class Select.
```

5. Print out the returned rows.

```
while (rs.next()) {
    id = rs.getInt(1);
    name = rs.getString("client_name");
    System.out.println(id + ": " +
    → name);
}
```

This loop will retrieve every record returned by the query (which should be five at the most). Then I use the getInt() and getString() methods to retrieve the value of an integer and a string column type, respectively. To use these functions, I refer to the column's indexed position in one case (the client_id is the first value returned) and the column's name in the other case.

6. Complete the try clause and catch any errors that might have occurred.

```
}
catch (SQLException e) {
    System.out.println("Problem: " +
    → e.toString());
}
```

continues on next page

7. Wrap up the class, closing all resources.

```
finally {
    if (rs != null) {
        try {
            rs.close();
        } catch (SQLException e) {
            // Do nothing with exception.
        }
        rs = null;
    }
    if (stmt != null) {
        try {
            stmt.close();
        } catch (SQLException e) {
            // Do nothing with exception.
        }
        stmt = null;
    }
    if (con != null) {
        try {
            con.close();
        } catch (SQLException e) {
            // Do nothing with exception.
        }
    }
}
} // End of main().
} // End of class Select.
```

Especially when dealing with SELECT queries, freeing up the resources of a statement and a result set is a good programming practice. This will be more and more true as your queries become more complex. In the finally clause, I attempt to close the result set, statement, and connection (in that order), if each has a value.

Finding the Number of Returned Rows

As you know, MySQL will report upon the number of returned rows for any SELECT query. There's no one function that will reveal this value in Java, but because you can move around within the returned rows easily, a little bit of code will suffice. For starters, run the query and assign the results to a ResultSet variable:

```
ResultSet rs = stmt.executeQuery
→ ("SELECT * FROM tablename");
```

Now move to the last row in the result set:

```
rs.last();
```

Assign this row number to a variable to determine the total number of returned rows:

```
int num = rs.getRow();
```

If you want to fetch the rows, move back to the first row, prior to your while loop:

```
rs.beforeFirst();
while (rs.next()) { …
```

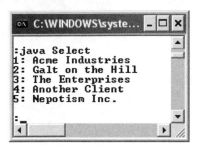

Figure 9.9 The Select class will run a query and display the results.

I'm no longer doing anything with any exceptions that might occur (as they shouldn't), but you could print them out or whatever.

8. Save the file as Select.java, compile, and run the application (**Figure 9.9**).

✔ Tips

■ As of JDBC 2.0, you can move through result sets using next()—as demonstrated in this section—and previous().

■ When using the getXXX() functions, referring to columns by their index is slightly faster than referring to columns by name.

■ The getMetaData() function can be used to find out information about a particular column, such as its name, data type, etc.

■ Most of the getXXX() functions will attempt to parse their type out of a value. For example, if you apply getString() to a number type, the number will be returned as a string.

■ If you are only fetching one row, you can do without the while loop but you still need to use next() to fetch that one row into the result set.

Retrieving the Insert ID

In Chapter 6, "MySQL Functions," I cover the LAST_INSERT_ID() function, which is a MySQL-specific tool for retrieving the value inserted into an auto-incremented field. You can do this with Java, too; it's just not as simple. I'll show the syntax and then explain it.

```
stmt.executeUpdate("INSERT INTO
→ tablename (table_id, column) VALUES
→ (NULL, 'value') ");
ResultSet rs = stmt.getGeneratedKeys();
rs.next();
int id = rs.getInt(1);
```

First some sort of INSERT query is run that invokes MySQL's AUTO_INCREMENT feature. Then a result set is assigned a value by calling the getGeneratedKeys() method. To fetch the first "row" in the result set, next() must be called. From that point, the actual value can be assigned to an integer by calling the getInt() function.

This technique will work as of Java 1.4 and is the preferred method for retrieving the insert ID. With this in mind, I'll create a new script, similar to Insert.java, that lets a user create an invoice and reports the new invoice number back to them.

To retrieve the insert ID:

1. Create a new Java application in your text editor or Java development tool (**Script 9.4**).

```
import java.sql.*;
public class AddInvoice {
    public static void main(String
→ args[]) throws Exception {
```

This class will be called *AddInvoice*.

continues on next page

Script 9.4 This program works like Insert but reports back the generated invoice ID.

```
1      import java.sql.*;
2
3      // Script 9.4 'AddInvoice.java'
4
5      public class AddInvoice {
6
7          public static void main(String args[]) throws Exception {
8
9              // Initialize variables.
10             Connection con = null;
11             Statement stmt = null;
12             ResultSet rs = null;
13             int affected = 0;
14             int id = 0;
15
16             try {
17
18                 // Connect to MySQL.
19                 String url = "jdbc:mysql:///accounting";
20                 Class.forName("com.mysql.jdbc.Driver").newInstance();
21                 con = DriverManager.getConnection(url, "username", "password");
22
23                 // Run the query.
24                 stmt = con.createStatement();
25                 affected = stmt.executeUpdate("INSERT INTO invoices (client_id, invoice_amount,
                   invoice_description) VALUES ('" + args[0] + "', '" + args[1] + "', '" + args[2] +
                   "')");
26
27                 // Confirm that the insert worked.
28                 if (affected == 1) {
29                     rs = stmt.getGeneratedKeys();
30                     rs.next();
31                     id = rs.getInt(1);
32                     System.out.println("Invoice number " + id + " has been created!");
33                 } else {
```

Script continues on next page

RETRIEVING THE INSERT ID

2. Initialize the variables.

```
Connection con = null;
Statement stmt = null;
ResultSet rs = null;
int affected = 0;
int id = 0;
```

Along with the three standard JDBC variables of type Connection, Statement, and ResultSet, this program needs two integers.

Script 9.4 *continued*

```
34                    System.out.println("The invoice could not be added to the database!");
35              }
36          }
37
38          // Catch exceptions.
39          catch (SQLException e) {
40              System.out.println("Problem: " + e.toString());
41          }
42
43          // Clean up.
44          finally {
45              if (rs != null) {
46                  try {
47                      rs.close();
48                  } catch (SQLException e) {
49                      // Do nothing with exception.
50                  }
51                  rs = null;
52              }
53              if (stmt != null) {
54                  try {
55                      stmt.close();
56                  } catch (SQLException e) {
57                      // Do nothing with exception.
58                  }
59                  stmt = null;
60              }
61              if (con != null) {
62                  try {
63                      con.close();
64                  } catch (SQLException e) {
65                      // Do nothing with exception.
66                  }
67              }
68          }
69
70      } // End of main().
71
72  } // End of class AddInvoice.
```

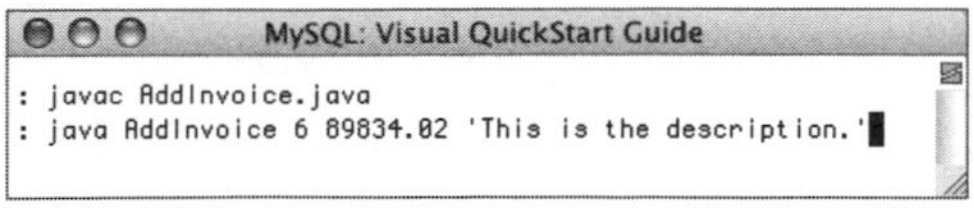

Figure 9.10 Once again the INSERT query will rely upon command-line arguments.

3. Establish a connection to the *accounting* database.

```
try {
    String url = "jdbc:mysql:///
    → accounting";
    Class.forName("com.mysql.jdbc.
    → Driver").newInstance();
    con = DriverManager.getConnection
    → (url, "username", "password");
```

4. Execute an INSERT query.

```
stmt = con.createStatement();
affected = stmt.executeUpdate
→ ("INSERT INTO invoices (client_id,
→ invoice_amount, invoice_description)
→ VALUES ('" + args[0] + "', '" +
→ args[1] + "', '" + args[2] + "')");
```

As with the Insert.java example, these values will be retrieved as command-line arguments typed when the application is run (**Figure 9.10**). To access their values, I refer to args[0] through args[2].

5. Report on the success of the INSERT.

```
if (affected == 1) {
    rs = stmt.getGeneratedKeys();
    rs.next();
    id = rs.getInt(1);
    System.out.println("Invoice number
    → " + id + " has been created!");
} else {
    System.out.println("The invoice
    → could not be added to the
    → database!");
}
```

Again, most of this code is exactly like that in the other INSERT example. The technique outlined earlier for retrieving the insert ID is incorporated, and that value will be printed.

continues on next page

RETRIEVING THE INSERT ID

6. Complete the `try` clause and catch any errors that might have occurred.

```
}
catch (SQLException e) {
   System.out.println("Problem: " +
   → e.toString());
}
```

7. Wrap up the class.

```
finally {
   if (rs != null) {
      try {
         rs.close();
      } catch (SQLException e) {
      }
      rs = null;
   }
   if (stmt != null) {
      try {
         stmt.close();
      } catch (SQLException e) {
      }
      stmt = null;
   }
   if (con != null) {
      try {
         con.close();
      } catch (SQLException e) {
      }
   }
}
} // End of main().
} // End of class Insert.
```

8. Save the file as `AddInvoice.java` and compile it.

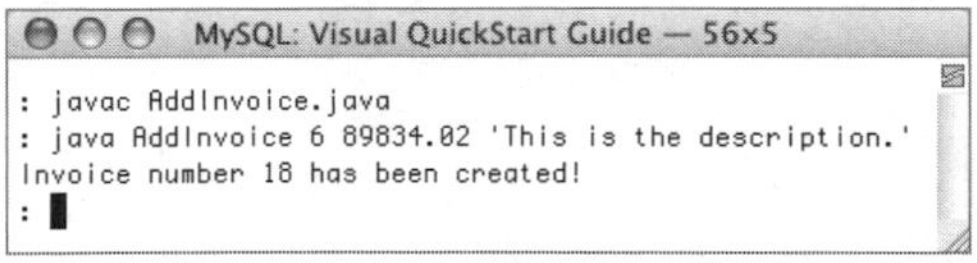

Figure 9.11 The invoice ID will be displayed for the user if it was successfully added to the database.

9. Run AddInvoice (**Figure 9.11**).

When running the program, add the three requisite arguments (for the client's ID, invoice amount, and invoice description):

```
java AddInvoice 2 4599.26 'Invoice
→ Description'
```

✔ Tip

■ You can also retrieve the incremented ID by running a SELECT LAST_INSERT_ID() query and fetching that result.

Using Prepared Statements

The last topic I'll discuss with respect to Java is the *prepared statement*. I'll run through the syntax and then explain the usefulness. To begin, create an object of type PreparedStatement. This object is fed the query to be run, using placeholders for its values.

```
PreparedStatement pstmt =
→ con.prepareStatement("INSERT INTO
→ tablename (column) VALUES (?)");
```

The question mark represents the data that will be added to the query. Note that no quotation marks go around the placeholder, even though it may represent string data (which otherwise has to be quoted in queries). Once you've prepared the query, you can then associate data with that placeholder:

```
pstmt.setString(1, "The actual
→ string.");
```

This has the effect of replacing the first placeholder in the query with the text *The actual string*. Along with setString(), you will also use setInt(), setFloat(), and so on. Essentially these are just the companions to the getXXX() functions listed in Table 9.1.

Finally, you can run the query:

```
pstmt.executeUpdate();
```

If you want to run the query again using new values, just repeat these last two steps. You only need to prepare the statement once.

Prepared statements offer two benefits. First, they are often a faster method of running queries, particularly in applications where the same query is run multiple times, using different values for each. The second benefit is that you do not need to worry about escaping problematic characters like apostrophes. They'll automatically be handled by the process.

To demonstrate this, I'll rewrite AddInvoice.java.

To use prepared statements:

1. Open AddInvoice.java (Script 9.4) in your text editor or IDE (if it is not already).

2. Change the class name to AddInvoice2 (**Script 9.5**).

continues on next page

Script 9.5 Prepared statements, used in the INSERT query here, can improve the performance and security of database interactions.

```
1   import java.sql.*;
2
3   // Script 9.5 'AddInvoice2.java'
4
5   public class AddInvoice2 {
6
7       public static void main(String args[]) throws Exception {
8
9           // Initialize variables.
10          Connection con = null;
11          PreparedStatement stmt = null;
12          ResultSet rs = null;
13          int affected = 0;
14          int id = 0;
15
16          try {
17
18              // Connect to MySQL.
19              String url = "jdbc:mysql:///accounting";
20              Class.forName("com.mysql.jdbc.Driver").newInstance();
21              con = DriverManager.getConnection(url, "username", "password");
22
```

Script continues on next page

3. Change the declaration of the `stmt` variable (line 11) to

`PreparedStatement stmt = null;`

You can also name the variable `pstmt` if you want to be more precise.

4. Remove the `createStatement()` line and replace it with

`stmt = con.prepareStatement`
`→ ("INSERT INTO invoices (client_id,`
`→ invoice_amount, invoice_description)`
`→ VALUES (?, ?, ?)");`

Another benefit of prepared statements, in my opinion, is that this syntax is a lot cleaner than that in the original script.

Script 9.5 *continued*

```
23          // Prepare the query.
24          stmt = con.prepareStatement("INSERT INTO invoices (client_id, invoice_amount,
            invoice_description) VALUES (?, ?, ?)");
25
26          // Assign values.
27          stmt.setInt(1, Integer.parseInt(args[0]));
28          stmt.setFloat(2, Float.parseFloat(args[1]));
29          stmt.setString(3, args[2]);
30
31          // Execute the query.
32          affected = stmt.executeUpdate();
33
34          // Confirm that the insert worked.
35          if (affected == 1) {
36              rs = stmt.getGeneratedKeys();
37              rs.next();
38              id = rs.getInt(1);
39              System.out.println("Invoice number " + id + " has been created!");
40          } else {
41              System.out.println("The invoice could not be added to the database!");
42          }
43      }
44
45      // Catch exceptions.
46      catch (SQLException e) {
47          System.out.println("Problem: " + e.toString());
48      }
49
50      // Clean up.
51      finally {
```

Script continues on next page

USING PREPARED STATEMENTS

5. Assign values to the placeholders.

```
stmt.setInt(1, Integer.parseInt
→ (args[0]));
stmt.setFloat(2, Float.parseFloat
→ (args[1]));
stmt.setString(3, args[2]);
```

Following the instructions already outlined, the setXXX() functions are used to assign specific values to the different placeholders. Each function matches the type of data expected by the database. The first argument in each is the placeholder number, starting at 1. The second argument is the actual value to be used. These correspond to command-line arguments used when running the program (see Figure 9.10).

continues on next page

Script 9.5 *continued*

```
52              if (rs != null) {
53                  try {
54                      rs.close();
55                  } catch (SQLException e) {
56                      // Do nothing with exception.
57                  }
58                  rs = null;
59              }
60              if (stmt != null) {
61                  try {
62                      stmt.close();
63                  } catch (SQLException e) {
64                      // Do nothing with exception.
65                  }
66                  stmt = null;
67              }
68              if (con != null) {
69                  try {
70                      con.close();
71                  } catch (SQLException e) {
72                      // Do nothing with exception.
73                  }
74              }
75          }
76
77      } // End of main().
78
79  } // End of class AddInvoice2.
```

Because all of the values are coming to the application as strings, the first two must be converted to their proper type. The `Integer.parseInt()` and `Float.parseFloat()` methods will accomplish this.

6. Execute the query.

```
affected = stmt.executeUpdate();
```

Replace the original `stmt.executeUpdate()` line with this one.

7. Save the file as `AddInvoice2.java` and compile.

8. Run `AddInvoice2` (**Figure 9.12**).

When running the program, add the three requisite arguments (for the client's ID, invoice amount, and invoice description):

```
java AddInvoice2 8 45.00 'Invoice
→ Description'
```

9. Run `AddInvoice2` using apostrophes in the description (**Figure 9.13**).

When running the program, add the three requisite arguments (for the client's ID, invoice amount, and invoice description):

```
java AddInvoice2 18 1002.48 "Larry's
→ Invoice Description"
```

✔ Tips

■ Prepared statements can be used with any type of query, not just INSERTs.

■ The process demonstrated here is also referred to as *bound variables*.

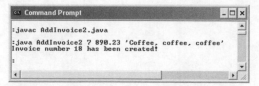

Figure 9.12 The application functions the same as it had before (Figure 9.11) as far as the end user is concerned.

Figure 9.13 Apostrophes in user-submitted data will no longer cause problems, thanks to the use of prepared statements.

ADVANCED SQL AND MySQL

10

Chapter 5, "Basic SQL," and Chapter 6, "MySQL Functions," discuss the fundamentals of both technologies. In those chapters I focus on the commands and functions that will do the vast majority of database-querying tasks. In this chapter, I cover a hodgepodge of topics that aren't used as often but are real time-savers when needed.

Many of these features have been added to MySQL in versions 4.0 and 4.1, so do pay attention to what I say about version support as I discuss a concept. Because these topics are unrelated to each other, most of the demonstrations will be independent and may require the creation of new tables. Instructions will be provided as needed.

Performing Transactions

Transactions are SQL queries executed as a two-step process. First you run the query (or queries) to see what the results will be. Then, if the results are acceptable, you enact the queries; otherwise, you undo their effects. While you have been able to build transaction support into MySQL ever since MySQL 3.23, current versions of MySQL always include a transaction-capable storage engine out of the box.

Transactions bring increased reliability to your databases. If you have a sequence of SQL queries that should either all work or not work at all, you can now trust that you'll never get stuck halfway through the sequence. In fact, you could say that transactions bring an undo feature to your database applications (up to a point, that is). To this end, transaction-safe tables are more secure and easier to recover should the server crash (since queries are run either completely or not at all). On the downside, transactions can be slower than standard queries would be, and your databases will require more laborious SQL or programming interfaces to adjust for their transactional nature.

Creating transaction-safe tables

The MySQL software supports several different table types, where a table's type is also called its *storage engine*. These are formally discussed in Chapter 4, "Creating a MySQL Database." MyISAM is the default storage engine (on non-Windows systems) and is your best choice for most situations. What MyISAM does lack is support for transactions, but storage engines like InnoDB do offer this feature (read the sidebar, though, about the available storage engines).

To make an InnoDB table, you'll proceed through the normal `CREATE TABLE` SQL but conclude it with `ENGINE=InnoDB`. This is true for assigning any table type, but when you do not specify a table type, MySQL assumes it to be the server's default type (which is MyISAM on non-Windows operating systems).

The classic (and really one of the best) examples for the need for transactions is banking. If you're transferring money from one account to another, guaranteeing that both queries (subtracting from one account, adding to the other) worked is critical. I'll create a simple table to demonstrate the concept.

Transaction-Safe Storage Engines

At the time of this writing, MySQL has two storage engines that support transactions: InnoDB and BDB (Berkeley Database). (The MySQL Cluster also supports transactions, but it's an entirely different beast from the MySQL products discussed in this book.) For better or for worse, the companies that make these products have both been purchased by Oracle, another database company. I mention this because it is unclear what the future holds for the available MySQL storage engines. My suspicion is that both InnoDB and BDB will disappear in future editions of MySQL, probably to be replaced by one built from scratch by the MySQL AB company.

In this chapter I will show you what steps to take to create a transaction-safe database using InnoDB, which is what MySQL has to offer at this time. Depending upon the version of MySQL you are using, you may need to use a different, as yet unnamed, storage engine instead. See Chapter 4 for instructions on identifying what storage engines your installation supports and how to choose among them.

To create transaction-safe tables:

1. Log in to mysql as a user capable of creating new tables in the *test* database.

2. Select the *test* database.

   USE test;

   Since this is just a demonstration, I'll use the all-purpose *test* database.

3. Create a new accounts table (**Figure 10.1**).

   CREATE TABLE accounts (

   id INT UNSIGNED NOT NULL
   → AUTO_INCREMENT,

   first_name VARCHAR(20) NOT NULL,

   last_name VARCHAR(40) NOT NULL,

   balance DECIMAL(10,2) NOT NULL
   → DEFAULT 0.0,

   PRIMARY KEY (id),

   INDEX (last_name)

) ENGINE=InnoDB;

   Obviously this isn't a complete table or database design. The most important aspect of the table definition is that its engine—InnoDB—allows for transactions.

4. Populate the table (**Figure 10.2**).

   INSERT INTO accounts VALUES

   (NULL, 'Sarah', 'Vowell', 5460.23),

   (NULL, 'David', 'Sedaris', 909325.24),

   (NULL, 'Kojo', 'Nnamdi', 892.00);

   You can use whatever names and values here that you want. The important thing to note is that MySQL will automatically commit this query, as no transaction has begun yet.

5. Confirm the structure and contents of the table (**Figure 10.3**).

   SELECT * FROM accounts;

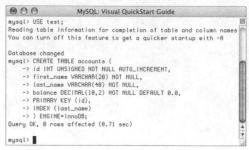

Figure 10.1 A new transaction-capable table must be created in order to demonstrate transactions.

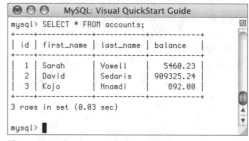

Figure 10.2 A few sample records are inserted into the table.

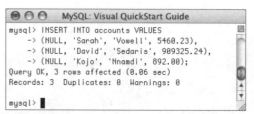

Figure 10.3 The account balances before any transactions.

✔ Tips

■ You can change an existing table's type using the command

   ALTER TABLE *tablename* ENGINE=InnoDB

■ The same database can, and commonly does, have tables of different types.

Using transactions

To start a transaction, you use the SQL term START TRANSACTION (prior to MySQL 4.0.11, you would just use BEGIN). Then you proceed with all of your queries as you otherwise would.

If you like the results of the transaction, enter COMMIT to enact the queries. Otherwise, enter ROLLBACK to retract their effect. After you have either committed or rolled back the queries, the transaction is considered complete, and MySQL returns to an *auto-commit* mode. This means that any queries you execute from that point on take immediate effect. To start another transaction, just type START TRANSACTION (or BEGIN).

It is important to also know that certain types of queries cannot be rolled back. Specifically those that create, alter, truncate (empty), or delete tables or that create or delete databases cannot be undone. Furthermore, using such a query has the effect of committing and ending the current transaction. So if you start a transaction, insert a couple of records, and then alter the table, those inserts are committed.

Finally, you should understand that transactions are particular to each connection. So one user connected through the mysql client has a different transaction than another mysql client user, both of which are different than a connected PHP script or Java application.

To use transactions:

1. Log in to the mysql client, if you have not already.

2. Select a database with transaction-safe tables.

   USE test;

   Remember that transactions can be used (in current versions of MySQL) only on InnoDB and BDB table types. The accounts table, created in the preceding set of steps, fits the bill.

3. Start a transaction (**Figure 10.4**).

   START TRANSACTION;

   Every query from here until I enter COMMIT, ROLLBACK, or another transaction-terminating query will be part of one transaction, even if unrelated. Again, if you are using an earlier version of MySQL, you'll need to use just BEGIN instead of START TRANSACTION.

4. Subtract $100 from David Sedaris' (or any user's) account.

   UPDATE accounts SET balance=
   → (balance-100) WHERE id=2;

   Using an UPDATE query, a little math, and a WHERE conditional, I can subtract 100 from a balance. Although MySQL will indicate that one row was affected, the effect is not permanent until the transaction is committed.

5. Add $100 to Sarah Vowell's account (**Figure 10.5**).

   UPDATE accounts SET balance=
   → (balance+100) WHERE id=1;

   This is the opposite of Step 4, as if $100 were being transferred from the one person to the other.

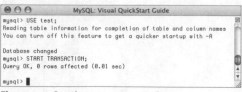

Figure 10.4 Starting a new transaction.

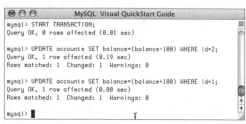

Figure 10.5 Because these queries are part of a transaction, they will not be truly enacted until the transaction is committed.

```
●○○        MySQL: Visual QuickStart Guide
mysql> SELECT * FROM accounts;
+----+------------+-----------+-----------+
| id | first_name | last_name | balance   |
+----+------------+-----------+-----------+
|  1 | Sarah      | Vowell    |   5560.23 |
|  2 | David      | Sedaris   | 909225.24 |
|  3 | Kojo       | Nnamdi    |    892.00 |
+----+------------+-----------+-----------+
3 rows in set (0.00 sec)

mysql>
```

Figure 10.6 You can see the results of the queries by reviewing the account balances (compare with Figure 10.3).

```
●○○        MySQL: Visual QuickStart Guide
mysql> ROLLBACK;
Query OK, 0 rows affected (0.02 sec)

mysql> SELECT * FROM accounts;
+----+------------+-----------+-----------+
| id | first_name | last_name | balance   |
+----+------------+-----------+-----------+
|  1 | Sarah      | Vowell    |   5460.23 |
|  2 | David      | Sedaris   | 909325.24 |
|  3 | Kojo       | Nnamdi    |    892.00 |
+----+------------+-----------+-----------+
3 rows in set (0.00 sec)

mysql>
```

Figure 10.7 The transaction is rolled back, undoing the effect of the two UPDATE queries (compare with Figures 10.3 and 10.6).

```
●○○        MySQL: Visual QuickStart Guide
mysql> COMMIT;
Query OK, 0 rows affected (0.01 sec)

mysql> SELECT * FROM accounts;
+----+------------+-----------+-----------+
| id | first_name | last_name | balance   |
+----+------------+-----------+-----------+
|  1 | Sarah      | Vowell    |   5560.23 |
|  2 | David      | Sedaris   | 909225.24 |
|  3 | Kojo       | Nnamdi    |    892.00 |
+----+------------+-----------+-----------+
3 rows in set (0.00 sec)

mysql>
```

Figure 10.8 After committing the transaction, the effect of the UPDATE queries is retained.

6. Confirm the results (**Figure 10.6**).

SELECT * FROM accounts;

As you can see in the figure, the one balance is 100 more and the other is 100 less than they originally were (Figure 10.3).

7. Roll back the transaction.

ROLLBACK;

To demonstrate how transactions can be undone, I'll negate the effects of these queries. The ROLLBACK command returns the database to how it was prior to starting the transaction. The command also terminates the transaction, returning MySQL to its autocommit mode.

8. Confirm the results (**Figure 10.7**).

SELECT * FROM accounts;

The query should reveal the contents of the table as they originally were (as shown in Figure 10.3).

9. Repeat Steps 3 through 5.

To see what happens when the transaction is committed, the two UPDATE queries will be run again. Be certain to start the transaction first, though, or the queries will automatically take effect!

10. Commit the transaction and confirm the results (**Figure 10.8**).

COMMIT;

SELECT * FROM accounts;

Once you enter COMMIT, the entire transaction is permanent, meaning that any changes are now in place. COMMIT also ends the transaction, returning MySQL to autocommit mode.

PERFORMING TRANSACTIONS

✔ Tips

- If the connection to the database is lost, all of the transactions are rolled back. This applies for a connection between the MySQL server and any type of client (`mysql`, a PHP script, etc.).

- When using tables that support transactions, if you fail to use the START TRANSACTION command, the queries will be automatically run much like they are on non-transactional tables (in other words, queries will be automatically committed).

- To alter MySQL's autocommit nature, use

  `SET AUTOCOMMIT=0`

  Then you do not need to use START TRANSACTION and no queries will be permanent until you type COMMIT (or use an ALTER, CREATE, etc., query). It is advised that you do not do this, though, as it's best to more manually control your transactions.

Using Savepoints

As of MySQL 4.0.14, you can use *savepoints* with your transactions. These are like bookmarks within a transaction, letting you roll back to a specific point.

To create a savepoint, type

`SAVEPOINT name`

Then you can continue on with your transaction. If you make a mistake or an error occurs, you can revert to the state of the database at that savepoint by entering

`ROLLBACK TO SAVEPOINT name`

You can create multiple savepoints (with different names) as you need. Every savepoint is cleared once you commit the transaction.

Full-Text Searching

Often, a database query contains a search where you're not exactly sure what you're looking for but you know it might be like this or that. You may have already seen this while using LIKE in a WHERE conditional. An alternative is the full-text search, which has two benefits over LIKE:

◆ You can search using multiple words.

◆ Full-text searches are much, much faster.

There are four gotchas when it comes to full-text searches:

◆ Full-text searches are case-insensitive.

◆ If you search using a term (or terms) that appears in more than half of the records, no rows will be returned, because that search will not be specific enough. One workaround is to use Boolean mode, discussed later in this chapter.

◆ There is a minimum word length for search terms, by default four characters. Shorter terms will never be found, even when you know they are present.

◆ Very popular words, called *stopwords*, are ignored.

Full-text searching is most important in situations where people will be entering keywords that must be searched against specific fields in a table, such as search engines. I'll first show you how to create the proper FULLTEXT index. Then I'll run through some simple full-text searches. Finally, you'll learn about the full-text Boolean mode, which allows for much more precise searching.

✔ Tips

■ MySQL comes with several hundred stopwords already defined. These are part of the application's source code. You can also specify your own custom stopword file to use as of MySQL 4.0.10.

■ The minimum keyword length—four characters by default—is a configuration setting you can change in MySQL.

Creating a FULLTEXT index

Before performing a full-text search, you need to prepare the database by creating an index of type FULLTEXT on the column or columns to be used in the searches. Currently, you can only create FULLTEXT searches on MyISAM tables.

To create a FULLTEXT index when defining a table, you would do something like this:

```
CREATE TABLE tablename (
col1 TEXT,
col2 TEXT,
FULLTEXT (col1, col2)
)
```

If the table already exists, you can add a FULLTEXT index using an ALTER query:

```
ALTER TABLE tablename ADD FULLTEXT
→ (columns)
```

I'll modify the expenses table (in the *accounting* database) to add a FULLTEXT index on the expense_description column.

To create a FULLTEXT index:

1. Log in to the mysql client as a user that can access and modify the *accounting* database.

2. Select the *accounting* database.
   ```
   USE accounting;
   ```

3. Make sure the expenses table is well populated (**Figure 10.9**).
   ```
   SELECT expense_description FROM
   → expenses;
   ```
   It doesn't really matter what SQL you use during these steps as long as you add records with good descriptions to the expenses table. The more records a table has, the more useful and accurate full-text indexing and searching becomes.

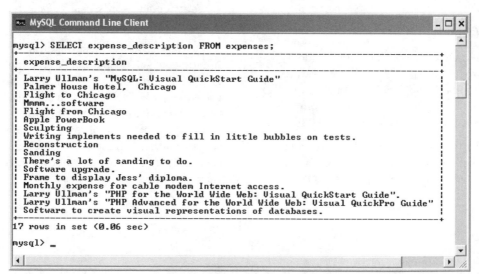

Figure 10.9 You'll need to have quite a bit of data in your table in order to best use full-text searches.

4. Create a full-text index (**Figure 10.10**).

```
ALTER TABLE expenses
ADD FULLTEXT (expense_description);
```

Before I run any full-text searches on a table, I must create a full-text index on the column or columns involved.

5. Confirm the table's structure by viewing its CREATE syntax (**Figure 10.11**).

```
SHOW CREATE TABLE expenses \G
```

You've already seen a couple of SHOW commands by now, so hopefully this one isn't too surprising. The SHOW CREATE TABLE *tablename* command asks MySQL to print out the SQL command used to create (or re-create) the named table. Using the \G trick makes the results easier to view.

✔ Tip

■ Inserting records into tables with FULLTEXT indexes can be much slower because of the complex index that's required. Similarly, adding a FULLTEXT index to an existing table can take some time, depending upon how much data is already there.

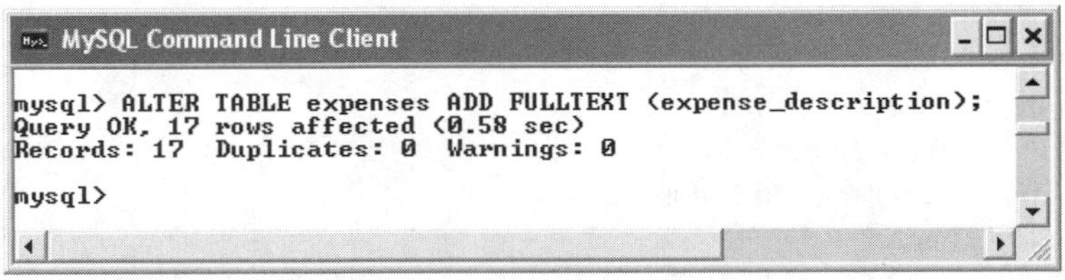

Figure 10.10 A FULLTEXT index is added to the expenses table.

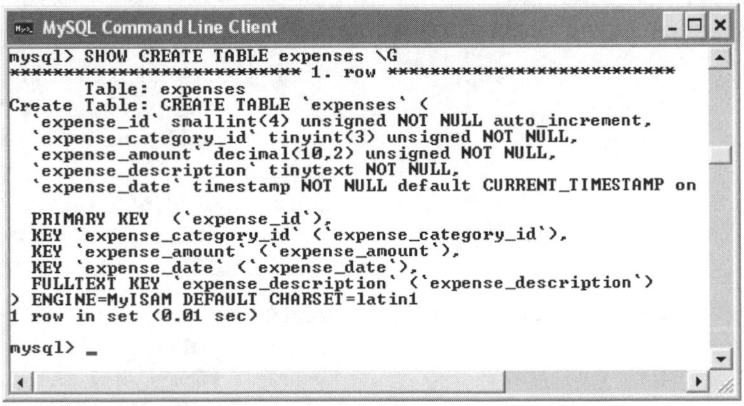

Figure 10.11 The SHOW CREATE TABLE query indicates what command would be used to make the table.

Performing basic FULLTEXT searches

Once you've established a FULLTEXT index on a column, you can start querying against it, using the MATCH and AGAINST keywords. The syntax for using full-text searching is

```
SELECT * FROM tablename WHERE MATCH
→ (column) AGAINST ('string')
```

The result of the query will be the rows returned in order of relevance from most to least. In other words, the rows in which *string* most matches the values in *column* will be listed first.

If you want to match against multiple words, you can do so, separating the words by spaces:

```
SELECT * FROM tablename WHERE MATCH
→ (column) AGAINST ('word1 word2')
```

With a query like this, rows that contain both words will rank higher than those that contain only one or the other (which would still qualify as a match). This behavior can be tweaked using the Boolean mode, discussed next in the chapter.

To view the relevance of a row returned by a match, you would select it:

```
SELECT somecolumn, MATCH (column)
→ AGAINST ('string') FROM tablename
```

FULLTEXT Indexes, Revisited

Your FULLTEXT index must be created on the same column or combination of columns that you use in your SELECT queries. If you create the index on one column, you can use only that one column in your query. If you create the index on two columns, you must use exactly both those columns in your queries:

```
ALTER TABLE tablename ADD FULLTEXT
→ (col1, col2)
```
```
SELECT * FROM tablename WHERE MATCH
→ (col1, col2) AGAINST ('string')
```

To use full-text searching:

1. Log in to the `mysql` client and select the *accounting* database, if you have not already.

   `USE accounting;`

2. Make sure the `expenses` table is well populated.

   If you are paying close attention, you'll note that this step was included in the preceding sequence. It's important, though. The more populated a table is, the more useful a full-text search is. In fact, a (non-Boolean mode) full-text search won't even work if you have fewer than three records in the table!

3. Do a full-text search using the word *visual* (**Figure 10.12**).

   `SELECT expense_id, expense_description`
   `FROM expenses WHERE`
   `MATCH (expense_description) AGAINST`
   `→ ('visual');`

   This query will return the `expense_id` and `expense_description` columns wherever *visual* has a positive relevance in the `expense_description` values. In other words, any record that contains the word *visual* will be returned.

   If you have different data in your table, you'll want to change the searched-for word accordingly.

   continues on next page

FULL-TEXT SEARCHING

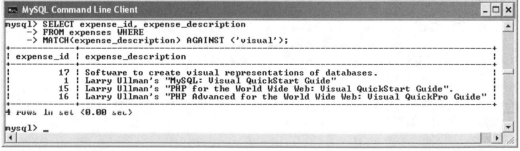

```
mysql> SELECT expense_id, expense_description
    -> FROM expenses WHERE
    -> MATCH(expense_description) AGAINST ('visual');
+------------+----------------------------------------------------------------------+
| expense_id | expense_description                                                  |
+------------+----------------------------------------------------------------------+
|         17 | Software to create visual representations of databases.              |
|          1 | Larry Ullman's "MySQL: Visual QuickStart Guide"                      |
|         15 | Larry Ullman's "PHP for the World Wide Web: Visual QuickStart Guide". |
|         16 | Larry Ullman's "PHP Advanced for the World Wide Web: Visual QuickPro Guide" |
+------------+----------------------------------------------------------------------+
4 rows in set (0.00 sec)

mysql>
```

Figure 10.12 A simple full-text search quickly returns all records that contain the word *visual* within the expense description.

4. Run a full-text search using the words *visual* and *guide* (**Figure 10.13**).

```
SELECT expense_id,
→ expense_description,
MATCH (expense_description) AGAINST
→ ('visual guide') AS rel
FROM expenses WHERE
MATCH (expense_description) AGAINST
→ ('visual guide') \G
```

This query differs from that in Step 3 in two ways. First, I'm also selecting the MATCH...AGAINST value so that the calculated relevance number is displayed. Second, I've included a second term to match. Those records with both terms will score higher than those with just one.

✔ Tips

■ You can weed out some results by using the MATCH...AGAINST() value in a WHERE clause:

```
SELECT expense_id, expense_description,
MATCH (expense_description) AGAINST
→ ('visual guide')
FROM expenses WHERE MATCH
→ (expense_description) AGAINST
→ ('visual guide') > .001
```

■ Remember that if a FULLTEXT search returns no records, this means either that no matches were made or that over half of the records match (when not using Boolean mode).

■ For sake of simplicity, I wrote all of the queries in this section as simple SELECT statements. You can certainly use FULLTEXT searches within joins or more complex queries.

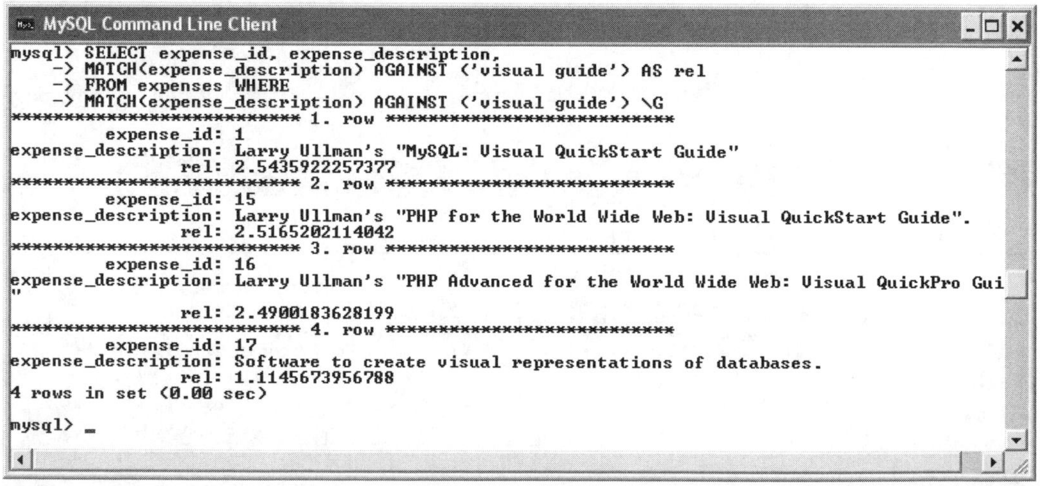

```
MySQL Command Line Client                                              _ □ ×
mysql> SELECT expense_id, expense_description,
    -> MATCH(expense_description) AGAINST ('visual guide') AS rel
    -> FROM expenses WHERE
    -> MATCH(expense_description) AGAINST ('visual guide') \G
*************************** 1. row ***************************
        expense_id: 1
expense_description: Larry Ullman's "MySQL: Visual QuickStart Guide"
               rel: 2.5435922257377
*************************** 2. row ***************************
        expense_id: 15
expense_description: Larry Ullman's "PHP for the World Wide Web: Visual QuickStart Guide".
               rel: 2.5165202114042
*************************** 3. row ***************************
        expense_id: 16
expense_description: Larry Ullman's "PHP Advanced for the World Wide Web: Visual QuickPro Gui
"
               rel: 2.4900183628199
*************************** 4. row ***************************
        expense_id: 17
expense_description: Software to create visual representations of databases.
               rel: 1.1145673956788
4 rows in set (0.00 sec)

mysql> _
```

Figure 10.13 This search returns every record that contains either *visual* or *guide* but ranks records with both higher.

Performing Boolean FULLTEXT searches

You can take your full-text searching one step further by using its Boolean mode (as of MySQL version 4.0.1). In Boolean mode the search terms can be preceded by special characters (**Table 10.1**) to indicate how their presence should be weighted with regard to relevancy.

```
SELECT columns FROM tablename WHERE
→ MATCH (column) AGAINST ('+word1 word2'
→ IN BOOLEAN MODE)
SELECT * FROM tablename WHERE MATCH
→ (column) AGAINST ('+database -mysql'
→ IN BOOLEAN MODE)
```

In the second example, a match will be made if the word *database* is found and *mysql* is not present. Alternatively, the tilde (~) is used as a milder form of the minus sign, meaning that the keyword can be present in a match, but such matches should be considered less relevant.

Table 10.1 These characters are specifically used to affect the importance of terms in full-text searches.

CHARACTER	MEANING	EXAMPLE	MATCHES
+	Word is required	+punk rock	*punk* is required and *rock* is optional
-	Word must not be present	+punk -rock	*punk* is required and *rock* cannot be present
" "	A literal phrase	"punk rock"	Occurrences of the phrase *punk rock* are weighted
<	Less important	<punk +rock	*rock* is required, and *punk* is less significant
>	More important	>punk +rock	*rock* is required, but *punk* is more significant
( )	Creates groups	(>punk roll) +rock	*rock* is required, both *punk* and *roll* are optional, but *punk* is weighted more
~	Detracts from relevance	+punk ~rock	*punk* is required, and the presence of *rock* devalues the relevance (but *rock* is not excluded)
*	Allows for wildcards	+punk +rock*	*punk* and *rock* are required, but *rocks, rocker, rocking*, etc., are counted

Special Boolean Mode Characters

The wildcard character (*) matches variations on a word, so cata* matches *catalog, catalina,* and so on. Two operators explicitly state what keywords are more (>) or less (<) important. Finally, you can use double quotation marks to hunt for exact phrases. Parentheses can be used to make subexpressions.

The following query would look for records with the phrase *Web develop* with the word *html* being required and the word *JavaScript* detracting from a match's relevance:

```
SELECT * FROM tablename WHERE
MATCH(column) AGAINST('>"Web develop"
→ +html ~JavaScript' IN BOOLEAN MODE)
```

When using Boolean mode, there are several differences as to how FULLTEXT searches work:

◆ If a keyword is not preceded by an operator, the word is optional but a match will be ranked higher if it is present.

◆ Results will be returned even if more than 50 percent of the records match the search.

◆ The results are not automatically sorted by relevance.

Because of this last fact, you'll also want to sort the returned records by their relevance, as I'll demonstrate in the next sequence of steps. One important rule that remains with Boolean searches is that the minimum word length (four characters by default) still applies. So trying to require a shorter word using a plus sign (+SQL) still won't work.

Control Flow Functions

One advanced topic that I don't cover in this book is the various control flow functions MySQL has to offer.

The basic function is an IF conditional, which acts like a ternary operator:

```
IF (condition, return_this_if_true,
→ return_this_if_false)
```

If the condition is true, the second argument is returned. Otherwise, the third argument is returned. This next example returns either *odd* or *even*, depending upon whether or not the remainder of dividing a column's value (e.g., 3) by 2 is equal to 1:

```
SELECT IF( (some_num_col % 2) = 1,
→ 'odd', 'even');
```

Along with the IF conditional, there are an IFNULL, a NULLIF, and a CASE. Each is really just a specific type of conditional. See the MySQL manual for syntax and examples of these.

To use Boolean mode:

1. Log in to the mysql client and select the *accounting* database, if you have not already.

   USE accounting;

2. Do a full-text search requiring both the words *visual* and *guide* (**Figure 10.14**).

   SELECT expense_id, expense_description,
   MATCH (expense_description) AGAINST
   → ('+visual +guide' IN BOOLEAN MODE)
   → AS rel
   FROM expenses WHERE
   MATCH (expense_description) AGAINST
   → ('+visual +guide' IN BOOLEAN MODE)
   → ORDER BY rel DESC \G

   This query adds two new features. First, the IN BOOLEAN MODE text is added, as well as the plus signs, indicating required words. Second, the results are ordered by their relevance, using an alias.

   continues on next page

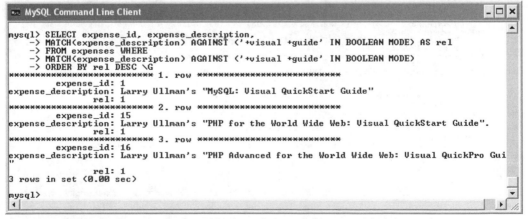

Figure 10.14 Both keywords are required, resulting in one less match (compare with Figure 10.13).

3. Do a full-text search requiring both the words *visual* and *guide* while stressing the word *quickpro* (**Figure 10.15**).

```
SELECT expense_id, expense_description,
MATCH (expense_description) AGAINST
→ ('+visual +guide >quickpro' IN
→ BOOLEAN MODE) AS rel
FROM expenses WHERE
MATCH (expense_description) AGAINST
→ ('+visual +guide >quickpro' IN
→ BOOLEAN MODE) ORDER BY rel DESC \G
```

I add *>quickpro* to my search terms to give preference to records containing this word.

✔ Tip

■ When you select the MATCH...AGAINST value, make sure that its terms are exactly the same as those in the WHERE clause.

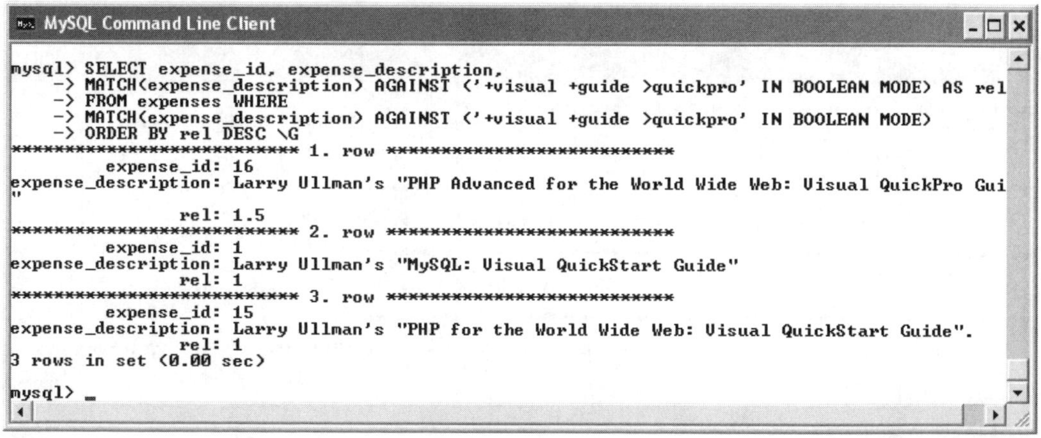

FULL-TEXT SEARCHING

```
mysql> SELECT expense_id, expense_description,
    -> MATCH(expense_description) AGAINST ('+visual +guide >quickpro' IN BOOLEAN MODE) AS rel
    -> FROM expenses WHERE
    -> MATCH(expense_description) AGAINST ('+visual +guide >quickpro' IN BOOLEAN MODE)
    -> ORDER BY rel DESC \G
*************************** 1. row ***************************
     expense_id: 16
expense_description: Larry Ullman's "PHP Advanced for the World Wide Web: Visual QuickPro Gui
"
            rel: 1.5
*************************** 2. row ***************************
     expense_id: 1
expense_description: Larry Ullman's "MySQL: Visual QuickStart Guide"
            rel: 1
*************************** 3. row ***************************
     expense_id: 15
expense_description: Larry Ullman's "PHP for the World Wide Web: Visual QuickStart Guide".
            rel: 1
3 rows in set (0.00 sec)

mysql> _
```

Figure 10.15 The relevance of the results was altered by placing extra importance on *quickpro* (compare with Figure 10.14).

Table 10.2 Here are the different special characters you can use when writing regular expressions.

Special Regular Expression Characters

CHARACTER	MATCHES
.	any single character
q?	zero or one *q*
q*	zero or more *q*'s
q+	at least one *q*
q{x}	*x* instances of *q*
q{x,}	at least *x* instances of *q*
q{,x}	up to *x* instances of *q*
q{x,y}	between *x* and *y* instances of *q*
^q	starts with *q*
q$	ends with *q*
(pqr)	grouping (matches *pqr*)
q|z	either *q* or *z*
[]	character classes (e.g., [a-z], [0-9])
\	escapes a special character (\., *, etc.)

Regular Expressions

In Chapter 5, "Basic SQL," I discuss and demonstrate how you can use the terms LIKE and NOT LIKE to match a string against the values in a column. Furthermore, you can use the single (_) and multiple (%) wildcard characters to add flexibility to what is matched. For example,

```
SELECT * FROM users WHERE first_name
→ LIKE 'John%'
```

In the preceding section of the chapter, I show you can do different types of searches, using FULLTEXT indexes. Thanks to regular expressions, which MySQL also supports, you can perform a third kind of search. With regular expressions you can define more elaborate patterns to match, rather than variations on literal values. You then use REGEXP and NOT REGEXP (or RLIKE and NOT RLIKE):

```
SELECT * FROM users WHERE first_name
→ REGEXP'^(Jo)h?n+.*'
```

This query differs from the LIKE query that precedes it in that it will match *John, Johnathon, Jon, Jonathon,* etc., whereas the earlier one would match only *John* or *Johnathon*. Since this may not make much sense to you if you are unfamiliar with regular expressions, I'll go over how patterns are written in a little more detail.

To define a pattern, you use a combination of literals (e.g., *a* matches only the letter *a*) and special characters (**Table 10.2**).

To match a string beginning with *ab*, you would use ^ab.*: the literal *ab* plus zero or more of anything (represented by the period). To match a string that contains the word *color* or *colour*, you would write col(or)|(our): the literal *col* plus either *or* or *our*.

Obviously, the hardest part of using regular expressions (in MySQL or anywhere else) is coming up with accurate and useful patterns. Defining this pattern is frequently a matter of finding a balance between one that is too lenient and another that is too strict.

To use REGEX and NOT REGEX:

1. Log in to the `mysql` monitor and select the *accounting* database.

   `USE accounting;`

2. Find which clients have a toll-free number (**Figure 10.16**).

   `SELECT client_name, client_phone`

   `FROM clients WHERE client_phone`

   `REGEXP '^[(]?8{1}(00|88|77)';`

   Toll-free numbers (in the United States and Canada) have an 800, 888, or 877 area code. The pattern in this regular expression will match any column whose value begins with one of those three.

   The pattern starts by saying that it must match the beginning of a string (^). Then it looks for zero or one (i.e., optional) opening parenthesis. Since this character already has special meaning within patterns, it's put within brackets to treat it literally. Next, exactly one *8* is required. After that, the string must have *00*, *88*, or *77*. So this pattern matches anything that starts with *(800*, *(888*, *(877*, *800*, *888*, or *877*.

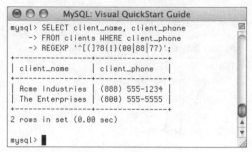

Figure 10.16 Regular expressions can add flexibility to your queries...

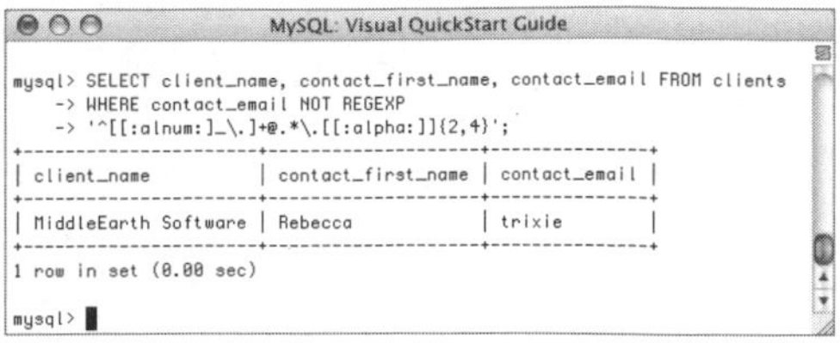

Figure 10.17 ...or assist in validating column values.

3. Retrieve all of the invalid contact email addresses (**Figure 10.17**).

```
SELECT client_name, contact_first_name,
→ contact_email FROM clients
WHERE contact_email NOT REGEXP
'^[[:alnum:]]_\.]+@.*\.[[:alpha:]]
→ {2,4}';
```

The pattern defined here for recognizing usable email addresses is very basic and perhaps overly lenient but should suffice for testing purposes. It just checks that an email address contains letters, numbers, the underscore or a period, followed by the ampersand, followed by anything, followed by a period, ending with between two and four letters. You can always make your patterns more (or less) exacting, per your needs.

✔ Tips

■ For more information about regular expressions, do a quick search online. You can come up with more thorough tutorials as well as example patterns.

■ Unless you specifically indicate that a pattern should match the beginning or end of a value, a match will be made if the pattern is found anywhere within the value. In other words, the query

```
SELECT client_name, client_phone FROM
→ clients WHERE client_phone
REGEXP '((800)|(888)|(877))';
```

would actually match a phone number like 312-888-1234 as well as anything starting with those three prefixes.

■ Regular expression searches can never take advantage of indexes, making them noticeably less efficient.

REGULAR EXPRESSIONS

User-Defined Variables

While not new to MySQL, user-defined variables are an unheralded feature. Such variables work as you would expect: you can temporarily store values in them and then use those variables where the values are needed.

You can use any alphanumeric character in your variable's name, as well as the underscore, period, and dollar sign. The variable's name is preceded by @, to indicate that it is a variable. Whatever name you use should be treated as if it were case-sensitive. This is just good form; as of MySQL 5.0 variable names are not case-sensitive.

To assign a value to a user-defined variable, use one of these SQL commands:

```
SELECT @var := 'value'
SET @var = 'value'
SET @var := 'value'
```

It doesn't matter whether you use SELECT or SET, but you must use := with SELECT, whereas SET can use = or :=. Regardless, note that you don't have to declare a variable before assigning a value to it. You can just do:

```
SET @num = 2
SET @name = 'Sam'
```

To define a variable using a value stored in a table, you can use a SELECT query:

```
SELECT @var:=some_column FROM tablename
→ WHERE condition
```

The only trick here is that you'll want just a single row and column returned so that just one value is assigned to the variable.

Using SQL Comments

A relatively minor topic is that of using comments within your SQL commands. MySQL supports three syntaxes for making comments. If you use # or – (two dashes followed by a space), all text until the end of the line is a comment. Examples:

```
SELECT NOW() # Comment
SELECT NOW() -- Comment
```

If running either of these queries within the mysql client, you would place the semicolon before the comment, or else the query would not be executed.

Comment blocks can be made using /* and */. Anything between these two indicators is a comment, even over multiple lines:

```
SELECT /* What
time is it? */ NOW()
```

A variation on this uses /*! and */. The premise is the same, but you can place MySQL-specific or version-specific SQL within the tags. When running the query on MySQL (or using the right version of MySQL), the SQL within the comment tags is executed. Otherwise, the SQL is ignored.

USER-DEFINED VARIABLES

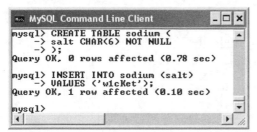

Figure 10.18 A special table, consisting of just one column, will be used to store the encryption salt value.

Once you've established any variable, it can be used in other queries:

INSERT INTO some_table (some_num_col,
→ some_text_col) VALUES (@num, @name)

The catch in such a query is the variable shouldn't be quoted, even if it is a string (like @name in that example).

As a demonstration of this I'm going to change how new accounts are added to the logins table (in the *accounting* database). The basic query is

INSERT INTO logins (client_id,
→ login_name, login_pass) VALUES
→ (*client_id*, AES_ENCRYPT('*name*',
→ 'w1cKet'), SHA1('*password*'))

At issue is the encryption salt (*w1cKet*), which is key to the encryption process. Having this value hard-coded into the query isn't very secure, particularly if the query is being run from PHP, Perl, or Java. Instead, I'll store the salt in a database table. To use it in a query, I will then select it and assign the value to a MySQL user variable.

To use a database-stored salt:

1. Log in to the mysql client and select the *accounting* database.

   USE accounting;

2. Create and populate a table (**Figure 10.18**).

   CREATE TABLE sodium (

   salt CHAR(6) NOT NULL

   );

   INSERT INTO sodium (salt) VALUES
   → ('w1cKet');

   This table, sodium, will store the encryption salt value in its one column. The INSERT query stores the salt, which will be retrieved and assigned to a user-defined variable as needed.

   You may also want to consider giving the table a less obvious name.

continues on next page

USER-DEFINED VARIABLES

3. Retrieve the stored salt value (**Figure 10.19**).

SELECT @salt:=salt FROM sodium;

This line retrieves the stored salt value from the sodium table and assigns this to @salt (the figure shows the results of the SELECT statement).

4. Add a record to the logins table (**Figure 10.20**).

INSERT INTO logins (client_id,
→ login_name, login_pass)

VALUES (3, AES_ENCRYPT('Isabella',
→ @salt), SHA1('atticus7'));

A standard INSERT query is run to add a record to the logins table. In this case, @salt is used in the query instead of a hard-coded salt value.

5. Decrypt the stored login names (**Figure 10.21**).

SELECT @salt:=salt FROM sodium;

SELECT client_id, AES_DECRYPT(login_
→ name, @salt) AS name FROM logins;

The first step retrieves the salt value so that it can be used for decryption purposes. (If you followed these steps without closing the MySQL session, this step wouldn't actually be necessary, as @salt would already be established.) The @salt variable is then used with the AES_DECRYPT() function.

✔ Tips

- User variables are particular to each connection. When one script or one mysql client session connects to MySQL and establishes a variable, only that one script or session has access to that variable.

- You cannot incorporate a user-defined variable as a parameter in a LIMIT clause.

- Never assign a value to and later reference a user-defined variable within the same SQL statement. These two steps must always be accomplished in two separate queries, as in these examples.

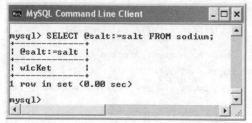

Figure 10.19 A user-defined variable is assigned the value retrieved from a table.

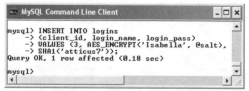

Figure 10.20 A new record is added, with the user-defined variable in place of the salt value.

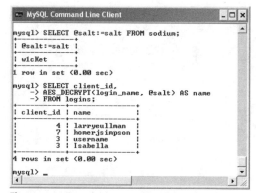

Figure 10.21 Every login record is retrieved and decrypted, again using @salt.

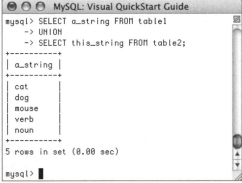

Figure 10.22 I'll use these two dummy tables to quickly demonstrate how UNIONs behave.

```
● ○ ○    MySQL: Visual QuickStart Guide
mysql> SELECT a_string FROM table1
    -> UNION
    -> SELECT this_string FROM table2;
+----------+
| a_string |
+----------+
| cat      |
| dog      |
| mouse    |
| verb     |
| noun     |
+----------+
5 rows in set (0.00 sec)

mysql> █
```

Figure 10.23 The contents of two unrelated columns from two unrelated tables are merged into one result set.

Introducing Unions

Added to MySQL in version 4.0 is the UNION. UNIONs are like JOINs in that they work on multiple tables (or the same table multiple times). With a JOIN, the returned results are normally based upon a condition, where a column in one table relates to a column in another. With a UNION, no such relationship is necessary, but the selected data from both tables should be of the same type. Specifically, the nth column selected in the first query should be of the same type as the nth column selected in the second query.

The basic syntax of a UNION is

SELECTquery1 UNION *SELECTquery2*

Assuming you have the two dummy tables shown in **Figure 10.22**, you can see the result of the following UNION in **Figure 10.23**.

SELECT a_string FROM table1 UNION
→ SELECT this_string FROM table2

You should notice a couple of things. First, the column names from the first table are used in the results. Second, any duplicate records will be removed (*cat* only appears once even though it's in both tables). This is true unless you add the ALL keyword (**Figure 10.24**):

```
SELECT a_string FROM table1
UNION ALL
SELECT this_string FROM table2;
```

I'll play with some examples in the following steps, but also see the sidebar for a discussion as to when UNIONs are most useful.

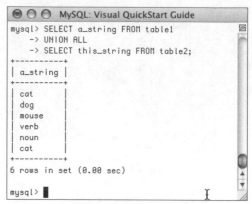

Figure 10.24 With a UNION ALL query, duplicates are not removed (compare with Figure 10.23).

When to Use UNIONs

Unions aren't needed often, but they can be a lifesaver. A common example of when to use them is if you have a query where two unrelated conditions could be met:

```
SELECT * FROM tablename WHERE col1='this value' OR col2='that value'
```

Such a query will work, but inefficiently (at least prior to MySQL 5.0). Instead you could use:

```
SELECT * FROM tablename WHERE col1='this value'
UNION
SELECT * FROM tablename WHERE col2='that value'
```

The other common situation for UNIONs is demonstrated in the steps. Specifically: selecting similar data from two unrelated tables.

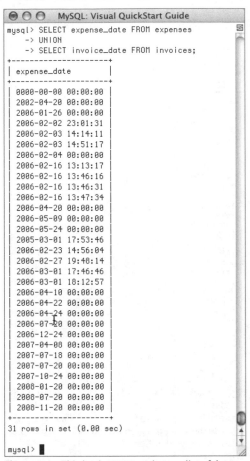

Figure 10.25 This basic UNION retrieves a list of dates and times.

To use UNIONs:

1. Log in to the mysql client and select the *accounting* database.

   USE accounting;

2. Find every date on which an accounting event (invoice date or expense date) took place (**Figure 10.25**).

   SELECT expense_date FROM expenses
   UNION
   SELECT invoice_date FROM invoices;

   The first SELECT retrieves every expense_date. The second retrieves every invoice_date. These are unrelated values but of the same type. The UNION will return them all together, with exact duplicates removed.

   continues on next page

3. Show the same dates formatted
(**Figure 10.26**).

```
SELECT DATE_FORMAT(expense_date,
→ '%M %e, %Y')
AS dates FROM expenses
UNION
SELECT DATE_FORMAT(invoice_date,
→ '%M %e, %Y')
FROM invoices;
```

This alteration on the previous query
uses the DATE_FORMAT() function to also
format the results. This has the added
effect of removing some records that
were returned by the other query
(because they happened on the same
date but not at the same time).

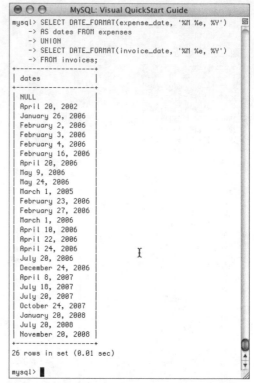

Figure 10.26 A side effect of formatting the returned
dates is that five fewer (non-distinct) records are
returned (compare with Figure 10.25). This occurred
because the formatting removed the time part of the
dates from consideration.

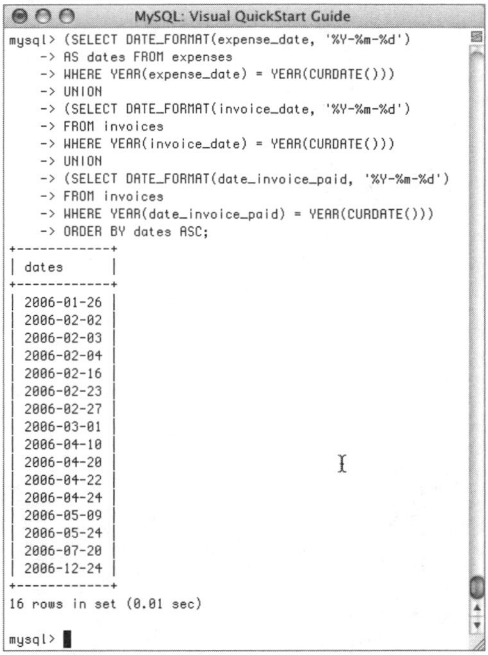

```
mysql> (SELECT DATE_FORMAT(expense_date, '%Y-%m-%d')
    -> AS dates FROM expenses
    -> WHERE YEAR(expense_date) = YEAR(CURDATE()))
    -> UNION
    -> (SELECT DATE_FORMAT(invoice_date, '%Y-%m-%d')
    -> FROM invoices
    -> WHERE YEAR(invoice_date) = YEAR(CURDATE()))
    -> UNION
    -> (SELECT DATE_FORMAT(date_invoice_paid, '%Y-%m-%d')
    -> FROM invoices
    -> WHERE YEAR(date_invoice_paid) = YEAR(CURDATE()))
    -> ORDER BY dates ASC;
+------------+
| dates      |
+------------+
| 2006-01-26 |
| 2006-02-02 |
| 2006-02-03 |
| 2006-02-04 |
| 2006-02-16 |
| 2006-02-23 |
| 2006-02-27 |
| 2006-03-01 |
| 2006-04-10 |
| 2006-04-20 |
| 2006-04-22 |
| 2006-04-24 |
| 2006-05-09 |
| 2006-05-24 |
| 2006-07-20 |
| 2006-12-24 |
+------------+
16 rows in set (0.01 sec)

mysql>
```

Figure 10.27 This query uses conditionals in each `WHERE` clause to limit the dates to the current year. It also performs the `UNION` on three query results.

4. Show all of the accounting events that took place this year, including any paid invoices (**Figure 10.27**).

```
(SELECT DATE_FORMAT(expense_date,
→ '%Y-%m-%d')
AS dates FROM expenses
WHERE YEAR(expense_date) =
→ YEAR(CURDATE()))
UNION
(SELECT DATE_FORMAT(invoice_date,
→ '%Y-%m-%d')
FROM invoices
WHERE YEAR(invoice_date) =
→ YEAR(CURDATE()))
UNION
(SELECT
DATE_FORMAT(date_invoice_paid,
→ '%Y-%m-%d')
FROM invoices
WHERE YEAR(date_invoice_paid) =
→ YEAR(CURDATE()))
ORDER BY dates ASC;
```

`UNION`s, like `JOIN`s, can involve multiple queries and tables. In other words, you can `UNION` two or more query results. To do so, you just continue on with the `UNION` syntax (*SELECTquery* `UNION` *SELECTquery2* `UNION` *SELECTquery3*).

Each `SELECT` query differs from the other ones in two ways. First, I've changed the formatting of the date so that I can sort it better. If I sorted the dates as they were formatted before, they would be sorted alphabetically, not chronologically. Second, each query uses a `WHERE` clause to restrict the returned results to only those that took place in the current year.

Finally, all of the results are ordered by the formatted date. Parentheses are used to clarify each query and to make clear that the `ORDER BY` applies to the whole `UNION`.

✔ Tips

■ You can apply a LIMIT clause to a UNION result, but you'll need to use parentheses to make clear where the LIMIT applies. Take these two slightly different examples:

SELECT *column* FROM *table1* UNION
→ SELECT *column* FROM *table2* LIMIT 5;

(SELECT *column* FROM *table1*) UNION
→ (SELECT *column* FROM *table2*) LIMIT 5;

The first query returns every row from the first table unioned with five rows from the second table. The second query takes everything from the first table unioned with everything from the second, and then returns only five records from that whole result.

■ You can also use ORDER BY clauses with your UNIONs. You can use them on either or both queries (within parentheses as with the LIMIT clauses) or use ORDER BY on the whole UNION (outside of any parentheses). If you do the former, you must also use a LIMIT clause or else the ORDER BY will have no effect. If you do the latter, you cannot use the *tablename.columnname* syntax. Instead, define an alias within the appropriate query and then refer to it. Step 4 (and Figure 10.27) is an example of a UNION with an ORDER BY.

An Introduction to Subqueries

Added to MySQL in version 4.1 is the ability to do subqueries, specifically subSELECT queries. The premise is simple: part of a query is based upon the results of another query.

The knock against a subSELECT is that you can often accomplish the same thing using a UNION or a more efficient JOIN. For this reason, and because the MySQL manual has a pretty good discussion of the topic, I'm not going to demonstrate the subquery in this book.

If you get bored with all of the other SQL you've learned, or otherwise think you might need to use subqueries, check out the manual or the handful of articles available online for the syntax and usage. But before going hog wild with subqueries, do some investigating to see if a JOIN isn't what you actually need. (You can use EXPLAIN to compare how MySQL executes a query.)

MySQL 5 Features

With each new major release of MySQL, often-requested features have been added. Many of these features have been present in rival database applications for years, although, to be fair, not supporting them has kept the MySQL software faster and leaner. A number of popular features were added in MySQL 4.0 and 4.1, some of which are discussed in Chapter 10, "Advanced SQL and MySQL."

In this chapter I cover three of the most important features new to MySQL 5. These are stored routines, triggers, and views. Obviously this chapter does assume you are using MySQL 5.0 or greater. As these features are new, it is possible that they will change (hopefully for the better) in subsequent releases of the software, but the following information was accurate at the time of this writing.

Stored Routines

Stored routines is the umbrella term for the combination of *stored procedures* and *stored functions*. Stored routines allow you to save a set sequence of code in the MySQL server, and then call that sequence as needed. As a rule of thumb, stored *functions* are used to determine and return a simple value; stored *procedures* are used to perform a sequence of steps and likely do not return any values (but not always).

Stored routines can offer several benefits over plain old SQL (remember that a stored routine is just an encapsulated invocation of SQL):

◆ **Security.** By placing code within a stored routine, you make that code less accessible, but the functionality remains the same.

◆ **Speed.** With the bulk of the code stored in the database, less information has to be transferred to the server.

◆ **Convenience.** If the same process is needed by 2 to 200 applications or interfaces, having it exist in only one location makes for easier maintenance.

Whether you experience all of these benefits or not depends upon your server setup, the stored routines themselves, and other factors. Stored routines aren't always the solution, but they often can be.

Stored routines make use of the proc table, found in the *mysql* database. This should have been installed when MySQL 5.0 was installed. If you upgraded your version of MySQL, you'll likely need to update the grant tables (see Chapter 1, "Installing MySQL") to create proc.

Because stored routines are like a mini-programming language unto themselves, a fair amount of basic syntax must be covered first. Then I'll show how to implement procedures and functions. And then you'll see even more syntax!

✔ Tips

- The implementation of stored routines differs from one database application to the next. All of the information provided here is MySQL-specific.

- Not all MySQL client programs support the creation and invocation of stored routines. You can create them within the mysql client, but third-party applications may not have this capability yet.

Permissions Issues

In order to create or execute stored routines, you'll need to log in as a MySQL user with the appropriate permissions. There are three relevant privileges.

The first is CREATE ROUTINE, which allows the user to, yes, make a stored routine. The second is ALTER ROUTINE. This lets a user both modify and/or drop a stored routine. Finally, there is EXECUTE, meaning a user can invoke a saved stored routine. Note that any user that has CREATE ROUTINE privileges automatically has EXECUTE privileges as well.

There are two reasons I'm highlighting these permissions issues. First, if you want to run through these steps and create or execute a stored routine, you must connect to MySQL as a user that has been granted said permissions. Second, as a security measure, one MySQL user can be allowed to create, alter, and drop stored routines, while others can be given permission to just execute them.

STORED ROUTINES

Basic stored routine syntax

To get the ball rolling, I'll introduce the very basic syntax for creating stored functions:

```
CREATE FUNCTION name (arguments) RETURN
→ type code
```

This is the syntax for creating stored procedures:

```
CREATE PROCEDURE name (arguments) code
```

I'll cover both in more detail later, but for now I want to focus on the *name*, *arguments*, and *code* sections, which are common to both.

For the routine's name, you should not use an existing keyword, SQL term, or function name. As with most things you name in MySQL, you should stick to alphanumeric characters and the underscore.

The arguments section is used to pass values to the routine. (In the case of a stored procedure, you can also return values through the arguments.) When a stored routine takes an argument, it's called exactly as you call MySQL functions:

```
SELECT ROUND(3.2)
```

The listed arguments are named and given types that correspond to the available data types in MySQL. Note that if your routine has no arguments, the parentheses are still required but are left empty.

The code section of this syntax is the most important. As your routines will normally contain multiple lines, you'll want to create a block by using BEGIN and END:

```
CREATE FUNCTION name (arguments)
→ RETURNS type BEGIN
    statement1;
    statement2;
END
```

STORED ROUTINES

Figure 11.1 The semicolons used to mark the end of a statement within a stored routine will cause problems in the mysql client (which uses the semicolon as the end of a command).

Within the code block, each statement ends with a semicolon. This can cause a problem: when you go to add this stored function using the mysql client, it will think that the semicolon indicates the end of a command to be executed immediately (**Figure 11.1**). To prevent this, you should, within the mysql client, establish a new delimiter before you define the stored routine:

```
DELIMITER $$
CREATE FUNCTION name (arguments) RETURNS
→ type BEGIN
    statement1;
    statement2;
END $$
```

The delimiter can be anything that will not appear in your code block. It could be \\ or ^:^--|. After you've defined the routine, reset the delimiter:

```
DELIMITER ;
```

✔ Tips

- Stored procedures can call other stored routines as part of their process.

- All stored routines are associated with a specific database (as of MySQL 5.0.1). This has the added benefit of not needing to select the database (USE *databasename*) when invoking them. This also means that you cannot have a stored routine select a database.

- Because stored routines are linked with databases, if you drop the database, you'll also drop any associated stored routine. However, because the routines are stored in the *mysql*.proc table, they won't be backed up when you back up a database unless you take special precautions.

STORED ROUTINES

Creating stored procedures

With a little bit of basic syntax in the bag, let's create a simple sample stored procedure. As I mentioned in the introduction to this concept, stored procedures normally execute a certain amount of code and may or many not return any values. For example, say you want a procedure that marks an invoice as paid. That might be defined like so:

```
CREATE PROCEDURE mark_invoice_paid
→ (id INT)
BEGIN
    UPDATE invoices SET
    → date_invoice_paid=NOW() WHERE
    → invoice_id=id LIMIT 1;
END
```

This procedure receives one argument, an integer that will be assigned to id. Then the procedure runs an UPDATE query using that value in a WHERE clause.

To invoke this procedure, you use the special CALL command:

```
CALL procedure_name (arguments)
CALL mark_invoice_paid (23)
```

One last thing to note: when referring to arguments within a stored routine, never quote that argument. Even if the argument is a string that's used in a query, you would not quote it. You'll see this in the example.

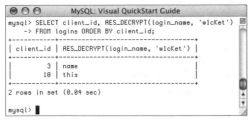

Figure 11.2 The logins table currently contains two records.

To create and call a stored procedure:

1. Log in to the mysql client as a user permitted to create stored procedures in the *accounting* database.

2. Select the *accounting* database.

   USE accounting;

3. View the current list of login accounts (**Figure 11.2**).

   SELECT client_id, AES_DECRYPT
   → (login_name, 'w1cKet')

   FROM logins ORDER BY client_id;

   The stored procedure you are about to create will add records to this table. To confirm that it worked, it'll help to know what or how many records are currently there.

   If you have problems with this query, see Chapter 6, "MySQL Functions," where it is first discussed (along with the encryption functions). This table is also created in that section.

4. Change the delimiter.

   DELIMITER $$

   Remember that this isn't part of stored procedures per se, but rather something that's necessary within the mysql client to avoid confusion and problems. After this line, statements in mysql are executed only upon entering $$.

continues on next page

5. Define a stored procedure for adding login records (**Figure 11.3**).

```
CREATE PROCEDURE add_login

(cid INT, name VARCHAR(20), pass
→ VARCHAR(20))

BEGIN

    INSERT INTO logins

(client_id, login_name, login_pass)

VALUES

(cid, AES_ENCRYPT(name, 'w1cKet'),
→ SHA1(pass));

END $$
```

One great example for using a stored procedure is to populate the `logins` table in the *accounting* database. This table is used to assign login accounts to clients. To populate it requires the preceding `INSERT` query. The problem is that any person or program that runs that query will therefore know what encryption algorithms are used and what the salt value is for `AES_ENCRYPT()`. By wrapping the query within a stored procedure, this is no longer a security risk.

The procedure takes three `IN` arguments: the client ID, the login name, and the login password. Notice that name and pass are not quoted in the query (...`AES_ENCRYPT` (`'name'`, `'w1cKet'`), `SHA1('pass')`...), as that would have the effect of using the literals *name* and *pass*, not the received values.

6. Change the delimiter back to the semicolon.

```
DELIMITER ;
```

If you don't do this, you'll need to keep ending statements and queries with $$.

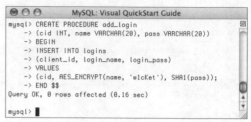

Figure 11.3 Creating the first stored procedure, which adds records to the `logins` table.

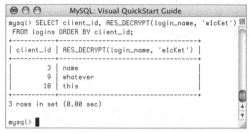

Figure 11.4 This invocation of the stored procedure will add one new record to the logins table.

```
● ○ ○        MySQL: Visual QuickStart Guide
mysql> SELECT client_id, AES_DECRYPT(login_name, 'w1cKet')
  FROM logins ORDER BY client_id;
+-----------+-----------------------------------+
| client_id | AES_DECRYPT(login_name, 'w1cKet')  |
+-----------+-----------------------------------+
|         3 | name                              |
|         9 | whatever                          |
|        10 | this                              |
+-----------+-----------------------------------+
3 rows in set (0.00 sec)

mysql>
```

Figure 11.5 The new record has been successfully added (compare with Figure 11.2).

7. Add a new login account by invoking the stored procedure (**Figure 11.4**).

CALL add_login (9, 'whatever',
→ 'mypass');

This line will have the effect of running the INSERT query in the stored procedure using these values.

8. Confirm that the new account has been added (**Figure 11.5**).

SELECT client_id, AES_DECRYPT
→ (login_name, 'w1cKet') FROM logins
→ ORDER BY client_id;

✔ Tips

■ As stored routines can involve a lot of typing, you may want to create them in a text editor, and then copy and paste them into mysql.

■ You can have a space between your routine name and its opening parenthesis when calling a stored routine. This differs from how you use a MySQL function, where a space would cause an error (unless you take special measures).

STORED ROUTINES

Creating stored functions

Stored functions are much like stored procedures but are often simpler. For starters, a stored function only takes IN parameters (this will mean more in time). They differ in that they also must contain a RETURN clause, indicating the type of value returned by the function:

CREATE FUNCTION *name*

(*arguments*) RETURNS *type*

Functions return scalar (single) values, like a number or a string. To do so, use

RETURN *data*

within the function's code body. The type of the data returned must match the type indicated in the function's initial definition line.

You cannot return a list of values from a stored function. Because of this limitation, you cannot use most SELECT statements, any SHOW queries, or any EXPLAIN queries in a stored function. However, because stored functions return scalar values, they can be used in queries like any of the existing MySQL functions. For example, the following stored function reformats a string so that only the first letter is capitalized:

```
CREATE FUNCTION capitalize
(str VARCHAR(30)) RETURNS VARCHAR(30)
BEGIN
    RETURN CONCAT(UPPER(LEFT(str, 1)),
    → SUBSTR(LOWER(str) FROM 2));
END
```

This may seem wordy, but it just returns the concatenation of two strings. The first string should be the first character in str, in uppercase. The second string is all of str, from the second character on, in lowercase. Once it is defined, you could use this function like so (**Figure 11.6** shows the first result):

```
SELECT capitalize('washington')
SELECT capitalize(contact_first_name)
→ FROM clients
```

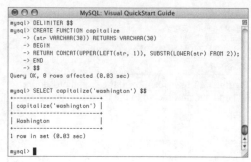

Figure 11.6 A stored function is usable like any MySQL function.

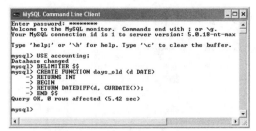

Figure 11.7 This stored function makes use of a MySQL function (two actually, including CURDATE()) and returns an integer result.

To create and use a stored function:

1. Log in to the mysql client as a user permitted to create stored functions in the *accounting* database, if you have not already.

2. Select the *accounting* database, if it is not already selected.

   USE accounting;

   Remember that all stored routines belong to a particular database.

3. Change the delimiter.

   DELIMITER $$

4. Define a stored function for calculating the number of days between the current date and a given date (**Figure 11.7**).

   CREATE FUNCTION days_old (d DATE)
   → RETURNS INT
   BEGIN
       RETURN DATEDIFF(d, CURDATE());
   END $$

   I want to create a function that will help me see how overdue some unpaid invoices are. To do so, I need to find out how late a payment is in days. The MySQL DATEDIFF() function returns the number of days between two given dates. In this function, it will be fed the current date as one of its arguments and the date sent to the function as the other. It returns an integer, which is the number of days different between the two dates.

5. Change the delimiter back to the semicolon.

   DELIMITER ;

continues on next page

STORED ROUTINES

6. Find every overdue invoice (**Figure 11.8**).

SELECT invoice_id, days_old(invoice_date)
→ AS days_unpaid FROM invoices WHERE
→ date_invoice_paid IS NULL ORDER BY
→ days_unpaid ASC;

The value returned by DATEDIFF(), and therefore by the stored routine, will be a negative number if the invoice date comes before the current date and a positive number if the opposite is true. In other words, unpaid invoices will have a negative value. This query gets me pretty close to my goal (of identifying unpaid invoices), but as you can see from the figure, it's not perfect. The main problem is that it lists *all* unpaid invoices, including recent invoices that aren't overdue or those in the future. This will be remedied in time. Regardless, you can see how the stored function was used within a query just like any MySQL function.

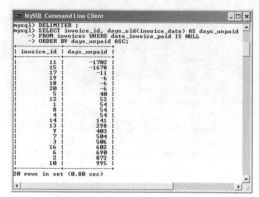

Figure 11.8 The stored function is used in a query to see how late each invoice is.

Declaring local variables

Now that you should have the basics of stored routines down, let's expand upon the topic. The examples demonstrated so far are perfectly legitimate, but there's so much more you can do. Stored routines are like small programs. They can even have their own variables. As with any programming language, it'll often be necessary to use variables as temporary storage within a stored routine. To do so, use the `DECLARE` statement:

```
DECLARE var_name var_type
```

The naming rules are pretty much the same as for everything else, but you absolutely want to make sure that your variables have unique identifiers. The types correspond to the MySQL data types:

```
DECLARE var1 INT
DECLARE var2 DECIMAL(5,2)
DECLARE var3 VARCHAR(20)
```

The only restrictions to declaring variables are:

◆ The declarations must take place within a `BEGIN...END` code block.

◆ The declarations must take place before any other statements (i.e., declarations must be immediately after the `BEGIN`).

When you declare a variable, you can also give it a default value:

```
DECLARE var_name var_type DEFAULT value
```

If not given a default value, a variable's value will be `NULL`.

Once you've declared a variable, you can assign it a value using `SET`:

```
SET name = value
```

As an implementation of this concept, I'll rewrite the `capitalize` function so that it will use variables. The new version will work just the same, but it will be easier to understand.

To use local variables:

1. Log in to the mysql client as a user permitted to create stored functions in the *accounting* database, if you have not already.

2. Select the *accounting* database, if it is not already selected.

   ```
   USE accounting;
   ```

   Actually, you can place this function in any database you want, as its usage won't be particular to *accounting*.

3. Change the delimiter.

   ```
   DELIMITER $$
   ```

4. Begin defining the stored function.

   ```
   CREATE FUNCTION capitalize
   (str VARCHAR(30)) RETURNS VARCHAR(30)
   → BEGIN
   ```

   This part of the function is unchanged from its early incarnation.

5. Declare two variables.

   ```
   DECLARE s1 CHAR;
   DECLARE s2 VARCHAR(29);
   ```

   The function will use two variables, one of type CHAR, the other of type VARCHAR. They've both been given simple but unique names. The first variable will store the single initial capital letter. The second will store the rest of the string. As the string is a maximum of 30 characters long (see the argument definition in Step 4), this variable can be up to 29 characters long (after subtracting the first).

6. Assign values to the variables.

   ```
   SET s1 = UPPER(LEFT(str, 1));
   SET s2 = SUBSTR(LOWER(str) FROM 2);
   ```

   The s1 CHAR variable is assigned the value of the first letter in str, capitalized. The s2 variable is assigned the rest of str, in lowercase form.

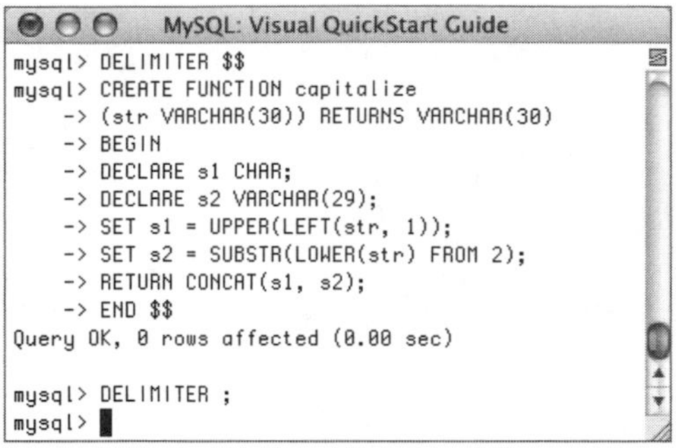

Figure 11.9 The capitalize function uses two local variables to break up its task into smaller pieces.

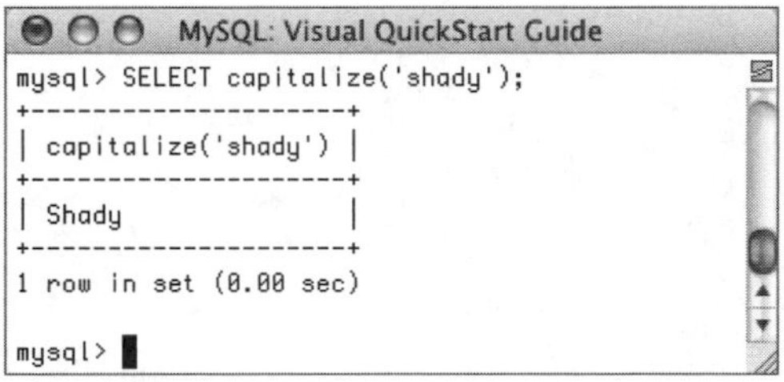

Figure 11.10 Applying the capitalize function to a random word.

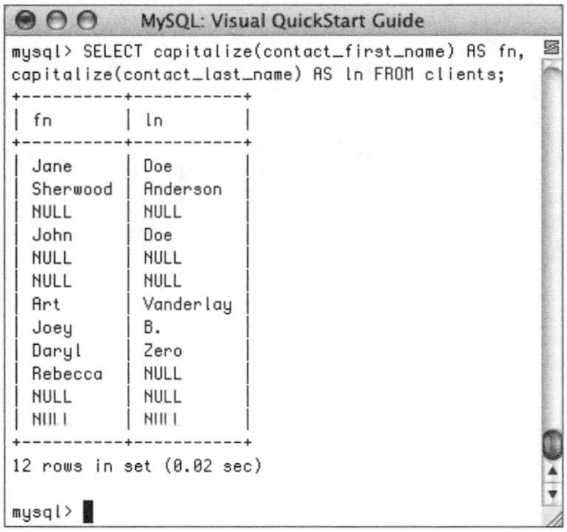

Figure 11.11 Applying the capitalize function to table columns.

7. Complete the function definition and change the delimiter back to the semi-colon (**Figure 11.9**).

```
    RETURN CONCAT(s1, s2);
END $$
DELIMITER ;
```

The last step in the function is to return the concatenated form of the two variables put together. Again, all of this is exactly what the first version of the function did, but it's less crammed together now.

8. Use the function to capitalize any word (**Figure 11.10**).

```
SELECT capitalize('shady');
```

9. Use the function to capitalize every client's contact person's name (**Figure 11.11**).

```
SELECT capitalize(contact_first_name)
→ AS fn, capitalize(contact_last_name)
→ AS ln FROM clients;
```

✔ Tips

■ Declared variables exist only within the BEGIN…END block. Once the END is reached, the variable no longer exists.

■ You can also use DECLARE to create conditions and handlers. Both are ways of dictating actions to take should a specific something happen. See the MySQL manual for syntax and usage of these.

■ Stored routines also support standard SQL variables (ones prefaced with @). These were introduced in Chapter 10, "Advanced SQL and MySQL."

STORED ROUTINES

Using control structures

Programming languages use both variables and control structures—conditionals and loops—to perform their tasks. You've already seen that stored routines support variables, so you might not be surprised to learn they support control structures as well.

For starters, there are two conditionals: IF and CASE (which is like a switch conditional in other languages). The syntax of the IF is natural:

```
IF condition THEN statements
ELSEIF condition2 THEN statements
ELSE statements
END IF
```

You can have as many ELSEIF clauses as you'd like. They are also optional, as is the ELSE. If present, though, the ELSE must come last. If you are only checking to see if something has a particular value, you can use CASE instead of an IF ELSEIF conditional:

```
CASE thing
WHEN value1 THEN statements
WHEN value2 THEN statements
ELSE statements
END CASE
```

Again, the ELSE is optional, but it acts as the default action if none of the WHEN cases are a match for the thing's value.

There are three kinds of loops you can use in a stored routine. The first is the WHILE:

```
WHILE condition DO
statements
END WHILE
```

Similar to WHILE is REPEAT, except that its condition is checked after executing the loop once (it will always execute its statements at least once):

```
REPEAT
statements
UNTIL condition
END REPEAT
```

Finally, there is the generic LOOP:

```
LOOP
statements
END LOOP
```

LOOP has no built-in way to exit the loop. Instead you must use the LEAVE command. It's normally used with a label to identify what exactly to leave:

```
myloop: LOOP
    statements
    IF condition
    THEN LEAVE myloop
    END IF
END LOOP myloop
```

The label—*myloop*—is optional and acts as a way for you to name a control structure. It can be used to label any control structure, including BEGIN...END. Just type *label_name:* before the control structure and END *structure_type label_name* after.

An alternative to LEAVE is ITERATE. It reenters the loop (it terminates the current iteration and begins another one). It works within LOOP, REPEAT, and WHILE.

This is a lot of information, but hopefully this is not the first time you've encountered control structures. Let's implement some of these in two stored routines. Before proceeding, I should point out that I include no semicolons in the preceding commands. But in the mysql client you will need to use semicolons to terminate statements and control structures. You'll see this in the following steps.

Altering and Deleting Routines

If you need to alter a stored procedure, first log in as a user with the proper permissions. Then select the appropriate database. From this point, you can change a stored routine using

```
ALTER {PROCEDURE | FUNCTION} name
→ [characteristics…]
```

Note that this only changes the characteristics of the stored routine, the characteristics being something I don't discuss in this chapter (see the manual). If what you really need to do is replace a routine's functionality, then first drop it:

```
DROP {PROCEDURE | FUNCTION} [IF
→ EXISTS] name
```

Again, you must be logged in as a user with permission to delete stored routines. The final syntax might be something like

```
DROP FUNCTION days_old
```
or
```
DROP PROCEDURE IF EXISTS add_login
```

After you drop the routine, you can create it anew.

To use control structures:

1. Log in to the mysql client as a user permitted to create stored functions in the *accounting* database, if you have not already.

2. Select the *accounting* database, if it is not already selected.

   USE accounting;

3. Change the delimiter.

   DELIMITER $$

4. Begin defining the stored function.

   CREATE FUNCTION is_overdue (d DATE)
   → RETURNS BOOLEAN

   BEGIN

   This new function is going to fix the problem with the days_old function. It takes one argument, a date, and returns a Boolean value (TRUE or FALSE).

5. Declare and assign a value to a variable.

   DECLARE num INT;

   SET num = DATEDIFF(d, CURDATE());

   The num variable will store the difference as a number of days between the invoice date (or any date provided to this stored function) and the current date.

6. Complete the function (**Figure 11.12**).

   ```
       IF num < -45 THEN RETURN TRUE;
       ELSE RETURN FALSE;
       END IF;
   END $$
   ```

   This is a simple conditional that checks if num is less than −45, which I'm using as the number of days when an invoice is considered overdue. Remember that DATEDIFF() returns a negative number if the first date comes before the second. So an invoice two months old would have a return value of −60 (approximately).

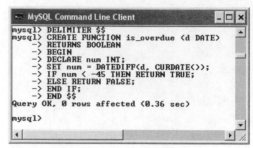

Figure 11.12 The is_overdue() function uses an IF ELSE conditional to return either TRUE or FALSE, depending upon the value of num.

STORED ROUTINES

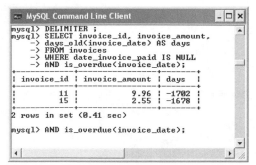

Figure 11.13 A more sophisticated stored function is used to whittle the list of unpaid invoices down to just the two overdue ones. Compare this with the results in Figure 11.8.

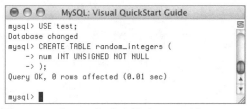

Figure 11.14 A new, simple table is created for demonstration purposes.

If num is less than −45, the function returns TRUE (saying that the invoice *is* overdue). Otherwise, the function returns FALSE. Notice that I use semicolons to conclude my statements (RETURN TRUE and RETURN FALSE) as well as the control structure (END IF).

7. Change the delimiter back to the semicolon and use this new function (**Figure 11.13**).

```
DELIMITER ;
SELECT invoice_id, invoice_amount,
days_old(invoice_date) AS days
FROM invoices WHERE date_invoice_paid
→ IS NULL
AND is_overdue(invoice_date);
```

As the function returns a Boolean value, it can be used in a WHERE conditional.

8. Select the *test* database.

```
USE test;
```

For this next example I'll create a dummy table in the *test* database. This does assume that you have a *test* database and that you are connected as a user that has permission to create stored routines in it.

9. Create a new table (**Figure 11.14**).

```
CREATE TABLE random_integers (
    num INT UNSIGNED NOT NULL
);
```

The table has only one column of type integer. It will be used to store some random integers (the table is well titled). The table will be populated by this next stored procedure.

continues on next page

STORED ROUTINES

10. Change the delimiter and begin defining a stored procedure.

```
DELIMITER $$

CREATE PROCEDURE populate (many INT)
BEGIN

    DECLARE i INT DEFAULT 1;
```

The function takes one argument, an integer indicating how many rows to create. Then the procedure declares a variable of type INT, with a default value of 1.

11. Create a loop.

```
WHILE i <= many DO
```

The loop's conditional is true as long as i is less than or equal to many. In other words, the loop will execute from i to many times.

12. Complete the loop.

```
    INSERT INTO random_integers
    → VALUES (FLOOR(1 + RAND() *
    → 100));
    SET i = i + 1;
END WHILE;
```

The loop contains two statements. The first is the INSERT query that will populate the random_integers table. To do so, it generates a random value between 1 and 100. Because the RAND() function returns a number between 0 and 1, this formula—1 + RAND() * 100—must be used to create integers. This is taken from the MySQL manual page for the RAND() function, so see that explanation if you find this confusing.

The second statement in the loop increases the value of i by 1. If you forget to do this, the loop will be infinite (which is bad, trust me).

Figure 11.15 This stored procedure uses a WHILE loop to execute an INSERT query a certain number of times.

Figure 11.16 Calling the stored procedure twice. Notice that the reported number of affected rows may not be accurate when calling stored procedures.

Figure 11.17 The query shows how the table was populated using a loop within a stored procedure.

13. Complete the procedure and change the delimiter back to the semicolon (**Figure 11.15**).

```
END $$

DELIMITER ;
```

14. Invoke the new procedure (**Figure 11.16**).

```
CALL populate (10);

CALL populate (5);
```

15. View the contents of the table (**Figure 11.17**).

```
SELECT * FROM random_integers;
```

✔ Tip

■ LEAVE can also be used to exit a stored routine (exit a BEGIN...END block). Therefore, it can be used to terminate a stored routine, if need be.

STORED ROUTINES

Using OUT Parameters

As I mentioned earlier in the chapter, stored procedures can have IN parameters (as you've seen) as well as OUT and INOUT parameters. IN parameters work just like those in stored functions. OUT parameters allow you to assign a value to a variable that exists outside of the stored procedure. INOUT can serve both purposes. MySQL assumes that all parameters are IN unless you say otherwise, by indicating such before the argument's name:

```
CREATE PROCEDURE myproc (OUT x INT,
→ INOUT y CHAR)…
```

When calling these procedures, you'll normally involve user-defined variables in the mysql client as the OUT argument (**Figure 11.18**):

```
DELIMITER $$
CREATE PROCEDURE assign (OUT n INT)
BEGIN
SET n = 10;
END $$
DELIMITER ;
CALL assign (@num);
SELECT @num;
```

The CALL line invokes the procedure, providing the user variable @num as its argument. In the procedure, this variable is given a value of 10. To see the variable's value, it must then be selected.

As an example of this concept, the next stored procedure will return the client ID if a user successfully enters the proper login name and password. This procedure also makes use of the SELECT…INTO query, which is introduced in the sidebar.

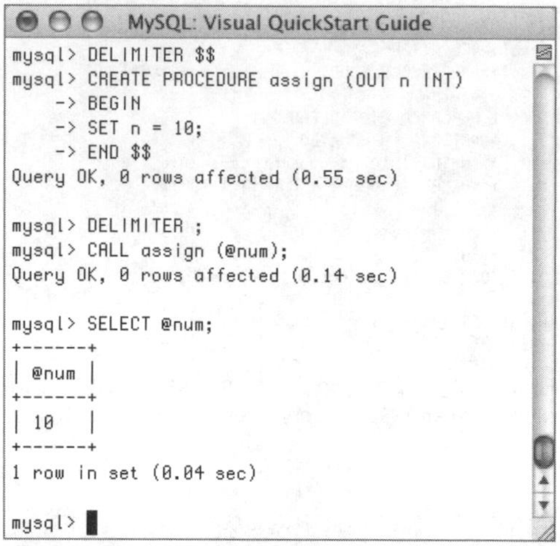

Figure 11.18 This trivial examples demonstrates how OUT arguments can assign values to user variables.

SELECT…INTO Queries

In this series of steps I use a special kind of SELECT query, referred to as SELECT…INTO. Such a query selects values and immediately assigns those values to variables. The general syntax is

```
SELECT col1, col2 INTO var1, var2
→ FROM tablename
```

You can have as many variables as you want, as long as they match the number of columns selected. You can also add WHERE and other clauses as needed.

To use OUT parameters:

1. Log in to the `mysql` client as a user permitted to create stored functions in the *accounting* database, if you have not already.

2. Select the *accounting* database, if it is not already selected.

   `USE accounting;`

3. Change the delimiter.

   `DELIMITER $$`

4. Begin defining the stored procedure.

   ```
   CREATE PROCEDURE check_login
   (name VARCHAR(20), pass VARCHAR(20),
   → OUT cid INT)
   BEGIN
   ```

   This procedure takes three arguments. The first two are of type **IN** and are both strings. The third is an **OUT** parameter of type integer.

5. Retrieve the client ID.

   ```
   SELECT client_id INTO cid FROM logins
   WHERE login_name=AES_ENCRYPT(name,
   → 'w1cKet')
   AND login_pass=SHA1(pass);
   ```

   This is a simple login query that returns the client ID associated with the password and username, assuming that the correct values were entered. The selected value, assuming there is one, will be immediately assigned to `cid`.

   Once again, the routine's arguments—`name` and `pass`, specifically—are not put within quotation marks even though they are strings.

   continues on next page

Cursors

If you need to fetch and handle a lot of data in a stored procedure (more than the single value returned by `check_login`), you'll need to make use of cursors. I don't discuss this topic in detail in the book, because:

◆ They aren't often necessary.

◆ Some people suggest that their use implies bad programming form (i.e., there's probably a better way to do what you're doing).

Still, if you're curious or think you need cursors, check out the MySQL manual. You'll also probably need to learn about declaring handlers, as cursors and handlers are often used together.

6. Complete the procedure and change the delimiter back to the semicolon (**Figure 11.19**).

```
END $$
DELIMITER ;
```

7. Test the procedure using both valid and invalid access information (**Figure 11.20**).

```
CALL check_login ('username',
→ 'password', @id);

SELECT @id;

CALL check_login ('bad', 'bad',
→ @id);

SELECT @id;
```

✔ Tip

■ The SELECT query in this procedure does assume that only one row will be returned. That is a safe assumption as long as the username/password combination is unique in the table.

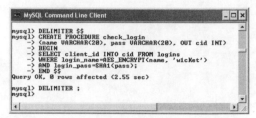

Figure 11.19 This procedure runs a SELECT…INTO query, assigning the returned value to an OUT argument.

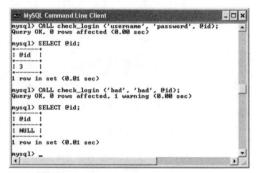

Figure 11.20 The user variable @id is used when calling the stored procedure. In the procedure, @id is assigned the client's ID, if the proper username and password combination is submitted.

Table 11.1 These three events are used in triggers. Notice that they don't apply to only INSERT, UPDATE, and DELETE queries, but rather when rows are inserted, updated, or deleted by any applicable query.

Trigger Events	
EVENT	APPLIES WHEN ROWS ARE…
INSERT	Added to the table, including through LOAD DATA
UPDATE	Updated
DELETE	Deleted

Triggers

New as of MySQL 5.0.2 is the *trigger*. A trigger is an action that automatically takes place when a specific something happens to a specific table. As triggers are associated with a table, they are therefore particular to that table and database. Furthermore, since they are automatically enacted, there is no way to invoke a trigger (other than taking whatever action invokes it).

The general syntax for making a trigger is

```
CREATE TRIGGER trigger_name time event
→ ON tablename FOR EACH ROW statement
```

The *trigger_name* value abides by pretty much the same rules as anything you name in MySQL—databases, tables, column, indexes: use alphanumeric characters, plus the underscore, avoid spaces and existing keywords, and so on. For the *time* value, this is either BEFORE or AFTER, indicating whether the trigger should run before the event takes place or afterward. For example, say that a trigger updates Table B every time a new record is added to Table A. Should that update happen before the insertion or after?

The event value corresponds to a type of action happening to the table. The possible events are listed in **Table 11.1.**

Finally, the statement part of the trigger is where the real magic happens. The code here will be much like that in a stored routine, using the same control structures, BEGIN...END blocks, and types of variables. Rather than give an example here, I'll show it to you in the following steps. But first, one last concept....

TRIGGERS

A complication can arise when working with triggers, as you often end up referring to columns whose values change. To remedy this, MySQL added the OLD and NEW keywords (case-insensitive) as a way to distinguish them. Both are used in the form of OLD.*columnname* and NEW.*columnname*. You'll want to use OLD anytime you are referring to an existing column changed by an UPDATE or DELETE. Note that you can use OLD either BEFORE or AFTER the UPDATE or DELETE. You'll want to use NEW to refer to the content used during an INSERT or UPDATE. It's often used to change data that's being entered into the table.

For my trigger examples, I'm going to create some new tables in a new database. The premise will be an e-commerce application that sells several types of doodads. Triggers will be used to manage the inventory as doodads are ordered or as orders get canceled.

To create a trigger:

1. Log in to the mysql client as a user that can create new databases.

2. Create a new database called *ecommerce* (**Figure 11.21**).

   CREATE DATABASE ecommerce;

   USE ecommerce;

3. Create the doodads table (**Figure 11.22**).

   CREATE TABLE doodads (

   doodad_id INT UNSIGNED NOT NULL
   → AUTO_INCREMENT,

   doodad_name VARCHAR(40) NOT NULL,

   doodad_price DECIMAL(10,2) UNSIGNED
   → NOT NULL,

   doodad_on_hand MEDIUMINT UNSIGNED NOT
   → NULL DEFAULT 0,

   PRIMARY KEY (doodad_id),

   INDEX (doodad_name),

   INDEX (doodad_price),

   INDEX (doodad_on_hand)

   );

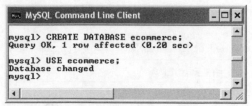

Figure 11.21 A new database will be created and used for the trigger examples.

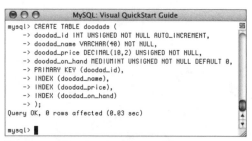

Figure 11.22 Creating the doodads table.

TRIGGERS

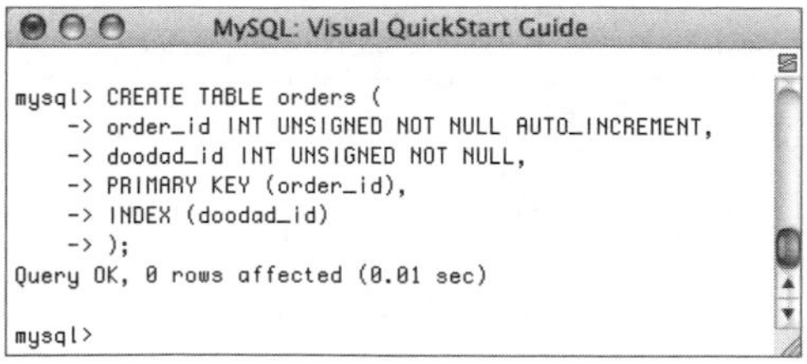

Figure 11.23 Creating the orders table.

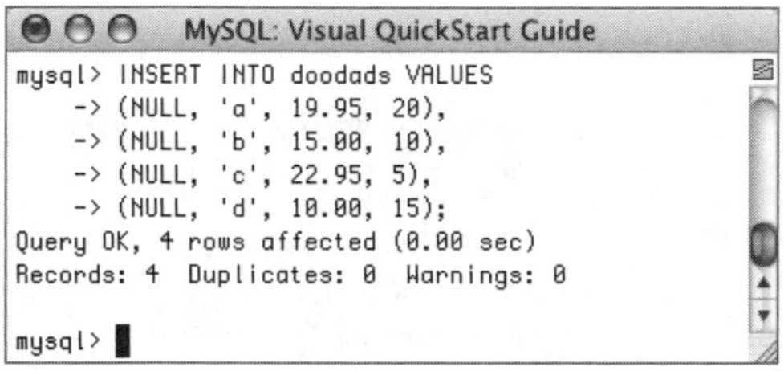

Figure 11.24 A few sample doodads are added to the database.

This is a very simple table with just four columns. No column can be NULL, and all merit having an index placed on them. A real e-commerce application would probably have descriptions, sizes, weights, and so forth in such a table.

4. Create the orders table (**Figure 11.23**).

```
CREATE TABLE orders (
order_id INT UNSIGNED NOT NULL
→ AUTO_INCREMENT,
doodad_id INT UNSIGNED NOT NULL,
PRIMARY KEY (order_id),
INDEX (doodad_id)
);
```

This table is also very simple, too simple really. Obviously in the real world there might be multiple products in an order or multiple quantities of the same product. Orders would also be associated with, you know, *clients*. But I'm using just the bare-bones stuff here in order to best focus on the triggers themselves.

5. Populate the doodads table (**Figure 11.24**).

```
INSERT INTO doodads VALUES
(NULL, 'a', 19.95, 20),
(NULL, 'b', 15.00, 10),
(NULL, 'c', 22.95, 5),
(NULL, 'd', 10.00, 15);
```

That'll be enough to demonstrate the concept. Now you can create the triggers that update the quantities in the doodads table when an order is placed.

6. Change the delimiter.

```
DELIMITER $$
```

Change the delimiter so that mysql doesn't choke when you use semicolons in the trigger's body.

continues on next page

TRIGGERS

7. Create the INSERT trigger (**Figure 11.25**).

```
CREATE TRIGGER update_qty_insert
AFTER INSERT ON orders FOR EACH ROW
BEGIN
UPDATE doodads SET
doodad_on_hand=doodad_on_hand-1
WHERE doodads.doodad_id=NEW.doodad_id;
END $$
```

To define the trigger, I start by giving it a unique name. Then I state that the trigger should take effect AFTER a row is INSERTed into the orders table.

The trigger itself runs one UPDATE query. The query subtracts 1 from the current doodad_on_hand value for the item being ordered. You can refer to this new (inserted) value by using NEW.doodad_id.

When you run this query:

```
INSERT INTO orders (doodad_id)
VALUES (3)
```

That INSERT triggers update_qty_insert. In the trigger, the UPDATE query uses the submitted value (3) in the WHERE conditional.

8. Create the DELETE trigger (**Figure 11.26**).

```
CREATE TRIGGER update_qty_delete
BEFORE DELETE ON orders FOR EACH ROW
BEGIN
UPDATE doodads SET
doodad_on_hand=doodad_on_hand+1
WHERE doodads.doodad_id=OLD.doodad_id;
END $$
```

This trigger differs from that in Step 7 in that it takes place BEFORE a DELETE query. (Technically, however, it could take place AFTER and still have the same effect in this particular instance.) The UPDATE query itself uses OLD.doodad_id to know which item was removed.

Note that the delimiter is still $$ until I change it back (in Step 9).

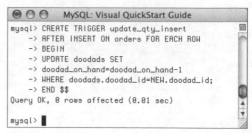

Figure 11.25 The first trigger updates a quantity when a new order is submitted.

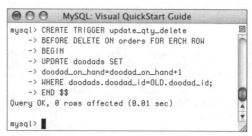

Figure 11.26 The second trigger updates a quantity when an existing order is cancelled (deleted).

Dropping Triggers

To remove an existing trigger, simply use

```
DROP TRIGGER trigger_name
```

You can also use the more formal

```
DROP TRIGGER database_name.trigger_name
```

Note that, at the time of this writing, there is no ALTER TRIGGER command. If you need to modify a trigger, you must drop and then re-create it.

```
○ ○ ○       MySQL: Visual QuickStart Guide
mysql> DELIMITER ;
mysql> INSERT INTO orders (doodad_id)
    -> VALUES (1), (2), (3), (1), (1);
Query OK, 5 rows affected (0.05 sec)
Records: 5  Duplicates: 0  Warnings: 0

mysql> █
```

Figure 11.27 Five orders are added to the orders table. Each invokes the trigger, which in turn updates the quantities in the doodads table (see Figure 11.28).

```
○ ○ ○       MySQL: Visual QuickStart Guide
mysql> SELECT * FROM doodads;
+-----------+-------------+--------------+----------------+
| doodad_id | doodad_name | doodad_price | doodad_on_hand |
+-----------+-------------+--------------+----------------+
|         1 | a           |        19.95 |             17 |
|         2 | b           |        15.00 |              9 |
|         3 | c           |        22.95 |              4 |
|         4 | d           |        10.00 |             15 |
+-----------+-------------+--------------+----------------+
4 rows in set (0.02 sec)

mysql> █
```

Figure 11.28 The on-hand values have been reduced in conjunction with the added records in the orders table.

```
○ ○ ○       MySQL: Visual QuickStart Guide
mysql> SELECT * FROM doodads;
+-----------+-------------+--------------+----------------+
| doodad_id | doodad_name | doodad_price | doodad_on_hand |
+-----------+-------------+--------------+----------------+
|         1 | a           |        19.95 |             18 |
|         2 | b           |        15.00 |              9 |
|         3 | c           |        22.95 |              4 |
|         4 | d           |        10.00 |             15 |
+-----------+-------------+--------------+----------------+
4 rows in set (0.00 sec)

mysql> █
```

Figure 11.29 After deleting order number 4, which was for doodad number 1, the doodad_on_hand value for that doodad is increased. Compare with Figure 11.28.

9. Change the delimiter back to the semicolon.

   DELIMITER ;

10. Add some items to the orders table (**Figure 11.27**).

    INSERT INTO orders (doodad_id)

    VALUES (1), (2), (3), (1), (1);

    Each of these inserted rows will trigger update_qty_insert.

11. Check the existing quantities (**Figure 11.28**).

    SELECT * FROM doodads;

    The results of this query should reveal how the doodad_on_hand values have been altered for each order.

12. Delete an order.

    DELETE FROM orders WHERE order_id=4;

    This will have the net effect of increasing the doodad_on_hand value of the corresponding doodad by 1.

13. Recheck the existing quantities (**Figure 11.29**).

    SELECT * FROM doodads;

✔ Tips

■ You cannot create two triggers on the same table with the same time and event. In other words, there cannot be two BEFORE INSERT or AFTER DELETE actions. If you need to do multiple things with the same time and event, just create one trigger with multiple steps in its body.

■ Stored routine, trigger, and view names are not case sensitive on any platform.

■ Triggers can call stored routines.

Views

Of the three new features in MySQL 5 that I discuss in this chapter, the view is the easiest to understand and implement. A view is simply a special kind of table, often based upon the structure and data of standard tables. For example, looking at the *accounting* database, you might often need to see how much in total dollars each client has been invoiced. You can establish a view that reflects just that information.

You might think that the view would then be a static look at some data: a snapshot taken at the time the view was created. But no! If you define a view based upon selecting data from other tables, when those tables are updated, so is the data in the view.

Views are available as of MySQL 5.0.1. If you upgraded to this version or later, make sure that you upgrade the grant tables so that the right permissions are enabled (see Chapter 1, "Installing MySQL"). Views, like stored routines and triggers, are specific to a database.

I'll show you how to create, use, modify, and drop views over the next several pages.

VIEWS

Figure 11.30 If you think about how SELECT query results look like tables, you'll understand what a view conceptually is.

Creating a view

You make a view using the CREATE VIEW command. The basic syntax is

CREATE VIEW *view_name* AS *select_query*

The *select_query* is the important part: it dictates the view's structure and populates it. The SELECT query can be more or less anything, including joins, unions, and subqueries. There are a few limitations: a view cannot:

◆ Contain a subquery in its FROM clause

◆ Use system or user variables

◆ Use prepared statements

The results of the SELECT query, which looks like a table (**Figure 11.30**), will be the view.

In order to create a view, you will need to have CREATE VIEW privileges within the database as well as SELECT privileges on the tables involved.

By default, the new view will be created using column names that match those retrieved by the SELECT statement. Say I define a view as

CREATE VIEW emp_directory AS SELECT
→ first_name, last_name, phone FROM
→ employees

Then the emp_directory view has three columns, called first_name, last_name, and phone. If you use an alias, that will be a column's name, just as it acts as the header in the returned results.

You can define your own column names by listing them:

CREATE VIEW *view_name* (*col1*, *col2*,
→ *col3...*) AS *select_query*

If you choose to do this, the number of columns must match the number returned by the query. Notice that you don't specify a data type for each column, as that will automatically be dictated by the defining SELECT statement.

To create a view:

1. Log in to the mysql client as a user with permission to create views on the *accounting* database.

2. Select the *accounting* database.

   USE accounting;

3. Show the total amount of expenses by category (**Figure 11.31**).

   SELECT expense_category AS category,

   SUM(expense_amount) AS total

   FROM expense_categories AS ec

   LEFT JOIN expenses

   USING (expense_category_id)

   GROUP BY ec.expense_category_id

   Before creating a view, you may want to run the SELECT query first to confirm that it works and has the results you desire. This is a join on two tables that also uses one of the aggregate functions.

4. Create a view that lists the total expenses in each category (**Figure 11.32**).

   CREATE VIEW total_expenses AS

   SELECT expense_category AS category,

   SUM(expense_amount) AS total

   FROM expense_categories AS ec

   LEFT JOIN expenses

   USING (expense_category_id)

   GROUP BY ec.expense_category_id;

   By slapping CREATE VIEW total_expenses before the query in Step 3, I can create a view whose contents will be the results from that query.

Figure 11.31 The SELECT query previews the view it will be used to create.

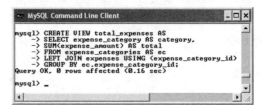

Figure 11.32 Creating a view.

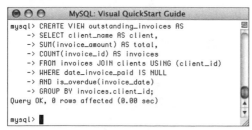

Figure 11.33 Creating another view.

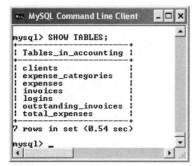

Figure 11.34 Views appear in the list of tables along with standard tables.

5. Create a view that lists the number and total amount of outstanding invoices for each client (**Figure 11.33**).

```
CREATE VIEW outstanding_invoices AS
SELECT client_name AS client,
SUM(invoice_amount) AS total,
COUNT(invoice_id) AS invoices
FROM invoices JOIN clients USING
→ (client_id)
WHERE date_invoice_paid IS NULL
AND is_overdue(invoice_date)
GROUP BY invoices.client_id;
```

This, as complicated as it may seem, works nicely. It returns three values: the client's name, the total amount of money that is past due, and the total number of invoices this involves. A join is used on two tables, and the stored function created earlier in the chapter determines which invoices are considered overdue.

6. View the database's tables (**Figure 11.34**).

```
SHOW TABLES;
```

VIEWS

✔ Tips

- You can see how a view was originally created by using SHOW CREATE VIEW *view_name*.

- Triggers cannot be associated with views. They can only be associated with tables.

- There are a couple of other clauses that can be added to your view definition. Two of these are related to security and who has permission to access a view. Another option is to dictate the algorithm used for managing the view. All of these are detailed in the MySQL manual but aren't needed for most views, particularly as you're just learning the concept.

Altering or Dropping a View

Once you've created a view, there are two ways to alter its definition. The first method is to use the CREATE VIEW syntax, with the added OR REPLACE clause:

CREATE OR REPLACE VIEW *view_name* AS *select_query*

You must have DROP VIEW privileges to execute this, though (as it drops the view and then creates the new one with the same name).

The second method is to use an ALTER VIEW statement. It looks a lot like a CREATE VIEW:

ALTER VIEW *view_name* AS *select_query*

Once you no longer need a view, you can delete it using

DROP VIEW *view_name*

To be extra cautious, you can add the IF EXISTS clause:

DROP VIEW IF EXISTS *view_name*

VIEWS

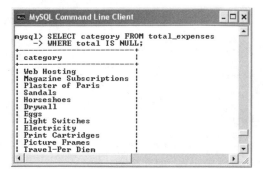

Figure 11.35 This simple query returns one column's values from a view.

```
mysql> SELECT * FROM outstanding_invoices;
+------------------+--------+----------+
| client           | total  | invoices |
+------------------+--------+----------+
| Another Client   | 2.55   | 1        |
| Fishmongers, Inc.| 466.51 | 2        |
+------------------+--------+----------+
2 rows in set (0.02 sec)

mysql>
```

Figure 11.36 SELECT * queries also work on views.

Using a view

As I already said, once you've created a view, you can use it like any other table. To really show what this means, let's try a few queries out.

To use a view:

1. Log in to the mysql client as a user with permission to use views on the *accounting* database.

2. Select the *accounting* database.
   USE accounting;

3. Show every expense category that has not yet been used (**Figure 11.35**).
   SELECT category FROM total_expenses
   WHERE total IS NULL;
   Because the view itself is based upon a join, I can now use a simple query to whittle down my results.

4. Reveal the entire contents of the outstanding_invoices view (**Figure 11.36**).
   SELECT * FROM outstanding_invoices;
   You can see both the column names and the row values in this view. For the column names, the original SELECT query's aliases are used.

continues on next page

VIEWS

Updating View Data

Just because a view acts like a table, that does not mean that you should always treat it like one. While it's safe to run SELECT queries on a view, I would argue against running any other, like INSERT, UPDATE, or DELETE. As the data in most views is based upon data stored in actual tables, you should, when necessary, alter the data in the underlying tables, not in the view.

As a matter of fact, the data in certain views cannot be modified regardless. This includes some views based upon multiple tables as well as ones whose SELECT query includes GROUP BY, DISTINCT, LIMIT, UNION, HAVING, or any of the aggregate functions.

5. Mark some of the invoices as paid
(**Figure 11.37**).

```
SELECT invoice_id, invoice_amount,
→ client_name
FROM clients JOIN invoices
USING (client_id)
WHERE is_overdue(invoice_date);
UPDATE invoices
SET date_invoice_paid=NOW()
WHERE invoice_id IN (11, 15);
```

The first query returns the invoice information along with the client's name for
each overdue invoice. Now I can decide
which of these invoices have been paid
(assuming they actually have been) and
mark them as such using the second query.

6. Reveal the entire contents of the
`outstanding_invoices` view again
(**Figure 11.38**).

```
SELECT * FROM outstanding_invoices;
```

You'll see how the view has been updated
so that only one outstanding invoice
remains.

✔ Tip

■ The queries I'm using in this views section
are based upon sample data that I have.
You may need to change them so that
they apply better to the data you have.
Also, as joins and `GROUP BY` queries can
be complex, often not giving the result
expected, rest assured that a fair amount
of experimentation went into making
them correct. This is my way of remind-
ing you not to sweat it if some queries
take you a while to get right.

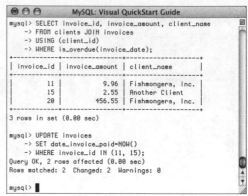

Figure 11.37 The information for the outstanding
invoices is first retrieved. This is then used to mark
two of the invoices as paid.

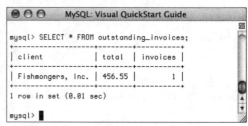

Figure 11.38 Changes to the tables on which the view
is defined immediately affect the contents of the view.
Compare this with Figure 11.36.

VIEWS

Techniques
for Programming

This, the fourth and final programming chapter of the book, will show you some specific ways of using programming languages to interface with MySQL. Whereas chapters 7 through 9 demonstrate how to do basic MySQL interactions with PHP, Perl, and Java, the focus here is more on theory and techniques: how to do certain things using a programming language. The particulars to be discussed include storing and retrieving binary data, generating query result pages, using transactions, and calling stored procedures.

The techniques demonstrated in this chapter cover a handful of what I believe are the more commonly needed programming topics. I'll be showing one workable solution to each of the quandaries. While you will most likely find yourself using slight variants on these techniques, following the steps for each topic should give you a sufficient sense of the theory behind them. I'll use one of the previously discussed languages (PHP, Perl, and Java) for each example, but you should be able to recognize and translate the techniques to whichever language you are using.

Storing and Retrieving Binary Data

One of the more common questions people ask regarding MySQL is how to store and retrieve binary data in a database. Binary data includes items such as an image, a PDF file, or a video clip. These items have to be handled differently than you would the things you normally file in a database: simple text strings, dates, and numbers.

For this example, I'll use PHP as the programming language. This is a logical choice, as Web content often includes binary data (specifically images). If you're using JSP or even CGI scripts written in Perl, you should still be able to follow along. I'll start by creating the database. Then I'll write one page that stores the binary data and lists all of the currently stored records. The third step will be to create a script that retrieves and displays the data.

Should You Store Binary Data?

In this chapter I teach how to store binary data, but there is some debate as to whether or not you *should* store binary data in your database. The alternative would be to store the file on the server in a convenient location, and then store the filename in the database. There are pros and cons to both methods.

On the one hand, storing binary data in a database allows you to back it up at the same time as you back up the rest of the data. It also makes those files accessible to anyone with access to the database. This means that the binary files can be accessible to multiple computers, as well.

On the other hand, you'll need to write extra SQL and code in order to store and retrieve this information. Your application may have decreased performance, too.

In the end, it's really up to the developer and the needs of the application as to which method you use, but it's great that MySQL offers different options. You should experiment with both approaches to see which you like the best.

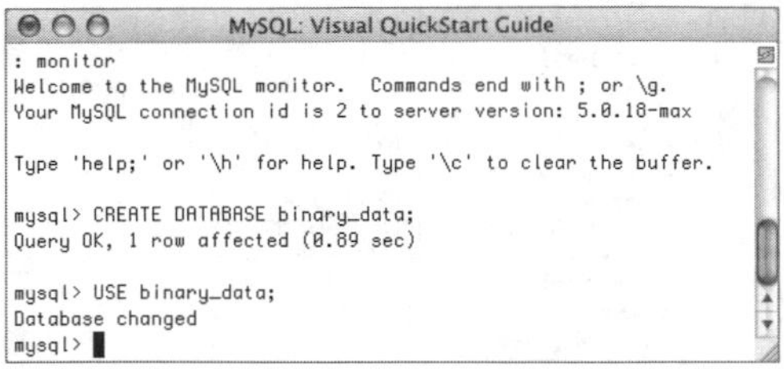

Figure 12.1 To begin this example, I make a new database using the mysql client.

Creating the database

To store binary data in your database, you should first make a column of type BLOB.

```
CREATE TABLE binary (
binary_item BLOB
)
```

MySQL supports different sizes of BLOBs—TINYBLOB, MEDIUMBLOB, BLOB, and LONGBLOB—even though the SQL standard does not. There's also BINARY and VARBINARY, which store smaller amounts of binary data, too small to use in this example.

For this example I will store images—JPEGs, GIFs, and PNGs—in a database. Along with the actual image, I will store the image's original name, its MIME type, its size in pixel dimensions, and its size in bytes. Of this metadata, the type is the most important, as PHP needs to know that information in order to properly show the image in a Web browser.

To create the database:

1. Log in to mysql as a user with permission to create a new database.

2. Create the new database (**Figure 12.1**).
   ```
   CREATE DATABASE binary_data;
   USE binary_data;
   ```

   continues on next page

STORING AND RETRIEVING BINARY DATA

3. Create the necessary table (**Figure 12.2**).

```
CREATE TABLE images (
image_id int(10) UNSIGNED NOT NULL
→ AUTO_INCREMENT,
image BLOB,
image_name VARCHAR(60) NOT NULL,
image_type VARCHAR(12) NOT NULL,
image_width MEDIUMINT UNSIGNED NOT
→ NULL,
image_height MEDIUMINT UNSIGNED NOT
→ NULL,
image_size INT UNSIGNED NOT NULL,
uploaded_date TIMESTAMP,
PRIMARY KEY (image_id),
INDEX (uploaded_date)
);
```

For demonstration purposes, I'll be creating a new images table within the *binary_data* database. The image's size is stored in two separate fields, both of type MEDIUMINT. I'm also adding an uploaded_date TIMESTAMP column that will reflect when an image was added to the database.

✔ Tip

■ In reality, a field of type BLOB is exactly like a TEXT field, except that it is case-sensitive, whereas TEXT fields are case-insensitive.

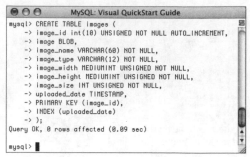

Figure 12.2 This single table will store all of the data this example requires.

Storing binary data

Once you've established a table field that can take binary data, you could use the LOAD_FILE() function to store data in it. Using the SET notation, an example INSERT would be:

```
INSERT INTO tablename SET image_col=
→ LOAD_FILE('/path/to/file.ext'),
→ SET other_col='value'…
```

The LOAD_FILE() function takes as its lone argument the full path and name of the file on the server (e.g., C:/data/myfile.xls). There are two requirements for using this method:

◆ The file must already exist on the same computer as the MySQL database.

◆ You must be connected to MySQL as a user with FILE permission.

This last requirement may be an issue, as, for security purposes, only administrators should have FILE permission.

An alternative to using LOAD_FILE() is to have your programming language read the file into a variable and then use that variable in a query, just as you would any other piece of data. Using this method, the first of the two preceding conditions still applies but the second does not.

To demonstrate this, I'll create a PHP script that uploads an image from a form and stores it in the database. I will use the Improved MySQL extension functions, discussed in Chapter 7, "MySQL and PHP." This assumes that you are using at least version 5 of PHP, with support for this extension (the version of MySQL will not matter in this example).

To store binary data:

1. Begin a new PHP script in your text editor (**Script 12.1**).

```
<!DOCTYPE html PUBLIC "-//W3C//DTD
→ XHTML 1.0 Transitional//EN"
"http://www.w3.org/TR/xhtml1/DTD/
→ xhtml1-transitional.dtd">
<html xmlns="http://www.w3.org/1999/
→ xhtml" xml:lang="en" lang="en">
<head>
    <meta http-equiv="content-type"
    → content="text/html; charset=
    → iso-8859-1" />
    <title>Storing Images in
    → MySQL</title>
</head>
<body>
<?php
```

This page will use a combination of XHTML and PHP to display a form and then handle a file upload. This is a standard XHTML header, followed by the initial PHP tag.

Script 12.1 The store_binary.php script allows the user to select an image to be stored in the database. It also lists the currently stored images.

```
1    <!DOCTYPE html PUBLIC "-//W3C//DTD XHTML 1.0 Transitional//EN"
2            "http://www.w3.org/TR/xhtml1/DTD/xhtml1-transitional.dtd">
3    <html xmlns="http://www.w3.org/1999/xhtml" xml:lang="en" lang="en">
4    <head>
5        <meta http-equiv="content-type" content="text/html; charset=iso-8859-1" />
6        <title>Storing Images in MySQL</title>
7    </head>
8    <body>
9    <?php
10
11   // ***** store_binary.php *****
12   // ***** Script 12.1 *****
13   // This script allows the user to upload an image.
14   // The image is then stored in the binary.images table.
15
16   // Connect to MySQL:
17   $dbc = @mysqli_connect('localhost', 'username', 'password', 'binary_data') or die ('Could not
     connect to MySQL: ' . mysqli_connect_error() . '</body></html>');
```

Script continues on next page

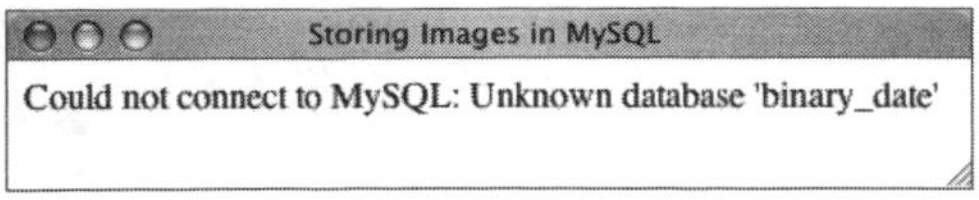

Figure 12.3 Connection errors are immediately reported, and the script then stops executing.

2. Connect to MySQL.

```
$dbc = @mysqli_connect('localhost',
→ 'username', 'password',
→ 'binary_data') or die ('Could not
→ connect to MySQL: ' . mysqli_
→ connect_error() . '</body></html>');
```

If the form has been submitted, an INSERT query is run. Whenever the page is viewed, whether or not the form has been submitted, a SELECT query is run. For this reason, the script will always need a database connection, so that's done first.

The code itself comes from Chapter 7. If a connection could not be made, the error is reported (**Figure 12.3**) and the HTML page is completed.

continues on next page

Script 12.1 *continued*

```
18
19   if (isset($_POST['submitted'])) { // If the form has been submitted...
20
21       // Check for an uploaded file:
22       if (isset($_FILES['upload'])) {
23
24           // Validate the type. Should be jpeg, jpg, gif, or png.
25           $allowed = array ('image/gif', 'image/jpeg', 'image/jpg', 'image/pjpeg', 'image/png');
26
27           if (in_array($_FILES['upload']['type'], $allowed)) { // OK
28
29               // Get the image's size in pixels:
30               $image_info = getimagesize($_FILES['upload']['tmp_name']);
31
32               // Read the uploaded file into a variable:
33               $image = fread(fopen($_FILES['upload']['tmp_name'], 'r'), $_FILES['upload']['size']);
34
35               // Secure the data:
36               $image = mysqli_real_escape_string($dbc, $image);
37               $name = mysqli_real_escape_string($dbc, $_FILES['upload']['name']);
38               $size = (int)$_FILES['upload']['size'];
39
```

Script continues on next page

3. Check if the form has been submitted.

```
if (isset($_POST['submitted'])) {
```

Since this script will both display and handle a form, a conditional has to check for the form's submission. This first part of code (from this point until the closing curly brace) will be run only if the form was submitted (and the POST variable submitted has a value).

Script 12.1 *continued*

```
40          // Generate the query:
41          $q = "INSERT INTO images (image, image_name, image_type, image_width, image_height,
            image_size) VALUES ('$image', '$name', '{$_FILES['upload']['type']}', $image_info[0],
            $image_info[1], $size)";
42
43          // Execute the query:
44          $r = mysqli_query ($dbc, $q);
45
46          // Print a message indicating success:
47          if (mysqli_affected_rows($dbc) == 1) {
48              echo '<p><font color="green">The image has been stored!</font></p>';
49          } else {
50              echo '<p><font color="red">The image could not be stored in the
                database!</font></p>';
51              echo '<p><font color="red">MySQL reported: '. mysqli_error($dbc) .'</font></p>';
52          }
53
54      } else { // Invalid type.
55          echo '<p><font color="red">Please upload a JPEG, GIF, or PNG image.</font></p>';
56      }
57
58      // Remove the file from the server:
59      if (file_exists($_FILES['upload']['tmp_name']) and
        is_file($_FILES['upload']['tmp_name'])) {
60          unlink ($_FILES['upload']['tmp_name']);
61      }
62
63  } else { // No file uploaded.
64      echo '<p><font color="red">Please upload a JPEG, GIF, or PNG image smaller than
        512KB.</font></p>';
65  }
66
67 } // End of submitted IF.
68
69 // Display the form:
70 echo '<h2>Use this form to store an image in the database:</h2>
71 <p>(Images must be of type JPEG, GIF, or PNG.)</p>
```

Script continues on next page

4. Check that a file of the proper type was uploaded.

```
if (isset($_FILES['upload'])) {
    $allowed = array ('image/gif',
    → 'image/jpeg', 'image/jpg',
    → 'image/pjpeg', 'image/png');
    if (in_array($_FILES['upload']
    → ['type'], $allowed)) {
```

The first step is to see if anything was uploaded at all. Then I create an array of allowable file types, using the MIME types as the possible values. If the uploaded file is of one of these types, then it can be stored in the database.

continues on next page

Script 12.1 *continued*

```
72    <form action="store_binary.php" method="post" enctype="multipart/form-data">
73    <input type="hidden" name="MAX_FILE_SIZE" value="524288" />
74    <p>Select an image to upload: <input type="file" name="upload" /></p>
75    <input type="hidden" name="submitted" value="true" />
76    <input type="submit" name="submit" value="Submit!" />
77    </form>
78    <br />';
79
80
81    // Show the current list of images.
82    // Link each to view_image.php.
83    echo '<h2>Currently Stored Images</h2><p>(Click an image\'s name to view it.)</p>';
84
85    // Create the query:
86    $q = 'SELECT image_id, image_name FROM images ORDER BY uploaded_date DESC';
87
88    // Execute the query:
89    $r = mysqli_query ($dbc, $q);
90
91    // Check the results:
92    if (mysqli_num_rows($r) > 0) {
93
94        // Display each item in a list.
95        echo '<ul>';
96
97        while ($row = mysqli_fetch_array ($r, MYSQLI_NUM)) {
98            echo "<li><a href=\"view_image.php?i=$row[0]\">$row[1]</a></li>\n";
99        }
100
```

Script continues on next page

5. Get the image's information and assign the uploaded image file to a string.

```
$image_info = getimagesize($_FILES
→ ['upload']['tmp_name']);
$image = fread(fopen($_FILES
→ ['upload']['tmp_name'], 'r'),
→ $_FILES['upload']['size']);
```

The first line just applies the getimagesize() function so that the script can know the image's height and width in pixels.

The second line is the most important one in the entire script. In this one step, the uploaded file (referred to by $_FILES['upload']['tmp_name') is read into a string called $image. To read the image, it is opened using the fopen() function, with the size of the file as the amount of data to read. The opened file is then read with fread() and assigned to $image. You can break this one line into two separate steps—fopen() and fread()—to make it easier to understand.

6. Secure the query data and define the query.

```
$image = mysqli_real_escape_string
→ ($dbc, $image);
$name = mysqli_real_escape_string
→ ($dbc, $_FILES['upload']['name']);
$size = (int)$_FILES['upload']
→ ['size'];
$q = "INSERT INTO images (image,
→ image_name, image_type, image_width,
→ image_height, image_size) VALUES
→ ('$image', '$name', '{$_FILES
→ ['upload']['type']}', $image_info[0],
→ $image_info[1], $size)";
```

Script 12.1 *continued*

```
101     echo '<ul>';
102
103     // Clean up:
104     mysqli_free_result($r);
105
106  } else { // No records returned.
107     echo '<p>There are currently no
        stored images.</p>';
108  }
109
110  // Close the database connection:
111  mysqli_close($dbc);
112
113  ?>
114  </body>
115  </html>
```

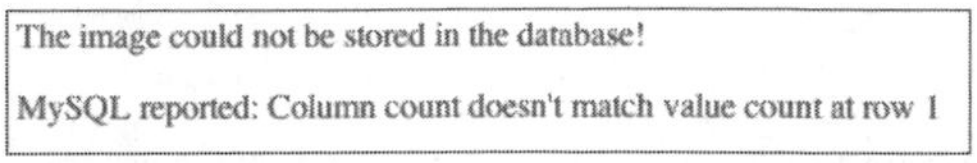

The image could not be stored in the database!

MySQL reported: Column count doesn't match value count at row 1

Figure 12.4 If the INSERT query fails, a message indicating such is printed. For debugging purposes, the MySQL error is also printed.

Binary data must be escaped prior to use in a query because it contains all sorts of problematic characters that will otherwise break the query. The `mysqli_real_escape_string()` function is used to accomplish this. The same function is also applied to the image's name, as that comes from the user's computer and could be dangerous. Finally, I type cast the file's size as an integer as an extra precaution.

The query itself is straightforward: a simple INSERT. Since $image has the value of the binary data that is the uploaded file, it can be used as if it were any other string of text.

7. Query the database and report on the success (**Figure 12.4**).

```
$r = mysqli_query ($dbc, $q);
if (mysqli_affected_rows($dbc) == 1) {
    echo '<p><font color="green">
    → The image has been stored!
    → </font></p>';
} else {
    echo '<p><font color="red">
    → The image could not be stored
    → in the database!</font></p>';
    echo '<p><font color="red">
    → MySQL reported: '. mysqli_error
    → ($dbc) .'</font></p>';
}
```

I've included a line for debugging purposes here, should the query fail. You can also print out the query to see what it is, although you'll print out a lot of gibberish in the process, that gibberish being the binary image data.

continues on next page

8. Complete every conditional and remove the file from the server.

```
        } else {
            echo '<p><font color=
            → "red">Please upload a
            → JPEG, GIF, or PNG
            → image.</font></p>';
        }
        if (file_exists($_FILES
        → ['upload']['tmp_name']) and
        → is_file($_FILES['upload']
        → ['tmp_name'])) {
            unlink ($_FILES['upload']
            → ['tmp_name']);
        }
    } else {
        echo '<p><font color="red">
        → Please upload a JPEG, GIF,
        → or PNG image smaller than
        → 512KB.</font></p>';
    }
}
```

The first else clause applies if the wrong type of file was uploaded (**Figure 12.5**). The second applies if no file was uploaded.

In the middle, the actual file on the server (which was put into a temporary directory upon upload) is deleted. This line applies if the wrong type of file was uploaded, if the file was uploaded and successfully stored in the database, or if the file was uploaded but couldn't be stored in the database because of a MySQL error.

Please upload a JPEG, GIF, or PNG image.

Figure 12.5 The script limits what kinds of files can be stored in the database.

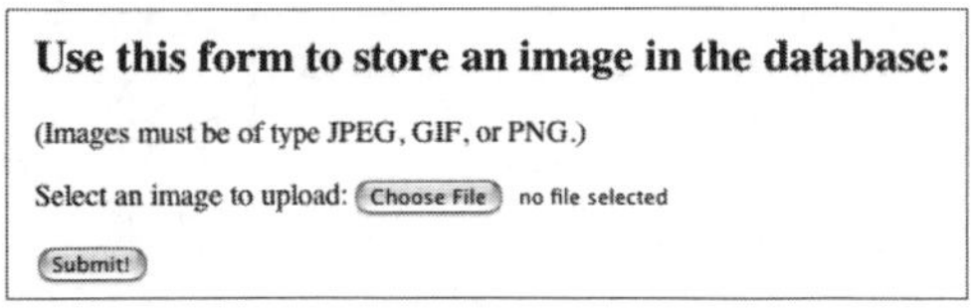

Use this form to store an image in the database:

(Images must be of type JPEG, GIF, or PNG.)

Select an image to upload: [Choose File] no file selected

[Submit!]

Figure 12.6 This HTML form will allow users to select an image on their hard drive that will be stored in the database.

9. Create the HTML form (**Figure 12.6**).

```
echo '<h2>Use this form to store an
image in the database:</h2>
<p>(Images must be of type JPEG,
→ GIF, or PNG.)</p>
<form action="store_binary.php"
→ method="post" enctype="multipart/
→ form-data">
<input type="hidden" name=
→ "MAX_FILE_SIZE" value="524288" />
<p>Select an image to upload: <input
→ type="file" name="upload" /></p>
<input type="hidden" name="submitted"
→ value="true" />
<input type="submit" name="submit"
→ value="Submit!" />
</form>
<br />';
```

The most important pieces of this form are the form's *action* (referring back to this same script), its *enctype* (which allows for a file to be uploaded), and the name of the file being uploaded (which should match the name used earlier in the script).

You should also adjust the MAX_FILE_SIZE value to accommodate the largest image you will want to store. In my example, up to a 512 Kbyte image will work just fine.

continues on next page

STORING AND RETRIEVING BINARY DATA

10. Show a list of currently stored images (**Figure 12.7**).

```
echo '<h2>Currently Stored
→ Images</h2><p>(Click an image\'s
→ name to view it.)</p>';
$q = 'SELECT image_id, image_name
→ FROM images ORDER BY uploaded_date
→ DESC';
$r = mysqli_query ($dbc, $q);
if (mysqli_num_rows($r) > 0) {
    echo '<ul>';
    while ($row = mysqli_fetch_array
    → ($r, MYSQLI_NUM)) {
        echo "<li><a href=
        → \"view_image.php?i=$row[0]\
        → ">$row[1]</a></li>\n";
    }
    echo '<ul>';
    mysqli_free_result($r);
} else {
    echo '<p>There are currently no
    → stored images.</p>';
}
```

This query retrieves every image ID and image name from the database. If some records are returned, they are printed within an unordered list. Each is linked to view_image.php, passing along the image's ID as an argument (**Figure 12.8**).

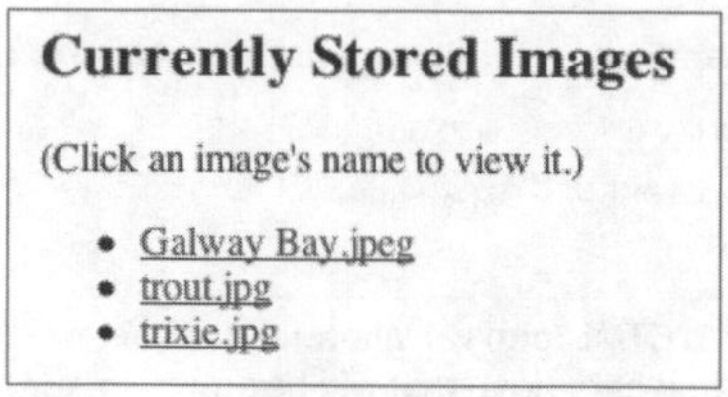

Currently Stored Images

(Click an image's name to view it.)

- Galway Bay.jpeg
- trout.jpg
- trixie.jpg

Figure 12.7 Each stored image is listed as a link to the view_image.php script.

```
<br /><h2>Currently Stored Images</h2><p>(Click an image's name to view
it.)</p><ul><li><a href="view_image.php?i=3">Galway Bay.jpeg</a></li>
<li><a href="view_image.php?i=2">trout.jpg</a></li>
<li><a href="view_image.php?i=1">trixie.jpg</a></li>
<ul></body>
```

Figure 12.8 The HTML source shows how each link passes the image's ID value to the view_image.php script.

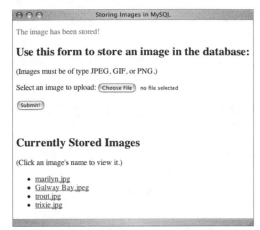

Figure 12.9 Another image has been uploaded and stored by this script.

11. Complete the script.

```
mysqli_close($dbc);
?>
</body>
</html>
```

12. Save the script as `store_binary.php`, upload it to your Web server, and test in your Web browser (**Figure 12.9**).

✔ Tips

- One potential problem with this script is that it relies upon the Web browser's identification of a file's MIME type. You could instead use a function like `mime_content_type()` for this purpose.

- If the uploaded image file does not contain an extension on the user's computer, it may not pass the validation tests.

Retrieving binary data

Now that I've written a script for storing images in a database, I'll create another that will retrieve and display the image in a Web browser. The retrieval part is easy: it's just a SELECT query. Getting the image to display from that point is a matter of telling the Web browser what kind of data to expect— an image of a certain type—and then sending the image to the browser. PHP's header() function can let the browser know what type of data is forthcoming, as you'll see in this script.

To retrieve and display binary data:

1. Create a new PHP script (**Script 12.2**).

   <?php

   No HTML is required by this script, as it only displays an image.

Script 12.2 The view_image.php script retrieves an image from a database and sends it to the Web browser.

```
1    <?php
2
3    // ***** view_image.php *****
4    // ***** Script 12.2 *****
5    // This script displays an image stored in the database.
6    // No HTML required as this page just shows an image.
7
8    if (isset($_GET['i'])) { // Need an image number.
9
10       // Type cast the number for security:
11       $i = (int) $_GET['i'];
12
13       if ($i > 0) { // Must be a positive integer!
14
15          // Connect to MySQL:
16          $dbc = @mysqli_connect('localhost', 'username', 'password', 'binary_data') or die
             ('Could not connect to MySQL: ' . mysqli_connect_error());
17
18          // Retrieve the image information.
19          $q = "SELECT image, image_name, image_type, image_size FROM images WHERE image_id=$i";
20
21          // Execute the query:
22          $r = mysqli_query ($dbc, $q);
23
```

Script continues on next page

```
MySQL: Visual QuickStart Guide
mysql> SELECT image_id, image_name, image_type,
    -> image_width, image_height, image_size
    -> FROM images;
+----------+----------------+------------+-------------+--------------+------------+
| image_id | image_name     | image_type | image_width | image_height | image_size |
+----------+----------------+------------+-------------+--------------+------------+
|        1 | trixie.jpg     | image/jpeg |        1280 |         1024 |     422205 |
|        2 | trout.jpg      | image/jpeg |         582 |          271 |      75645 |
|        3 | Galway Bay.jpeg | image/jpeg |        832 |          624 |      95915 |
|        4 | marilyn.jpg    | image/jpeg |         516 |          513 |      40521 |
+----------+----------------+------------+-------------+--------------+------------+
4 rows in set (0.00 sec)

mysql>
```

Figure 12.10 The records in the `images` table after uploading a few images.

2. Check for and validate an image number.

```
if (isset($_GET['i'])) {
    $i = (int) $_GET['i'];
    if ($i > 0) {
```

This page will be called by using the syntax *view_image.php?i=x*, where *x* refers to the `image_id` in the database for the corresponding image (**Figure 12.10**). This conditional first checks that `$_GET['i']` exists and then checks that it has an integer value greater than 0.

3. Connect to the database.

```
$dbc = @mysqli_connect('localhost',
→ 'username', 'password',
→ 'binary_data') or die ('Could not
connect to MySQL: ' .
→ mysqli_connect_error());
```

continues on next page

Script 12.2 *continued*

```
Script
            // Check the results:
            if (mysqli_num_rows($r) == 1) {

                // Retrieve the image information:
                $row = mysqli_fetch_array ($r, MYSQLI_ASSOC);

                // Clean up:
                mysqli_free_result($r);

                // Send the image to the browser:
                header ("Content-Type: {$row['image_type']}\n");
                header ("Content-disposition: inline; filename=\"{$row['image_name']}\"\n");
                header ("Content-Length: {$row['image_size']}\n");
                echo $row['image'];

            }

            // Close the database connection:
            mysqli_close($dbc);

        }

    }
    ?>
```

4. Retrieve the image and image information from the database.

```
$q = "SELECT image, image_name,
→ image_type, image_size FROM images
→ WHERE image_id=$i";
$r = mysqli_query ($dbc, $q);
if (mysqli_num_rows($r) == 1) {
    $row = mysqli_fetch_array ($r,
    → MYSQLI_ASSOC);
    mysqli_free_result($r);
```

The query returns the image itself (the binary data), its name, and its size in bytes from the table based upon the `image_id` value (which corresponds to i, passed to the script). If the query is successful, an array of information is assigned to the `$row` variable.

5. Send the image to the Web browser.

```
header ("Content-Type:
→ {$row['image_type']}\n");
header ("Content-disposition: inline;
→ filename=\"{$row['image_name']}\"\
→ n");
header ("Content-Length:
→ {$row['image_size']}\n");
echo $row['image'];
```

The first use of the `header()` function will tell the browser what type of data to expect, which is the stored MIME type of the image. Then the browser is told to display this data inline (in the Web browser) and the image's name is provided. The content-length value is also sent, which isn't required but is a good idea. The length value is the size of the image in bytes. Finally, after all of this preparation, the image itself is sent to the browser by simply echoing it.

Figure 12.11 The `view_image.php` script retrieves an image from the database and sends it to the Web browser.

6. Complete the script.

```
    }
    mysqli_close($dbc);
  }
}
?>
```

7. Save the file as `view_image.php`, upload it to your Web server, and test in a Web browser (**Figure 12.11**) by clicking the links in `store_binary.php`.

✔ Tips

- You can use the `view_image.php` script to display images anywhere within a Web page by using the code `<img src= "view_image.php?i=89" />`. You can use the stored image width and height to add that information to this image tag.

- Depending upon your Web server, you may find that the page loads and the image is displayed rather slowly. This is the performance issue mentioned earlier, and it may be a reason not to use this technique.

- If your image only partially displays, this is probably because it was too big for the blob column in the database. Change the column's definition, perhaps to `LONGBLOB`, so that more data can be stored.

Making Query Result Pages

Except for limited queries on small databases, most SELECT statements will return tens, hundreds, or even thousands of records. When printing these records (to a Web page or wherever), you will presumably not want to display them all at one time. In such cases, you will need to make query result pages so that page one will display the first 25 records, page two the next 25, and so forth until all of the records have been displayed. This is called *pagination*.

Depending upon the programming language being used and the needs of the application, there are two logical ways of developing query result pages:

◆ Assign the query's resource link to a variable that gets passed from page to page (see the sidebar "Using a Resource Link").

◆ Reapply the query on each page, changing the start and end points (the LIMITs) accordingly.

For this example, I will use PHP, which must use the slightly more complex second method (as PHP closes a database connection when the script stops running). As my example, the script will browse through all of the records in a *movies* database by movie title. To start off, you'll need to create and populate the database.

Using a Resource Link

Assuming that you are using a programming language that does not automatically close a database connection when a script runs (or that allows for permanent connections), you can simplify the steps outlined in this section. Here's how:

Normally when you query a database, the result of that query can be assigned to a variable. The value of this variable is essentially a link to the database for that particular query. Normally data is retrieved within a loop, fetching a record through this link with each iteration. But if you can get the link to exist beyond the scope of a single script, it can be passed from page to page, allowing you to access rows as needed, without requerying the database every time.

If you're creating an application, it could show X number of records, wait for the user to press a button, and then show the next X number. In such a case it's just a matter of using the same resource link, user input, and some loops.

Movies Database

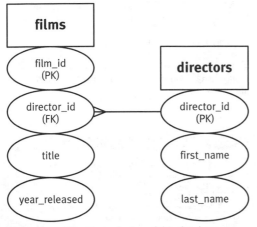

Figure 12.12 The simple design of this database.

Creating the database

This database will store information about movies and directors. For the sake of focusing on the task at hand (paginating query results), I'm going to implement a minimal version of this database. I'll just define two tables: one that stores directors and another that stores information about films. A one-to-many relationship will exist between the two, as each film has only one director (by the Director's Guild rules) and each director can make several films (**Figure 12.12**). If you'd like to expand upon this design, you could start by fleshing out these first two tables: adding biographic information about the director, production information about a film, and so on. Then you could create an actors table and an actors_films table that's an intermediary between actors and films (as there's a many-to-many relationship there).

To create the database:

1. Log in to the mysql client as a user capable of creating new databases.

2. Create and select a movies database.

   CREATE DATABASE movies;

   USE movies;

   Instead of using an existing database, I'll be making a new one for storing movie information. The database being used in this example has not previously been designed or implemented. If you followed the steps in Chapter 2, "Running MySQL," you may have created a *movies* database, but without any tables (when creating users). If you've already created this database, you can skip the first SQL command and just use the second to select it.

continues on next page

MAKING QUERY RESULT PAGES

3. Create a new table called *directors*
(**Figure 12.13**).

```
CREATE TABLE directors (
director_id INT UNSIGNED NOT NULL
→ AUTO_INCREMENT,
first_name VARCHAR(20),
last_name VARCHAR(30) NOT NULL,
PRIMARY KEY (director_id),
INDEX (last_name)
);
```

This is the bare-bones directors table.
It just stores each director's first and last
names. I've put an index on the last name,
as that is likely to be used in queries.

4. Create the second table (**Figure 12.14**).

```
CREATE TABLE films (
film_id INT UNSIGNED NOT NULL
→ AUTO_INCREMENT,
director_id INT UNSIGNED NOT NULL,
title VARCHAR(100) NOT NULL,
year_released YEAR NOT NULL,
PRIMARY KEY (film_id),
INDEX (director_id),
INDEX (title),
INDEX (year_released)
);
```

The films table has a little more to it,
but not much. I index the director_id
field, as it will be used in joins. I also
index the film's title and year of release,
as these are likely to be used in WHERE or
ORDER BY clauses.

5. Populate the directors table
(**Figure 12.15**).

```
INSERT INTO directors
(first_name, last_name)
VALUES
('Wes', 'Anderson'),
('Joel', 'Coen'),
('Paul Thomas', 'Anderson'),
```

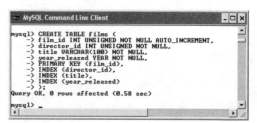

Figure 12.13 Creating a table to store information about directors.

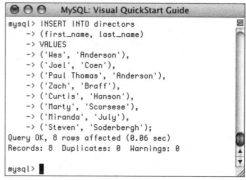

Figure 12.14 Creating a table to store information about films.

Figure 12.15 A few records are added to the directors table.

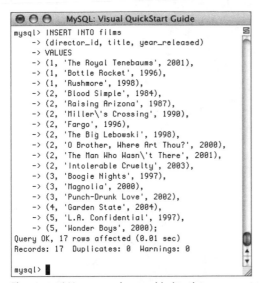

```
mysql> INSERT INTO films
    -> (director_id, title, year_released)
    -> VALUES
    -> (1, 'The Royal Tenebaums', 2001),
    -> (1, 'Bottle Rocket', 1996),
    -> (1, 'Rushmore', 1998),
    -> (2, 'Blood Simple', 1984),
    -> (2, 'Raising Arizona', 1987),
    -> (2, 'Miller\'s Crossing', 1990),
    -> (2, 'Fargo', 1996),
    -> (2, 'The Big Lebowski', 1998),
    -> (2, 'O Brother, Where Art Thou?', 2000),
    -> (2, 'The Man Who Wasn\'t There', 2001),
    -> (2, 'Intolerable Cruelty', 2003),
    -> (3, 'Boogie Nights', 1997),
    -> (3, 'Magnolia', 2000),
    -> (3, 'Punch-Drunk Love', 2002),
    -> (4, 'Garden State', 2004),
    -> (5, 'L.A. Confidential', 1997),
    -> (5, 'Wonder Boys', 2000);
Query OK, 17 rows affected (0.01 sec)
Records: 17  Duplicates: 0  Warnings: 0

mysql>
```

Figure 12.16 Many records are added to the films table.

('Zach', 'Braff'),

('Curtis', 'Hanson'),

('Marty', 'Scorsese'),

('Miranda', 'July'),

('Steven', 'Soderbergh');

This is just some sample data I'm using. Fill in your own favorites as you see fit.

6. Populate the films table (**Figure 12.16**).

INSERT INTO films

(director_id, file_title,

→ year_released)

VALUES

(1, 'The Royal Tenenbaums', 2001),

(1, 'Bottle Rocket', 1996),

(1, 'Rushmore', 1998),

(2, 'Blood Simple', 1984),

(2, 'Raising Arizona', 1987),

(2, 'Miller\'s Crossing', 1990),

(2, 'Fargo', 1996),

(2, 'The Big Lebowski', 1998),

(2, 'O Brother, Where Art Thou?', 2000),

(2, 'The Man Who Wasn\'t There', 2001),

(2, 'Intolerable Cruelty', 2003),

(3, 'Boogie Nights', 1997),

(3, 'Magnolia', 2000),

(3, 'Punch-Drunk Love', 2002),

(4, 'Garden State', 2004),

(5, 'L.A. Confidential', 1997),

(5, 'Wonder Boys', 2000);

Each of these films corresponds to one of the directors that have already been added.

7. Repeat Steps 5 and 6 until the directors and films tables are well populated.

In order to adequately demonstrate the concept of pagination, you'll need quite a lot of records to retrieve.

✔ Tip

■ All of this SQL is available for download from the book's corresponding Web site.

MAKING QUERY RESULT PAGES

Paginating PHP pages

Now that you have a populated database, you can make the query results pages. As I mention in the introduction to this section, to achieve the pagination, I'll display X number of results on each page. To make sure that the right results are displayed, I use a LIMIT clause on my query.

For the first page, I should display the first X records, so my query would end with LIMIT X, or the more formal LIMIT 0, X (take X records starting from 0, which is the first record returned). For the second page, I've already seen the first X records, so I'll want to use LIMIT (X * 1), X. If you're displaying ten records per page, this means LIMIT 10, 10. In other words, start with the eleventh item (which is number 10 when you start counting from 0) and show the next ten. For the third page, you'd want LIMIT (X * 2), X. And so on.

In short, the LIMIT formula for pagination will be

LIMIT (X * (Y - 1)), X

where X is the number of records being displayed per page and Y is the page number. You have to subtract 1 so that the first page starts at 0 (X * (1 - 1)), the second at X (X * (2 - 1)), etc.

That's the hardest part. The only other tricks are:

◆ The first time the page is run, it must determine how many records are returned by the query.

◆ The page must pass back to itself all of the LIMIT and other values.

To create a query result page:

1. Begin a new PHP script in your text editor (**Script 12.3**).

```
<!DOCTYPE html PUBLIC "-//W3C//DTD
→ XHTML 1.0 Transitional//EN"
"http://www.w3.org/TR/xhtml1/DTD/
→ xhtml1-transitional.dtd">
<html xmlns="http://www.w3.org/1999/
→ xhtml" xml:lang="en" lang="en">
<head>
    <meta http-equiv="content-type"
    → content="text/html;
    → charset=iso-8859-1" />
    <title>Browse the Movie Titles
    → </title>
</head>
<body>
<?php
```

continues on next page

Script 12.3 This PHP script demonstrates how easily you can paginate your query result pages.

```
1    <!DOCTYPE html PUBLIC "-//W3C//DTD XHTML 1.0 Transitional//EN"
2         "http://www.w3.org/TR/xhtml1/DTD/xhtml1-transitional.dtd">
3    <html xmlns="http://www.w3.org/1999/xhtml" xml:lang="en" lang="en">
4    <head>
5         <meta http-equiv="content-type" content="text/html; charset=iso-8859-1" />
6         <title>Browse the Movie Titles</title>
7    </head>
8    <body>
9    <?php
10
11   // ***** browse_movies.php *****
12   // ***** Script 12.3 *****
13   // This script generates query result pages
14   // of movie titles in the movies database.
15
16   // Number of records to show per page:
17   $display_number = 5;
18
19   // Connect to MySQL:
20   $dbc = @mysqli_connect('localhost', 'username', 'password', 'movies') or die ('Could not connect
     to MySQL: ' . mysqli_connect_error() . '</body></html>');
21
22   // Determine how many records there are:
23   if (isset($_GET['np'])) {
```

Script continues on next page

2. Establish the number of records to show per page.

`$display_number = 5;`

For sake of convenience, I prefer to set this number as a variable. This way, I can change how the script works by changing only one value (even though the number will be used several times over the course of the script).

Since my database isn't that full yet, I'm using a small number.

Script 12.3 *continued*

```
24
25      $num_pages = (int) $_GET['np'];
26
27  } else {
28
29      // Find out how many records there are.
30      $q = 'SELECT COUNT(*) FROM directors, films WHERE directors.director_id=films.director_id';
31
32      // Get the number.
33      $r = mysqli_query($dbc, $q);
34      list($num_records) = mysqli_fetch_array($r, MYSQLI_NUM);
35      mysqli_free_result($r);
36
37      // Calculate the number of pages:
38      if ($num_records > $display_number) {
39          $num_pages = ceil ($num_records/$display_number);
40      } else {
41          $num_pages = 1;
42      }
43
44  }
45
46  // Determine where in the database to start returning results:
47  if (isset($_GET['s'])) {
48      $start = (int) $_GET['s'];
49  } else {
50      $start = 0;
51  }
52
53  // Define the query:
54  $q = "SELECT CONCAT(directors.first_name, ' ', directors.last_name) AS Director, title AS Title
        FROM directors, films WHERE directors.director_id=films.director_id ORDER BY films.title ASC
        LIMIT $start, $display_number";
55
```

Script continues on next page

3. Connect to the database.

```
$dbc = @mysqli_connect('localhost',
→ 'username', 'password', 'movies')
→ or die ('Could not connect to
→ MySQL: ' . mysqli_connect_error() .
→ '</body></html>');
```

As always, you could place this information in a separate configuration file for added security.

continues on next page

Script 12.3 *continued*

```
56    // Run the query:
57    $r = mysqli_query ($dbc, $q);
58
59    // Display all of the records:
60    while ($row = mysqli_fetch_array ($r, MYSQLI_ASSOC)) {
61        echo "{$row['Director']} <i>{$row['Title']}</i><br />\n";
62    }
63
64    // Clean up:
65    mysqli_free_result ($r);
66    mysqli_close($dbc);
67
68    // Make the links to other pages, if necessary:
69    if ($num_pages > 1) {
70
71        echo '<hr width="50%" align="left" />';
72
73        // Determine what page the script is on:
74        $current_page = ($start/$display_number) + 1;
75
76        // If it's not the first page, make a Previous button:
77        if ($current_page != 1) {
78            echo '<a href="browse_movies.php?s=' . ($start - $display_number) . '&np=' . $num_pages
             . '">Previous</a> ';
79        }
80
81        // Make all the numbered pages:
82        for ($i = 1; $i <= $num_pages; $i++) {
83
84            // Don't link the current page:
85            if ($i != $current_page) {
86                echo '<a href="browse_movies.php?s=' . (($display_number * ($i - 1))) . '&np=' .
                 $num_pages . '">' . $i . '</a> ';
```

Script continues on next page

4. Determine how many pages will need to be used to display all of the records.

```php
if (isset($_GET['np'])) {
    $num_pages = (int) $_GET['np'];
} else {
    $q = 'SELECT COUNT(*) FROM
    → directors, films WHERE directors.
    → director_id=films.director_id';
    $r = mysqli_query($dbc, $q);
    list($num_records) =
    → mysqli_fetch_array
    → ($r, MYSQLI_NUM);
    mysqli_free_result($r);
    if ($num_records > $display_
    → number) {
        $num_pages = ceil ($num_records/
        → $display_number);
    } else {
        $num_pages = 1;
    }
}
```

This is the first step in generating query result pages: seeing how many records will be displayed and therefore how many pages will be needed.

Script 12.3 *continued*

```
000                                           Script
87          } else {
88              echo $i . ' ';
89          }
90
91      }
92
93      // If it's not the last page, make a Next button:
94      if ($current_page != $num_pages) {
95          echo '<a href="browse_movies.php?s=
            ' . ($start + $display_number) . '&np=' . $num_pages . '">Next</a> ';
96      }
97
98  }
99
100 ?>
101 </body>
102 </html>
```

If the URL has an *np* value (for the number of pages), this means that the number has already been calculated and does not need to be determined again. If *np* does not have a value, it will need to be derived.

To calculate the number of pages, a modified version of the query is run to count how many records will be returned. If there are more rows than will fit on one page, I divide the number of rows by the number of rows to display per page and round this value up to the next higher integer. Otherwise, one page will suffice.

5. Determine with what record the query should start displaying.

```
if (isset($_GET['s'])) {
    $start = (int) $_GET['s'];
} else {
    $start = 0;
}
```

As I explain in the introduction to these steps, the query itself will use a LIMIT clause to show up to *X* records per page, starting from $X * (Y - 1)$. For this reason I need to determine whether the LIMIT should start at 0 (which is the first record) or elsewhere. If the *s* value (for *start*), appended to the URL, has a value, the query will use it. Otherwise, it will begin at 0.

continues on next page

MAKING QUERY RESULT PAGES

6. Display all of the records for this particular page.

```
$q = "SELECT CONCAT
→ (directors.first_name, ' ',
→ directors.last_name) AS Director,
→ title AS Title FROM directors,
→ films WHERE directors.director_id=
→ films.director_id ORDER BY
→ films.title ASC LIMIT $start,
→ $display_number";
$r = mysqli_query ($dbc, $q);
while ($row = mysqli_fetch_array
→ ($r, MYSQLI_ASSOC)) {
    echo "{$row['Director']}
    → <i>{$row['Title']}</i><br />\n";
}
```

The query in this step returns the actual records and uses a LIMIT clause. Aside from the query itself, this section of the script merely displays each record in a basic format (**Figure 12.17**).

7. Clean up the database resources.

```
mysqli_free_result ($r);
mysqli_close($dbc);
```

8. Begin making hyperlinks to the other query result pages.

```
if ($num_pages > 1) {
    echo '<hr width="50%"
    → align="left" />';
    $current_page = ($start/
    → $display_number) + 1;
```

If the query requires multiple pages, I'll need to make links so that the user can browse through them all. In this example, the navigation will have a previous link, a next link, and numbered links for every page (with the current page unlinked, **Figure 12.18**).

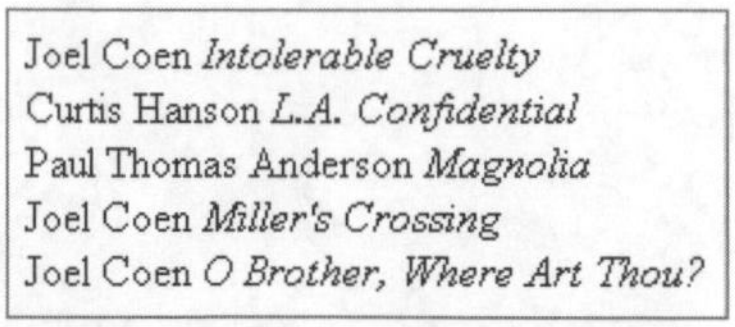

Joel Coen *Intolerable Cruelty*
Curtis Hanson *L.A. Confidential*
Paul Thomas Anderson *Magnolia*
Joel Coen *Miller's Crossing*
Joel Coen *O Brother, Where Art Thou?*

Figure 12.17 Each movie's director and title are displayed by the page.

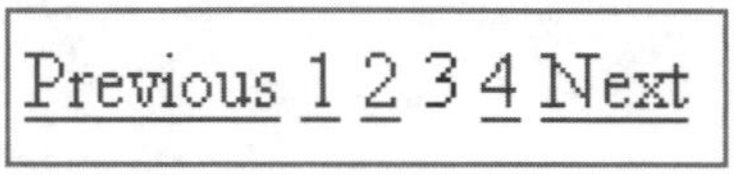

Previous 1 2 3 4 Next

Figure 12.18 The links to the paginated pages.

To calculate the current page, I add 1 to the division of the start number divided by the display number. For example, the first page will have a `$start` of 0 and a `$display_number` of 5. Zero divided by 5 is zero, plus 1 is 1. Hence, it's the first page. The fourth page will have a `$start` value of 15 (because it's showing the fourth group of five records from the database) and a `$display_number` of 5 still.

9. Create the *Previous* link.

```
if ($current_page != 1) {
    echo '<a href=
    ↪ "browse_movies.php?s=' .
    ↪ ($start - $display_number) .
    ↪ '&np=' . $num_pages . '">
    ↪ Previous</a> ';
}
```

If it is not the first page, I want to make a link to the previous page. The link is a URL of the format *browse_movies.php?s=A&np=B*, where *s* is the number to start with and *np* is the number of total pages. The *A* value will be based upon the current start value minus the number of records to display per page (in other words, the previous page should begin `$display_number` of records prior to this one). The *B* value will be based upon the calculated number of pages.

continues on next page

MAKING QUERY RESULT PAGES

10. Generate the numbered links.

```
for ($i = 1; $i <= $num_pages; $i++) {
    if ($i != $current_page) {
        echo '<a href=
        → "browse_movies.php?s=' .
        → (($display_number * ($i -
        → 1))) . '&np=' . $num_pages
        → . '">' . $i . '</a> ';
    } else {
        echo $i . ' ';
    }
}
```

So that the user can immediately jump through the list of movies, I want to make numbered links. To do so, I loop through the numbers 1 to the total number of pages, creating a link for each number except for the current page (no reason to link a page to itself). The *s* value here is calculated as $i minus 1, multiplied by the number of records displayed per page. For the second page, $i minus 1 is 1, times 5 is 5, meaning that the second page should begin with the second group of five records out of the database.

11. Make the *Next* page link.

```
if ($current_page != $num_pages) {
    echo '<a href=
    → "browse_movies.php?s=' .
    → ($start + $display_number) .
    → '&np=' . $num_pages . '">Next
    → </a> ';
}
```

Every page except for the final one will have a *Next* link.

Figure 12.19 Upon first viewing browse_movies.php, the first five movies in the database (alphabetical by title) are displayed, along with links to the other pages.

Figure 12.20 Clicking any numbered link brings the user to that page.

Figure 12.21 The last page will not have a *Next* link, just as the first does not have a *Previous* link (Figure 12.19).

12. Close the links conditional and complete the HTML page.

```
}
?>
</body>
</html>
```

13. Save the file as browse_movies.php, upload it to your Web server, and test in a Web browser (**Figures 12.19**, **12.20**, and **12.21**).

✔ Tips

- One potential flaw in this system is that if the database changes between the different executions of the query, it could throw off the result pages.

- In order for this process to work, the two queries—the one that returns the number of records and the one that actually retrieves the records—must have comparable results. Always test both queries to ensure this is the case.

- If your query uses any other variables, such as a search term, they must also be passed from page to page (in the URL) or else the paginated pages will not work.

MAKING QUERY RESULT PAGES

Using Transactions with Perl

In Chapter 10, "Advanced SQL and MySQL," I discuss transactions, which you can do in MySQL as long as you are using a transaction-safe storage engine. During that discussion, I demonstrate the transaction process within the `mysql` client. You can also use transactions from a programming language, though.

For most languages, this is a four-step process:

1. Turn off MySQL's autocommit mode.

2. Run your queries.

3. Commit or roll back the queries.

4. Turn MySQL's autocommit mode back on.

In PHP, this would look like:

```
mysqli_autocommit($dbc, FALSE);
$r = mysqli_query($dbc, query);
// Do whatever else.
mysqli_commit($dbc);
// or
mysqli_rollback($dbc);
mysqli_autocommit($dbc, TRUE);
```

This assumes you've already established a valid connection and assigned it to the `$dbc` variable. I'm also referencing the MySQL Improved extension functions, which are available as of PHP 5.

With Java, the code would be:

```
con.setAutoCommit(false);
Statement stmt = con.createStatement();
stmt.executeUpdate(query);
// Do whatever else.
con.commit();
// or
con.rollback();
con.setAutoCommit(true);
```

Script 12.4 This Perl script uses transactions to guarantee that a common banking sequence—the transfer of funds from one account to another—works.

```
1    #!/usr/bin/perl -w
2
3    # Script 12.4 - transfer_money.pl
4    # This script lets a user transfer money
5    # from one account to another.
6
7    # Use what needs to be used.
8    use strict;
9    use DBI;
10
11   # Needed variables:
12   my ($dbh, $sql, $sth, @row, $balance,
     $affected, $from, $to, $amount);
13
14   # Print a message.
15   print "Use this program to transfer
     money.\n\n";
16   print "Accounts (Account ID):\n";
17
18   # Connect to the database.
19   $dbh = DBI->connect("DBI:mysql:test:
     localhost", 'username', 'password',
     {RaiseError => 1});
20
21   # Show the current accounts with their
     IDs.
22   $sql = "SELECT CONCAT(last_name, ', ',
     first_name) AS name, id FROM accounts
     ORDER BY last_name, first_name ASC";
23   $sth = $dbh->prepare($sql);
24   $sth->execute();
25   while (@row = $sth->fetchrow_array()) {
26       print "$row[0] ($row[1])\n";
27   }
28   $sth->finish();
29
30   # Get the information from the user.
31   print "\nFROM whose account is the money
     being transferred? ";
32   $from = <STDIN>;
33   print "\nINTO whose account is the money
     being transferred? ";
34   $to = <STDIN>;
35   print "\nHOW MUCH money is being
     transferred? ";
36   $amount = <STDIN>;
37
38   # Validate the input (omitted).
39
```

Script continues on next page

Again, this assumes that a database connection has been made and assigned to con.

Finally, in Perl, the code would look like (where $dbh is the connection):

```
$dbh->{'AutoCommit'} = 0;
$dbh->do(query);
$dbh->commit();
// or
$dbh->rollback();
$dbh->{'AutoCommit'} = 0;
```

I'll go through a demonstration of the Perl technique by creating a script that transfers money from one record in the *test*.accounts table to another. If you don't have this table in your database, see Chapter 10 for its CREATE command.

To perform transactions using Perl:

1. Create a new Perl script in your text editor, starting with the standard lines of code (**Script 12.4**).

   ```
   #!/usr/bin/perl -w
   use strict;
   use DBI;
   ```

   If you have any questions about any of the Perl, see Chapter 8, "MySQL and Perl."

2. Identify what variables are needed.

   ```
   my ($dbh, $sql, $sth, @row,
   → $balance, $affected, $from, $to,
   → $amount);
   ```

   Rather than using my for each individual variable, I'm identifying them all here.

   continues on next page

3. Print an introductory message and connect to the database.

```
print "Use this program to transfer
→ money.\n\n";

print "Accounts (Account ID):\n";

$dbh = DBI->connect("DBI:mysql:
→ test:localhost", 'username',
→ 'password', {RaiseError => 1});
```

Script 12.4 *continued*

```
40   # Confirm that the FROM account can afford the transfer.
41   $sql = "SELECT balance FROM accounts WHERE id=$from";
42   $sth = $dbh->prepare($sql);
43   $sth->execute();
44   $balance = $sth->fetchrow_array();
45   $sth->finish();
46
47   # Can they afford it?
48   if ($balance >= $amount) { # Transact!
49
50       # Start the transaction.
51       $dbh->{'AutoCommit'} = 0;
52
53       # Subtract the amount.
54       $affected = $dbh->do("UPDATE accounts SET balance=(balance - $amount) WHERE id=$from");
55       if ($affected == 1) { # Good!
56
57           # Add the amount.
58           $affected = $dbh->do("UPDATE accounts SET balance=(balance + $amount) WHERE id=$to");
59           if ($affected == 1) { # Commit.
60
61               $dbh->commit();
62               print "\nThe transaction is complete! \n";
63
64           } else { # Rollback.
65
66               $dbh->rollback();
67               print "\nAn error occurred! The transaction was rolled back. \n";
68
69           }
70
71       } else { # First UPDATE didn't work.
72
73           # Cancel the transaction.
74           $dbh->rollback();
75
```

Script continues on next page

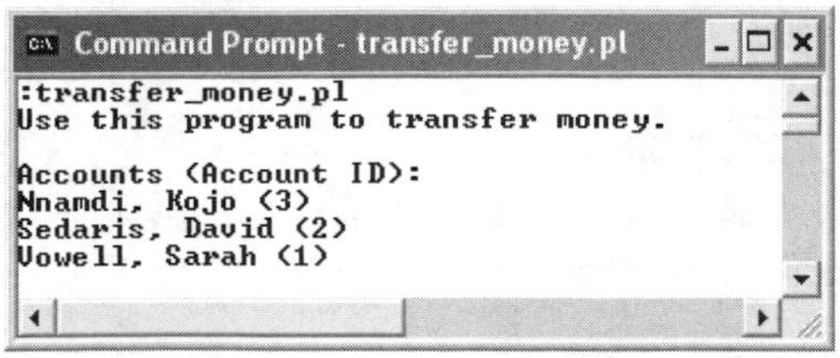

Figure 12.22 Every existing account is listed so that the user can pick the two accounts involved in the transaction.

4. Show the current accounts with their IDs.

```
$sql = "SELECT CONCAT(last_name, ',
→ ', first_name) AS name, id FROM
→ accounts ORDER BY last_name,
→ first_name ASC";
$sth = $dbh->prepare($sql);
$sth->execute();
while (@row = $sth->fetchrow_array()) {
    print "$row[0] ($row[1])\n";
}
$sth->finish();
```

The script starts by listing every account by name, showing the account ID in parentheses (**Figure 12.22**). The program user will reference the account ID in Step 5.

continues on next page

Script 12.4 *continued*

```
76        print "\nAn error occurred! The transaction was rolled back. \n";
77
78    }
79
80  } else { # Can't afford it!
81      print "\nNon-sufficient Funds! \n";
82  }
83
84  # Disconnect.
85  $dbh->disconnect;
```

5. Get all of the necessary information from the user.

```
print "\nFROM whose account is the
→ money being transferred? ";

$from = <STDIN>;

print "\nINTO whose account is the
→ money being transferred? ";

$to = <STDIN>;

print "\nHOW MUCH money is being
→ transferred? ";

$amount = <STDIN>;
```

The user will be prompted for three pieces of input (**Figure 12.23**). The first is the ID number of the account from which the money is coming. The second is the ID number of the account into which the money is going. The third is the amount of money.

You'll likely want to perform some validation on these values, although I omitted it from the script. See Chapter 8 for suggestions.

6. Confirm that the "from" account can afford the transfer.

```
$sql = "SELECT balance FROM accounts
→ WHERE id=$from";

$sth = $dbh->prepare($sql);

$sth->execute();

$balance = $sth->fetchrow_array();

$sth->finish();

if ($balance >= $amount) {
```

Before trying to transfer some money, you ought to check that the user has that much money available. To do so, the current user balance is retrieved from the table.

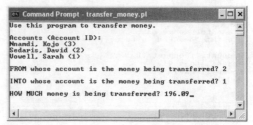

Figure 12.23 The script's user enters the ID numbers of the involved accounts and then the amount of money being transferred.

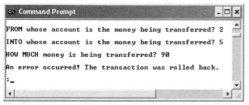

Figure 12.24 The transaction was a success!

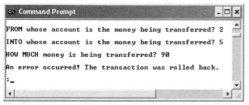

Figure 12.25 A problem occurred, so neither UPDATE was committed.

7. Begin the transaction.

`$dbh->{'AutoCommit'} = 0;`

From this point forward, MySQL is in transaction mode.

8. Subtract the dollar amount.

`$affected = $dbh->do("UPDATE accounts → SET balance=(balance - $amount) → WHERE id=$from");`

`if ($affected == 1) {`

A simple UPDATE query is run. The results are then checked to make sure that exactly one row was affected.

9. Add the dollar amount to the other account.

`$affected = $dbh->do("UPDATE accounts → SET balance=(balance + $amount) → WHERE id=$to");`

`if ($affected == 1) {`

This is the inverse of the query in Step 8. Again the results are confirmed to ensure the transaction worked.

10. Commit or roll back the transaction.

```
    $dbh->commit();
    print "\nThe transaction is
    → complete! \n";
} else {
    $dbh->rollback();
    print "\nAn error occurred! The
    → transaction was rolled back.
    → \n";
}
```

If both UPDATE queries affected one row, the transaction can be committed (the first line here). If the second UPDATE query failed, the transaction should be nullified by rolling it back (this takes place within the else clause). Messages indicate success (**Figure 12.24**) or failure (**Figure 12.25**).

continues on next page

USING TRANSACTIONS WITH PERL

11. Complete the two conditionals.

```
    } else {
        $dbh->rollback();
        print "\nAn error occurred!
        → The transaction was rolled
        → back. \n";
    }
} else {
    print "\nNon-sufficient Funds! \n";
}
```

The first `else` clause is the companion to the one in Step 10. It applies if the first `UPDATE` query fails. The second `else` clause applies if the "from" account does not have enough money (**Figure 12.26**).

12. Disconnect from the database.

```
$dbh->disconnect;
```

13. Save the file as `transfer_money.pl`, change the permissions (if necessary), and run the script.

✔ Tips

- In Perl you can also turn off the auto-commit mode when you connect:

```
$dbh = DBI->connect("DBI:mysql:
→ test:localhost", 'username',
→ 'password', {RaiseError => 1,
→ AutoCommit => 0});
```

- You may want to also add some error reporting to this script. Further, you should check that a valid "from" account was entered, or you may see an error message as `$balance` ends up with no value.

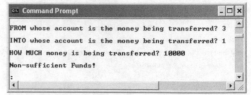

Figure 12.26 The script will not allow a negative balance in any account.

Calling Stored Procedures

In Chapter 11, "MySQL 5 Features," I cover stored procedures. These are memorized bits of code that are stored in the database. The topic, unfortunately, is not as easily demonstrated using programming languages, as each supports the concept to different degrees. Instead of a full-on example, I'll mention the basic idea for each language.

With PHP, you can call a stored procedure as you would execute any SQL command using `mysqli_query()`:

```
$r = mysqli_query("CALL procedure_name ($var1, $var2));
```

If the procedure has several `SELECT` statements that return several result sets, use `mysqi_multi_query()` instead.

With Java, you need to create a

`CallableStatement` object:

```
CallableStatement stmt = con.prepareCall("{CALL procedure_name(?, ?)}");
```

Then you bind the values to the statement and execute it. The MySQL manual has a couple of examples of this.

As for Perl, sadly the DBD::mysql driver doesn't support stored procedures at the time of this writing. There is a patch that can kind of get this to work, but not reliably.

Stored routines are normally used exactly like the existing MySQL functions. Therefore, you can use stored routines in a query as you would a MySQL function.

USING TRANSACTIONS WITH PERL

MySQL ADMINISTRATION

There are several facets to administering a MySQL server, from the obvious and critical backing up of data to improving security and performance. Fortunately the reliability of MySQL demands little in the way of maintenance, but should the need arise, this, too, is easily accomplished.

Historically, pretty much every administrative task could be accomplished using one of two methods. First, there are several utilities that MySQL distributes with the server itself. These are each run from a command-line interface, just like the `mysql` client. Second, most tasks can also be accomplished within the `mysql` client using the proper SQL command. I will briefly mention these options, as applicable, for the tasks I discuss in this chapter. But for the most part, I will focus on the exciting new product called the MySQL Administrator. Released by the company that makes MySQL, it places all of the necessary administrative tools within one graphical interface.

The MySQL Administrator

A very welcome addition to the MySQL family of products is the free (free!) MySQL Administrator. This is a graphical tool that will run on most operating systems, starting with Windows, Mac OS X, and Linux. The application works with MySQL servers versions 4.0 and greater.

You can perform all of your MySQL administration using this tool. This includes backing up and restoring databases, repairing tables, optimizing performance, and so on. In short, the MySQL Administrator can do everything that the individual utilities MySQL comes with can.

In this first section of the chapter, I'll talk about getting, installing, and running the application. In subsequent sections, I'll demonstrate how you use the MySQL Administrator to manage particular administrative tasks.

Note that I've taken the screenshots using both Mac OS X and Windows. For some reason, there are many differences in the application on different operating systems: different layouts, different labels, etc. It's almost as if each version was put out by a separate company! Nevertheless, the functionality is the same regardless of the operating system in use.

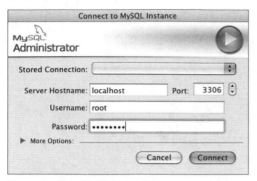

Figure 13.1 Start MySQL Administrator, connecting as *root* or another superuser.

To use the MySQL Administrator:

1. Download the MySQL Administrator from www.mysql.com.

At the time of this writing, the latest version is 1.1, which supports MySQL versions 4.0 through 5.0. (The precise version numbers are 1.1.9 on Windows, 1.1.6 on Unix, and 1.1.3 on Mac, unless you build it from the source code.)

2. Install the application on your computer.

Windows users will download and run a Windows Installer file (.msi). Mac users need to mount the downloaded disk image and then copy the application to your hard drive. Linux users just need to untar the download.

3. Start the application.

Windows users can use the Start menu shortcut. Mac users can double-click the application itself. Linux users should move into the program's installation directory (/opt/mysql-administrator/bin) and start the application from there.

4. At the first prompt (**Figure 13.1**), enter the correct username, hostname, and password combination.

To administer MySQL running on the same computer, you'll likely want to enter *localhost* as the host. You'll then want to use either *root* or another administrative account, and the correct password for that user. These values correspond to the users and permissions established within the MySQL server.

continues on next page

5. Click OK or Connect, depending upon your version of the application, to take you into the application.

Assuming that you used a valid administrative username/hostname/password combination, this will connect to the MySQL server. **Figure 13.2** shows the result on Windows; **Figure 13.3** is the Mac OS X view.

6. Use the Server Information (Windows) or Information (Mac OS X) pane to learn about the MySQL and system status (Figures 13.2 and 13.3).

This includes information such as the version of MySQL, how much RAM the server has installed, the server's IP address, and so on.

7. Use the Service Control (Windows) or Service (Mac OS X) pane to start, stop, and control the MySQL service.

The Windows version of this window (**Figure 13.4**) contains more options than the Mac version. With Windows, what you can do here is similar to what you can do in the Windows Services control panel (see Chapter 2, "Running MySQL").

8. Use the Server Connections (Windows) or Connections (Mac OS X) pane to view the active MySQL connections.

You can also terminate any connections in this window. If you're running MySQL on your own computer without a lot of activity, you won't see much here.

Figure 13.2 MySQL Administrator on Windows, showing the Server Information pane.

Figure 13.3 MySQL Administrator on Mac OS X, showing the Information pane.

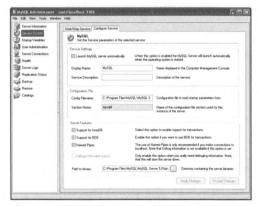

Figure 13.4 The Service pane starts and stops the MySQL server.

Figure 13.5 Enable the System Tray tool on Windows to give yourself really easy access to common MySQL utilities and commands.

9. Go into User Administration (Windows) or Accounts (Mac OS X) to manage the MySQL users.

   You can manage all of the MySQL users—set their passwords, usernames, hosts, privileges, and more—in this application instead of using SQL commands with the mysql client. I don't cover this feature in this chapter, but if you poke around it's easy enough to use.

10. Continue through the rest of the chapter to use the MySQL Administrator for specific tasks.

✔ Tips

- You can connect to multiple MySQL servers simultaneously using the MySQL Administrator. Just create a new connection for each. This also means that you can connect to the same MySQL server using different login information.

- On Windows, in the application's Tools menu, there's a shortcut for quickly connecting to MySQL through the mysql client. The connection will use the same access information as provided to the MySQL Administrator. You can also enable the MySQL System Tray Monitor, which puts quick access to common MySQL information and tools in the Windows System Tray (**Figure 13.5**).

- On Windows, under Tools > Options, you can set how the MySQL Administrator behaves. This includes saving passwords and connections. On Mac OS X, you can find the equivalent by select MySQL Administrator > Preferences.

- You may or may not also have a Replication Status pane in your MySQL Administrator. If present, this pane would be used to view the status of any replication you have established. Replication is where one MySQL server mimics the behavior of another: any changes made to a database on one will also be made to the other.

Backing Up Databases

A common reason to use the MySQL Administrator is to easily back up and restore your data. The process is simple, but there are quite a few options, so I'll lead you through the entire sequence in these next steps.

If you cannot use the MySQL Administrator or otherwise don't want to, you can use MySQL's built-in `mysqldump` utility or the SQL commands discussed in the sidebar.

Using mysqldump

This utility can re-create the SQL queries used to build—and more important, to populate—your tables and data. An added benefit of this formal backup is that your databases can be easily transferred to another operating system or even another database application by importing the SQL queries there.

Because `mysqldump` is a separate utility, it is run from the command line. The syntax for `mysqldump` is

`mysqldump [options] databasename`

The `[options]` section is, naturally, optional. In general, the easiest, most fail-safe configuration option for `mysqldump` is to use `--opt`. This setting will automatically initiate a standard set of parameters, and it will generate one large text file. In this case you should specify the filename to be created as a backup:

`mysqldump --opt databasename > /path/to/filename.sql`

You can back up every database at once using

`mysqldump --opt --all-databases > /path/to/filename.sql`

Figure 13.6 You can create as many backup projects as you want or need.

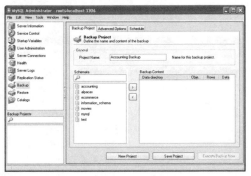

Figure 13.7 Use an appropriate title for each backup project.

Figure 13.8 You can back up multiple databases or just individual tables.

To back up your database:

1. Open the MySQL Administrator and connect to the MySQL server.

   You only need to connect as a user with permission to access the database you'll be backing up.

2. Click Backup.

3. Click New Project (Windows) or click the plus button at the bottom of the Backup Projects window (Mac OS X, **Figure 13.6**) to start creating a new backup project.

   You can establish any number of projects, each of which performs a different backup (different databases or different backup options).

4. In the Project Name window, give the backup a descriptive name (**Figure 13.7**).

5. Select the tables and databases to back up (**Figure 13.8**).

   From the left-hand column, which lists the databases (also called the *schemata*), click a database name. Then click the "greater than" button to move the database into the Backup Content window. Then check or uncheck any individual table to include it in a backup.

   Repeat this simple sequence for any other databases to be included.

   continues on next page

BACKING UP DATABASES

6. Click Advanced Options to change any settings (**Figure 13.9**).

You should start by making sure that the Backup Execution value corresponds to the type of tables being backed up. Also note that, ironically, the "normal backup" should be avoided. In any case, read the nice descriptions and choose the right Backup Execution method.

With the output file options, these will also affect how you restore a database using a backup. I personally like the "Add DROP Statements" option (or "Add DROP Table" option on Mac), which will drop any existing tables before going to re-create them (during a restore).

7. Click Schedule to establish routine and automatic backups (**Figure 13.10**).

You can automatically schedule the execution of a backup project. If you are the kind of person who tends to forget these things until it's too late, you may want to strongly consider this option.

8. On Windows, click Save Project to complete the process.

You do not need to take this step on Mac OS X.

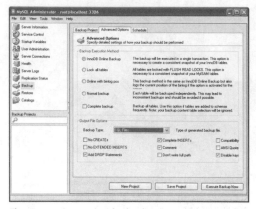

Figure 13.9 Customize the backup to suit the storage engines used and what kind of output you want to generate.

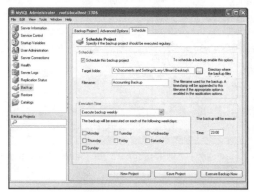

Figure 13.10 Schedule frequent and regular backups to prevent data loss in case of a server problem.

✔ Tips

■ You can click Start Backup (Mac) or Execute Backup Now (Windows) at any time in order to immediately back up the selected tables.

■ Another way to back up your databases is to use the `mysqlhotcopy` Perl script that comes with Unix and Mac OS X MySQL installations. This is the fastest way to back up a database, but it must be run on the same computer as MySQL, can only be used to back up MyISAM tables, and assumes that you have Perl installed.

An SQL Equivalent, Part 1

With most versions of MySQL you can back up a table using a SELECT INTO query:

```
SELECT * INTO OUTFILE '/path/to/
→ filename.txt' FROM tablename
```

This command will allow you to create a more specialized query and store the results in a text file. This method will only store the data, not the structure of a table.

Two caveats with using SQL to back up your databases are that MySQL must have permission to create the file in the directory that you name and that you must be logged in as a user with FILE permissions (which may also mean you can only do this while working directly on the server).

Importing Data

Once you've learned how to back up your databases, you should understand how to reconstruct them. If you used the `mysqldump` utility (see the sidebar in the preceding section), its counterpart, `mysqlimport`, will reinstate the databases (see the sidebar here). If you used the MySQL Administrator's Backup option, then its Restore option can be used to re-create your databases using the backed up files. I'll show you how.

To restore a database:

1. Open the MySQL Administrator and connect to the MySQL server.

   You only need to connect as a user with permission to access the database you'll be restoring.

2. Click Restore.

3. Click Open Backup File (Windows) or Choose File (Mac OS X, **Figure 13.11**) to select the backup file.

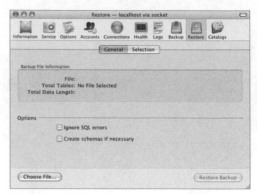

Figure 13.11 The Restore pane lets you restore a database using an existing backup file.

Using mysqlimport

This application takes the data stored in a text file and inserts it into a table. Like `mysqldump`, it's run from a command-line interface.

The syntax for using `mysqlimport` is

```
mysqlimport -u username -p databasename '/path/to/filename.sql'
```

With `mysqlimport`, there are two assumptions: first, that the table the data is being inserted into already exists; and second, that the text file containing the records to be inserted has the same name as the table.

The `mysqlimport` utility is actually just an implementation of the `LOAD DATA INFILE` without directly using the `mysql` client. I discuss this SQL alternative in a separate sidebar.

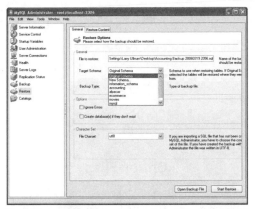

Figure 13.12 Select the schema where the data should be restored.

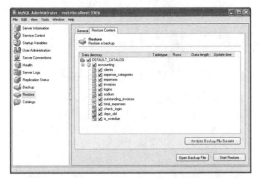

Figure 13.13 The backup file lists all of the tables that can be restored. On Windows this includes the views and stored procedures.

4. Select the file to use.

   The button clicked in Step 3 creates an Open dialog box for you to select the source file on your computer. This file should be the one created by the Backup pane in the preceding section of this chapter.

5. On Windows, choose the target database (**Figure 13.12**).

   Windows users have the option of restoring the data to the original database (or schema) or to another one.

6. Click Restore Content (Windows) or Selection (Mac) to customize the restoration.

   You can choose to back up specific tables instead of the entire database. On Windows, you'll need to click Analyze Backup File Content to see the list of tables (**Figure 13.13**).

7. Select the tables you want to restore.

   By default, all of the tables are checked. Just uncheck a table to not restore its data.

8. Click Start Restore (Windows) or Restore Backup (Mac) to restore the data.

IMPORTING DATA

An SQL Equivalent, Part 2

There are two different ways to import data into your database using SQL. The first is RESTORE, and the second is LOAD DATA.

RESTORE is the complement to the SQL command BACKUP and is used to re-create a table based upon files stored in a directory. LOAD DATA INFILE is the complement of the SELECT...INTO OUTFILE SQL query.

```
LOAD DATA LOCAL INFILE '/path/to/filename.txt' INTO TABLE tablename
```

To use the LOAD DATA technique, you will need FILE permissions, and you will need to start mysql with the --local-infile option if you are loading a file from a client machine to a separate server computer.

MySQL Logging

One subject that any database administrator should be familiar with is that of logs. There are different types of logs MySQL uses; I'll focus on two: the error log, which records server problems, and the tracking log, which keeps a history of queries.

MySQL's error log will be located in the data directory and titled *hostname*.err. Normally this will mean that the file is something like /usr/local/mysql/data/localhost.err or C:\Program Files\MySQL\MySQL Server *x.x*\data*computername*.err. The error log will record every error reported, like those caused by a failure to start the MySQL server. For this reason, checking the error log can greatly facilitate debugging any problems you have with running the server.

The second type of log, an update log, will record track all of the SQL statements that have been run. There are two types of tracking logs: The first is a general one that records all queries, whether or not they succeed. The second is a binary log that records only those queries that succeeded and that, in some way, modified a database. The binary log is also in chronological order, meaning that it could be used to restore a database.

There are two caveats with using update logs. First of all, they'll eat up space on your hard drive, particularly the general tracking log. Second, as these logs contain lots of information about your database, they can be a security risk. Make sure that the directory where they are stored is not accessible by non-administrative users.

I'll demonstrate how to use the MySQL Administrator to both enable and view logs.

Option Files

An option file, also called a configuration file, is a special text file where you can define values to be used when an application starts. The MySQL software supports two types of options files:

- Those that affect how the MySQL server runs

- Those that are used by other MySQL applications (like the mysql client)

Many sections of the MySQL Administrator write to the first kind of option file. The second kind can be created or edited in any text editor.

Any parameter that can be added when starting an application from the command line (e.g., --database or --host) can be stored in an option file. For a client file, you would start with something like this:

[client]
user=*username*
password=*password*

On Mac OS X and Unix, you would save the file as ~/.my.cnf (where ~ is your Home directory). On Windows, you would want to call this file my.ini and place it in the directory where MySQL is installed (e.g., C:\Program Files\MySQL\ MySQL Server *x.x*). This file likely already exists, so just open it and edit the [client] or [mysql] section.

MYSQL LOGGING

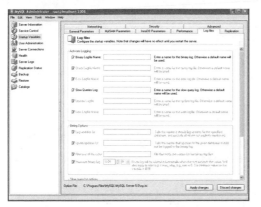

Figure 13.14 The Log Files pane on Windows.

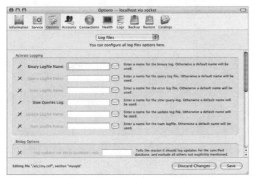

Figure 13.15 The Log Files pane on Mac OS X.

To use and view logs:

1. Open the MySQL Administrator and connect to the MySQL server.

   You should connect as an administrative user, as you'll be changing how MySQL runs.

2. Click Startup Variables (Windows) or Options (Mac).

   The first step will be to enable logging, which can be done within this area of the application.

3. Click Log Files (Windows) or choose Log Files from the drop-down menu (Mac).

4. In the Activate Logging area (**Figures 13.14** and **13.15**), enable all the logs you want.

   To enable a log, click the little icon to the left of the log's name. This tells the MySQL Administrator to write the change to the MySQL options file. By doing so, you have this change take effect whenever MySQL is started.

   You can optionally give the log a name, if you want other than the default. On Mac, you can also use the button on the right of the text box to choose a location where the log should be stored.

   Of the available logs, the error log is automatically enabled. I am also opting to enable the binary log (discussed in the introduction to these steps) and the Slow Queries log (to monitor specific performance problems).

continues on next page

MySQL Logging

5. In the Binlog Options area, adjust the binary log's attributes.

This is a nice little feature, letting you log only specific databases, ignore specific databases, and state how large each binary log is allowed to get (in terms of file size on the server). For each attribute, again just click the icon to the left and then enter a value on the right.

6. Repeat for the Slow Queries log (**Figure 13.16**).

If you enable this log, you can also state what qualifies as a slow query.

7. Click Apply Changes (Windows) or Save (Mac) to enact the changes.

8. Restart the MySQL server.

The logging changes will not take effect until the next time the MySQL server is started. At that time it will use the options that were written to the option file by the MySQL Administrator.

9. Use the Server Logs (Windows) or Logs (Mac) pane to view the logs (**Figure 13.17**).

Each log has its own pane or tab. You can easily scroll and search within each log, making this the best way to view them.

✔ Tip

■ For extra safety and reliability, you could place the MySQL data directory on one hard drive on your computer and the logs on another (this assumes you have multiple hard drives, of course). Once you have done this, if one drive fails, the other will have a copy of the recorded queries, from which your databases can be resurrected (at least in part).

Figure 13.16 Adjusting the behavior of the Slow Queries log within the Advanced log options area.

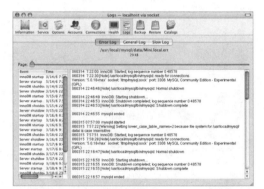

Figure 13.17 The MySQL Administrator provides the best interface for viewing any type of MySQL log.

MySQL Logging

Figure 13.18 View, edit, and maintain your databases in the Catalogs pane.

Database Maintenance

Part of administering a database, besides maintaining backups of the data, is checking the integrity of the database files. To check for and repair corrupted files, one option is to use the `myisamchk` utility. This only works on MyISAM tables, though, and is really my least favorite of the three options for maintaining tables.

The second option is to use SQL commands within the `mysql` client or other interface. These commands are discussed in the sidebar.

The final option is to use our new friend the MySQL Administrator.

To check and repair your tables:

1. Open the MySQL Administrator and connect to the MySQL server.

   You should connect as an administrative user.

2. Back up all of the databases you'll be checking.

   Since you could be affecting the data files themselves in this sequence of steps, it's always smart to back up everything first. To do so, use one of the methods discussed earlier in the chapter.

3. Click Catalogs (Windows or Mac, **Figure 13.18**).

   This area of the application is for managing the database files.

   continues on next page

4. Click a database in the Schemata listing to select it (**Figure 13.19**).

You can now see all of the tables, views, and stored procedures in this database. You can also see each table's storage engine, how many rows each has, the total size of each table's data and index, and the last time the table was updated. At the bottom of the window is a synopsis of the entire database.

5. Select a table from the display on the right, and then click Maintenance (Windows) or select Check Table from the Table Actions menu (Mac, **Figure 13.20**).

You can also select multiple tables, if you'd like. On Windows, this brings up the Table Maintenance dialog box (**Figure 13.21**), in which you should choose Check Tables and click Next.

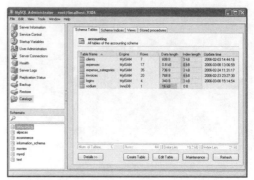

Figure 13.19 An overview of the tables in the *accounting* database.

Figure 13.20 On Mac OS X, the MySQL Administrator places the maintenance options within a drop-down menu.

Figure 13.21 On Windows, choose a maintenance option within this box.

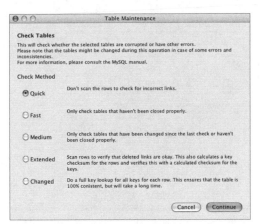

Figure 13.22 Choose what type of check you would like to perform on the already-selected tables.

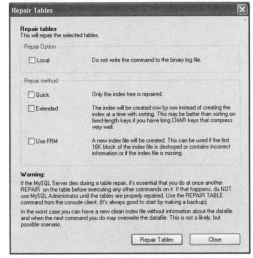

Figure 13.23 Have MySQL repair any tables that were marked as problematic when analyzed.

6. Select a Check method, and then click Check Tables (Windows) or Continue (Mac, **Figure 13.22**).

Each option is well documented, so you shouldn't need to guess as to which is appropriate. Just read the descriptions and factor in things like:

▲ How much data there is

▲ How often you perform checks

▲ How active the databases are

▲ How busy the server currently is

For example, if you regularly check your tables, you might want to go with Changed here. If the server isn't being used much at the moment and it's been a long time since you've done a check, opt for Extended.

7. If any problems are reported by the check, repeat Steps 3 and 4, choosing Repair Tables from the Table Maintenance dialog box (Windows) or Table Actions menu (Mac).

Again, you'll be given choices as to what kind of repair to make (**Figure 13.23**).

✔ Tips

- If you select a table and then click Edit Table (Windows) or select Table Actions > Edit Table (Mac), you'll bring up the Table Editor (**Figure 13.24**). This is a wonderful tool that's kind of hidden in the MySQL Administrator. With it you can do anything that you might otherwise use an ALTER command for. For example, you can: modify columns; change the storage engine, charset, or collation; add, edit, or drop indexes; and much more.

- Similarly, the ability to edit stored procedures within the MySQL Administrator is really convenient, particularly when you consider how cumbersome it is to add and edit them within the mysql client. On Windows you can even run the stored procedure from the editing window.

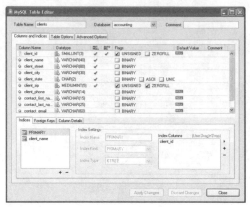

Figure 13.24 You can modify every aspect of a table using the Table Editor.

An SQL Equivalent, Part 3

Once again, you have the option of performing maintenance using SQL within the mysql client rather than the dedicated utility. To quickly analyze a table, use

CHECK TABLE *tablename*

Unlike myisamchk, this query will work on both MyISAM and InnoDB table types.

You can change the level of checking performed by changing the SQL to

CHECK TABLE *tablename* EXTENDED

If the CHECK TABLE query indicates a problem, run

REPAIR TABLE *tablename* EXTENDED

The commands ANALYZE TABLE *tablename* and OPTIMIZE TABLE *tablename* can also be used to test and improve the performance of your tables.

Improving Performance

MySQL was created with the express purpose of being a fast and reliable database. Still, there are ways to improve performance even within the existing framework of the software.

The first way to improve the performance of MySQL is to upgrade the server itself. The connection from the client to the server (via the Internet, for example) is one potential bottleneck, and the processor speed, amount of RAM, and type of hard drive all affect MySQL's performance. Since, in the end, MySQL is constantly reading and writing from files on the hard drive, it's easy to see how outdated or slow hardware can inhibit performance. Ideally, if you have a dedicated server with a RAID array, that would be a great place to place the MySQL data directory. And, of course, installing more RAM is always a benefit.

The second way to spruce things up is to manipulate how the MySQL server (`mysqld`) runs. You can do this by specifying different options, such as the following:

- `key_buffer` (the amount of memory reserved for indexes)

- `max_connections` (how many connections can be handled at one time)

- storage engine settings

A third way to improve performance is to optimize your tables. To do so, you would follow the analysis and repair techniques shown in the preceding section, but choose Optimize Tables instead. Similarly, you could run the `OPTIMIZE` command within the `mysql` client.

I'll show you where to go within the MySQL Administrator to tune the server's performance. Unfortunately, there are no universally correct answers as to what exact values you might want to use. For more information on any of the options, as well as what indicators you should be looking for, see the MySQL manual or search the Web. Also remember that the Health pane of the MySQL Administrator will show you the current memory usage and performance of your server. This information will often indicate if you need to change how MySQL runs.

To optimize MySQL:

1. Open the MySQL Administrator and connect to the MySQL server.

   You should connect as an administrative user (of course).

2. Click Startup Variables (Windows) or Options (Mac).

   This section of the application is where you control how the MySQL server runs.

3. Increase the Key buffer size if using MyISAM tables (**Figure 13.25**).

   The buffer has a default value of 8 MB, which should be increased if you have a lot of memory and your computer primarily runs MySQL. It only affects MyISAM tables, though.

   As with every setting within this area of the MySQL Administrator, click the icon to the left of the item in order to enact the changes (you only need to do this if the icon has a red slash or X on it).

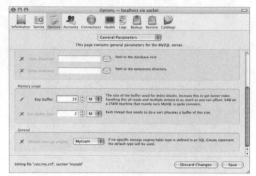

Figure 13.25 Increasing the key buffer is one of the first optimization changes you should make, if you use a lot of MyISAM tables.

Figure 13.26 There are many adjustments you can make as to how MyISAM tables are used in MySQL.

Figure 13.27 The InnoDB storage engine (while it lasts in MySQL) offers another bevy of adjustments.

4. Click MyISAM Parameters (Windows, **Figure 13.26**) or select MyISAM Parameters from the drop-down menu (Mac).

In this area you can establish the parameters for just the MyISAM tables. In terms of performance, look under Advanced Settings at the bottom. Generally speaking, increasing the values will improve the performance, but don't go randomly changing things unless you understand what they mean (read the descriptions, then see the manual for more) and know you have a need.

5. Repeat Step 4 for the InnoDB Parameters (**Figure 13.27**).

The InnoDB storage engine has its own options you can set. There's no absolutely right answer for what settings you should use, so read the descriptions and pay attention to your server's health and performance, then adjust accordingly.

continues on next page

6. Click Performance (Windows) or select Performance from the drop-down menu (Mac).

This is the last of the performance areas to peek into. At the time of this writing, there are only four options (**Figure 13.28**), each of which is easy to comprehend. These performance settings adjust how MySQL caches queries and results. When MySQL caches a query, the results of that query can be pulled from memory, without your having to requery the database. This is a major performance boost.

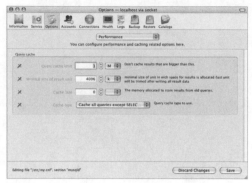

Figure 13.28 Increasing the cache size will improve the MySQL server's performance.

✔ Tips

■ By using and analyzing slow query logs, you can find and fix particularly problematic queries. You can also use EXPLAIN to see how MySQL executes a query (see the MySQL manual or the Web for more).

■ Your database's performance is also highly dependent upon the decisions you made when designing and implementing it. This includes how you define your columns and indexes. See Chapter 4, "Creating a MySQL Database," for more.

■ As mentioned in the steps, the key buffer value is specific to the MyISAM table type. If you are not using this kind of table, you can improve MySQL's performance by setting this value as small as possible.

Using Batch Files

For the most part, throughout the course of this book I have run queries directly in the mysql client. The MySQL software also allows you to run queries without entering the mysql client itself. To do so is to use mysql in what is called *batch mode*. Instead of entering queries directly, you can store them in a text file and then run the text file through mysql. From a command prompt, you would do something like the following:

```
bin/mysql -u username -p <
→ '/path/to/filename.txt'
```

Since you will presumably be running the queries on a particular database, you will often use the -D option to select it in advance:

```
bin/mysql -u username -p -D
→ databasename < '/path/to/filename.txt'
```

As just one example of this technology, I will run a batch script that creates a table and populates it.

To use batch files:

1. Download the SQL commands for this book from the book's corresponding Web site (www.dmcinsights.com/mysql2).

   Every SQL command I use in the entire book is available in a single text file. You'll find this on the Extras page.

2. Unzip the downloaded file.

   I've archived the text file in Zip format, so you'll need to expand it.

3. Open the text file in a text editor.

   You can edit this in any text application, although Notepad (and perhaps some others) will not handle the line breaks properly.

   continues on next page

4. Copy any SQL commands you want to run into a new text document.

You absolutely, positively should not run the entire SQL file as is! Doing so would take forever and make all sorts of messes. Instead, copy just the SQL commands you need at this time.

In this specific example, I will use a batch file to re-create and populate the `expense_categories` table, so I will need to copy its `CREATE` and `INSERT` statements. You can find them under the "Chapter 4" and "Chapter 5" headings in the text file.

5. Save the new file as `ec.sql`.

It doesn't really matter what name you use or where you save it, as long as you know where it is and what it's called.

6. Access your server from a command-line interface and move into the MySQL `bin` directory.

These instructions are in the second chapter, if you do not know how to do this.

7. If desired, create a new database (**Figure 13.29**).

```
./bin/mysqladmin -u root -p create
→ accounting2
```

Since I already have an *accounting* database with this table (that I don't want to mess up), I'll create a new database.

8. Run the batch file (**Figure 13.30**).

```
./bin/mysql -u root -p -D accounting2
→ < '/path/to/ec.sql'
```

You'll need to change the */path/to/* `ec.sql` part so that it corresponds to the name and location of the file on your server. This might be `C:\Documents and Settings\My Name\Desktop\ec.sql` on Windows or `~/Desktop/ec.sql` on Mac OS X (where ~ is your home directory).

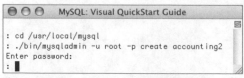

Figure 13.29 In order to practice using batch files without altering my existing database, I'll create a new database using `mysqladmin`.

Figure 13.30 To re-create the `expense_categories` table without retyping my SQL, I can use the batch mode.

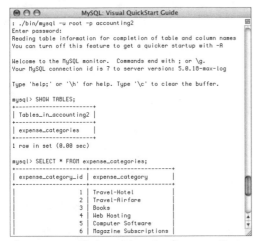

Figure 13.31 Verify the results using the mysql client.

9. Confirm that the SQL commands worked (**Figure 13.31**).

```
./bin/mysql -u root -p accounting2
SHOW TABLES;
SELECT * FROM expense_categories;
```

✔ Tips

■ If you want to save the result of a batch file as its own text file, add

`> '/path/to/output.txt'`

to your code. The line

```
bin/mysql -u username -p <
→ '/path/to/input.txt' >
→ '/path/to/output.txt'
```

creates a file containing the results of the queries.

■ To have mysql continue executing a batch file even if it encounters errors, add --force to the execution line.

■ Batch files can also be run from within the mysql client, if you'd prefer. Just log in, select your database, and then type

`source /path/to/filename`

■ You should not have any comments (lines that begin with #) as the first lines in your batch script or else it will not run.

TROUBLESHOOTING

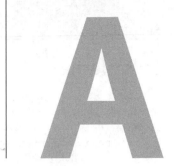

Like any software, MySQL can occasionally cause those bang-your-head-against-the-wall moments, so this book includes a trouble-shooting appendix to help address the most common problems. On the bright side, once it gets going, MySQL tends to run for extended periods of time with few to no issues. On the other hand, sometimes getting the server itself to start, before you even attempt to connect to it, can be unduly troublesome.

This section of the book will address the most frequently witnessed problems, giving a sense of what the cause is and what can be done to remedy the situation. As you might expect, you can always turn to the MySQL manual (or visit your friendly neighborhood search engine) for a more complete list of problems and solutions. In fact, the first appendix in the MySQL manual is also about troubleshooting.

I'll go through this appendix in rough sequential order: installing MySQL, starting it, accessing MySQL using a client or programming language, and debugging odd query results. The appendix ends with two specific issues that you hopefully may not face,

Installation

For better or for worse, you won't discover most installation-related problems until you go to run the software. That being said, some issues to be aware of when configuring and installing MySQL are

◆ You must run the `mysql_install_db` script (found in the `mysql/scripts` directory) to set up the users and privileges tables, unless you are copying over existing databases (**Figure A.1**).

◆ You'll like need to run the script `mysql_fix_privilege_tables` after upgrading MySQL to a new major version (e.g., going from 4.0 to 4.1 or 4.1 to 5.0).

◆ Be sure to use the `–prefix=`/*path*/*to*/*mysql* parameter when configuring MySQL if you are installing from the source.

◆ When installing a new version of MySQL from the source, first delete the previous configuration by typing `rm config.cache` followed by `make clean`.

◆ On Windows platforms, install MySQL in the default location if at all possible. If not, you'll need to tell the server where the data directory is (by using an option file or a command-line argument).

✔ Tips

■ For more information on configuration issues, see the MySQL manual or type `./configure –help` (**Figure A.2**) within the source code directory.

■ Instead of clearing out a previous configuration as a two-step process, you can run `make distclean`.

Figure A.1 The `mysql_install_db` script establishes the *mysql* database that is used to grant access to users.

Figure A.2 The configuration step (when installing from the source files) has dozens of parameters that can be adjusted for your server.

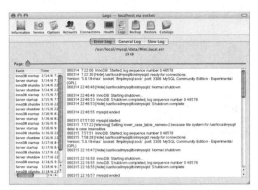

Figure A.3 Use the MySQL Administrator to view your error logs.

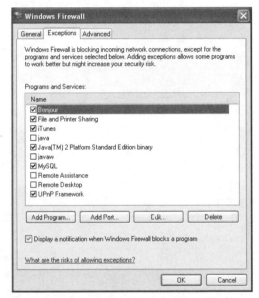

Figure A.4 A firewall, like this one built into Windows, can cause complications unless you specifically allow MySQL access to port 3306.

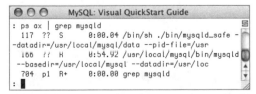

Figure A.5 The command ps ax | grep mysqld should show that safe_mysqld and mysqld are running.

Starting MySQL

Starting the MySQL server can be a common cause of problems, particularly when you go to install it for the first time. Your absolutely best first step should MySQL fail to start is to view the error log. It will record any messages indicating why MySQL could not be started. You can read logs in a text editor, or more easily in the MySQL Administrator (**Figure A.3**, see Chapter 13, "MySQL Administration").

Here are some common problems and solutions for starting MySQL:

◆ If MySQL cannot find the data directory, set the value when you start mysqld using the `--basedir=/path/to/mysql/data` argument. You can also establish this in an option file.

◆ If MySQL claims that it cannot find `host.frm` or `mysql.host`, it means that it cannot read the grant tables in the *mysql* database. Check that you ran the `mysql_install_db` script and that MySQL has permission to access the *mysql* files.

◆ If you are running a firewall, this may prevent MySQL from starting. Turn off the firewall to confirm this is the problem. If so, allow MySQL's port (3306 by default) an exception in your firewall (**Figure A.4**).

✔ Tips

■ On Windows, you can have difficulty starting MySQL as a service if there is a space in the pathname, e.g., `C:\Program Files\MySQL\MySQL Server x.x`, or if part of the pathname is too long. Either move into the MySQL directory and then execute the command, or use double quotation marks around the entire pathname.

■ On Unix and Mac OS X, to check if MySQL is already running, type `ps ax | grep mysqld` in a shell (**Figure A.5**).

Accessing MySQL

Once you know that MySQL has been successfully installed and is running, getting access to a database can be the next hiccup you encounter. The three most important variables for connecting to MySQL are the hostname, username, and password. These values will be matched against the records in the *mysql* database to approve access.

Next, MySQL will check to see if the user has the permission to run specific queries on specific databases (see Chapter 2, "Running MySQL," for more information). However, an inability to connect to MySQL as a whole is a far more common issue than an inability to run a particular query.

Common solutions to access denied errors are

◆ Reload MySQL after altering the privileges so that the changes take effect. Use either the mysqladmin tool or run FLUSH PRIVILEGES in the mysql client.

◆ Double-check the password used. The error message *Access denied for user: 'root@localhost' (Using password: YES)* normally indicates that the password is wrong or mistyped. (This is not always the cause but is the first thing to check.)

◆ Use the PASSWORD() function when setting privileges or updating a password.

◆ If you are having trouble using a hostname, try omitting the hostname, using a different hostname (such as *localhost* if you are working directly on the computer), running mysqladmin flush-hosts (**Figure A.6**), starting mysqld with --skip-name-resolve, or changing the host setting for the user within the *mysql* database.

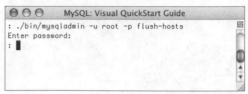

Figure A.6 If you are having particular difficulty with a hostname, flush MySQL's host cache with the mysqladmin tool.

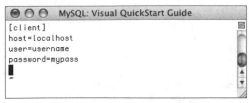

Figure A.7 Settings in a `.my.cnf` file can affect access to a MySQL utility without your awareness.

◆ If you are using a `.my.cnf`, `my.cnf`, or `my.ini` file to establish parameters for client programs, don't forget to check these settings (**Figure A.7**). Also inspect any `my.cnf` or `my.ini` files.

◆ The error message *Can't connect to...* (error number 2002) indicates that either MySQL is not running or is not running on the socket or TCP/IP port tried by the client. First check that MySQL is running, and then attempt to connect using a different port or socket.

◆ Another common reason why you cannot connect to MySQL is because the client program cannot find the `mysql.sock` file. This is a Unix and Mac OS X issue, which I discuss next.

The absolutely most important step you should take in debugging an access issue is to confirm that MySQL is running! All too frequently, a failure to start MySQL is the cause.

mysql.sock Problems

Client programs use the `mysql.sock` socket to access the `mysqld` server on Unix and Mac OS X systems (MySQL on Windows uses TCP/IP). Should the client application—for example, `mysql` or a PHP script—be unable to find the socket, you'll encounter problems accessing MySQL. There are two reasons why this might occur:

◆ The `mysql.sock` file has been deleted.

◆ The `mysql.sock` file is located other than where the client program is looking for it.

Normally, `mysql.sock` is stored in the `/tmp` directory. On some installations, the socket will be in `/var/lib/mysql` instead. Mac OS X Server puts the MySQL socket in `/var/mysql`.

You can prevent the first problem by protecting the `mysql.sock` so that it cannot be deleted.

To protect mysql.sock:

1. Access your server using a terminal application.

2. Add a "sticky bit" to the `/tmp` directory.

   `sudo chmod +t /tmp`

   Adding a sticky bit to a directory means that all of the files therein can be deleted only by the owner of the file or by a super-user. One of the reasons MySQL may not be able to find the socket is that it has been inadvertently deleted by another user or application. This step will prevent that from occurring again.

3. Enter the computer's administrative password at the prompt (**Figure A.8**).

4. Restart MySQL.

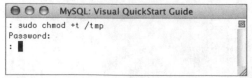

Figure A.8 On Unix and Mac OS X, the chmod command can be applied to the /tmp directory to protect the mysql.sock socket.

Figure A.9 I can tell the mysql client where the socket is so that it can communicate with the MySQL server.

Figure A.10 MySQL needs to be able to find the mysql.sock socket in order for clients to connect to the server. So I first find out for myself where it is.

Figure A.11 By creating a symbolic link, I assure that my client applications will be able to find the socket.

For the second problem, there are two fixes. First, you can tell the client programs where to find mysql.sock. This is editable within the php.ini file, and you can indicate the socket when connecting via the mysql client (**Figure A.9**). The second option is to create a symbolic link so that where the client thinks the socket should be (e.g., /tmp/mysql.sock) points to where the socket actually is (e.g., /var/mysql/mysql.sock). I'll show you how to do that now.

To create a symbolic link:

1. Access your server using a terminal application.

2. Locate the mysql.sock socket (**Figure A.10**).

   sudo find / -name 'mysql.sock'

   This command will search through the entire server to find mysql.sock. This assumes, of course, that the MySQL server is currently running.

   Enter the computer's administrative password at the prompt.

3. Create a symbolic link from where MySQL thinks the socket should be to where the socket actually is (**Figure A.11**).

   sudo ln -s /path/to/actual/mysql.sock
   → /tmp/mysql.sock

   A symbolic link will trick MySQL into thinking that /tmp/mysql.sock is the real socket, even when it is not.

✔ Tips

- As a reminder, the mysql.sock file only exists on Unix computers (and Mac OS X) and while the MySQL server is running. It's possible that a client could not find the socket because the server is not running.

- You can also specify the socket's location by using either an option file or the --socket parameter when mysqld is started.

Queries That Return Strange Results

A problem many MySQL users come across, particularly when accessing the database using PHP, Perl, or Java, is that a script or application does not give the intended results. There are many places for a problem to occur:

◆ In connecting to and selecting a database

◆ In executing the query

◆ In the SQL of the query itself

◆ In the MySQL results of the query

◆ In how the query results are handled by the program

(If you're not using a programming language, you'll be limited to just the third and fourth issues.) To debug such situations, you need to identify the actual cause of the problem.

To debug query problems:

1. If using a programming language to create an SQL query, print out the query so that you know exactly what is trying to be executed. Frequently, the program is not assembling a query as you would expect.

2. Run the query on the database via another method, such as using the `mysql` client. Doing so will validate both the SQL and the results.

3. In a programming language, use the methods available for reporting any MySQL errors.

4. If the query results are bad, rewrite the query in its most basic form. Then keep adding dimensions back in until you discover which clause is causing the problem.

5. Pay attention to what versions you are using (of MySQL and the languages) and reread any applicable manual pages to see if this is a version-specific issue.

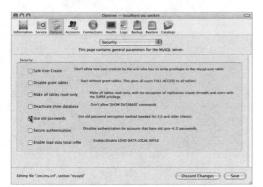

Figure A.12 If absolutely necessary, you can tell the MySQL server to use the old-style password algorithm.

Authentication Protocol Problems

As of version 4.1 of MySQL, a new algorithm is used for handling user passwords. While this change is more secure, it has led to many confusing problems, including the "Client does not support authentication protocol" error. This error is caused by using an older client to connect to a newer installation of MySQL. I've seen it most frequently when using PHP's older MySQL functions (mysql_*) to connect to MySQL 4.1 or 5. There are several solutions to this problem:

◆ Use an older version of MySQL. This is an easy option, although not ideal.

◆ Tell the newer version of MySQL to behave, with respect to the authentication protocol, like the old version. To do so, start the server with the --old-passwords setting. You can opt for this within the MySQL Administrator, too (**Figure A.12**).

◆ Similarly, you could use the old-style password algorithm for just certain users. Update their password within the MySQL monitor by using this command:

```
SET PASSWORD FOR
→ 'username'@'hostname' =
→ OLD_PASSWORD('thepassword')
```

◆ The third solution is to upgrade the client. For PHP in particular, this means switching to the new MySQL Improved Extension functions (mysqli_*).

Resetting the Root Password

I know it happens, because I've done it myself: You go to log in to MySQL as the *root* user and access is denied. You cannot remember the correct password or get a new password to work. Effectively you've locked yourself out of MySQL and all hope is lost. Luckily, there is an easy enough work-around when (or if) this does occur: You need to reset the root password.

Resetting an access password involves starting MySQL without the user/privilege system in use. Then anyone can access the database, make the alterations, and restart MySQL.

To reset the root password:

1. Use the MySQL Administrator to disable the grant tables (**Figure A.13**).

   This option tells MySQL to run without concern for user and access privileges. While this is an obvious security issue, it's the only way to reset the *root* password. This, of course, does assume that the MySQL Administrator has remembered your administrative password (although it's unrecoverable by you). See Chapter 13, "MySQL Administration," for more information on the MySQL Administrator, in case you're not familiar with it.

   Checking the box here will write the value to the proper option file. The new value— disabling the grant tables—will take effect the next time MySQL is started.

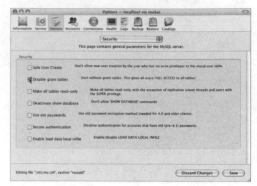

Figure A.13 Disabling the grant tables when starting MySQL allows you to circumvent the user/privilege system.

If you cannot use the MySQL Administrator to set this option, then you must start MySQL from the command line (in Step 3), using the `--skip-grant-tables` argument. See Chapter 2 for ways to start MySQL manually. Alternatively, you could manually edit a MySQL option file (see Chapter 13) to accomplish the same effect.

2. Stop the MySQL server.

The next step is to stop MySQL so that you can restart it without the grant tables. To do so:

▲ On Windows, where MySQL is running as a service, go into the Administrative Tools > Services panel to stop MySQL. You can see the specific steps in Chapter 2, if you need.

▲ On Mac OS X and Unix, issue the following command in the Terminal:

```
sudo kill `cat /path/to/mysql/
→ data/hostname.pid`
```

▲ On these operating systems you'll likely need to use this strong-arm technique to stop a running MySQL server. You'll need to find the `pid` file on your computer and use that path and name here. It should be in your MySQL data directory. Note that those are backticks around the `cat` code, not single quotation marks.

3. Start MySQL.

If you were able to use the MySQL Administrator or an option file to disable the grant tables, you can start MySQL as you normally would. If not, then you must start MySQL with the `--skip-grant-tables` argument.

continues on next page

4. Update the root password using `mysqladmin`.

```
mysqladmin -u root password
→ 'newpassword'
```

This step is exactly the same as the one used to first establish a root password (see Chapter 2). No password is required to make this change, since the grant tables were skipped. You could also log in to the `mysql` client (without using a password to get in) and then run a SET PASSWORD command.

5. Undo the effects of Step 1.

Now that you've reset the password, it's important that you re-enabled the grant tables. If you used the MySQL Administrator in Step 1, you should uncheck that box (see Figure A.13). If you manually edited an option file, you should re-edit it. If you didn't do any of this but instead used the `--skip -grant-tables` flag when starting MySQL, you do not need to do anything here.

6. Stop and restart MySQL.

Since `mysqld` is currently running without verifying access, you'll need to stop and restart the server. Use the techniques taught in Chapter 2 to stop and restart it. You will not need to use a password to stop MySQL, as it doesn't currently require them.

SQL AND MYSQL REFERENCES

This appendix should stand as a quick reference for your SQL and MySQL needs. In this section you'll find tables from elsewhere in the book—sometimes in a more complete form—along with other terminology and function listings. The tables and references here have been loosely grouped by subject and generally follow the same outline as the content of the book as a whole. For information not listed, or to see the most current specifications for a newer version of MySQL, check the MySQL manual.

SQL AND MYSQL REFERENCES

Basic SQL

MySQL aims to have full ANSI SQL support, although some considerations are made in the interest of performance and features. This first section of the appendix deals with SQL-specific standards, whereas the other sections refer to more MySQL-specific issues. To start, **Table B.1** lists the most common SQL terms.

Here are some examples as to how these queries would be used:

◆ CREATE DATABASE *databasename*

(Creates a new database.)

◆ CREATE TABLE *tablename* (*columnname1* → *column_definition*, *columnname2* → *column_definition*)

(Creates a new table, structured according to the column definitions.)

◆ DELETE FROM *tablename* WHERE → *columnname* = '*value*'

(Removes every record from the table where *columnname* is equal to *value*.)

◆ DROP TABLE *tablename*

(Deletes the table and all of its columns, rows, and data.)

◆ DROP DATABASE *databasename*

(Deletes the database and all of its tables, columns, rows, and data.)

◆ INSERT INTO *tablename* VALUES ('x', → 'y', 'z')

(Inserts the values *x*, *y*, and *z* into the three columns of a new row in *tablename*. This syntax will work only if the number of values specified exactly matches the number of columns.)

Table B.1 These are the eight most common SQL query types.

SQL Terminology	
TERM	**USED FOR**
ALTER	Changing the structure of a table
CREATE	Creating a table or database
DELETE	Deleting records from a table
DROP	Deleting entire tables or databases
INSERT	Adding records to a table
SELECT	Retrieving information from a database
SHOW	Displaying information about the structure of a database or table
UPDATE	Modifying a database entry

- INSERT INTO *tablename* (*column1name*, → *column3name*) VALUES ('x', 'y')

  (Inserts the value *x* into the first and the value *y* into the third column of a new row. This syntax will work as long as the specified columns exist.)

- INSERT INTO *tablename* VALUES ('x', → 'y', 'z'), ('a', 'b', 'c')

  (Inserts two rows into the table. This is a MySQL addition to the SQL standard and will not necessarily work in every database application.)

- SELECT * FROM *tablename*

  (Returns every column of every row.)

- SELECT *column1name*, *column2name* FROM → *tablename*

  (Returns just the two columns for every row.)

- UPDATE *tablename* SET *columnname* = 'x'

  (Sets the value of *columnname* to *x* for every row in the table.)

ALTER Commands

While every SQL term can be used in many ways to accomplish different goals, ALTER may be the most complex. In general, ALTER is used to change the structure of a table, by:

◆ Changing its name

◆ Adding or deleting indexes

◆ Modifying its columns

Table B.2 lists some of the common ALTER clauses, all of which would begin with the phrase ALTER TABLE *tablename*. For example:

```
ALTER TABLE my_table ADD COLUMN my_column
→ INT UNSIGNED
ALTER TABLE my_table DROP INDEX my_index
```

Table B.2 The ALTER SQL command can be used to modify tables in numerous ways.

ALTER TABLE Clauses

CLAUSE USAGE	MEANING
ALTER TABLE *tblname* ADD COLUMN *colname coltype*	Adds a new column to the end of the table.
ALTER TABLE *tblname* CHANGE COLUMN *colname newcolname newcoltype*	Allows you to change the data type and properties.
ALTER TABLE *tblname* DROP COLUMN *colname*	Removes a column from a table, including all of its data.
ALTER TABLE *tblname* ADD INDEX *indexname* (*columns*)	Adds a new index on the listed column(s).
ALTER TABLE *tblname* DROP INDEX *indexname*	Removes an existing index.
ALTER TABLE *tblname* RENAME AS *newtblname*	Changes the name of a table.

Table B.3 These operators and comparators can be used in conjunction with parentheses to create different expressions in SQL queries.

Operators and Comparators	
OPERATOR	**MEANING**
+	Addition
-	Subtraction
*	Multiplication
/	Division
%	Modulus
<	Less than
>	Greater than
<=	Less than or equal to
>=	Greater than or equal to
=	Equals
!= (also <>)	Not equal to
%	Multiple wildcard character (used with LIKE)
_	Single wildcard character (underscore) (used with LIKE)
IS NOT NULL	Has a value (including an empty string or zero)
IS NULL	Does not have a value
BETWEEN	Within a range
NOT BETWEEN	Outside of a range
IN	Is one of a listed set of values
NOT IN	Is not one of a listed set of values
OR (also ||)	Where at least one of two conditionals is true
AND (also &&)	Where both conditionals are true
NOT (also !)	Where the condition is not true
OR NOT (also ^)	Where only one of two conditionals is true
LIKE	Where the value matches a string
NOT LIKE	Where the value does not match a string
REGEXP	Where the value matches a pattern
NOT REGEXP	Where the value does not match a pattern
MATCH AGAINST	Where the values matches against a series of words

SQL Clauses

With most of your queries, normally you will want to use clauses to limit the information returned. This especially true for UPDATE and DELETE commands.

The four common clauses are WHERE, GROUP BY, ORDER BY, and LIMIT (LIMIT is an extension to the SQL standard). Examples:

◆ SELECT * FROM *tablename* ORDER BY
→ *columnname* DESC

(Retrieves every column and every record from the table, sorted by *columnname* in descending order.)

◆ SELECT * FROM *tablename* ORDER BY
→ *column1name* ASC, *column2name* DESC

(Retrieves every column and every record from the table, sorted by *column1name* in ascending order, then by *column2name* in descending order.)

◆ SELECT * FROM *tablename* LIMIT 10

(Retrieves every column of the first ten records from the table.)

◆ SELECT * FROM *tablename* LIMIT 100, 50

(Retrieves every column of the 101st through 150th records from the table.)

You can also, and frequently will, use multiple clauses in the same query. The clauses always go in this order:

SELECT *columns* FROM *tablename* WHERE
→ *clause* GROUP BY *columnname* ORDER BY
→ *columnname* LIMIT *x*

Clauses can be applied just to a column name, or they can be used in conjunction with parentheses and operators to create more elaborate conditionals. **Table B.3** lists the operators and comparators you'll commonly use.

MySQL Privileges

The user privilege system built into MySQL dictates who can do what within each particular database. The *mysql* database stores the specifics in terms of users, passwords, hosts, and database access. It also records what individual, allowable actions particular users can do—in other words, what SQL commands they can run on the database. As newer features are added to MySQL, such as stored procedures and views, those permissions are added to the *mysql* database as well.

Tables B.4, **B.5**, and **B.6** list the available privileges. I've grouped them into my own rough categories: basic, administrative, and new. These are entirely artificial distinctions of my own making but should help give you a sense of how to assign privileges based upon the version of MySQL you are using and what a user needs to be able to do. As a rule, always give each user the minimum required privileges on a database.

Table B.4 This is the list of basic privileges that can be assigned to MySQL users on a case-by-case basis. It is generally safe to assign these to users for a specific database (except for the *mysql* database, which must be kept off-limits).

Basic MySQL Privileges	
PRIVILEGE	ALLOWS FOR
SELECT	Reading of rows from tables
INSERT	Adding new rows of data to tables
UPDATE	Altering existing data in tables
DELETE	Removing existing data in tables
SHOW DATABASES	Listing the available databases
INDEX	Creating and dropping indexes in tables
ALTER	Modifying the structure or properties of a table
CREATE	Creating new tables or databases
CREATE TEMPORARY TABLES	Creating temporary tables
DROP	Deleting existing tables or databases

Table B.5 These privileges should be given only to administrative users and preferably on specific databases.

Administrative MySQL Privileges	
PRIVILEGE	ALLOWS FOR
RELOAD	Reloading the grant tables (and therefore enact user changes)
SHUTDOWN	Stopping the MySQL server
FILE	Importing data into tables from text files
GRANT OPTION	Creating new users with the same permissions as current user
CREATE USER	Creating new users
REVOKE	Removing the permissions of users
PROCESS	Showing currently running processes
SUPER	Terminating running processes

Table B.6 These privileges have been added in newer versions of MySQL (mostly 5.0 and up). Note that it's safer and normal for some users to be able to use a view or run a stored procedure, whereas limited users can create or modify them.

Newer MySQL Privileges	
PRIVILEGE	ALLOWS FOR
CREATE VIEW	Creating a view
SHOW VIEW	Using a view
ALTER ROUTINE	Modifying a stored procedure
CREATE ROUTINE	Creating a stored procedure
EXECUTE	Running a stored procedure
LOCK TABLES	Locking tables
REPLICATION CLIENT	Showing replication status
REPLICATION SLAVE	Performing replication

MySQL Data Types

Selecting the proper column type for your tables is key to a successful database. **Tables B.7**, **B.8**, and **B.9** define the different string, number, and other types you can use, along with how much space they will take up on the server's hard drive. When choosing a type for each column, you should use the most efficient (i.e., the most size-frugal) data type in terms of the largest possible value for the column.

Further, I should mention that MEDIUMINT, SET, ENUM, as well as the different-sized BLOB and TEXT column types are all MySQL-specific extensions of the SQL defaults. Finally, when it comes to defining columns, remember that any column type can be NULL or NOT NULL, integers can be UNSIGNED, and any number can be ZEROFILL. A column can also be defined as having a DEFAULT value, should a value not otherwise be supplied for it.

Table B.7 Here are most of the available numeric column types for use with MySQL databases. For FLOAT, DOUBLE, and DECIMAL, the *Length* argument is the maximum total number of digits, and the *Decimals* argument dictates the number of that total to be found after the decimal point. (As of MySQL 5.0.3, the size of DECIMAL column is based upon a formula.)

MySQL Numeric Types

TYPE	SIZE	DESCRIPTION
TINYINT[*Length*]	1 byte	Range of –128 to 127 or 0 to 255 unsigned.
SMALLINT[*Length*]	2 bytes	Range of –32,768 to 32,767 or 0 to 65535 unsigned.
MEDIUMINT[*Length*]	3 bytes	Range of –8,388,608 to 8,388,607 or 0 to 16,777,215 unsigned.
INT[*Length*]	4 bytes	Range of –2,147,483,648 to 2,147,483,647 or 0 to 4,294,967,295 unsigned.
BIGINT[*Length*]	8 bytes	Range of –9,223,372,036,854,775,808 to 9,223,372,036,854,775,807 or 0 to 18,446,744,073,709,551,615 unsigned.
FLOAT[*Length*, *Decimals*]	4 bytes	A small number with a floating decimal point.
DOUBLE[*Length*, *Decimals*]	8 bytes	A large number with a floating decimal point.
DECIMAL[*Length*, *Decimals*]	*Length* + 1 or *Length* + 2 bytes	A DOUBLE with a fixed decimal point.

Table B.8 Here are the most common column types for storing text in a MySQL database.

MySQL Text Types

TYPE	SIZE	DESCRIPTION
CHAR[*Length*]	*Length* bytes	A fixed-length field from 0 to 255 characters long.
VARCHAR(*Length*)	String length + 1 or 2 bytes	A fixed-length field from 0 to 255 characters long (65,535 characters long as of MySQL 5.0.3).
TINYTEXT	String length + 1 bytes	A string with a maximum length of 255 characters.
TEXT	String length + 2 bytes	A string with a maximum length of 65,535 characters.
MEDIUMTEXT	String length + 3 bytes	A string with a maximum length of 16,777,215 characters.
LONGTEXT	String length + 4 bytes	A string with a maximum length of 4,294,967,295 characters.
BINARY[*Length*]	*Length* bytes	Similar to CHAR but stores binary data.
VARBINARY[*Length*]	Data length + 1 bytes	Similar to VARCHAR but stores binary data.
TINYBLOB	Data length + 1 bytes	Stores binary data with a maximum length of 255 bytes.
BLOB	Data length + 2 bytes	Stores binary data with a maximum length of 65,535 bytes.
MEDIUMBLOB	Data length + 3 bytes	Stores binary data with a maximum length of 16,777,215 bytes.
LONGBLOB	Data length + 4 bytes	Stores binary data with a maximum length of 4,294,967,295 bytes.
ENUM	1 or 2 bytes	Short for *enumeration*, which means that each column can have one of several possible values.
SET	1, 2, 3, 4, or 8 bytes	Like ENUM except that each column can have more than one of several possible values.

Table B.9 These are the available date and time column types for MySQL.

MySQL Date and Time Types

TYPE	SIZE	DESCRIPTION
DATE	3 bytes	In the format of *YYYY-MM-DD*
DATETIME	8 bytes	In the format of *YYYY-MM-DD HH:MM:SS*
TIMESTAMP	4 bytes	In the format of *YYYYMMDDHHMMSS*; acceptable range ends in the year 2037
TIME	3 bytes	In the format of *HH:MM:SS*
YEAR	1 byte	In the format of *YYYY*, with a range from 1901 to 2155

MySQL Functions

Preformatting the results returned by a query makes your data more usable and can cut down on the amount of programming interface required. To do so, you make use of MySQL's built-in functions, first introduced in Chapter 6, "MySQL Functions." Of course, you can also use functions in your clauses to limit what records are returned, to group them, and more.

Table B.10 shows the functions used with strings. **Table B.11** has most, but not all, of the number-based functions. **Table B.12** lists date-related functions. **Table B.13** has the formatting parameters for the DATE_FORMAT() and TIME_FORMAT() functions. **Table B.14** covers the aggregate or grouping functions. **Table B.15** discusses most of the encryption functions and **Table B.16** is the catchall for miscellaneous functions.

Most every function can be applied either to the value retrieved from a column or to a literal one:

```
SELECT ROUND (3.142857, 2)
SELECT ROUND (columnname) FROM tablename
```

Table B.10 These functions are used for manipulating string values, in columns or otherwise.

Text Functions	
FUNCTION AND USAGE	PURPOSE
FIND_IN_SET(*string, set*)	Returns a positive number if *string* is found in *set*; returns 0 otherwise.
LEFT(*string, x*)	Returns the leftmost *x* characters from a string.
LENGTH(*string*)	Returns the length of the string.
LOCATE(*substring, string*)	Returns the first instance of *substring* in *string*, if applicable.
LOWER(*string*)	Turns the string into an all-lowercase format.
LTRIM(*string*)	Trims excess spaces from the beginning of the string.
REPLACE(*string, find, replace*)	Returns the string with every instance of *find* substituted by *replace*.
RIGHT(*string, x*)	Returns the rightmost *x* characters from a string.
RTRIM(*string*)	Trims excess spaces from the end of the stored string.
STRCMP(*string1, string2*)	Returns 0 if the strings are the same, –1 or 1 otherwise.
SUBSTRING(*string, start, length*)	Returns *length* characters from *string* beginning with *start* (indexed from 1).
TRIM(*string*)	Trims excess spaces from the beginning and end of the string.
UPPER(*string*)	Capitalizes the entire string.

Table B.11 Here are some of the numeric functions MySQL has, excluding the trigonometric and more esoteric ones.

Numeric Functions

FUNCTION AND USAGE	PURPOSE
ABS(*num*)	Returns the absolute value of *num*.
CEILING(*num*)	Returns the next-highest integer based upon the value of *num*.
FLOOR(*num*)	Returns the integer value of *num*.
FORMAT(*num*, *y*)	Returns *num* formatted as a number with *y* decimal places and commas inserted every three spaces.
GREATEST(*num1*, *num2*, *num3*...)	Returns the greatest value from a list.
LEAST(*num1*, *num2*, *num3*...)	Returns the smallest value from a list.
MOD(*x*, *y*)	Returns the remainder of dividing *x* by *y* (either or both can be a column).
POW(*x*, *y*)	Returns the value of *x* to the *y* power.
RAND()	Returns a random number between 0 and 1.0.
ROUND(*x*, *y*)	Returns the number *x* rounded to *y* decimal places.
SIGN(*num*)	Returns a value indicating whether *num* is negative (–1), zero (0), or positive (+1).
SQRT(*num*)	Calculates the square root of *num*.

Table B.12 MySQL uses several different functions for working with dates and times in your databases. In the usage examples, *dt* could represent a date, a time, or a datetime.

Date and Time Functions

FUNCTION AND USAGE	PURPOSE
HOUR(*dt*)	Returns just the hour value of *dt*.
MINUTE(*dt*)	Returns just the minute value of *dt*.
SECOND(*dt*)	Returns just the second value of *dt*.
DATE(*dt*)	Returns just the date value of *dt*.
DAYNAME(*dt*)	Returns the name of the day of *dt*.
DAYOFMONTH(*dt*)	Returns just the numerical day of *dt*.
MONTHNAME(*dt*)	Returns the name of the month of *dt*.
MONTH(*dt*)	Returns just the numerical month value of *dt*.
YEAR(*dt*)	Returns just the year value of *dt*.
DATE_ADD(*dt*, INTERVAL *x type*)	Returns the value of *x* units added to *dt*.
DATE_SUB(*dt*, INTERVAL *x type*)	Returns the value of *x* units subtracted from *dt*.
ADDTIME(*dt*, *t*)	Returns the value of *t* time added to *dt*.
SUBTIME(*dt*, *t*)	Returns the value of *t* time subtracted from *dt*.
DATEDIFF(*dt*, *dt*)	Returns the number of days between the two dates.
TIMEDIFF(*dt*, *dt*)	Returns the time difference between the dates or dates and times.
CONVERT_TZ(*dt*, *from_zone*, *to_zone*)	Converts *dt* from one time zone to another.
CURDATE()	Returns the current date.
CURTIME()	Returns the current time.
NOW()	Returns the current date and time.
UNIX_TIMESTAMP(*dt*)	Returns the number of seconds since the epoch or since the date specified.

Table B.13 The DATE_FORMAT() and TIME_FORMAT() functions make use of these special characters to format a date or time.

DATE_FORMAT() and TIME_FORMAT() Parameters

TERM	MEANING	EXAMPLE
%e	Day of the month	1–31
%d	Day of the month, two digit	01–31
%D	Day with suffix	1st–31st
%W	Weekday name	Sunday–Saturday
%a	Abbreviated weekday name	Sun–Sat
%c	Month number	1–12
%m	Month number, two digit	01–12
%M	Month name	January–December
%b	Month name, abbreviated	Jan–Dec
%Y	Year	2002
%y	Year	02
%l	Hour	1–12
%h	Hour, two-digit	01–12
%k	Hour, 24-hour clock	0–23
%H	Hour, 24-hour clock, two-digit	00–23
%i	Minutes	00–59
%S	Seconds	00–59
%r	Time	8:17:02 PM
%T	Time, 24-hour clock	20:17:02
%p	AM or PM	AM or PM

Table B.14 The grouping functions are frequently tied to a GROUP BY clause to aggregate values in a column.

Grouping Functions

FUNCTION AND USAGE	PURPOSE
AVG(column)	Returns the average of the values of the column.
COUNT(column)	Counts the number of rows.
COUNT(DISTINCT column)	Counts the number of distinct column values.
GROUP_CONCAT(values)	Returns a concatenation of the grouped values.
MIN(column)	Returns the smallest value from the column.
MAX(column)	Returns the largest value from the column.
SUM(column)	Returns the sum of all of the values in the column.

MySQL Functions

Table B.15 Different encryption functions are available as of new releases of MySQL, so know what version you are using!

Encryption Functions

FUNCTION	VERSION	NOTES
MD5()	3.23.2	Returns a 32-digit hash.
SHA1()	4.0.2	Returns a 40-digit hash.
AES_ENCRYPT()	4.0.2	Encrypts data using AES algorithm.
AES_DECRYPT ()	4.0.2	Decrypts AES_ENCRYPT() data.
ENCODE()	3.x	Older encryption function.
DECODE()	3.x	Decrypts ENCODE() data.
DES_ENCRYPT()	4.0.1	Encrypts data using DES algorithm, requires SSL.
DES_DECRYPT ()	4.0.1	Decrypts DES_ENCRYPT() data.
ENCRYPT()	3.x	May not be available on Windows; no decryption possible.
PASSWORD()	3.x	Used by the *mysql* database; do not use yourself.

Table B.16 These various functions are for everything from encryption to concatenation.

Other Functions

FUNCTION AND USAGE	PURPOSE
CONAT(*column1*, ' - ', *column2*)	Combines the elements in parentheses into one string.
CONCAT_WS(' - ', *column1*, *column2*)	Combines the elements with the one common separator.
DATABASE()	Returns the name of the database currently being used.
LAST_INSERT_ID()	Returns the previous auto-incremented value.
USER()	Returns the name of the user of the current session.

MySQL Functions

Table B.17 These characters all have special meanings when used in queries. The letters are all case-sensitive! The percentage character and the underscore are necessary because these characters, when not escaped, can be used as wildcards in searches.

Escape Characters

CHARACTER	MEANING
\'	Single quotation mark
\"	Double quotation mark
\b	Backspace
\n	Newline
\r	Carriage return
\t	Tab
\\	Backslash
\%	Percentage character
_	Underscore character

Other References

The last three references for this appendix include **Table B.17**, how to store special characters in a database; **Table B.18**, how to weight keywords in a binary-mode full-text search; and **Table B.19**, significant characters for regular expressions.

Table B.18 As of version 4 of MySQL, you can perform full-text searches in binary mode, using these symbols.

Special Boolean Mode Characters

CHARACTER	MEANING	EXAMPLE	MATCHES
+	Word is required	+punk rock	*punk* is required and *rock* is optional.
-	Word must not be present	+punk -rock	*punk* is required and *rock* cannot be present.
""	A literal phrase	"punk rock"	Occurrences of the phrase *punk rock* are weighted.
<	Less important	<punk +rock	*rock* is required and *punk* is less significant.
>	More important	>punk +rock	*rock* is required but *punk* is more significant.
()	Creates groups	(>punk roll) +rock	*rock* is required, both *punk* and *roll* are optional, but *punk* is weighted more.
~	Detracts from relevance	+punk ~rock	*punk* is required, and the presence of *rock* devalues the relevance (but *rock* is not excluded).
*	Allows for wildcards	+punk +rock*	*punk* and *rock* are required, but *rocks, rocker, rocking*, etc., are counted.

Table B.19 When using REGEX and NOT REGEX, you'll need to define patterns with the characters listed here.

Special Regular Expression Characters

CHARACTER	MATCHES	CHARACTER	MATCHES
.	Any single character	q{x,y}	Between *x* and *y* instances of *q*
q?	Zero or one *q*	^q	Starts with *q*
q*	Zero or more *q*'s	q$	Ends with *q*
q+	At least one *q*	(pqr)	Grouping (matches *pqr*)
q{x}	Exactly *x* instances of *q*	q|z	Either *q* or *z*
q{x,}	At least *x* instances of *q*	[]	Character classes (e.g., [a-z], [0-9])
q{,x}	Up to *x* instances of *q*	\	Escapes a special character (\., *, etc.)

RESOURCES

Because a book can only be so thorough and so current, I like to include a list of useful resources in each one I write. Here you'll primarily find links to Web sites I consider valuable along with other, miscellaneous resources such as book titles and mailing lists.

Your first reference for MySQL-related issues should be MySQL's official Web site, located at www.mysql.com. After that, I hope you will frequent this book's home page, found at www.DMCinsights.com/mysql2. The site was designed with the express intention of supporting this book, and thus you will find there:

◆ More Web links (over 300 at last count)

◆ A support forum for questions and issues arising from this book

◆ An errata page, listing printing errors (which unfortunately do happen)

◆ And more, as the mood strikes me

All of the resources listed in this chapter are items I have come across that may be useful to the average reader. Referencing something here does not constitute an endorsement, nor does it imply that each of these is the best possible resource or tool for your needs.

MySQL-Specific

The absolutely very first resource you should consider is the MySQL manual, available through the company's Web site (www.mysql.com) in many different forms. The main online version has the added advantage of being searchable. You'll also find user-submitted comments that are often helpful. I also keep a copy of the manual on my hard drive for whichever version of MySQL I am running (in case your Internet connection goes down).

Once you've performed an exhaustive search through the MySQL manual, you can consider turning to one of several MySQL-dedicated mailing lists (there are no official MySQL newsgroups). Each list has a different subject:

- Announcements

- General

- Java

- Windows

- .NET

- C++

- Perl

- ODBC

Most of these are available in a digest form so that you can receive two large emails per day rather than many individual ones. Plus these lists are available in other languages. It is recommended that every MySQL user subscribe to the announcements list to keep up to date.

Figure C.1 You can access information from the MySQL mailing lists by subscribing or by searching the respective archives.

Figure C.2 Frequently asked MySQL questions—and their answers—are available through the FAQTs site.

Through another link at the MySQL site—http://lists.mysql.com (**Figure C.1**)—you can perform searches through the mailing list archives. Doing a quick search here before posting a question to a mailing list (and presumably after you've scoured the MySQL manual) will save you lots of time.

And if the manual and mailing lists aren't enough, MySQL runs a number of support forums (http://forums.mysql.com). If you need more personal and time-sensitive help, you could consider purchasing one of MySQL's support plans.

You may also want to keep abreast of Planet MySQL (www.planetmysql.com). The focus here is on general news and opinion, rather than technical documentation, although it is also associated with the MySQL AB company.

Finally, some good general, common knowledge can be found at the FAQTs page for MySQL (http://mysql.faqts.com, **Figure C.2**). You might also like the "gotchas" section at sql-info.de (http://sql-info.de/mysql/).

Third-Party MySQL Applications

As I mention in Chapter 3, "Database Design," you can use dedicated applications to help you with your database scheme. One such program is MYdbPAL (http://www.it-map.com/html/mydbpal_.html). This free program runs on Windows and will help you both design and implement a MySQL database. DB Tools Software (www.dbtools.com) also makes an application for designing and implementing MySQL databases. It runs on Windows and is available in both free and inexpensive versions.

For an easy-to-use and powerful database administration tool, one of the hands-down favorites is phpMyAdmin, created by the talented people at phpWizard.net (www.phpwizard.net). It requires that you have a Web server and PHP installed but allows you to interact with MySQL through a Web browser, rather than the mysql client (**Figure C.3**).

There are literally dozens and dozens of other third-party applications you can use to interact with MySQL. Many are now obsolete thanks to the MySQL Query Browser and the MySQL Administrator (both of which are free), but if these two applications don't suit your needs, just do a search online for alternatives.

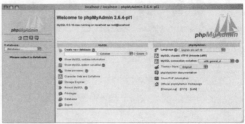

Figure C.3 The phpMyAdmin software, developed by phpWizard.net, is an excellent way to interact with MySQL.

Figure C.4 The W3Schools site includes tutorials on lots of subjects, including SQL.

Figure C.5 Andrew Cumming's A Gentle Introduction to SQL is a user-friendly discussion of the language.

SQL

Since SQL is used by MySQL and other databases, you can find an endless supply of resources for this language. While generic SQL references will not necessarily show you how to get the most out of a MySQL database, they should remind you of the fundamentals. A few online SQL references include

◆ SQL Course, `www.sqlcourse.com`

◆ W3Schools.com, `www.w3schools.com/sql/default.asp` (**Figure C.4**)

◆ A Gentle Introduction to SQL, `www.sqlzoo.net` (**Figure C.5**)

◆ SQL Course 2, `www.sqlcourse2.com`

Many bookstores stock texts dedicated to the language. You may find, however, that an entire book on SQL is more knowledge than all but the advanced database developer requires. Further, you'll see that MySQL does not support a number of features that would be discussed in an all-purpose SQL text. And, MySQL has its own extensions that you may not find in a general SQL book.

SQL

PHP

In Chapter 7, "MySQL and PHP," I demonstrate how to interact with a MySQL database from a PHP script. Because of the language's popularity, there are dozens of PHP-related sites on the Internet. The three most important and useful are

◆ The PHP home page, www.php.net (**Figure C.6**), where you'll find the manual and more

◆ Zend, www.zend.com (**Figure C.7**), which contains articles and sample code

◆ PHPBuilder, www.phpbuilder.com, a great repository of PHP tutorials, forums, and code

As a reminder, if you are using PHP 5 or greater with MySQL 4.1 or greater, you have the option of using the MySQL Improved Extension functions. With older versions of PHP or MySQL, you must use the standard MySQL functions.

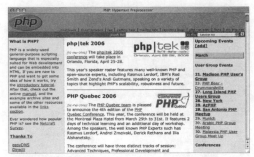

Figure C.6 PHP.net is the home page of the PHP scripting language...

Figure C.7 ...whereas Zend.com supports the language in many different ways.

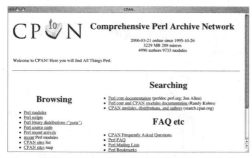

Figure C.8 To access a MySQL database from a Perl script, you use some of the CPAN modules.

Figure C.9 The DBI Documentation pages include both Perl and general database information.

Perl

In Chapter 8, "MySQL and Perl," I interface with a MySQL database using Perl. There, I include some URLs to visit for more information, such as:

◆ The official Perl home page, `www.perl.com`

◆ CPAN (Comprehensive Perl Archive Network), `www.cpan.org` (**Figure C.8**), where you can get the modules necessary to interact with MySQL

◆ ActiveState, `www.activestate.com`, where you can download ActivePerl for running Perl on Windows

◆ DBI Documentation, `http://dbi.perl.org` (**Figure C.9**), which contains links to various Perl DBI resources

PERL

Java

In Chapter 9, "MySQL and Java," I introduce the topic of using JDBC to access MySQL from a Java application. The corresponding Web links for that topic are:

◆ Java home page, http://java.sun.com (**Figure C.10**)

◆ JDBC home page, http://java.sun.com/products/jdbc

◆ Javaboutique, http://javaboutique.internet.com, which has sample code and articles

◆ JavaWorld, www.javaworld.com, which also has sample Java code and tutorials

Also check out MySQL's pages on the MySQL Connector/J, which is used to connect to a MySQL server from a Java application.

Figure C.10 Sun, the maker of Java, maintains the language and its documentation.

Figure C.11 Apple's Developer Connection pages are a must-use resource for more advanced OS X users.

Other

Finally, I'll throw out a couple miscellaneous resources that do not fall under the previous categories. For starters, people using Mac OS X (of which I'm obviously a big fan) should get to know

◆ Apple Developer Connection, `http://developer.apple.com` (**Figure C.11**)

◆ Entropy, `www.entropy.ch`, which supports Mac OS X development in many ways

SourceForge.net, `www.sourceforge.net`, claims to be the world's largest repository of open-source applications (and there's good cause to believe that). Thousands of different technologies are developed through and hosted by SourceForge.net.

Developer Shed, `www.devshed.com`, is a general development site that includes articles discussing the various programming languages and technologies you are likely to use.

WebMonkey, `www.webmonkey.com`, is very similar to Developer Shed, although it is broader in scope.

If you are intrigued by the open-source community and projects such as MySQL, see `www.opensource.org`.

OTHER

INDEX

E

R

S